COMMUNICATING ACROSS CULTURES

COMMUNICATING ACROSS CULTURES

MAUREEN GUIRDHAM

Ichor Business Books
An Imprint of
Purdue University Press
West Lafayette, Indiana

First Ichor Business Book edition, 1999.

Published under license from Macmillan Press Ltd, Houndmills, Basingstoke, Hampshire, RG21 6XS

This edition available only in the United States and Canada.

03   02   01   00   99   5   4   3   2   1

Library of Congress Cataloging-in-Publication Data

Guirdham, Maureen.
    Communicating across cultures / Maureen Guirdham.
    p. cm.
    Includes bibliographical references (p.).
    ISBN 1–55753–166–8 (alk. paper)—ISBN 1–55753–167–6 (pbk.: alk. paper)
    1. Communication in personnel management.   2. Diversity in the workplace.
3. Intercultural communication.   I. Title.
HF5549.5.C6G84   1999
658.4'5—dc21   99–12005
                                                  CIP

Printed in Great Britain

CONTENTS

LIST OF TABLES AND FIGURES

TABLES

FIGURES

PREFACE

The impetus behind the writing and publication of this book has been a utilitarian one: there is a widespread and urgent need to improve the ability of people at work to understand and be understood by others whose different backgrounds mean that they communicate differently. Ironically, this need is greatest where it is least recognised, among the members of the dominant groups in society. The members of the 'minority' groups have accommodated so well and the cultural sensitivity of the dominant groups has been so poor that the latter do not, in the main, realise that ways of communicating other than their own exist, persist and have validity; nor that, by imposing their own way, they limit their ability to understand those with whom they work and lose the potential benefits of diversity. In the UK, acknowledgement of the issue is largely confined to a weak complaint that 'We are not very good at learning languages'. Only in the field of international business is there any real sense that something is amiss.

Therefore, my purpose in this book is a focused one: to help the need for intercultural communication skills at work to become better recognised and to contribute my understanding of the knowledge and skill areas required. For this reason, the aspects of subjects such as culture and communication which are covered are those I deem central to this purpose. I realise that others may disagree with my selection and/or the fact that I have not attempted complete coverage of subjects which are foundation disciplines for my study nor argued my epistemological and ontological positions nor entered the postmodernism debate. I hope that readers will nevertheless find the book useful.

The book is dedicated to my children, Damon and Oliver.

ACKNOWLEDGEMENTS

My thanks are due to several people who have been kind enough to read and comment on draft chapters of this book – especially to Alan Bennett and E.D. Berman, MBE; to my many friends and colleagues in Bulgaria, the Czech Republic, Hungary, Kazakhstan, Poland, South Africa, the UK, the USA and Uzbekistan, from whom I have learnt by experience and through shared discussion; and to individuals and organisations who generously gave of their time and ideas for the interviews which formed an important part of my research.

Every effort has been made to contact all copyright holders but if any have been inadvertently omitted the publishers will be pleased to make the necessary arrangement at the earliest opportunity.

1 COMMUNICATING WITH DIVERSITY AT WORK

Managers of all types, business executives, members of the professions and people at work generally need to be able to communicate with others successfully. Increasingly, they must communicate in a 'new world' of diverse colleagues, clients and customers and of international operations. Modern societies and organisations are composed of people who differ widely in terms of nationality, ethnicity, gender, sexual orientation, age, education, social class or level of (dis)ability – in other words in terms of their demographic profile or social background. At work, therefore, individuals are now likely to interact with a highly diverse range of people as colleagues, subordinates, managers, clients, patients, customers, students, professional advisers and other service providers, sales representatives and other interface workers. Because societies such as Europe are becoming increasingly integrated, markets increasingly global and workforces increasingly diverse, more people than ever before now interact with 'different others' in these varying roles. (Different others are people whose demographic profile or social background is different from an individual's own.) It is their face-to-face communication in such interactions which is the subject of this book.

In the last two decades of the twentieth century, the need to adapt for cultural difference became a major concern of management, marketing and organisational literature. One major impulse behind this concern was the increasing globalisation of business. Another was the work done in the 1970s and 80s by researchers who demonstrated that the cultural differences between modern societies are profound, have significant effects on how people work and consequently on how they are most effectively to be managed, and show no signs of disappearing despite the homogenisation of some aspects of life in the late twentieth century. The importance of culture for international business and the problems managers have in dealing with it were summarised by Fons Trompenaars as follows:

> As markets globalize, the need for standardization in organizational design, systems and procedures increases. Yet managers are also under pressure to adapt their organization to the local characteristics of the market, the legislation, the fiscal regime, the socio-political system and the cultural system. (p. 3)

1

> Culture still seems like a luxury item to most managers, a dish on the side. In fact, culture pervades and radiates meanings into every aspect of the enterprise. (p. 16)[1]

Similarly, cultural differences are known to affect what and how people consume and therefore the most effective ways of marketing to them. With spreading globalisation, more and more organisations are impelled to take these differences into account.

Another growing concern is with diversity. Gary P. Ferraro, an anthropologist, has pointed out that organisations have many:

> social components that come from different backgrounds, hold contrasting values and attitudes and have conflicting loyalties. It is not at all likely that the company vice president will have much in common with the assembly line worker, the union representative… or many members of that diverse group called the buying public. And yet, if the organization is to function effectively, that high management official needs to know about the values, attitudes, expectations, concerns and behaviour patterns of all these people, and others as well. This is particularly true today as more and more minorities are brought into domestic work forces under equal opportunity employment laws.[2]

In an article entitled 'Managing cross-national and intra-national diversity', Rosalie Tung[3] argued that there are important similarities, as well as differences, in the processes and dynamics of managing diversity in cross-national and intra-national contexts. There is a need, however, for an increased emphasis on the domestic issue rather than the international one. In a later presentation, Tung explained why:

> (First) due to the localization policies of most host countries and the rising costs of expatriation, there will be a decrease in the number of expatriates. In comparison, the problem of managing intra-national diversity is definitely increasing in size and magnitude…; (second)… expatriates involved in managing cross-national diversity do so on a short-term basis (2 to 3 years). In contrast, in light of the changing demographics of the… workforce, those involved in managing intra-national diversity are expected to have a long-term (permanent) commitment to such policies and practices.[4]

Thus globalisation of both marketing and production, plus the increasing diversity of workforces, domestic markets and populations mean that few organisations can afford to ignore cultural difference. At the same time, increased understanding of its significance has encouraged those concerned with management, either as practitioners or scholars, to take an interest in the matter.

A third trend has been an increasing concern with 'capturing individual capabilities and motivating the entire organisation to respond to the demands of the environment'. Earlier, multinational companies were mainly concerned with strategy; organisational structures were designed to support strategy. Companies believed that by changing their structure they automatically changed the 'shared norms, values and beliefs that shape the way individual managers think and act' (Bartlett and Ghoshal, 1989).[5] Because these assumptions of managerial responsiveness were false, many organisations were incapable of carrying out the sophisticated strategies they developed, as Box 1.1 illustrates.

BOX 1.1

CORPORATE FANTASISING

'We (the human resource department) have done an audit of the top 250 staff, and found, much as we expected, that the company does not have the capabilities it needs. We found that, even if all the other factors like marketing and finance were in place, we would still trip up because there is no way we could resource the strategies that the company is dreaming up. For instance, there's a target for 50% of our business to come from international markets by the year 2001. You could count on the fingers of one hand the number of people in this company who could carry out an international assignment. And we don't have the lead time to buy in the expertise, even if it were out there, which it isn't because this is an industry-wide problem – the few people who have the experience are highly marketable and volatile – more likely to set themselves up in competition than stay with us.

'Another example – they've planned to do international telemarketing (we already do some domestically). There's been no real thought about how to resource this. Most of them think that if we recruit some school leavers with GCSE French, we'll be able to telemarket in France!'

Source: Interview with a human resource manager in an insurance company, 1996, author's research.

Recognition of the constraints placed on strategy implementation by individuals' limitations has brought a shift in organisational priorities; there is a new emphasis on individual capabilities and motivations as key intervening variables. Growth, development and prosperity are seen to depend on developing a creative, consultative culture in which individuals can contribute fully. Human capital is often regarded as the strategic resource of the future;[6] the role of managers has been changing from directing to facilitating, coaching and counselling.[7] Organisations are trying to build into their very structure the capacity for individual learning and development.[8]

However, despite the growing interest in cultural diversity and individual development, one aspect of the subject has received scant attention up to now. This is arguably the aspect where the impact of cultural difference is most direct and experienced by most people: interpersonal communication at work. In the words of Gillian Khoo:

> It is simply not enough for us to know how and why people differ culturally. We also need to know to what extent such differences can be generalized across situations, and especially to interactions with culturally different individuals. The need for a more global understanding of people, organizations, attitudes, norms, group processes, values, and ways of operating can be enhanced by examining how people interact and transact both among themselves as well as with culturally different individuals.[9]

Although Khoo was addressing her remarks to intercultural researchers in particular, there seems no reason to doubt that they also apply to anyone concerned with cultural difference and its impact on work and organisations.

The lack of attention to the effect of culture on interaction is the more surprising because a fourth major trend in management concerns and organisational literature over the period has been with communication. Communication as an object of study has been described as a 'revolutionary discovery' of the twentieth century,[10] energised by technological development, increasing global literacy, and 'the philosophies of progressivism and pragmatism, which stimulated a desire to improve society through widespread social change'.[11] In the world of work and organisations, many writers now acknowledge the central role of communication and there is a large literature devoted to it.[12] It is true that most of the attention has been given to impersonal or mass communication, perhaps because of an overhang from the days when organisations commonly had workforces of hundreds of thousands who were often treated as intelligent cogs in a machine, so that one-way communication rather than dialogue was seen as appropriate. Until recently there was a relatively prevalent naive view that interpersonal communication is 'natural' and so unproblematic. This naive view usually recognised that individuals might have deficiencies in social skills but not that there were any broad issues affecting organisational effectiveness or individual performance. This reasoning led to regarding analysis of interpersonal communication as academic, on the one hand, and trivial, on the other.

However, the new recognition that in order to compete modern organisations need to tap the creativity, expertise and knowhow of all their (generally much reduced numbers of) employees places a premium on interpersonal communication. There is considerable evidence that individual achievement in organisations is closely related to communication abilities and that good communication – both good communication systems and having staff with high interpersonal skills – is related to organisational effectiveness.

From the point of view of individual achievement the relationship has been demonstrated through a systematic line of research which found, that in a large insurance company and two other organisations, persuasive ability was a relatively strong predictor of performance appraisal ratings, job level and upward mobility.[13] It has also been shown that small business owners who give directions and control to their employees in a 'person-centred' way – that is, skilfully adjust their instructions and feedback to the characteristics of the individual employee – are perceived more positively as leaders by their employees. Person-centred communication by doctors has been found to be linked to health outcomes, including the degree to which patients comply with 'doctors' orders'.[14] There is a developing body of work showing that teacher communication methods influence student empowerment.[15]

A study published in 1996 investigated the link between communication abilities and organisational achievement among 394 employees of three south-east US organisations – a state-owned not-for-profit retail store, a state human services agency and a private mail-order company (from which came 203 participants). This research established that communication abilities and achievement are closely linked for both men and women.[16] The researchers concluded that 'The results lend additional support to the claim that these abilities help people attain desired social outcomes.'

There is clear evidence that organisations should value skilled interpersonal communication extremely highly. Tompkins and Cheney (1985),[17] for instance, have argued that concertive control is more effective than the other three kinds – simple control, technical control or bureaucratic control. Concertive control uses interpersonal relationships and teamwork to achieve a shared reality and shared values, thus leading to higher identification of employees with the organisation's assumptions and an increased likelihood that the decisions they will make will be consistent with the organisation's objectives and mission. Rosabeth Moss Kanter in *The Changemasters* (1983)[18] depicted the high-performing organisations in her study as highly participative and able to manage high levels of complexity successfully through effective communication. She argued that 'to produce innovation, more complexity is essential: more relationships, more sources of information, more angles on the problem, more ways to pull in human and material resources, more ways to walk around and across the organisation'.

In sum, attention, long overdue, is at last being paid to the needs of managers and other workers for an increased understanding of how to communicate effectively face to face; but there is still a lack of focus on communication with people from different backgrounds.

Parallel to and as important as the needs of managers for intercultural communication skills are the needs of the large numbers of service providers who interact with a public which continues to become more and more diverse. A straw poll of 20 university lecturers, librarians, doctors, lawyers, architects, social workers, policemen and dental receptionists known to the author revealed that they estimated that no more than 15–20% of their students, patients and clients were similar to themselves in terms of nationality, ethnicity, religious affiliation, gender, sexual orientation and social class. Perhaps it is surprising that the percentage is as high as it is.

Professional workers' concerns with communication are steadily increasing. For example, until recently the most that was expected of a doctor's communication with patients was to have a 'good bedside manner'. This meant, generally, having an avuncular and authoritative communicative style, disclosing little information but providing reassurance. No understanding of the communication needs of patients, relatives or the bereaved was expected. Now the subject of health communication is beginning to gain significance among practitioners, signalled by compulsory courses for medical students and at least one journal. However, on medical courses training in how to deal with people from different ethnic backgrounds is still exceptional and it is rare for any distinction to be made between the empathic needs of women and men.

Training for professionals, other service providers and interface workers in how to deal with people appropriately is gradually being introduced; similarly, equal opportunities awareness training is now widespread. However, most of the interpersonal skills training is generic, in the sense that little help is given in making it 'person centred' by adjusting to the different values, attitudes and motives of different individuals; and most of the equal opportunities awareness training omits any serious treatment of communication. It is true that adaptation at the individual level can only be achieved through sensitivity, active listening and gaining feedback; nevertheless, awareness of cultural and subcultural difference and knowledge of how to communicate with different others is an important underpinning for such adaptation.

The problem of communicating across cultural barriers is possibly better recognised by individuals than educationalists, trainers and writers. Gudykunst's (1983)[19] research indicates that people behave differently when they are interacting with others whom they perceive as culturally dissimilar: they ask more questions, but self-disclose less; they seek out information about dissimilarities instead of information about similarities. They are less willing to draw inferences about the attributes of people from other cultures. Gudykunst's conclusion is that 'people know how to get to know other people from the same culture but not from different cultures'. Gudykunst's findings suggest that people experience intercultural contact as different, even difficult, and attempt to handle it differently.

Rationale for the topics covered in the book

- In most fields, working effectively requires good face-to-face communication skills.
- While natural endowments vary, they can be enhanced by understanding, learning, experience and practice.
- There is an increasing diversity of people met at work.
- Differences of background create differences in ways of communicating which in turn constitute barriers to good communication.
- Overcoming barriers can be learned and tools are available in the form of theories with practical implications.

One question that may be raised by consideration of this rationale is whether the work context obliterates differences in communication and behaviour resulting from differences in backgrounds: whether, to adapt the words of Wanous (1977):

> When social behavior is regulated by other, less diffuse social roles, as it is in organizational settings, behavior... primarily reflect(s) the influence of these other roles and therefore lose(s) much of its... stereotypical character.[20]

Wanous, however, answers this question from her own research findings on leadership styles:

> Nevertheless, women's leadership styles were more democratic than men's even in organization settings. This sex difference may reflect underlying differences in female and male personality or skills (for example women's superior social skills) or subtle differences in the status of women and men who occupy the same organizational role.

While, clearly, there are constraints on differences in behaviour at work, the evidence that will emerge in this book I believe confirms overwhelmingly that such differences still obtain, are significant and need to be taken into account more than is currently practised. In the presentation referred to earlier, Tung identified the core competencies required of both domestic and international managers in the twenty-first century as an 'ability to balance the conflicting demands of global integration versus local responsiveness; an ability to work in teams comprised of peoples from multiple functions/disciplines, different companies, and diverse industry backgrounds; an ability to manage and/or work with peoples from diverse racial/ethnic backgrounds'. These three competencies all depend on intercultural communication skills and all assume that cultural differences remain potent despite the work setting.

This point is reinforced by a second: the prevailing modes of interpersonal communication at work undoubtedly reflect the preferred style of one cultural and subcultural group. In Western societies, with some exceptions (such as Body Shop), the dominant style is that of the individualistic, monochronic, universalistic male; in other societies, other modes prevail: communication in Hong Kong Chinese businesses, for instance, tends to the high context – that is, to a less explicit style than is usual in Western businesses. There is evidence that work and organisational effectiveness can be enhanced if more diverse communication modes operate, allowing entry and influence to the diverse values, attitudes and ideas of the diverse populations now involved.

Third, for the large numbers of people who interface with the public in the course of their work, the behaviour of their clients, patients, students or customers may not be greatly affected by the work context, so the social and cultural influences on their co-interactors' behaviour are still likely to be paramount and need to be understood.

Chapter 2 has two purposes: to argue the growing prevalence of intercultural communication in work settings and to begin the process of describing its context. Some of the material in this chapter serves both purposes – sets of 'objective' facts about the size and employment position of different societal groups both tend to demonstrate the amount and range of intercultural encounters which must be happening and are relevant to the beliefs and attitudes and so to the communication behaviours of the participants. Admittedly there is a problem with this last point: it is people's perceptions which influence their beliefs and attitudes rather than any 'objective' facts, and in individual cases the two may diverge quite widely. Nevertheless, the facts are useful as an overall foundation for understanding how interactors view the intercultural social world of work.

A discussion of discrimination and harassment at work is included in this chapter because there is clear evidence that these are part of the everyday realities of working life for some groups and so an essential part of the context. Descriptions of organisational diversity policies and 'attitudes' are also included here because they significantly affect the climate for intercultural interactions at work, especially between colleagues.

Chapter 3 draws on the last quarter century of cross-cultural research which has firmly established that there are differences in the ways that members of different societal groups behave, both in private life and at work. The chapter sets out to analyse culture and cultural differences, in terms both of underlying factors, such as values, and of communication, using Hall's 'high-context/low-context' distinction and cultural identity theories; it also discusses certain conceptual issues, including the generalisability of cultural concepts to subcultural groups.

Chapters 4 and 5 cover face-to-face communication at work and the effects of (sub)cultural difference. The subject of human communication is a huge one and radical selection has been necessary for this book: it has been done by selecting those elements of general communication which differ between cultures, such as the concept of 'politeness', and those which feed directly in to intercultural communication, such as 'elaborated and restricted codes'. Chapter 4 deals with analyses of overt communication behaviour at an individual level; Chapter 5 expands the analysis into the psychological factors and processes affecting behaviour, on the one hand, and on the other the reconceptualisations resulting from viewing communication as an interactive, dynamic process where the unit of analysis is supra-individual.

Chapter 6 presents the argument that intercultural communication at work is problematic in particular ways and describes the wide range of barriers which obtain. It both builds on the analyses of Chapters 3, 4 and 5, by showing how (sub)cultural differences create barriers, and deals with 'universal' factors, such as stereotyping and prejudice, which also impede intercultural communication. It refutes by demonstration the argument that the work situation so over-rides individual differences and prejudices that intercultural communication problems are insignificant in that context.

Chapter 7 provides a theoretical underpinning for the last two chapters of the book, which give practical guidance on how to communicate interculturally at work. Intercultural communication theory as a subject is in its infancy: there is no holistic theory and the theories presented here are a disparate collection reflecting the particular interests or beliefs of the scholars developing them. The amount of empirical research support they have received is limited, although growing. Nevertheless, brought together, they cover a considerable area of the potential behavioural ground, ranging from the motivations (goals), emotions (anxiety) and cognitions (uncertainty, identity, episode representations, expectations) of the intercultural encounter to the processes involved in effective intercultural interactions (anxiety and uncertainty management, identity and face negotiation, communication accommodation).

Chapter 8 covers both theoretic and atheoretic approaches to intercultural communication skills. These range from guidance on inclusive language to the practical application of Ellingsworth's adaptation theory. Attention is paid to behaviours and traits, such as tolerance for ambiguity, mindfulness and self-monitoring, for whose efficacy there is empirical evidence.

Chapter 9 is another practically orientated chapter, which deals with the different situation which arises when the work context is that of a culture other than the individual's own – that is, it provides guidance for sojourners and people on international assignments.

Terminology in the rest of the book

While references to cultures and subcultures as distinct concepts use the terms without brackets, to cover the combined concepts the terms (sub)culture and (sub)cultural are generally used here; however, when referring to communication and interactions between members of different groups, I prefer the term 'intercultural', to avoid the clumsiness of 'inter(sub)cultural'. To refer to members of groups other than a communicator's own, I generally use the terminology, which is gradually becoming current, of 'different others', and to capture the quality of their difference, 'otherness'. However, certain of the theories covered in Chapter 7 use the term 'strangers' instead of 'different others' and where that is so, the author's original terminology is used. Again, I generally use the term 'interpersonal' to mean 'between people' or 'face to face', but in some writings on intercultural communication it is used in contrast to 'intergroup' and 'intercultural', in the sense that an encounter, even between only two people, may occur on an intergroup, intercultural or interpersonal level. Again, in these cases I follow the terminology of the writer but try to make the difference clear.

Labels for societal groups are always problematic – the subject is discussed in the next chapter and a section on inclusive language is given in Chapter 8. The term 'minority' is often used not literally, but to define a group in a subordinate position irrespective of relative size; for example it can be applied to women in

Britain or black people in South Africa, both of whom are numeric majorities. This usage can be sensitive because of its indirect reference to subordinate status, but in the absence of any other accepted general term and because it is adopted by the Commission for Racial Equality, it will be used (in inverted commas) in this book.

REFERENCES

1. Trompenaars, F. (1993) *Riding the Waves of Culture*, London: Nicholas Brealey.
2. Ferraro, G.P. (1994) *The Cultural Dimension of International Business* (2nd edn), Englewood Cliffs, NJ: Prentice-Hall.
3. Tung, R.L. (1993) 'Managing cross-national and intra-national diversity', *Human Resource Management*, **32**(2): 18–34.
4. Tung, R.L. (1996) 'Managing diversity for international competitiveness'. Paper presented at David See-Chai Lam Centre For International Communication: Pacific Region Forum on Business and Management Communication. Simon Fraser University At Harbour Centre. Posted on the Internet: hoshi.cic.sfu.ca/forum/RTung96–12–23.html.
5. Bartlett, C.A. and Ghoshal, S. (1989) *Managing Across Borders, The Transnational Solution*, Cambridge, MA: Harvard Business School Press.
6. Chalofsky, N.E. and Reinhart, C. (1988) *Effective Human Resource Development*, San Francisco: Jossey-Bass.
7. Naisbitt, J. and Aburdene, P. (1985) *Re-inventing the Corporation*, New York: Warner Books.
8. Savage, C.M. (1990) *5th Generation Management*, Bedford, MA: BARD Productions, Digital Press.
9. Khoo, G. (1994) 'The role of assumptions in intercultural research and consulting: Examining the interplay of culture and conflict at work'. Paper given at the Simon Fraser University at Harbour Centre, David See-Chai Lam Centre for International Communication: Pacific Region Forum on Business and Management Communication.
10. Barnett Pearce, W. (1979) *Communication and the Human Condition*, Carbondale: Southern Illinois University Press.
11. Delia, J.G. (1987) 'Communication research: a history' in Berger, C.R. and Chaffee, S.H. (eds) *Communication Science*, Newbury Park, CA: Sage.
12. See, for instance, Allen, M.W., Gotcher, M.M. and Seibert, J.H. (1993) 'A decade of organizational communication research' in Deetz, S. (ed.) *Communication Yearbook*, **16**: 252–330.
13. Sypher, B.D. and Zorn, T.E. (1986) 'Communication abilities and upward mobility: a longitudinal investigation', *Human Communication Research*, **12**: 420–31.
14. Kline, S.L. and Ceropski, J.M. (1984) 'Person-centred communication in medical practice' in Wood, J.T. and. Phillips, G.M. (eds) *Human Decision-Making*, Carbondale: Southern Illinois University Press, pp. 120–41.
15. Frymier, A.B., Shulman, G.M. and Houser, M. (1996) 'The development of a learner empowerment measure', *Communication Education*, **45**: 181–99.
16. Zorn, T.E. and Violanti, M.T. (1996) 'Communication abilities and individual achievement in organizations', *Management Communication Quarterly*, **10**(2): 139–67.
17. Tompkins, P.K. and Cheney, G. (1985) 'Communication and unobtrusive control in contemporary organizations' in McPhee, R.D. and Tompkins, P.K. (eds) *Organizational Communication: Traditional Themes and New Directions*, Beverly Hills, CA: Sage.

18. Kanter, R.M. (1983) *The Changemasters: Innovation and Entrepreneurship in the American Corporation*, New York: Simon & Schuster.
19. Gudykunst, W.B. (1983) 'Similarities and differences in perceptions of initial intra-cultural and intercultural encounters: an exploratory investigation', *The Southern Speech Communication Journal*, **49**: 49–65.
20. Wanous, J.P. (1977) 'Organizational entry: newcomers moving from outside to inside', *Psychological Bulletin*, **84**: 601–18.

2

DIVERSITY AT WORK

The workforce of the early twenty-first century, in the UK as in many other countries, will be diverse – that is, it will consist of people from many different national and ethnic backgrounds and of women to the same degree as men. Diversity will be increased by the inclusion of more people with disabilities, social recognition that people are entitled to differing sexual orientations, religious affiliations and family structures and, in the European Union, the cumulative effects of the open labour market. What is more, for most people the diversity of the people they meet through work – as patients, students, pupils and their parents, clients, customers, suppliers, advisers, accountants, bankers and lawyers – is already wider than that among their colleagues alone and is growing. For business executives and managers, for instance, the diversity of the backgrounds of their contacts will increase even faster than the rate at which it increases among colleagues, owing to globalisation. For the caring professions, because people are living longer and as they age need more medical and support services, mainly young or middle-aged nurses, doctors and care workers are dealing with more and more elderly or very elderly people; women live longer than men and so are disproportionately served by doctors who are still predominantly male; members of ethnic minorities have a higher birth rate and so use more maternity services and so on.

This chapter is intended to show the context of communication at work in terms of diversity. It therefore provides information on the numbers and proportions, legal and employment status and de facto position in society and at work of different groups within the UK and Europe. It begins by discussing the position of national and ethnic minorities, then that of the female 'minority', and then those of other groups. Discrimination and harassment are an unavoidable part of that context and are discussed in that light. Finally, organisational goals, policies and and how they are changing are examined, for they, too, are part of the context of intergroup communication at work.

2.1   NATIONALITY AND ETHNICITY

'Nationality', as the term is used here, is decided by a person's national status, which is a legal relationship involving allegiance on the part of an individual and (usually) protection on the part of the state. This usage distinguishes nationality from ethnicity, since a nation may be composed of many ethnic groups but of course only one nationality. However, the importance of nationality itself to how people behave and so to its impact on work communication is far from clear; in terms of culture, the concept of nation is rather vague, because in multi-ethnic nations many peoples contribute to the creation of a national culture.

According to Smith (1986),[1] an ethnic unit is 'a population whose members believe that in some sense they share common descent and a common cultural heritage or tradition, and who are so regarded by others'. Mary Collier's (1988) definition of ethnic identity reflects the same idea: it is 'identification with and perceived acceptance into a group with shared heritage and culture'.[2]

Unfortunately, definitions of ethnicity are controversial and may in themselves be racist. 'Ethnic', as the term is commonly used in Britain, refers to those who are different from some indigenous norm; ethnicity is seen as an attribute of others – not of the dominant group: the English see themselves as individuals, others as members of groups. Responsibility for disadvantage is laid at the door of those who 'fail' to change – that is, to adopt 'our ways'.[3] Mason[4] has pointed out that in Britain 'ethnic minority' is widely understood to denote a category of people whose recent origins lie in the countries of the New Commonwealth and Pakistan. It is not so often used of people of Polish origin, for instance, but is conflated with skin colour and therefore designates as ethnic minorities members of the long-established black communities in, for example, Liverpool and Cardiff, who are culturally similar to their white neighbours. This terminology is even used in official statistics: the Labour Force Survey, whose statistics will be used, perforce, in this chapter, conflate 'European' minorities with the 'white' majority, so that ethnic minorities refers to 'black' ethnicity. The terminological challenge, Mason contends, is to:

- avoid assimilist assumptions – that is, assuming that minorities 'should' assimilate to the culture of the majority in the way implied by terms such as immigrant
- avoid racist biological determinism assumptions
- recognise diversity
- focus on culture.

Ethnic groups share a sense of heritage, history and origin from an area outside or preceding the creation of their present nation-state; they often also share a language or dialect. Unlike nationality, ethnicity is situational; it is possible to be simultaneously English, British and European, stressing these identities more or less strongly in different aspects of everyday life. Similarly, the same person might identify as Gujerati, Indian, Hindu, East African, Asian or British depending on the situation, their immediate objectives and the responses and behaviour of others.

The growing significance of national and ethnic differences for communication at work

Growth in the volume of international trade is one, albeit crude, indicator of growth in the amount of international communication, since doing business obviously requires contact and communication. The volume of world exports rose substantially between 1993 and 1997, despite various economic shocks such as the Asian crisis and the halving of the oil price. The UK participated in this growth, with both exports and imports nearly doubling by value between 1981 and 1995; both the UK and European Union (EU) experienced substantial growth in exports, imports and intra-EU dispatches and arrivals during the early 1990s. While some of this activity is no doubt cyclical, some is due to the opening of new markets (like those of the former Communist bloc) and some to globalisation: the long-term trends are for continuing growth.

The growing national diversity of the UK resident and working population, especially in London and other major cities, is obvious to anyone who travels about by public transport: a straw-in-the-wind indicator is the BBC news report of 20 May 1998 that 100,000 French people had come to live in Britain since 1990. These were mostly young people in search of work who were taking advantage of the common labour market of the European Union. From outside the EU, 40,000 Japanese people were also reported (in 1997) to be resident and (mainly) working in London, especially in the financial services industries.

The total number of foreign nationals working in the UK in 1993 was 862,000, 3.4% of the total working population. The largest single national group was from the Republic of Ireland, which accounted for 27% of all foreign workers in the UK; a further 15% were from the rest of the European Union. Most foreign workers were concentrated in London (44%) or the south east outside London (19%). Immigration in 1992 into the nine EU countries able to provide data was substantial and diverse, including 400,000 former Yugoslavians, 130,000 Poles, 110,000 Romanians, 90,000 Turks and 75,000 Russians.

There are now over 3 million people of minority ethnic origin who are UK citizens, constituting about 6% of the population. The largest category is people of Indian ethnicity, at 1.5% of the population, followed by Pakistani at 0.9% and black-Caribbean at the same level. Among those originating in other European Union countries, Germans constitute the largest group apart from those from Eire; there are large groups of people of Polish, Cypriot, Turkish and Jewish origin.[5] In 1991, ethnic categories were used for the census of Great Britain and Northern Ireland. This was the first time that 'country of origin' was not used for the census; the same ethnic categories are now adopted by the Commission for Racial Equality as those which it recommends for ethnic monitoring purposes. The categories are those shown in Table 2.1.

Labour market participation by ethnic minority members in Britain is roughly equal to that of the majority, although differently distributed, with slightly higher percentages of minority males being economically active and lower for minority females.

Table 2.1   **Ethnic group percentages in Great Britain 1991**

White	94.5
Black-Caribbean	0.9
Black-African	0.4
Black – Other	0.3
Indian	1.5
Pakistani	0.9
Bangladeshi	0.3
Chinese	0.3
Any other ethnic group	0.9

Source: Commission for Racial Equality.

Successive studies have shown that persons of minority ethnic origin are at a consistently higher risk of unemployment than are white people.[6] According to the Labour Force Survey, in 1995/96 the unemployment rate for people from ethnic minorities (18%) was more than double the rate for white people (8%). The duration of unemployment was also greater, for black people especially: men and women in the black groups were most likely (19% and 23% respectively) to be unemployed for 1–2 years, compared with only 15% and 13% for white men and women respectively. Among the young, the disparities were even greater, with 36% and 39% of economically active black female and male 16–24 year olds unemployed in 1995 compared with 17% and 12% of whites.[7]

There is evidence that unemployment among people from minority ethnic groups is 'hypercyclical': in times of recession, the rate rises faster than that of white people, while in times of recovery it falls more rapidly – thus showing that some employers treat minority groups as a residual labour force.[8] Male members of the ethnic minorities also experience higher rates of part-time employment, with its usual connotations of poor pay, lack of security, pensions, sick pay and holiday pay. The 1991 census shows that self-employment is generally more common among minority ethnic groups than among whites. In 1995, average hourly earnings of full-time employees from ethnic minorities were about 92% of those of white employees. However, the overall figures disguise some significant differences: 49% of all Pakistani and Bangladeshi workers earned less than £4.50 per hour compared with 31% of white workers and 21% of black workers.

A long series of studies of the employment status of members of minority ethnic groups has shown that in general terms they are employed in less skilled jobs, at lower job levels, and are concentrated in particular industrial sectors. However, male members of some minority ethnic groups are beginning to experience employment patterns which approximate those of white men. This is true of African, Asian, Chinese and Indian men, where proportions are close to or more than those of white workers in management, administrative, professional and technical jobs. However, although they are more likely to be professionals, minority men are considerably less likely to be senior, especially in large enterprises.

There are various explanations given for the evident employment disadvantage of members of ethnic minorities:

- Employers commonly claim that such workers have 'communication difficulties'; there is some truth in this as regards some small groups such as older Asian women in Coventry, but the disadvantage also applies to the much larger and growing part of the population which was born and educated in the UK.
- Employers also claim that ethnic minority members have skill or education deficits. However, several studies have shown that when educational qualifications are allowed for, ethnic minority workers are still more likely to be unemployed or at lower job levels. There is also evidence that discrimination blocks ethnic minority young people at the earlier training stage.

| 2.2 | GENDER |

Gender has been defined as: 'patterned, socially produced distinctions between female and male... Gender is not something that people are... rather for the individual and the collective, it is daily accomplished.'[9] The term gender therefore refers to:

- a society's beliefs about the differences between the sexes
- society's rules for appropriate behaviour for males and females.

The growing significance of gender differences at work

In Europe as a whole, women outnumber men by 105 to 100 (1995) compared with a slight advantage in men's favour worldwide (98.6 women for 100 men). Twenty-four per cent of European households had a woman as the head of the family in 1990.

The role of women in the labour market of the European Union became increasingly important over the decade 1985–95. Their proportion of the labour force and total employment rose steadily, although there were still considerable differences between member states such as Sweden, where women have an approximate 48% share of the labour force, and Spain and Ireland, where the figure is approximately 26%.[10] In the UK workforce women occupy a numerically greater niche than men, as Table 2.2 illustrates. In all EU countries, with the exception of the UK, Finland and Sweden, the proportion of women among people in employment is lower than their proportion of the labour force. As a corollary, they are over-represented among the EU unemployed. The country by country European figures for the percentage of women (15 years old and more) in the total active employed population in 1994 appear to reflect cultural differences such as religion and recent ideological history – thus the two countries with the highest participation rates for women were Slovenia with 50% and Bulgaria with 48%; those with the lowest were Malta at 23% and Spain at 25%. Russia had 45% and the UK 43%.

Table 2.2   **United Kingdom employment data for men and women 1994 and 1997**

	Males			*Females*		
	Spring/ Summer 1994	*Spring 1997*	*+/– 1994–97*	*Spring/ Summer 1994*	*Spring 1997*	*+/– 1994–97*
All aged 16 or over (thousands)	22,050	22,341		23,416	23,557	
Workforce %	71.2	69.4	–1.8	52.5	53.4	0.9
In employment as % workforce	69	75	6	87	90	0.9
Claimant unemployed as % workforce	12.7	7.9	–4.8	5	4	–1
Self-employed as % all aged 16 or over	11	11	0	3.3	3.6	3.6

Source: Labour Force Survey (1997) Government Statistical Office. London: Her Majesty's Stationery Office.

From the bare employment figures given in Table 2.2, it appears that women in the UK are well treated by the labour market. Between 1994 and 1997 there was an increase in the percentage of women who were economically active, continuing a long-term trend, while the percentage of economically active males continued to fall. Equally, the percentage of women in the workforce in jobs was higher than that for men both at the start and the end of the period, although rising slightly more slowly than for the other gender. Fewer women were claimant unemployed (although there may be many explanations for such a figure, including the possibility that women who lose their jobs are more likely than men to leave the workforce rather than claim benefits). Fewer women than men were self-employed.

However, according to Colgan and Ledwith (1996)[11], this picture disguises some harsher realities. They claim that, for women already in employment and for the new supply of women flooding into the labour market in the early 1990s, the going rate of pay remained low, nearly half the work was part time (but this was less true among ethnic minority women, two-thirds of whom work full time), casual and flexible. With the deconstruction of the employment contract, job security became ever more tenuous. The effect of gender-segregated labour markets was that over 80% of women worked in the service sector, compared with 56% of men. Women's employment is skewed towards economic sectors where pay is lower, terms of employment are worse and job security may be less. Women's employment is also skewed in terms of occupational groups. For instance, in the UK, 51% of all working-age women in employment work in four occupational groups – clerical, secretarial, sales and personal service occupations. These occupations account for only 16% of men in the UK. By the same token, 92% of all receptionists, 87% of all nurses, 73% of all local government administrators, 75% of clerks and secretaries and 63% of all teachers are women; in contrast only 6% of all engineers and technologists, 12% of workers in protective services such as police and fire and 18% of computer systems analysts are women. The sectors and occupations in which women predominate are also those which attract relatively low pay and status and where most part-time working is to be found.

BOX 2.1

THE MOST IMPORTANT BARRIERS
ARE INTANGIBLE

Carol Hymowitz, who originated the term 'glass ceiling', wrote that 'the biggest obstacle women face is also the most intangible: men at the top feel uncomfortable beside them'. Could the same be true for homosexuals, people from minority ethnic or religious groups and people with disabilities?

Source: Hymowitz, C. and Weissman, M. (1997) *A History of Women in America,* London: Bantam Books.

However, the marked skewing of female employment away from industry and towards services, which is so notable a feature of Western European countries, is less marked in the former Communist countries of Europe, where women also have a higher share in professional categories such as professional and technical, administration and management and sales force (see Table 2.3).

Table 2.3   **Percentage of women's share in the main professional categories, Eastern and Western Europe 1990**

	Eastern Europe	Western Europe
Professionals and technicians	56	15
Administration and management personnel	33	18
Office clerks and similar	73	63
Sales force	66	48
Production and transport operators and manual workers	27	16

Source: Women's Indicators and Statistics Database (United Nations).

Women in management form an extremely broad group. They include fast food restaurant managers, CEOs of large corporations, accountants, underwriters, administrators and officials, financial managers, medicine and health managers, and other occupations. The supply of women qualified for management jobs continues to increase as more women accumulate work experience and complete management and professional education programmes. However, although women have made progress in attaining management jobs, their median weekly earnings continue to be well below those of male managers and the statistics still paint a discouraging picture of Europe in terms of seniority and power at work and in society generally. There are only six countries where more than 25% of directors and senior managers are women (Bulgaria, Finland, Germany, Hungary, Norway and Sweden). In both Eastern and Western Europe, women are under-represented in positions of power; however, the comparative position varies between the two regions in respect of senior positions in the public and private sector and in representational roles. In Eastern Europe, women have done better in the private sector but worse in public administration; in representational assemblies, the 1987 position in which there were more women in parliaments in the East was reversed following the end of Communism there – indeed, the position has shown an absolute decline, while in Western Europe women improved their position. In the UK, the 1997 election increased women's representation in parliament by more than 100 members of parliament.

> **BOX 2.2**
>
> ## AFFIRMATIVE ACTION – GOOD OR BAD?
>
> 'My boss is a woman; she's terrifically good at the job, but she would never have got it, because a long career break to raise her family meant she didn't have the same length of experience as a man. However, the corporation had a jobs quota for women, so she got the job, and she's shown that she's fully competent. Of course, she has to work about sixty hours a week – but so do I.'
>
> *Source:* Interview with a broadcaster, author's research.

Ethnicity/gender interactive effects

Ethnicity and gender can be expected to produce combined effects on the employment positions of ethnic minority women, although there is some debate about whether the combination tends to make for 'double jeopardy' or to be mutually compensatory. Ethnic minority women are less likely to be unemployed than their male equivalents, but to a lesser degree than white women are in comparison with their male counterparts. They are less likely to be in part-time employment than white women (33% against 46%) although more than three times as likely as ethnic minority men (10%) and nearly five times as likely as white men (7%). Earnings of women from ethnic minorities were on average roughly the same as those of white women. Most of the difference in earnings of ethnic minority workers compared to white was due to different pay rates for white and ethnic minority men.

2.3   PEOPLE WITH DISABILITIES

Disabilities are physical, sensory or mental impairments that can make performing an everyday task more difficult. Most disabilities are not 'handicaps' in the sense of making people unable to work and take part in community life on an equal footing with others. This includes severe disabilities such as being confined to a wheelchair. Often it is only the fact that an environment is not adapted – there are no wheelchair ramps or lifts – that makes full participation difficult for people with such impairments. A qualified person with a disability is someone who, with or without reasonable adjustment by the employer, can perform the essential function of the employment position that she or he holds or desires.

Until the second half of the twentieth century it was rare to find the simple recognition that, apart from their specific impairment, people with disabilities have the same needs, abilities and interests as the mainstream population. For many people with disabilities, the greatest handicap has been the image of them as a 'breed apart' who were often pitied, ignored or placed in institutions that offered mere custodial care.[12]

There are over 6 million registered disabled people in the UK (12% of the population); in the EU, the proportion of people with disabilities varies between 9.3% and 15.2% by country, averaging about 12%. Disability increases with age in a rising curve.

People with disabilities are a significant part of the workforce. In the UK, nearly 1.5 million people with disabilities are employed full time; a further 600,000 or more work part time. They are, however, disproportionately likely to suffer unemployment, as Figure 2.1, for nine EU countries, illustrates.

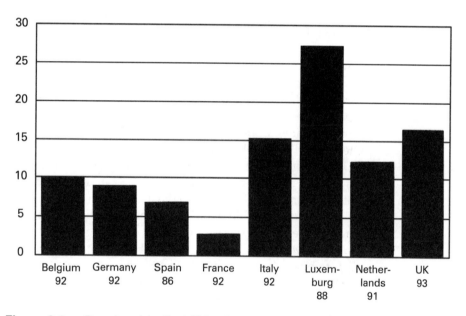

Figure 2.1   People with disabilities looking for a job as a percentage of all unemployed – various years

In the words of the European Statistical Office, Figure 2.1 shows that 'in general disabled persons are over-represented in the total unemployed population. The percentage of disabled persons unemployed is in fact generally higher than 10% of all unemployed persons, although their percentage of working age in the total population varies between 6% and 8%.'

2.4 OTHER SOCIETAL GROUPS

Religious groups. In Great Britain there are about two million active members of the Anglican Communion, 160,000 Baptists, nearly one million Roman Catholics, over 400,000 Methodists, and about one million adherents of other Christian churches; there are 360,000 Hindus, 300,000 Jews, 400,000 Sikhs, and at least one million Muslims. Worldwide, there are about 900 million Christians (mainly Roman Catholic), 800 million Hindus, 1,000 million Muslims, over 12.5 million Jews and 12.5 million Sikhs.

In France, Germany and Italy, statutes ban discrimination on the grounds of religion as well as ethnicity, gender and so on, but there is no legislation to ban discrimination on the basis of religion in Britain, except in Northern Ireland. There, the amended Fair Employment Act 1989, in addition to banning discrimination, requires all employers of over ten people to report annually on the religious composition of their workforce and to review it at least every three years. Non-compliance can bring heavy penalties. The Act was a response to the evident imbalance in employment opportunities for Catholics in the Province.

Younger people. In the late 1990s there were a million fewer 16- to 19-year-olds in the UK than a decade before. The story was similar in the rest of Europe. Despite this, EU-wide unemployment of people under 25 was 21.3% in 1997, a figure which had hardly changed since 1993. Since this figure is substantially above the average of 11%, it points to a serious disadvantage for young people; however, the predominant cause is less likely to be discrimination than labour market rigidities: the difficulty for younger people is to gain entry. Most job opportunities arise only as the total number of jobs expands or as natural wastage creates vacancies. People in the age group 25 to 49 tend to have a degree of tenure in the jobs they occupy.

Older people. About 25% of the UK population in 2006 is projected to be aged between 45 and 65, compared with 22.7% in 1996, and this figure is set to continue rising. In February 1996 the number of workers aged over 49 unable to find employment within two years or more had doubled since 1990. In this case, there is evidence that discrimination is part of the cause as Section 2.5 will show.

Homosexuals. Estimates for the numbers of male homosexuals and lesbians are, for obvious reasons, unreliable: the figures quoted range from 2% to 10%. Anecdotal evidence suggests that homosexuals often attain seniority at work more rapidly than the majority population; this is sometimes attributed to their greater commitment, owing to the higher demands of family life on heterosexuals. Despite instances of persistent discrimination, such as the armed forces and the Church of England, the workplace in general is now perhaps not a prime problem area for homosexuals as a group.

Household composition. In 1994, 11% of the UK population lived in 'atypical' households – that is, not as heterosexual couples or two-parent families – and a further 10% lived alone; 15% of UK children lived in single-parent households.

Social class and education. Social class is one dimension on which societies like the UK became less diverse during the last quarter of the twentieth century, with the growth of a large category of 'intermediate' and other non-manual workers and a decrease in the percentage of all manual workers, especially the unskilled. This came about largely as a result of the decline of manufacturing and heavy industry. These trends are set to continue, reinforced by government policies which see an increase in the educational and technical skill levels of the population as essential to the country's international competitiveness.

Final educational level is undeniably a major source of difference among individuals in the workplace. There is, for instance, undoubtedly a considerable amount of initial job segregation of graduates, 18-year-old school leavers with higher level school qualifications (such as A Level), 16-year-old school leavers with qualifications and those who leave school at the earliest legal date without qualifications. In this respect, the UK is still, despite recent changes, elitist compared with some international competitors, such as USA or South Korea, where about 70% of the population receive university-level qualifications. In 1991–92, in the UK, 23% of 16- to 20-year-olds entered full-time higher education, up from 16% in 1985/86; 32% of all 17-year-olds obtained one or more A Level or Scottish Certificate of Education Higher Certificate; and half of school leavers with no higher level qualifications obtained one or more graded GCSE or SCE O or standard grade result. In crude terms, among younger workers, about a third have no academic qualifications (but may have one of a range of vocational qualifications), a quarter are graduates, and the rest have intermediate qualifications. In older age groups, the proportion with advanced qualifications is lower.

Other educational/professional differences also create significant differences among groups of people at work. Examples include subject specialisation (especially science versus arts), independent versus state-maintained schooling (because of its perceived implications for social class) and professional training (for instance, the problems created by legal jargon, 'academese' and civil servant speak).

Thus far this chapter has shown that, numerically, both the population at large and the workforce in the UK, EU and Europe as a whole are diverse and are continuing to become more so. This implies a significant increase in the amount, and therefore the importance, of intergroup (intercultural) face-to-face communication at work. It has also shown that despite legislation and an improvement in their societal position, minorities' earnings, employment rates and career prospects are still below those of the majority groups in both UK and Europe; these facts are part of the context of intercultural communication at work.

2.5	DISCRIMINATION

All 'minority' groups, including people with disabilities, religious minorities, homosexuals and older people as well as ethnic minorities and women, are affected by prejudice and discrimination both at work and in society more generally. A wide range of people – not just women – are affected by harassment. Understanding and knowing about this is essential background for communicating across barriers created by difference. Without such understanding and knowledge, there can be no possibility of the awareness of sensitive issues, which, as Chapter 8 will show, is vital. Of course, the actual relevant variables are 'perceived' rather than 'actual' prejudice and discrimination. Thus a section such as this, which deals with actuals, can only heighten consciousness rather than provide the needed information, which will have to be obtained face to face, person by person. Nevertheless, consciousness raising is an important part of the process of improving intercultural communication effectiveness.

In modern usage the term 'prejudice' usually means an irrationally unfavourable or hostile attitude towards the members of another group. 'Discrimination' means any situation in which a group or individual is treated unfavourably on the basis of arbitrary grounds, especially prejudice. Discrimination is a manifestation of prejudice which is often institutionalised and pervasive throughout an organisation. Discrimination seriously reduces 'minority' groups' chances of obtaining employment, equal earnings and promotion. (Discrimination is part of the context within which intercultural communication takes place and so is treated in this chapter; prejudice is a direct barrier to communication and is covered in Chapter 6.)

Few women or minority men ever compete for the top managerial jobs in the large corporations or government agencies; this is often cited as an argument that they do not want them, but the lack of opportunities earlier in their careers mean that few are 'qualified'. Getting a top job depends on trust (which in turn is linked to social similarity) and access to informal networks. As a result:

> In the private sector, glass ceilings exist for most white male managers and professionals as well as for women and minorities. The pressures for social similarity and trust are so extreme at the top of large corporations that race and gender are joined by social class and school background, corporate and foundation connections beyond the corporation and even social club memberships as screening devices in the selection of the 'inner circle' of economic power. In smaller firms, of course, being a member of the owning family is the primary screening device.[13]

In addition to this well-known glass ceiling, organisations may contain glass walls, which keep women and minority men out of some functional areas (for example manufacturing) and locked into others (for example human resource management). Glass walls are the equivalent for managers of job segregation in employment more generally. Usually, the areas from which 'minorities' are excluded are the ones which are most likely to lead to reaching the top of the organisations – they may even be those where experience is essential to get there. For example, in a multinational company a woman or ethnic minority man may be less likely than members of the majority group to get an overseas posting, but international experience may be a requirement for board-level jobs; or, in an industrial marketing company, where all male graduate trainees may undertake a period of experience as sales representatives, which is regarded as basic for promotion above a certain level, women graduate trainees may not be allowed to 'go on the road' – theoretically for their protection.

BOX 2.3

RACISM IN THE BRITISH ARMED
FORCES – OFFICIAL

1. A five-month investigation by the Office for Public Management, published on 20 March 1997, unearthed widespread racist attitudes among armed forces personnel who thought black people were 'lazy' and Asians were 'sly'. The Royal Navy was singled out, with the report saying senior officers turned a blind eye to taunts among lower ranks. 'The conventions of a sea-faring tradition result in a level of awareness of cultural diversity which is 10 or 20 years behind that of a society at large and which can reasonably be said to constitute institutional racism.'

2. Ex-Royal Marine: 'I thought enduring racism was part of my training.'

   Commentator: 'Unless the Army does something to sort it out, they will continue to lose good soldiers who are being driven out purely because of their colour.'

Sources: Guardian, 21 March 1997; Channel 4 programme, 20 March 1997.

In general, the UK has been found to exhibit high levels of discrimination against 'minorities'. For example, in the findings of the 1996 World Competitiveness Report,[14] issued by an independent body based in Geneva, out of 48 nations surveyed, the UK ranked 38th for career opportunities for women and 39th for equal opportunities regardless of background. (It is interesting and significant, of course, that the Report links discrimination and competitiveness.) The US State Department Report on Human Rights for 1997 said of the UK:

Although the law prohibits discrimination based on race, persons of African or South Asian origin face substantial unofficial discrimination. ...Several studies showed that ethnic minorities were less likely to obtain jobs and mortgages and more likely to live in overcrowded housing than were whites.[15]

<table>
<tr><td>

Ethnic groups

</td></tr>
</table>

BOX 2.4

RACISM AFFECTS NURSES

In 1995 a health Trust accused of racism agreed a £35,000 settlement with five black nurses. The nurses, whose case was to have been heard by a Birmingham industrial tribunal, claimed a computerised personality test unfairly discriminated against them. Ten white and ten black staff were invited to apply for the nine remaining jobs at the Coventry Healthcare NHS Trust's psychiatric unit at Walsgrave Hospital, Coventry, where nursing posts were cut from 20. All nine vacancies were filled by white applicants. Five of the black nurses claimed racial discrimination; five other black nurses made no formal claim.

Deputy ward sister Alice Mommerville claimed the interview procedure was rigged and the result was a foregone conclusion. The Trust refused to give a full breakdown of individual awards.

Source: Guardian, 17 October 1995.

According to Mason (1995)[16] there is 'overwhelming evidence that discrimination is a continuing and persistent feature of the experience of Britain's citizens of minority ethnic origin'. A common method for obtaining such evidence has been to submit job applications from candidates matched in every way except ethnic origin. Using methods such as this, Brown and Gay (1985)[17] revealed continuing systematic discrimination, despite the many years of race relations legislation. The probable explanation is that employers are very unlikely to be caught.

Discrimination applies to the top 100 companies from *The Times* 1,000 Index. When matched letters of enquiry about employment were sent by fictitious applicants called Evans and Patel, presented as MBA students who were about to qualify and already had relevant experience, even 48% of companies with equal opportunities statements in their annual reports did not treat both candidates equally and where they did not do so they favoured the white candidate in proportions greater than those in companies without statements.[18]

Equally serious is indirect discrimination – where selection criteria are applied equally to everyone but disproportionately affect members of particular groups.

> Many of the ordinary, routine aspects of the recruitment market and the labour market may give rise to indirect discrimination – for example the notion that candidates must 'fit in'. If selectors hold stereotypes of minority ethnic groups which mean they do not 'fit in', indirect discrimination follows.

Changing work patterns only add to this – female Asian workers are recognised as loyal, hardworking and uncomplaining; but new labour demands are for flexibility and the ability to exercise initiative and responsibility for checking one's own work. There is an implicit assumption that just because these women workers are the former, they cannot be the latter.

Some of the UK's most respected institutions – the police, the bar, the law – are among those which in recent years have been exposed as bastions of ethnic discrimination:

- In 1993 a report by Her Majesty's Inspectorate of Constabulary published by the Home Office identified continuing problems of unchallenged racist banter among police officers and a general scepticism about senior officers' commitment to equal opportunities.[19] The Chair of the UK Commission for Racial Equality said, launching 'Race and Equal Opportunities in the Police Service', 'Currently only 1.7% of police officers in England and Wales are from ethnic minorities, against 5.2% of the economically active population. All police services will benefit from the provision of equality of opportunity.' He said it would help the police to have a better relationship with the rest of society if they reflected the population more closely.
- A 1995 inquiry conducted by the Council for Legal Education, a non-governmental organisation, found that racial discrimination by barristers was a key factor in the high failure rate among black students attempting to qualify for the bar. The report recommended a series of reforms.
- Referring to the Commonwealth Immigrants Act 1962, the Commonwealth Immigrants Act 1968, the Immigration Act 1971 and the Nationality Act 1981, Mason (1995) wrote: 'It is no accident that the clearly consistent theme in immigration and citizenship legislation since 1962 has been a distinction between those who were thought of as "white" and those who were not.'[20]

Other recent examples of possible discrimination against ethnic groups are given in Box 2.5.

BOX 2.5

EXAMPLES OF ETHNIC DISCRIMINATION AT WORK

1. Contract cleaners at Heathrow Airport – a large employer of Asian women, most working in catering or cleaning – on average earned £2 an hour. They also complained of racism, sexism and bad working conditions. When the Transport and General Workers Union formed a special branch, the airport management refused to recognise the union for collective bargaining. (It was entitled to do this under British law but would not be in most other European Union states.) The union officer was barred from meeting employees at work and had to rely on home visits. The women – in any case suspicious of white union officials – worked shifts. Membership rose from only 6 to a mere 50 out of a possible 1,000.

2. Race as a factor in job placement. In a large US commercial bank research revealed a statistically significant tendency to assign new employees to supervisors of the same ethnic group; and among those who were subsequently re-assigned within 5 months, the level of such identity-based homophily increased significantly further. Four alternative non-racial hypotheses that might have explained the pattern of reassignments were investigated and rejected – viz. that those re-assigned were less capable or less liked by their initial supervisor or not deemed differentially qualified or had lower average performance ratings. 'At present, no explanations are available for the processes underlying the pattern of intra-organisational "ethnic drift".'

Sources: Virdee, S. and Wrench, J. (1995) 'Organising the Unorganised: Race, Poor Work and Trade Unions', Research Paper 21, Centre for Research in Ethnic Relations, University of Warwick; Lefkowitz, J. (1994) 'Race as a factor in job placement: serendipitous findings of "ethnic drift"', *Personnel Psychology*, **47**: 497–513.

Women

Recent evidence for direct discrimination against women is less explicit than that for discrimination against some ethnic groups, although the statistical story told in Section 2.2 combined with the evidence of women's suitability for modern employment and management are strong pointers. In addition, there are undoubtedly sectors, such as the insurance industry where, as Box 2.8

shows, prejudice and discrimination are overt. Indirect discrimination may, however, currently be having more damaging effects on women at work. Indirect discrimination ranges from the lack of family-friendly policies in many organisations to the gendering of organisations.

'Family-friendly policies' is the term for the provision of childcare (and elder-care) resources and facilities, such as workplace nurseries, part time, flexitime, work-at-home, job sharing, compressed work weeks, extended lunch breaks and maternity and parenting leave. Most UK employers, including very large employers of women, provide few if any of these benefits. Even where they exist, there is a widespread belief that the use of leave and flexible working arrangements involves sacrificing career advancement, at least in the short term, and perhaps permanently. Second, it has been shown that an individual's immediate supervisor or manager is a key influence, with considerable effect on the level of work/family conflict, perceived trade-offs between work and personal life and the repercussions of using family-friendly policies. Attitudes of such supervisors and managers are key and may often be prejudiced. Third, research has shown that family-friendly resources are more likely to be available to senior echelon and non-minority staff, which means they may actually reinforce the glass ceiling.[21]

Organisational gendering refers to the existence and persistence of a male-dominant organisational culture and climate which occur through four distinct but interrelated processes:

1. the construction of gender divisions, with men almost always in the highest positions of organisational power
2. the construction of symbols and images that explain, express or reinforce those divisions, such as language, dress and media image
3. the gendered components of individual identity and presentation of self
4. the demands for 'gender-appropriate' behaviour and attitudes.[22]

One explanation for the gendering of organisations is given by Burrell,[23] who wrote that 'the suppression of sexuality is one of the first tasks the bureaucracy sets itself'. This is in order to try to control the interferences and disruptions to the 'ideal functioning of the organisations' caused by sexuality, procreation and emotions. There is a view that the integration of women into bureaucratic structures will alter these structures in a significant way, but Colgan and Ledwith[24] argue that it is more likely that women will become co-opted – that is, will function like men in order to operate effectively at senior levels.

Despite their progress in the last thirty years of the twentieth century, women as a group are still comparatively in low power positions at work. In the words of Nina Colwill:

> The lack of women in management is an issue, not of education and training, but of power. Time, patience and women's self-improvement do not appear to be the solution. The solution, in fact, is similar to the problem: power.[25]

People with disabilities

Organisations are often frightened of the cost of employing people with disabilities. However, a US analysis of more than 10,000 disabled employees showed that 31% of their hirings required no added cost for special training or facilities, 50% were under $50 and 69% cost less than $500. Only 1% cost over $5,000. Studies show that building a new facility that is accessible adds only one half of 1% to the building's cost.

BOX 2.6

DO ORGANISATIONS FOR PEOPLE WHO ARE BLIND DISCRIMINATE AGAINST THEM?

A woman who was registered as blind said in a broadcast interview: 'I applied for a managerial job with an organisation which advises blind people on education. I was turned down because I don't have a driving licence. Here was an organisation set up to help blind people, setting conditions which made it impossible for a blind person to get the post. I don't think it had ever occurred to them that a blind person might apply for a senior management job.'

Source: BBC Television News, 31 October 1995.

In the USA, the Americans with Disabilities Act 1990 is credited with being in part responsible for the fact that a million new jobs for people with disabilities were created between then and 1998. In the UK a 1996 Act, the Disability Discrimination Act, introduced new laws and measures aimed at ending the discrimination which many people with disabilities face. The Act gave people with disabilities new rights in the areas of employment, access to goods, facilities and services and buying or renting land or property. In addition the Act required schools, colleges and universities to provide information for people with disabilities, allowed the government to set minimum standards so that people with disabilities can use public transport easily and set up the National Disability Council (in Northern Ireland, the Northern Ireland Disability Council) to advise the government on discrimination against people with disabilities.

Other societal groups

Religious groups. Some of the discrimination affecting 'minority groups' is so accepted that even liberal members of the dominant (sub)culture are barely aware of it. For instance, societies such as that of the UK provide a double bind for people from religious backgrounds other than the dominant Protestant Christian one, so far as accommodating their religious practices is concerned. The working week is built around the practice of Sunday worship, even though the majority of the population takes no active part, while the secular tone means that organisations and individual managers often underestimate the priority which people from religious backgrounds give to having time free for worship. For Moslems being able to attend a mosque on Fridays, for Hindus time free for festivals and ceremonials, for Jews being home before sunset on Fridays are considerations which they are forced to trade off against earnings or career.

BOX 2.7

A POSSIBLE CASE OF RELIGIOUS DISCRIMINATION

It was reported on 18 October 1995 that Patricia Campbell, an Ulster Catholic, had filed a religious discrimination complaint with the Fair Employment Tribunal against the Ulster Unionist Party. She claimed she was unfairly treated in not being shortlisted for the post of party public relations officer. Ms Campbell, 30, said: 'I have stuck my neck out by becoming the first Catholic of my generation to become involved in the Ulster Unionist Party. Look at how my pioneering courage has been repaid. So much for the claim that there is no bar to Catholic advancement in the party.'

Source: Various newspapers, 18 October 1995.

Older people. Ageism, a term originating in the early 1970s, is prejudice or discrimination against people, usually older people, on the grounds of their age. Ageism has been blamed for being a cause why people age poorly in Western society. Prejudice directed against older people is largely a problem of individualistic Western cultures – in collectivist cultures elderly people are usually highly respected and their contribution is acknowledged. Fear of growing old among the young and middle aged is a powerful factor in ageism.

Ageism in the workplace begins to bite at the age of 42. Two-thirds of employees claim to have been excluded from job interviews or offers because of age. One economist has estimated that most people have one promotion in them after the age of 40 – and then they are out. The story goes that in most companies people over 50 are either chairperson or doing the cleaning. Some growth industries, such as public relations and media, are very image conscious – and older people have the wrong image. Age discrimination affects women particularly, as it reduces career prospects for women returning to work after childrearing.

The continuing process of downsizing, followed by new recruitment, leads to elimination of older workers (downsizing is often achieved through early retirement) while new jobs go to younger ones. Causes include the fact that final-salary pension schemes and higher wages make older workers expensive while younger managers may be prejudiced against older workers, arguing they must be mediocre, unambitious or tired if they have failed to progress. Older workers tend to have experience and perspective, which may be valuable for work, but is not valued per se.

In 1993 the UK Liberal Democrat Party committed the party in a Policy Paper to 'entrench equal rights for older people by outlawing discrimination on the basis of age'. In September 1995 the Labour Party undertook a similar commitment, but by September 1998, after more than a year in government, had not announced an intention of bringing legislation forward.

A Private Members' Bill to outlaw 'ageist' job advertisements which specify upper-age limits for applicants was voted on in the UK House of Commons on 9 February 1996. The vote was lost, but it was taken as an indication that moves are now afoot to break the 'last barrier' of legalised workplace discrimination. The sponsor of the Bill said that discrimination on the grounds of sex, race and disability were now all illegal and that legislation was urgently needed to deal with age bias. Soon afterwards 90 large companies, including Marks & Spencer and Royal Bank of Scotland, agreed to oppose age discrimination. On 13 May 1996, it was announced that a collection of eighteen top organisations, including British Airways, British Telecom, Marks & Spencer and Sainsbury's, had come together to form the Employers' Forum on Age. They launched a campaign to ban age discrimination and warned about the cost of releasing older staff. The B&Q store in Macclesfield, staffed entirely by older staff, is 18% more profitable than other stores, and workers in their twenties at WH Smith are four times as likely to leave as older colleagues.

Homosexuals. According to *The Economist* of 6 January 1966, there is a global shift towards reducing prejudice and discrimination against homosexuals. *The Economist* argued that there are four factors promoting this favourable change: scientific evidence of homosexuality as innate; a worldwide development of a middle class, a category into which many gays fall; democratisation (democratic societies are more permissive) and the use of the Internet for global information sharing and resistance to oppression.

Despite such favourable tides, there are many persisting bastions of discrimination against homosexuals. For instance, in May 1996 a vote in the UK House of Commons went 188/120 against relaxing the ban on gays in the armed forces. The debate scarcely mentioned the 'moral' issue and almost all the arguments in favour of retaining the ban rested on the point that the presence of gays in the armed forces was unacceptable to current servicemen and women.

2.6   HARASSMENT

Dictionaries define harassing as 'vexing by repeated attacks'. Definitions of what constitutes sexual harassment depend on gender, with women consistently defining more experiences as harassing than men. The differences in definition create comparability problems for studies of harassment incidence; however, there seems little doubt that it is widespread in the workplace. A study in Tanzania found that *all* women in the sample had experience of sexual harassment at work. In general, men harass women who are junior to them. As one man put it: 'In principle, a woman can refuse without repercussions, but in practice she cannot.' A study of 1,800 UK police women found that 62% had experienced some form of sexual harassment, including touching, by male colleagues and 6% had suffered 'serious sexual assault'.[26] A 1993 Industrial Society report estimated that only 5% of workers who experienced harassment filed a formal complaint. Another survey suggested that women victims doubted that their complaints would be taken seriously or that adequate action would be taken against someone found guilty.

Research into the problem of sexual harassment has tended to focus on harassment that occurs within overt power relationships, for example, bosses and employees, teachers and students, doctors and patients, lawyers and clients. However, sexual harassment often occurs between peers – persons whose relationship is not based on an overt power or status differential. One study found that sexual harassment was pervasive both in terms of the numbers of female and male who had been victims/targets of peer sexual harassment, the relationship of the harassers to their victims, the settings in which harassment occurred, and the verbal and non-verbal behaviours communicated.[27]

Many feminists regard sexual harassment as a patriarchal control strategy used by men to keep women 'in their place': men are seen as intentionally or unintentionally reducing women employees to sexualised beings. In addition, feminists assert, men often subscribe to a 'male sexual drive discourse', in which their sexuality is treated as 'incontinent', 'out of their own control' and essentially biologically driven. The psychodynamics of sexual harassment maintain an unequal power structure between the sexes, forcing women into compliance with nurturant or sexual aspects of the traditional sex role.

As the case of Jenny in Box 2.8 illustrates, women in service sector employment can be vulnerable to sexual harassment from male 'clients'. In general, women in less traditional forms of employment for women are more vulnerable to harassment; especially in such cases, managers may believe that harassment claims result from women's inability to cope with the added pressure of non-traditional work.[28] There is some evidence that harassment can be worse for women who enter managerial work.

Direct and indirect discrimination, job segregation, the glass ceiling and sexual harassment are still part of the context of work for many people from 'minority' groups and so are likely to affect their attitudes and communication behaviours.

BOX 2.8

THE SEXUAL HARASSMENT OF WOMEN IN INSURANCE SALES

An in-depth case study published in 1996 revealed the following situation:

Jenny, an insurance sales representative, was subjected to provocation by Dick, her supervisor, and harassment by a potential client who said he felt 'spurned' because he'd heard that she acquired business through sleeping with clients and felt they could come to some arrangement. Her complaints about sexual harassment not only fell on deaf ears, but got her labelled a 'complaining feminist' and denied the promotion which would normally have followed her consistent performance as her area's highest selling representative; she eventually left the company.

John, the manager of the division and Jenny's line manager, recognised that brokers often made improper suggestions to saleswomen, but was unwilling to define this as sexual harassment, saying 'It's a fact of life, it's out there and usually the girls [sic] have handled it very well' – by which he meant that they had not reacted in front of the brokers. He had placed women under Dick because 'selling was a high pressure job which entailed dealing with men all day' and exposure to a manager like Dick was a test of their suitability for the job. 'The problem with Jenny was that she wanted to change the culture within sales and that did not go down too well with the men.'

The study's authors commented that 'In these conditions of extensive harassment, female isolation and the absence of support from superiors, it is extremely difficult for women to respond in effective ways to sexual harassment in non-traditional work. Whether by resistance, integration, indifference, distancing or denial, all failed to deal effectively and all were then redefined and criticised by line managers as a means of claiming that the women were incompetent/unable to "fit in".' They concluded that whatever response a woman makes to sexual harassment, she is 'punished' for it and that management operate divide and control strategies, with which some women collude.

Source: Collinson, M. and Collinson, D. (1996) 'It's only Dick: the sexual harassment of women managers in insurance sales', *Work, Employment and Society,* **10**(1): 29–56.

2.7   ORGANISATIONAL POLICIES AND CULTURES

As Section 2.4 showed, within organisations the segregation of people into separate spheres and the status differences between them in general reflect the conditions of the wider society. Feminist writers argue that organisations are gendered, embedding the values, attitudes and norms of one gender, usually the male. Writers on race comment on 'the silencing of the importance of race in organizations' (Nkomo 1992)[29] and ask 'why so much attention [has] been given to race and ethnicity outside of organizations and why so little inside'.[30]

Organisations and their managers are generally highly conscious of the disadvantages of diversity. They are particularly aware of the difficulties involved in reaching agreement, standardising procedures and working in parallel on aspects of a project when individuals from a range of cultural or subcultural backgrounds are involved. These activities have even been called 'convergent' activities, implying that there is a problem with divergence or non-conformity. Additionally, for many organisations the cost of diversity is highly visible. It includes obeying equal opportunities law and the negative reactions to diversity in the workplace by some employees. Indeed, for many organisations, their overarching diversity goal might be described as to minimise the costs it entails.

Organisations are less inclined to notice the organisational benefits of diversity. These are of two kinds: the first kind has been defined as affecting divergent activities. These are those activities where creativity is required, which range from strategy generation to writing advertising copy, from new product development to systems improvements. Cross-fertilisation of perspectives and approaches from people of different ethnic, national, gender, religious, sexual orientation, social class and specialist backgrounds help ferment ideas while the tests applied by such a cross-section help filter out the good from the bad. Diversity also helps guard against the dangers of over-conformity and groupthink which are real perils in organisations.

The second category of benefits of diversity in organisations is that it gives them an increased capacity for dealing with the inescapable diversity that exists in the environment: for domestic and international organisations alike in markets, user groups and publics, and, for international organisations, in governments.

While an increasing number of organisations have explicit and well-articulated diversity goals, many do not. Perhaps a senior employee of an airport authority captured their attitude when he said: 'Although the airline industry and airport industry are fairly diverse, I don't think we have a particular view as to how we deal with it – it's sometimes a bit hand-to-mouth' (author's research).

Many organisations' diversity goals are limited to the largely negative ones of avoiding the penalties of disobeying the law or the moral odium of unfairness to certain population groups. There is a marked difference between these and the more positive goals of managing diversity to gain the benefits of using people's talents as fully as possible, creating fertile learning communities and gaining competitive advantage.

BOX 2.9

EQUAL OPPORTUNITIES VERSUS DIVERSITY MANAGEMENT

'I work for a local authority, and I think it still has quite a dogmatic approach to having an equal opportunities policy, rather than what I understand by a diversity policy. It's a very large organisation and it's obviously made up of diverse sections of people, but in terms of the policies which are followed, I don't think they are at all adequate... There's a lot of time and resources put into equal opportunities (EOpps), but EOpps deals with large groups of people, assumes that all black people have similar interests and needs, and that's the way that the policy is followed, I think, where I work; whereas diversity recognises that all people have varying needs and that they don't follow stereotypes, really, which is what EOpps assumes.'

Source: Interview with a local authority human resources manager, author's research.

Corporate goals

In managing diversity these can include:
- obeying the law
- ethical conduct
- using the pool of talent to the full
- building learning communities
- meeting the needs of diverse user populations

Obeying the law. In the UK, as in many countries, there is an extensive legal framework governing the treatment of 'minorities', and those laws have teeth. Despite that, the position of 'minorities' in regard to work in those same countries is by no means acceptable, pointing to the fact that organisations in many cases are evading the law. The Appendix describes the position with regard to discrimination at work in four European countries – France, Germany, Italy and the UK – and shows that it is far from eliminated.

However, for the majority of organisations, obeying the law is a basic tenet. The legal prohibitions of discrimination against 'minorities' have therefore undoubtedly been a major influence on the improving position of 'minorities' in employment. It has often been argued that ending discrimination will only come with a change of attitudes, not by legal means, but there are numerous examples of legal changes ultimately affecting people's attitudes. This happens particularly in democracies, where matters are publicly debated and receive considerable media exposure before they become law, and where people recognise that principles embodied in law usually have majority support.

BOX 2.10

EXAMPLES OF GOOD ORGANISATIONAL PRACTICE FOR PEOPLE WITH DISABILITIES

IBM Canada provides high-quality jobs for people with varying degrees of intellectual impairment in a sheltered data-processing environment.

When Embassy Suites realised that they had many jobs that persons with disabilities could do, they also had to make some accommodation such as widening bathroom doors for wheelchair access. They found that hiring and accommodating persons with disabilities had financial benefits. The most obvious was that an accessible place invites business from clients with disabilities and that the presence of such employees makes such clients more comfortable. It can also help the organisation stay aware of possible barriers to service. But they also had to teach other employees to be sensitive to those with disabilities.

Source: Stack, B. (1990) 'Disabled workers are top performers', *Management Review*, **23**: 35–44.

Ethical Conduct. A growing number of organisations are actively committed to operating ethically. For example, the management of the successful restaurant chain Thank God It's Friday is adamant that business ethics is fundamental to an understanding of how the company runs itself. Not all organisations share this commitment. For example, until its actions provoked an outcry, Shell International had a statement of principles drafted in the 1970s that ran:

> Shell shall not be influenced by those pressure groups that would have corporations make or withhold investment not on commercial criteria but in order to influence the course or pattern of political society. The latter is the role of citizens and governments, not business organisations.

However, there is undoubtedly a marked trend towards organisations adopting ethical principles, which are often embodied in 'mission' statements. It has been described as an 'ethical boom'. Organisations adopting such principles are likely to make active support for equal opportunities a platform of their ethical conduct. Even in these organisations, however, the 'hidden presumption' often is that the moral values of the social majority will prevail, and that individuals who adhere to other values will adjust. For example, most UK organisations would make no commitment to supplying food prepared in ways which are acceptable to people of Jewish or Islamic faith. These minorities among employees are simply expected to make their own arrangements for eating according to their religion.

Using the pool of talent to the full. Many organisations need more tangible reasons than ethical principles for embracing diversity, as the following extract from a letter published in a newspaper in 1995 shows:

> The moral imperative is hardly foremost in the minds of those companies struggling to survive – and there is legislation in place to deal with that issue. Therefore the working group set up... to improve equal opportunities in the (construction) industry has focused on the business case, because it is the most persuasive and constructive argument for change... To survive, the construction industry must change to attract and retain the best people for the job. The benefits will be for men, women, the industry and the clients it serves.[31]

For many organisations, a strong business case argument for actively supporting equal opportunities is that it positively affects the motivations of staff. This applies both to existing staff and to potential staff. Many organisations believe that developing appropriate multicultural provision will affect how far employees identify with the organisation and feel loyal to it, with all the accompanying advantages of improved attendance, motivation and self-discipline. Job advertisements that carry the statement 'X is an equal opportunities employer' generally attract a greater number and higher calibre of applicants than those that do not. This is particularly true of younger staff, whom many companies are especially eager to attract.

BOX 2.11

OPPORTUNITY 2000 GOALS IN THE NATIONAL HEALTH SERVICE

1. Increase the number of women in general management posts from 18% in 1991 to 30% in 1994. (28% achieved by April 1995.)
2. Increase the number of qualified women accountants in the NHS.
3. Increase the percentage of women medical consultants from 15.5% in 1991 to 20% by 1994, necessitating an annual increase of 10%.
4. Increase the representation of women as members of authorities and trusts from 29% in 1991 to 35% by 1994.
5. Introduce a programme allowing women aspiring to management positions to go through a development centre with a view to establishing their own personal development needs.
6. Introduce incentives for recruitment and retention to ensure that the number of qualified nurses and midwives leaving the profession does not rise.
7. Ensure that, following a maternity leave or career break, all women (including those returning to part-time nursing or as a job share) are able to return at a grade commensurate with their leaving grade and to work of similar status.
8. Monitor the time taken for nurses to reach management positions to ensure that men and women have equal access to these positions.

Source: Opportunity 2000 goals in the National Health Service (1996), Department of Health.

A second business case argument is that existing staff, who represent a major fixed cost for most organisations, constitute a resource or capacity. Increasingly, organisations are recognising that underutilisation of that capacity as a result of discriminatory barriers is inefficient, just as the underutilisation of any other resource is.

Building learning communities. Some organisations now aim to become 'learning organisations'. This means that they try to ensure that learning from organisational experience and learning about environmental change are embedded in the structures, processes and culture of the organisation. The goal is a continuous transfer of understanding and knowledge from individuals to groups, an openness to the outside world and a capacity for renewing the organisation.

In general, aiming to become a learning organisation is a response to environmental pressures. These include:

- the speed and variety of technological change
- the existence of global competition, much of it low cost
- the short lifespan of competitive advantages gained by innovation
- the entry of new competitors in traditional markets (such as retailers in financial services)
- the opening up of new and diverse markets, both nationally and internationally, and the changes in the composition and attitudes of societies, including labour forces.

Within the context of the goal of being a learning organisation, diversity acquires an intrinsic value; people from different backgrounds, whether those are technical, educational, social, ethnic or gender based, are attuned to different aspects of the environment. Providing the mechanisms exist for them to pool and transfer the information they gain through this attuning, the organisation can tap into a much larger and wider range of environmental information.

Meeting the needs of diverse user populations. In earlier sections of this chapter, the diversity of the population of the UK, EU and Europe were briefly described. All these people of differing nationalities, ethnicity, genders, sexual orientations, levels of physical and mental ability, religions and age groups are potential users of services or are in the market for products. From libraries to confectionery manufacturers, hospitals to house builders, the users and consumers of services and products are highly diverse. With diversity comes diversity of needs and wants. Public service providers such as libraries, hospitals, schools, government and local authority agencies and many charities can only fulfil their role properly if they meet the needs of these diverse user groups. Marketing, for commercial organisations, implies 'meeting consumer needs profitably'; some companies target their products at niche markets (such as hair detensioners); much of the UK market for 'universal' products come from 'minority' groups. In some cases, the main form of adaptation for market diversity is in the product advertising: confectionery countlines appeal to individuals across the cultural spectrum. For other companies, a more fundamental adaptation is needed for diverse markets: the media, for instance, comprise a large category of commercial provider with a particular need to understand and reflect the market (audience), because their products are so visible and explicit that they can easily offend large sections of the market.

In many organisations, however, diversity is treated as the province of the human resources department. This can result in neglecting the diversity of their users and consumers, with adverse effects on profits or consumer satisfaction. For example, a UK survey of women car drivers by Condé Nast, published in February 1996, showed that more than half the women polled felt they were patronised by the car industry. Portrayal of women drivers as spoilt children who drive cars bought by their indulgent fathers (Renault Clio), or women with hair blowing through the sun roof (Ford Fiesta) were particularly offensive.

They also disliked commercials that showed macho images of cars speeding or going over cliffs because these contained little practical information about safety features or prices. Most of the 700 women surveyed said that safety, service contracts and power were their criteria in choosing a car.[32] Equally offensive to some user groups, such as people with disabilities and ethnic minorities, is their invisibility in advertisements, as Box 2.12 illustrates.

BOX 2.12

HOW NOT TO MARKET TO 'MINORITIES'

1. A television news item in February 1996 showed that a brochure by Ford Motor Company, issued four years previously with a photograph showing the diversity of its workforce, had been reissued with four members from ethnic minorities 'brushed' out and replaced by white faces. The company said it was an administrative error: the new brochure had been versioned for Poland and reflected the ethnic composition there; it had been used in the UK by mistake. A Ford manager, acting as spokesperson, said 'I apologise for any offence the brochure might have caused employees or customers, and we have taken steps to ensure it does not happen again.' A union representative said 'If it's good enough for black workers to make the product, it's good enough for black workers to also advertise the product.' The editor of an advertising magazine described it as a 'major own goal' for Ford, the TV reporter as 'an expensive episode for Ford in terms of negative publicity'.

2. Organisational personnel concerned about diversity among consumers often face an uphill struggle: 'We have trouble getting support round the company. For instance, the advertising department almost never shows a member of the ethnic minorities. The department is only interested if we are talking about a significant percentage of the target market and, of course, at 6% in all, no one ethnic group is. The advertising treats women better – they are a big group, and they both influence family car purchases and are major buyers in their own right.'

Sources: BBC Television News, 20 February 1996; interview with the personnel director and assistant personnel director of a major car manufacturer, author's research.

Against this, some companies are very conscious of the need to be diverse, have strong programmes supporting diversity and to reflect that diversity in their public face. A human resources manager for a television company, interviewed by the author, said that:

> We believe that it is in the best interests of the company to recruit, select, promote and train on merit. We aim to operate within the spirit as well as the letter of the law on Equal Opportunities. We have numerous positive action schemes, which we do not see as positive discrimination; they are designed to create a level playing field. We have a commitment to creating a comfortable culture/atmosphere for workers in this organisation. The community we serve (our viewers) contains a high level of ethnic minorities. We have both to have a work force that reflects that and to reflect it in our programmes.[33]

Organisational cultures

These can be analysed in a variety of ways, for instance as externally driven versus internally driven, task or people focused. Geert Hofstede[34] identified six dimensions, which are closely related to his concepts of culture (see Chapter 3) and also significant for the likely impact of the culture on diversity within the organisation. The six differences, Hofstede asserts, seem to result from historical factors like the philosophy of the founders and are:

1. Process-orientated versus results-orientated cultures. Process-orientated work cultures emphasise technical and bureacratic routines; results-orientated cultures have a common concern for outcomes. The latter may well be more supportive of diversity, since within them a range of approaches can be tolerated, provided the results are satisfactory.
2. Job-orientated versus employee-orientated cultures. Organisations with employee-orientated cultures assume a broader responsibility for employees' well-being than do those with job-orientated cultures. Obviously, in organisations with a diverse workforce, an employee-orientated culture is more likely to ensure that all individuals have opportunities for advancement.
3. Professional versus parochial cultures. This is a distinction which corresponds to an older one between individuals with a cosmopolitan outlook and those with a local outlook. In terms of organisational culture, parochialism is likely to be associated with a degree of xenophobia or distrust of outsiders, which can be inimical to diversity and raise its cost in terms of the adaptation required of existing employees.
4. Open system versus closed system cultures. Here the reference is to the corporate style of internal and external communications, and to the ease with which outsiders and newcomers are admitted. Hofstede found that the Danish organisations studied were more open than the Dutch – and that this was the only difference found between them. Closed systems cultures are likely to be less capable of benefiting from the increased sensitivity to the environment which diversity makes possible as well as less accessible to minorities than open systems.

5. Tightly versus loosely controlled cultures. The difference here concerns the degree of formality and punctuality; which culture applies in an organisation is partly a function of its technology – banks, for example, are more tightly controlled than advertising agencies – but some variation occurs within the same technology. More loosely controlled systems are better able to tolerate the behavioural differences which come with diversity; tightly controlled systems require all individuals to conform to a single model.

6. Pragmatic versus normative cultures. Pragmatic cultures have flexible ways of dealing with the environment, especially customers; rigid cultures do not. The distinction reflects the organisation's degree of 'customer orientation'. Since flexibility is both a necessary condition and an outcome of diversity, pragmatic cultures are better adapted to benefit from it.

> Corporate goals in relation to diversity range from evading legal requirements such as equal opportunities laws to fully embracing the benefits of diversity in every sphere. Moreover, multiple goals and various diversity policies can be overlapping and mutually reinforcing. Organisational cultures vary in their supportiveness or incompatibility with diversity, with those which are results orientated, employee orientated, professional, open, loosely controlled and pragmatic being more favourable than those which are process orientated, job orientated, parochial, closed, tightly controlled and normative.
>
> The goals, policies and culture of the organisation or organisations for which communicators work create a climate which will impact strongly on their communication and which they need to take into account.

2.8 EXPLANATIONS OF THE DIFFERENCES IN EMPLOYMENT REALITIES AND OPPORTUNITIES FOR DIFFERENT GROUPS

It is often argued in the USA that differences in self-investment by individuals in their own education and training explain earnings gaps; this is an argument which can be expected to be heard more in the future in countries such as the UK, which until recently had a 'free' university education system, but one which is increasingly becoming not free. However, research in the USA shows that only a small percentage of gender and about one-third of ethnic earnings inequalities can be explained in this way. There are substantial inequalities that cannot be explained by differences in education, labour market experience or organisational tenure.

The following are some sources of inequality:

● Substantial numbers of jobs are 'advertised' only through informal networks, which some employers use as screening devices.

43

- Gender- and ethnicity-specific training and job search information are provided by some employment and training agencies.
- Corporate practice (in personnel and human resource departments) includes steering all candidates to jobs that are deemed appropriate to their ethnicity or gender and specifically away from jobs requiring long training, either off or on the job, thus reducing their prospects of career development; this helps account for the fact that earning disparities widen with age.
- Stereotypical beliefs about women and ethnic minorities feed into these first three points.
- Prejudiced co-workers exclude women and minority members from informal networks in which opportunities for career-enhancing experience are circulated.
- Job segregation: although less well understood than discrimination, this is increasingly recognised by researchers as a common source of employment disadvantage for 'minorities'.

Thus discrimination and harassment are only two of the many causes of unemployment inequality.

However, the material in Sections 2.2 to 2.4 could give an impression that there exists a substantial group (25–40-year-old, majority nationality, ethnicity and religion, degree-bearing, heterosexual males of intermediate or professional social class status living in traditional nuclear families) that is not only privileged and exempt from discrimination but that also holds power and uses it to exclude members of other groups. If such a group still exists, the facts suggest it is now small – numerically a tiny minority – and under threat, both from the demands of the 'minority' groups and from the pressures of global competition.

2.9 CONCLUSION

This chapter provides evidence of the growing significance of intercultural communication at work, resulting from population shifts, increased international trade and workforce participation by minority groups. It also bears witness to the continuing disadvantages of some groups, which must be understood by all intercultural communicators as potentially present in the thoughts, emotions and attitudes of those with whom they interact.

REFERENCES

1. Smith, M.G. (1986) 'Pluralism, race and ethnicity in selected African countries', in Rex, J. and Mason, D. (eds) *Theories of Race and Ethnic Relations*, Cambridge: Cambridge University Press.

2. Collier, M.J. and Thomas, M. (1988) 'Cultural identity: an interpretive perspective' in Kim, Y.Y. and Gudykunst, W.B. (eds) *Theories in Intercultural Communication*, Newbury Park, CA: Sage.
3. Wallman, S. (ed.) (1986) *Ethnicity at Work*, London: Macmillan.
4. Mason, D. (1995) *Race and Ethnicity in Modern Britain*, Oxford: Oxford University Press.
5. European Commission (1995) *Europe in Figures* (4th edn), Luxembourg: Office for Official Publications of the European Communities, pp. 183–85.
6. Owen, D. (1993) *Country of Birth: Settlement Patterns*, University of Warwick Centre for Research in Ethnic Relations, National Ethnic Minority Data Archive, 1991 Census Statistical Paper no. 5.
7. Government Statistical Office (1997) *Labour Force Survey*, London: Her Majesty's Stationery Office.
8. Jones, T. (1983) *Britains' Ethnic Minorities*, London: Policy Studies Institute.
9. Acker, J. (1992) 'Gendering organizational theory' in Mills, A.J. and Tancred, P. (eds) *Gendering Organizational Analysis*, London: Sage.
10. European Commission (1995) op. cit.
11. Colgan, F. and Ledwith, S. (1996) 'Women as organisational change agents' in Colgan, F. and. Ledwith, S. (eds) *Women in Organisations*, Basingstoke: Macmillan.
12. Bram, L.L. and Dickey, N.H. (1994) 'Disabled People', *Funk and Wagnalls Encyclopaedia*, Cleveland, OH: World Almanac Edition.
13. Taylor, C. Jr and Smolinksi, C. (1994) *Managing Diversity and Glass Ceiling Initiatives as National Economic Imperatives*, US Dept of Labor, Glass Ceiling Commission Report. Posted on the Internet: http:www.auaa.org/library/glasceil.html.
14. World Economic Forum (1995) *World Competitiveness Report*. Posted on the Internet: http:www/issues/edfi/worldrep.html.
15. US State Department (1997) *Human Rights Report*. Posted on the Internet: http:www3.ituint/MISSIONS/US/hrr97/97hrp_report_toc.html.
16. Mason, D. (1995) op. cit.
17. Brown, C. and Gay, P. (1985) *Racial Discrimination: Seventeen Years after the Act*, London: Policy Studies Institute.
18. Noon, M. (1993) Racial discrimination in speculative applications: evidence from the UK's top 100 firms, *Human Resource Management Journal*, 3(4): 35–47.
19. Home Office (1993) *Report on the Police and Racism*, London: Her Majesty's Stationery Office.
20. Mason, D. (1995) op. cit.
21. Schwartz, D.B. (1994) *An Examination of the Impact of Family-Friendly Policies on the Glass Ceiling*, US Dept of Labor, Glass Ceiling Commission Report.
22. Acker, J. (1992) op. cit.
23. Burrell, G. (1984) 'Sex and organizational analysis', *Organization Studies*, **5**: 97–118.
24. Colgan F. and Ledwith, S. (1996) op. cit.
25. Colwill, N. (1995) 'Women in management: power and powerlessness' in VinniCombe, S. and Colwill, N.L. (eds) *The Essence of Women in Management*, Hemel Hempstead: Prentice-Hall.
26. Gutek, B.A. and Cohen, A.G. (1992) 'Sex ratios, sex role spillover and sex at work' in Mills, A.J. and Tancred, P. (eds) *Gendering Organizational Analysis*, London: Sage.
27. Ivy, D.K. and Hamlet, S. (1996) 'College students and sexual dynamics: two studies of peer sexual harassment', *Communication Education*, **45**: 149–66.
28. Collinson, M. and Collinson, D. (1996) 'It's only Dick: the sexual harassment of women managers in insurance sales', *Work, Employment and Society*, **10**(1): 29–56.
29. Nkomo, S. (1992) 'The emperor has no clothes: rewriting "race" in organizations', *Academy of Management Review*, **17**: 487–513.
30. Alderfer, C.P. and Smith, K.K. (1988) 'Studying intergroup relations embedded in organizations', *Administrative Science Quarterly*, **27**: 5–65.

31. From a letter to the *Independent*, 16 November 1995 from Sandi Rhys Jones, Chairwoman, Construction Industry Board.
32. *The Times* 9 February 1996 (Alexandra Frean).
33. Interview at Thames Television: author's research.
34. Hofstede, G. (1994) *Cultures and Organizations: Software of the Mind*, London: HarperCollins.

3

HOW CULTURES DIFFER

Chapter 2 described some of the important differences of background and societal position that increasingly exist between people who interact at work. This chapter considers some explanations how those differences arise and of how they can affect the organisational environment of work communication.

Section 3.1 gives some definitions of the term culture and mainstream accounts of cultural difference, largely in terms of psychological factors such as values; Section 3.2 considers theories which differentiate cultures on the basis of communication; Section 3.3 looks at the impact of national cultural differences on the immediate context for much work communication: the organisation. The concluding section discusses issues such as cultural change and convergence, how cultural influences on communication and behaviour can be distinguished from other influences and the generalisability of cultural theories and research findings to subcultures such as gender or occupation.

It must be remembered in reading what follows that cultural orientations represent central tendencies; that is, in general, individual members of these cultures are most likely to act in a manner consistent with these findings, but it should not be expected that everyone will do so.

3.1 EXPLANATIONS OF CULTURAL DIFFERENCE

The previous chapter has, I hope, established that, in any field of work, in the twenty-first century many of the people will be of varying sexes, genders, sexual orientations, ethnicities, nationalities, religions, social classes, educational, technical, professional and experiential backgrounds or physical, mental or sensory abilities. Whether this fact matters not at all, very little or a great deal depends on how much and how those differences of background affect people's behaviour, including their ways of communicating. The contention of this chapter, which is consistent with current thinking on the subject, is that they affect them a great deal, although not to the extent of determining them – and indeed that there is great variety in how much different individuals in different work settings will be affected by the same or similar factors in their personal background.

The key concept in understanding behavioural differences resulting from differences of background is culture. This is a subject which has received a huge amount of attention in both the communication and the management literature over the past 20 or so years. What have we learned?

There are many and various definitions of culture. As early as 1952, Kroeber and Kluckhohn[1] analysed 160 definitions of the concept and concluded that the definitions fell into six major groups based on the emphasis given by the author of the definition. By synthesis they produced this definition:

> Culture consists of patterns, explicit and implicit, of and for behaviour acquired and transmitted by symbols, constituting the distinctive achievements of human groups, including their embodiments in artifacts; the essential core of culture consists of traditional (that is historically derived and selected) ideas and especially their attached values; culture systems may, on the one hand, be considered as products of action, on the other as conditioned elements of further action. (p. 181)

Thus the core of Kroeber and Kluckhohn's concept of culture is the following:

● The members of a culture system share a set of ideas, and, especially, values.
● These are transmitted (particularly from one generation to another) by symbols.
● Culture is produced by the past actions of a group and its members.

So, for example, Scottish culture supports the value of courage in the face of overwhelming odds, symbolised in the stories of 'William Wallace and the spider' and 'Bonnie Prince Charlie's rebellion'; these symbols derive from Scotland's history as a small nation resisting English domination and it may well be that the Scots' reputation for producing soldiers renowned for their valour can be attributed to this aspect of their culture.

The culture which is relevant to the theme of this book is not high culture – art, music, theatre – nor even popular culture in the sense of popular music and films, but anthropological culture, which is, broadly speaking, the ways in which one group or society of humans live that are different from the ways in which other groups live.

Anthropologists often draw a distinction between surface culture and deep culture. Surface culture consists of the things which are obviously different to visitors to a foreign country – differences in dress, things people eat or their music, gestures and artifacts plus more subtle things such as norms and roles. The elements of surface culture can be summarised as its shared symbols.

BOX 3.1

TAKING NOTE OF SURFACE CULTURE

1. A guide published by the UK National Housing Federation and the Home Housing Trust in August 1998 recommended that architects and designers should take cultural, religious and social needs into account when creating housing for minority communities. The report's advice included:

   - A private, sheltered outdoor space will be needed in some Bangladeshi, Indian and Pakistani households for sun-drying foods such as poppadums.
   - A space for barbecueing should be provided in housing for Turks and Cypriots, for whom it is a popular social ritual.
   - Orthodox Jews need the edge of the property clearly demarcated by, for instance, a high fence, as they are prohibited by their religion from carrying any object beyond the home's boundaries on the Sabbath.
   - For some Vietnamese it is important to have a pond, or, better still, a stream with a bridge, as water symbolises happiness.
   - Bedroom design for Chinese people should take into account that some cannot have a bed facing any door, including that of a wardrobe; the colour white should be avoided in their homes.
   - Niches and shelves are needed in homes for Buddhists, Confucians and Taoists who use them for shrines and for Greek Orthodox people who use them for icons and candles.

2. 'Driving in from Trivandrum airport, I saw that the roads were thronged with "autorickshaws" [three-wheeled taxis], highly decorated lorries often bearing scenes of Hindu myths and the occasional bullock cart; that the answer to the question "Do Indians drive on the right or the left" appeared to be "neither – straight down the middle – or both"; that all the women wore beautifully coloured saris or shalwar kameez and many of the men wore dhotis or lunghis; that many carried pots or bundles gracefully on their heads; that there were single cows grazing everywhere by the sides of the roads or being led along by ropes; that the many huge billboards were painted and so semi-permanently carried the same advertisement; that many of the houses were in "bungalow" style with a deep verandah; that rice and tapioca were growing among the innumerable coconut palms; and that we passed several buildings offering computing courses or Internet and e-mail services.'

Sources: Reports in various newspapers, 13 August 1998; a letter to the author from a friend who was visiting Kerala, India, in 1997.

Deep culture is the hidden part that cannot be accessed directly by the human sensory organs. It is 'any of the customs, worldview, language, kinship systems, social organisation and other taken-for-granted day-to-day practices of a people which set that group apart as a distinctive group'.[2]

Worldview refers to a 'culture's orientation toward such things as God, humanity, nature, the universe, and the other philosophical issues that are concerned with the concept of being'. An example often used is a comparison between Euro-American and Native American relationships to nature. While the Native American views the human relationship to nature as one of unity (being at one with nature), the Euro-American views the world as human centred. Rhetorical forms such as religious, philosophical, and scientific discourses help to create a coherent worldview for a culture.

Language is an essential part of culture, both because the other elements, such as worldview, can only be transmitted through language and because language itself helps mould the way the people who use it think.

Social organisation refers to the way societies organise relationships among members of a group. In general, cultures differ in their kinship systems, family types and rules of descent. 'Kinship systems' refers to the point that, for instance, such relationships as mother's brother have much more significance in some societies than others; 'family types' range from monogamy (one husband – one wife) to polyandry (one wife – several husbands); and rules of descent specify ways in which persons in a society trace their ancestry – patrilineally, matrilineally, bilaterally or ambilineally.

Deep culture is not only hard for outsiders to see, it is also a fluid, multidimensional process and 'a woefully complex, maddeningly dynamic phenomenon that does not lend itself easily to causal analysis' (Ruben).[3]

We have already seen that, according to Kroeber and Kluckhohn's definition, *values* play a central role in culture. More recently, Lachman *et al.* (1994)[4] have also argued that values play a central role in the impact of culture: 'Values... determine and provide legitimacy for (or sanction) collective and individual preferences for certain states of affairs and modes of conduct over available alternatives.' Thus, values serve as a mechanism of social control. However, these authors assert, within a culture some values are more important than others; some are core, others peripheral. Core values are stabilising mechanisms, although they can change, slowly and with difficulty; peripheral values, however, change comparatively easily.

Lachman *et al.* put forward a framework that distinguishes core and peripheral values, while recognising that they are part of a continuum. Values can be arranged in a hierarchy based on:

- their relative importance
- their durability
- the level of acceptance and agreement attached to them
- their involvement in social control.

BOX 3.2

IS CULTURE GOING TRIBAL?

It was reported in *The Economist* that the sales and profits of Hennes and Mauritz (H&M), a Swedish fashion retailer, grew faster over the decade to 1998 than those of any other clothes retailer in the world. Its CEO, Stefan Perrson, believes that national tastes are disappearing, 'a result of feeding the MTV generation from Tokyo to London the same diet of satellite television, movies and music'.

The view that tastes are crossing national frontiers is supported by a survey of some 35,000 consumers in 35 countries published in March 1998 by Roper Starch Worldwide, a marketing group. Its MD says consumers are now divided, not by country, but into 'global tribes'.

Source: *The Economist*, 28 February 1998, p. 84.

Which values are core and which peripheral vary across cultures – for instance, the status of women is a core value in Argentina, Chile, India and Israel, but less so in China, where the Confucian hierarchical concept of relations between individuals is more core (and has not been changed by Maoism). Similarly, to a third-generation American, the value of the democratic right to free speech might be core, but to her Singaporean cousin it might be peripheral, something to be traded off against the value of having a low-crime, drug-free society to live in.

A rather different definition of culture that has useful implications is that 'culture is a shared system of perceptions and values, or a group of people who share a certain system of perceptions and values' (Robinson 1997).[5] This definition appears simple but it carries some far-reaching implications:

- The use of the term 'system' means that a culture is a rigid constellation of interactions between certain values – thus for many Americans, for instance, belief in the value of democracy is interlocked with belief in the importance of freedom of expression and information; for Jains, religious belief is inseparable from the moral imperative not to take any life.
- However, individual members of any culture have values beyond those they have in common with other members of that culture – an American democrat may or may not be very concerned about the environment or be a born-again Christian. This point implies that a person can be part of more than one cultural system simultaneously, and that cultural conflict can occur within a person as well as between people.

- The boundaries of cultures are ill-defined – a culture can be shared by people from one or many different geographical locations, so long as they share the same system of interactions between values; emigrants usually take many of the values of their natal culture with them, although over time they may integrate them with values of the society into which they have immigrated.
- Values and systems of interactions between values can change over time, both for individuals and for a society (or culture) as a whole.

It is generally agreed that culture is an exclusively human phenomenon, which, in the words of *Webster's Dictionary*, 'depends on man's [sic] capacity for learning and transmitting knowledge to succeeding generations'. Thus culture emerges from differences in different human groups' historical experience – in the case of national or ethnic groups, for instance, this includes their historical, physical and climatic environment, their experience of conquering or being conquered, and their exposure to different religions or myths. The solutions the groups have found to the problems presented by those experiences are an equally important part of their culture.

Over the past thirty years there has been a substantial effort of theorising and research devoted to cultural difference, much of which has attempted to reduce the bewildering variety of its manifestations to a small set of central variables. These central variables are usually related to deep culture. The first widely considered such set, put forward by the anthropologists Kluckhohn and Strodtbeck (1961),[6] identified five core variables corresponding to the solutions to basic problems which they argued are faced by humankind:

1. What is the relationship of the individual to others (relational orientation)? Is a higher value placed on the individual or the group?
2. What is the temporal focus of human life (time orientation)? Is time to be reckoned as precisely as possible or more loosely? What are the relative values of the near future, the far future, the past or the present?
3. What is the modality of human activity (activity orientation)? Are people expected to try actively to meet their desires or to accept their fates?
4. What is a human being's relation to nature (person–nature orientation)? Should people co-exist with nature, attempt to control it, or attempt to dominate it?
5. What is the character of innate human nature (human–nature orientation)? Are people naturally good or evil?

Following Kluckhohn and Strodtbeck, in the late 1960s and 1970s, Geert Hofstede undertook the most exhaustive cross-cultural study to date, using questionnaire data from 80,000 IBM employees in 66 countries across seven occupations.[7] From this research Hofstede established four dimensions of culture:

1. *Individualism–collectivism* (IC) is defined by the extent to which individuals' behaviours are influenced and defined by others: individualists prefer self-

sufficiency while collectivists give more recognition to their interdependent roles and obligations to the group. Studies of social categorisation and intergroup relations show that people 'group' others using salient characteristics as the basis. The group that the categoriser feels similar to and identifies with is called the 'ingroup' and other groups are called 'outgroups'. People from all types of culture categorise others in this way, but the importance of the distinction is much greater for people from collectivist cultures. Whereas individualistic societies are loosely knit social frameworks in which people primarily operate as individuals or in their immediate families, collectivist societies are composed of tight networks in which people operate as members of ingroups and outgroups, expect to look after other members of their ingroup in need and expect their group to look after them.

This dimension is associated with relational behaviour – determining the relevance of others. For people in collectivistic cultures, the personal relationship prevails over the task, whereas the opposite is the case for those in individualistic cultures.

For scores on individualism, five of the top six countries out of the 66 researched by Hofstede are 'Anglo' countries – Australia, Canada, Great Britain, New Zealand and the USA – with the Netherlands occupying position five. Five of the lowest in individualism (highest in collectivism) are South American and the sixth is Pakistan. France is eleventh highest in individualism and Germany fifteenth.

Individualism–collectivism as a concept long antedates Hofstede's work and has been by far the most widely applied of all the cultural constructs to analyses of cultural difference of all kinds. It will recur frequently in this book.

2. *Power distance* (PD) is defined by the degree of separation between people of various social statuses or, to put it another way, the extent to which the less powerful members of a society expect and accept that power is distributed unequally. Low-PD cultures endorse egalitarianism, high-PD cultures endorse hierarchies. In high-PD societies relations between unequals are formal, often patron–client in format, information flow is formalised and restricted, and companies are organised in rigid vertical hierarchies. In low-PD societies relations are open and informal, information flows are functional and unrestricted, and companies tend to have flat hierarchies and matrix organisations.

    Countries particularly high on power distance are Malaysia, the Philippines and four South American countries; those particularly low on this variable are Austria, Ireland, Israel, New Zealand, and the four Scandinavian countries. Great Britain is tenth from the bottom in power distance, Germany eleventh, and the USA is sixteenth; France, however, is fifteenth from the highest.

3. *Uncertainty avoidance* (UA) refers to the extent to which a culture prefers to avoid ambiguity and the way in which it resolves uncertainty. High-UA cultures prefer rules and set procedures to contain the uncertainty, low-UA cultures tolerate greater ambiguity and prefer more flexibility in their responses. In high-UA societies, families, groups and organisations tend to be closed to outsiders, to stress compliance and obedience, to punish error and non-conformity, and to reward conformity, loyalty and attention to detail. Low-UA societies tend to accept outsiders at all levels, stress personal choice and decision making, reward initiative, teamplay, and risk taking and stress the development of analytical skills.

   Two Southern European countries – Greece and Portugal – and two South American – Guatemala and Uruguay – are highest on uncertainty avoidance, while the six lowest in this characteristic are four small nations, Hong Kong, Ireland, Jamaica, Singapore, and two Scandinavian countries. Great Britain is low, at position seven from the lowest, so is the USA, at eleven, but Germany is about halfway and France is thirteenth from the highest.

4. *Masculinity/femininity* (MAS) defines quality of life issues, high-MAS cultures endorsing assertiveness, competition and aggressive success, low-MAS cultures preferring modesty, compromise and cooperative success. In high-MAS societies people tend to believe that matters of material comfort, social privilege, access to power and influence, status and prestige, and ability to consume are related to ability and that with enough opportunity any individual who wants these benefits of society can have them. The corollary is that those who do not have the ability, or the character, cannot and should not have them, since they are essentially a reward for hard work and success. High-MAS societies tend to reward financial and material achievements with preferential social prestige and status, and to attribute strong character and spiritual values to such high achievers.

   In some low-MAS societies, living well in material comfort and having other high standard of living factors are believed to be matters of birth, luck, or destiny. In some other low-MAS societies, material comfort and lifestyle are considered less an indication of a person's character and value than their religious devotion, their social conscience, their intellectual or artistic abilities, their stature as a wise elder, or (and this probably applies in Scandinavia) their rights as a fellow member of a caring society.

   On the MAS variable, Japan is significantly higher than any other nation while Austria, Venezuela, Italy and Switzerland are in positions two to five; four Northern European countries are highest on the 'feminine' end of the dimension. Great Britain and Germany are high on MAS at positions nine and ten, somewhat above the USA at 15, and substantially above France at 35. This was the only dimension on which Hofstede found significant differences between men and women, although, even then, not consistently. In the most 'feminine' countries, there was no real difference, but in the most 'masculine' countries, men scored 50% higher than women, and correspondingly for the countries in between. It was because this was the only dimension on which men and women differed that Hofstede labelled it 'masculine'/'feminine'. Since sexism can be read into these labels, some writers have renamed its poles 'achievement' and 'relational' orientations. This terminology is followed in this book.

Hofstede's research found that some of the variables are correlated, so there are clusters of countries on their intersection; however, there are exceptions to these relationships, so the dimensions are probably independent although related statistically. Figure 3.1 shows the location on power distance and individualism–collectivism of a selected set of countries.

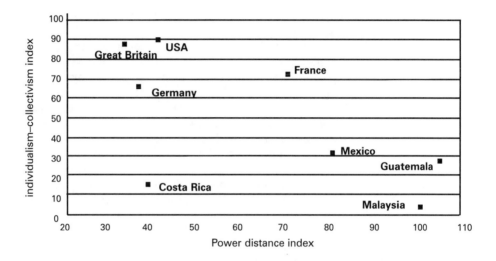

Figure 3.1 Power distance and individualism–collectivism interactions for eight countries

Hofstede's definition and analyses of culture are not intended to be rigid categorisations of behaviour or people: he argues that the culture of a country – or any other category of people – is not a combination of properties of the 'average citizen' or 'modal personality'. He says that one person from a culture may react in one way (such as feeling nervous), another from the same culture in another way (such as wanting rules to be respected). These would both be manifestations of a common cultural tendency to avoid uncertainty. In addition, such reactions need not be found within the same persons or in all persons from the culture, but only statistically more often in the same society. Few people fall entirely into one or the other cultural pattern, but the tendency is there.

For F. Trompenaars, culture is 'often intangible and difficult to define'.[8] However, Trompenaars, like earlier researchers, produced a taxonomy of cultures, drawing in part on the orientations concepts of Kluckhohn and Strodtbeck and the 'pattern' categories of Parsons (1951).[9] His analysis was derived partly from fifteen years of training of managers and more specifically on academic research using minimum samples in each of 30 countries of 100 people with similar backgrounds and occupations (75% managers, 25% general administrative staff) from a variety of multinational companies.

BOX 3.3

SOME DEVELOPMENTS FROM
HOFSTEDE'S FINDINGS

1. Triandis *et al.* (1988) found by research that when respondents were asked to give 20 descriptions of themselves by completing 20 sentences that started with 'I am...' people from collectivistic cultures used 35–45% group-related attributes such as 'I am the third daughter of my family' to describe their sense of person-hood, while people from individualistic cultures used only 15% group-related attributes.
2. Ashleigh Merritt of the University of Texas at Austin undertook a replication study for eighteen countries to answer the question 'To what extent do Hofstede's dimensions of national culture, derived from personnel in a large multinational company in the late 1960s and early 1970s, apply to commercial airline pilots flying in the 1990s?'

   For individualism he found higher levels overall and lower differences between countries than Hofstede: possible explanations were that forces of economic modernisation might have produced more individualism in previously low-individualistic countries; or that pilots are at the forefront of modernity and self-select into an individualistic profession.

   Power distance and uncertainty avoidance results discriminated between countries fairly well and correlated fairly well with those of Hofstede. Masculinity/femininity failed to discriminate well, probably because of unique attributes of the pilot profession. A strong cluster of the six 'Anglo' countries were found among the 18 yielding data; this result may provide strong statistical evidence for the cultural similarities of these countries.

Sources: Triandis, H.C., McCusker, C. and Hui, C.H. (1990) 'Multi-method probes of individualism-collectivism', *Journal of Personality and Social Psychology*, **59**: 1006–20; Merritt, A.C. (1997) 'Replicating Hofstede: a study of pilots in eighteen countries'. Posted on the Internet: http://www/psy.utexas.edu/psy/helmreich/hofrep.htm.

For Trompenaars there are three main categories and eight sub-categories of cultural dimension:

● Relationships with people
 – universalism versus particularism
 – individualism versus collectivism
 – neutrality versus emotionalism
 – specificity versus diffuseness
 – achievement versus ascription
● Attitudes to time
 – future versus past orientation
 – polychronic versus monochronic time
 – time as a stream or a cycle
● Attitudes to the environment.

Universalism and particularism contrast a preference for drawing general principles versus a preference for the anecdotal or itemised. For example, where one
person might say 'One of the characteristics of modern Western life is for
married women with children to work', another might say 'It's a curious fact,
but three of my friends – all married women with children – have got themselves
jobs. There's Mrs X running a playgroup, Mrs Y working at the supermarket and
Mrs Z training to be a solicitor.' These preferences for the universal or the particular are, however, complementary, not opposing preferences – therefore they are
reconcilable. In most situations, universalistic and particular judgements reinforce one another. Much of the research into this cultural dimension has come
from the USA, and is influenced by American cultural preferences.

Individualism and collectivism. Trompenaars sees this dimension slightly differently from Hofstede – as a conflict between what each of us wants as an individual and the interests of the group we belong to. Individualism is 'a prime
orientation to the self', collectivism is a 'prime orientation to common goals and
objectives'.[10] For Trompenaars, writing in the early 1990s, the success of the
'Five Dragons' – Japan, Hong Kong, Singapore, South Korea and Taiwan –
raised 'serious questions about both the success and the inevitability of
individualism'.

Neutrality and emotionalism. The main emphasis on this dimension is the
display of feeling, rather than the level or range of emotions experienced.
Trompenaars contends that emotional display is a major difference between
cultures and argues that 'there is a tendency for those with norms of
emotional neutrality to dismiss anger, delight or intensity in the workplace as
"unprofessional"'.

Specificity and diffuseness. This distinction is based on the concept of 'life
spaces'. People have different senses of what is the domain of the public and the
private and of how compartmentalised different aspects of life should be. For
example, Swiss and Japanese people do not readily invite business contacts into
their homes; North Americans are much freer in this respect.

Achieved and ascribed status. This is a matter of the importance attached to what a person has done or is doing – what they have achieved through their own efforts – versus their position resulting from external factors. Trompenaars counters the Western ethnocentric view that ascription is inferior to achievement for determining status by contending that some ascriptions make good sense in predicting business performance: he refers to age and experience, education and professional qualifications.

Concepts of time. There are several ways in which concepts of time vary between cultures – time as a cycle or a sequence (linear); past, present and future emphasis (the British emphasise the past, North Americans the future); time as a precious resource which must not be wasted versus a more leisurely approach. A major distinction is between polychronic and monochronic notions of activity: people from Anglo-Saxon cultures find their sense of order disrupted if work is not clock regulated, if they are expected not to do things one at a time or find others around them doing several things at once. For example, a British person feels uncomfortable if they enter someone's office for an appointment, are waved to a seat and smiled at while the person they have come to see continues a telephone conversation and making notes. For an Argentinian, this would be quite normal and acceptable.

Concepts of the environment. Is the environment to be controlled or harmonised with?

BOX 3.4

IS TIME OF THE ESSENCE?

An international executive from the UK, interviewed for this book, said that a Russian colleague once said to him that he was a typical Westerner. When he asked why, the Russian said, 'You are always planning for the future or analysing the past, but you never want to talk about what we are doing here and now.'

Source: Author's research.

Critiques of dimensional approaches to culture

Treatments of culture such as those of Kluckhohn and Strodtbeck, Hofstede and Trompenaars, which provide lists of shared background characteristics such as worldviews, values and behavioural characteristics, have been criticised for being oversimplified, static and lacking a basis for determining whether two cultures are different. Trompenaars' work also attracts the criticism that, while his variables are intended to be a continuum, only lip service is paid to this; in reality they are treated as dichotomous – for instance he writes of 'the ascriptive culture' although 21 out of 39 countries in his research fall between 25% and 33% on this measure and of 'the achievement-orientated culture', although again 21 countries fall between 61% and 70% on this measure. Hofstede's work, although much admired and widely applied, has been criticised primarily on two grounds: that it omits important values (Hofstede himself subsequently identified a fifth value – long- and short-term time orientation) and that it is non-dynamic. The comment of Tayeb (1996)[11] is typical of these criticisms: 'A country's culture is too vibrant and complex an entity to be simplified and described only in terms of these dimensions.'

Other criticisms focus on their lack of explanatory power. Kim,[12] for instance, comments that 'When broad dimensions such as individualism–collectivism… are invoked to account for cultural differences, it is uncertain exactly how or why these differences occur. The use of culture as a post hoc explanation of observed differences does little to help us understand the underlying causes of behavior.' Collier and Thomas (1988),[13] too, criticise taxonomic conceptualisations because they do not supply answers to how many of the characteristics need to be different for there to be a cultural difference, because the characteristics vary in their impact on different cultures and their salience is not usually attended to and because such definitions may not capture the experience of the participants.

These criticisms certainly have some force, but despite their limitations, dimensional approaches have generated a large amount of empirical research and provided the most widespread increase in our awareness and understanding of cultural difference and its implications for work behaviour.

> Cultures are more fruitfully differentiated on the basis of deep culture, which means underlying values, worldviews and ways of social organisation, than on the basis of surface culture differences such as dress or food. A number of dimensions of culture, purporting to reflect underlying values, have been tested and found to be effective ways of differentiating national cultures. Although these dimensions, like all models, certainly simplify and may distort reality, their 'workability' means that they have been widely and productively applied to understanding intercultural encounters of all kinds, including those which occur at work.

3.2 COMMUNICATION AS THE BASIS OF CULTURAL DIFFERENCE

A somewhat different approach to culture and cultural difference is taken by a group of theorists who come out of a communications tradition. They take varying views on how much language and communication affect people but agree in placing communication at the centre of cultural differentiation. For Kincaid et al.,[14] communication is the work required to sustain a human group; it consists of the transfer of information among individuals, groups or cultures. Groups cluster together according to common beliefs, values and behaviour. Cultures are nothing more than common ways of thinking and acting, which develop because of relatively isolated within-group communication. Cultures differ from one another because there is less contact between cultures than within them. If everybody communicated with people outside their culture as much as they do with people within it, cultures would soon disappear.

Haslett (1989)[15] held that culture and communication are acquired simultaneously: neither exists without the other. Culture by definition is a 'shared, consensual way of life and sharing and consensus are made possible only by communication'; in turn, humans communicate in a cultural milieu that constrains the form and nature of communication. As a result of communication, members of a culture share a perspective, although members may not share that perspective equally or in every facet of experience.

Two communication theories and their related concepts are particularly relevant for distinguishing cultures:

- high-context, low-context communication
- cultural identity theory.

High-context, low-context communication

Edward Hall (1976)[16] used communication styles to provide a taxonomic approach to analysing cultures. He drew a distinction between high-context communication and low-context communication and used the distinction as the basis for differentiating cultures. In high-context cultures (HCCs), people rely heavily on the overall situation to interpret messages – and so the messages which are explicitly spoken can be elliptical; in low-context cultures (LCCs) people rely more on the explicit verbal content of messages. Members of HCCs, for instance Japanese people, use non-verbal cues and information about a person's background to a greater extent than members of LCCs, such as the British.

In a high-context culture, 'most of the information [to be communicated] is either in the physical context or internalized in the person, while very little is in the coded, explicit, transmitted part of the message'. In contrast, in a low-context society, 'the mass of the [communicated] information is vested in the explicit code'.

People in high-context cultures adopt a role-orientated style. Role-orientated communication emphasises the social roles that the participants hold and different scripts are used depending on role relationships. Work meetings in Eastern countries, for instance, are usually very formal by Western standards. As a result, interaction is formal and ritualistic. In contrast, people in low-context cultures use a personal style. A personal style emphasises personal identity over social position. Because role relationships and status differences are less important, communication is less formal and often more intimate.[17] Weldon[18] and Ting-Toomey (1988)[19] link conflict management behaviour to low- versus high-context communication style.

Cultural identity theory

Within this approach, too, communication and culture are inextricably intertwined. Culture is defined as a historically transmitted system of symbols, meanings and norms. Symbols and meanings define what groups of people say, do, think and feel; it is not the people but the communication that links them together. This interpretation of culture is radically different from those described earlier in which cultural status is determined mainly by birth rather than by subscribing to a system of symbols and meanings.

Core symbols are particularly important. At this point Mary Jane Collier,[20] one of the leading advocates of cultural identity theory, refers across to the values theorists; she suggests that, for example, a core symbol for collectivistic cultures, such as Mexico's, may be bondedness, whereas a core symbol for a more individualistic culture, such as mainstream culture in the US, may be personal accomplishment. Meanings include metaphors, stories and myths. Norms are patterns of appropriate ways of communicating; attached to norms are prescriptions, proscriptions and social sanctions while stories that are told often relate to norm violations and how they are punished. For example, the Biblical story of Sodom and Gomorrah refers to Hebrew norms against certain sexual practices; also, the folk tale of the fisherman who was granted three wishes, but lost everything through asking for too much, refers to a widespread norm against greed.

There are different types of culture corresponding to different types of groups which, according to cultural identity theorists, meet the requirements for being a culture. Groups with histories include corporations, support groups, national groups, or civil rights groups; cultural groups are any such historical groups that are bounded (have restricted membership) and salient to individuals. Symbols and norms change over the life of culture systems, but there is enough consistency in what is handed down to make it possible to define the boundaries between systems and distinguish members of one cultural system from members of another. This is why each individual has a range of cultures to which she or he belongs. The experience of the participants is the basis for conduct, so studies need to focus on the participants' communication about, and identification with, particular culture groups. Figure 3.2 shows cultural identification theory in diagrammatic form.

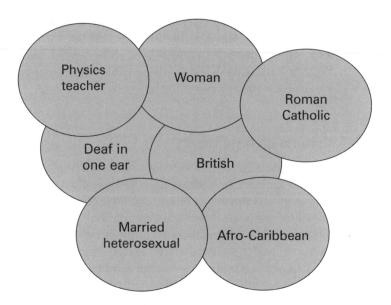

Figure 3.2   An example of cultural identities at work according to cultural identity theory

Thus, for cultural identity theorists, national culture is only one type among many. In fact, because many people contribute to the creation of a national culture's symbols, meanings and norms, national culture is fairly diffuse, so predictions about language use and what symbols mean can only be generalised. Ethnic cultural groups share a sense of heritage, history and origin from an area outside or preceding the creation of their present nation-state. Gender, profession, geographical area and organisation are other bases for cultural difference. Cultural identities are enduring yet dynamic; thus the idea of what it means to be a woman has changed considerably during the twentieth century, but the underlying idea of difference from men persists, of course.

In new or unusual settings, an identity to which someone normally pays little attention becomes more important to them. This might happen when they meet for the first time with people whom they perceive to have a different cultural identity – for example, when they travel abroad. This point will be seen to have considerable importance when intercultural communication theories are considered (Chapter 7).

BOX 3.5

DOES COMMUNICATION CREATE GENDER?

The significance of communication practices is no less important in the arena of gender and communication than in national or ethnic culture. In fact, Laurie Arliss argues that 'Communication is thought to be, at once, the process by which we learn to be male or female, and the product of our attempts to behave sex appropriately.' In describing feminist criticism, rhetorical critic Sonja Foss posits that 'Its focus is on a fundamental element of human life – gender – and it is dramatically changing the form and content of knowledge about rhetoric.' That is, gender is both an influence on and a product of communication.

Communicative practices, according to these writers, not only reflect notions about gender, but they also create cultural concepts of gender. Message sources privileged by society as legitimate knowledge generators create a web of socially compelling discourses. Thus, religious, mythic, philosophic, and scientific discourses teach us, among other things, about society's values and rules related to gender.

Sources: Mulvahaney, B.M. 'Gender Differences in Communication: an Intercultural Experience'. Posted on the Internet: http://snyside.sunnyside.com/cpsr/gender/mulvaney.txt; Arliss, L.P. (1991) *Gender Communication*, Englewood Cliffs, NJ: Prentice-Hall, p. 10; Foss, S.K. (1989) *Rhetorical Criticism: Exploration and Practice*, Prospect Heights, IL: Waveland, p. 151.

Cultural identification is a process which happens in a constantly changing socio-economic, political environment and which is also affected by contact with other cultures. Cultural identities are negotiated, co-created, reinforced and challenged through communication. Whereas social psychological perspectives view identity as a characteristic of the person and the self as centred in social roles and social practices, a communication perspective views identity as something that emerges when messages are exchanged between persons. Throughout life, cultural identities are emergent, not created or completed.

In summary, the cultural identity approach can be used to identify similarities and differences in behaviours, interpretations and norms. It acknowledges that all individuals have many potential cultural identities.

Communication is of central concern when addressing cultural issues: it in part determines what is considered knowledge (for example the worldview) and what values are espoused. It is basic to ways of thinking (linguistic relativity and high context, low context) and to how an important part of a person's identity, the cultural identity, is created. Communicative practices therefore not only reflect culture, as Chapters 4 and 5 will show, they also help create the cultures themselves.

The classificatory variables used to distinguish cultures can interact to affect behaviour. For instance, in a high-power distance, high-context communication culture, such as Burundi, status is a very important part of the (unstated) context. However, the 'contextualism' of communication is relative. Even in low-context cultures like Britain's, cultural values such as low-power distance or low uncertainty avoidance are not generally explicitly stated, but 'understood'.

3.3 CULTURAL DIFFERENCES AT WORK

Cultural factors have considerable impact on the context for face-to-face communication at work – the organisation and its management. Cultural values have a strong influence on the structures, processes and predominant managerial styles of organisations in different societies. For example, in a culture which is high on measures of uncertainty, formalisation and centralisation are prominent features of organisational structure; decision making, authority, responsibility and communication are distributed according to a hierarchical pattern, and the climate is reserved – in fact, the organisation is characterised by the obvious features of a Weberian bureaucracy; in a low uncertainty avoidance culture, on the other hand, the structure is informal and decentralised, decision-making authority and all that goes with it is widely distributed and an open climate of discussion and bargaining prevails.

This section will discuss aspects of cultural differences in work practices and relations which depend on or impact on communication: work roles and norms, groupwork, manager/subordinate relations, management style and organisational cultures. A final subsection will look at some related issues such as the question of whether technological universality and cultural convergence make discussion of cultural difference in organisational arrangements obsolete.

Work roles are extensively affected by cultural values: high-power distance leads to steep hierarchies and narrow spans of control (and vice-versa for low-power distance); high uncertainty avoidance to strict adherence to job descriptions and formality (and vice-versa for low uncertainty avoidance); individualism to an emphasis on personal responsibility; collectivism to an emphasis on group responsibility; high achievement orientation to prioritising task completion; high relationship orientation to concern with maintenance.

Norms exist to 'enforce' values, so their link to culture is also strongly marked, as shown in Table 3.1.

Table 3.1   Effects of cultural values on work norms

Cultural values	Work norms
High-power distance	Penalties for breaches apply more to lower members; higher ones are 'above the law'; norms imposed by leaders rather than emerge by consensus
High achievement	Norm adherence more enforced and methods of norm enforcement more punitive
High uncertainty avoidance	Norms more rigid – less scope for different interpretations
High collectivism	Special emphasis on norms concerned with loyalty to the group, treatment of ingroup versus outgroup members

Behaviour during *groupwork*, although less obviously affected by some dimensions of culture than norms, is still strongly influenced, as Table 3.2 shows. However, while individualists are likely to behave to some degree in the same competitive way in most groups, collectivists will behave differently in groups composed of their ingroup, where cooperativeness will predominate, and those composed of their outgroups, where they may be more inclined to compete or, in the case of conflict arising, to behave, 'uncharacteristically', with confrontation.

Table 3.2   Effects of culture on groupwork

Effect of	High	Low
Power distance	Difficulty in working in an unchaired or unsupervised group	Lack of 'respect' for authority
Uncertainty avoidance	Preference for agendas and sticking to them, structured discussion, clear outcomes, minutes	Preference for informality
Achievement values	Task orientation predominant	Maintenance orientation predominant
Individualism	Competitive atmosphere	Cooperative atmosphere
Time orientation	Long: exploration of all issues before decision sought	Short: sense of urgency, pressure for closure

In a comparison of management in six nations – British, French, German, American (USA), Japanese and Arab – Torrington (1994)[21] highlighted a number of differences in *manager/subordinate relations*; these differences can be understood in terms of Hofstede's dimensions:

- The British are willing to 'listen' to subordinates (being low in uncertainty avoidance) and are addicted to 'old boy networks' (high in masculinity).
- The French are high in power distance (preserved through formality) and individualism (expressed through 'intellectualism').
- The Americans are high on individualism and achievement, leading them to embrace a 'tough', results-orientated approach to manager–subordinate relations.
- The Japanese, although high on achievement, are strongly collectivistic, which produces the 'nurturing father' type of manager.
- The Germans are high on uncertainty avoidance, shown in adherence to routines and procedures; and are in close control of subordinates who are seen as apprentices.
- Arab countries are intermediate on all dimensions except power distance, where they are high: the distance between manager and subordinate is maintained through the high value placed on loyalty and the avoidance of interpersonal conflict.

Research has pointed to significant national differences in *management style*. For instance, a general management survey on perceptions of national management style was given to 707 managers representing diverse industries from Indonesia (177), Malaysia (192), Thailand (182) and the USA (156). It found significant differences in formality of structures and controls, individual versus team development, employee involvement in setting goals and the appraisal process, intrinsic versus extrinsic rewards and frequency of feedback.[22]

In addition to these national differences, there are well-researched differences between women and men as managers. Finnish studies, for instance, have found that women tend to encourage their subordinates to use their abilities and to cut through bureaucratic red tape. To a greater extent than men, they do this by facilitating informal contacts between leaders and workers, introducing new working methods and training, disseminating information and taking workers' views into consideration.[23] Female supervisors' communication style is perceived as placing more emphasis on interpersonal relations than that of male supervisors.

A meta-analysis by Eagly and Johnson[24] of 370 studies compared men's and women's leadership styles: 289 in natural organisational settings, 56 in assessment situations, 25 in laboratory studies; some were self-reports, some ratings by managers, supervisors, subordinates, peers or independent judges; the average age was the late thirties and positions ranged from first-line supervision to top management. Their conclusions were that 'The strongest evidence... for a sex difference in leadership style occurred on the tendency for women to adopt a more democratic or participative style and for men to adopt a more autocratic or directive style... 92% of the available comparisons went in the direction of more democratic behaviour from women than men.' They attributed this difference, which occurred in all three situations, to women's greater interpersonal skills and complexity.

Hofstede warned that national cultures have a direct influence on *organisational cultures*; for this reason, he argued, it is very difficult for organisational cultures to cross geographical boundaries.

BOX 3.6

IS THERE A 'FEMALE ADVANTAGE' AT WORK?

Miller (1986) reframed the so-called 'female' personality characteristics of vulnerability, empathy, and emotionality as representing a unique 'female advantage'. In the past decade or so, the 'female advantage' perspective has invaded the organisation and management knowledge-making communities, as well as the popular management press, in a major way. Scholars writing from this point of view have suggested that incorporation and greater valuing of the characteristics associated with the 'women's voice' or 'female advantage' would bring much needed softening and connection to organizational life and offer competitive advantage in an age of global competition (Adler and Izraeli, 1994).

Sources: Aaltio-Marjosola, I. and Williams Jacobson, S. (1997) 'Researching the experience of women in "man"agement across cultures: A feminist standpoint approach'. Posted on the Internet: http://www.anderson.ucla.edu/research/conferences/scos/papers/aaltio.htm; Adler, N.J. and Izraeli, D. (1994) *Competitive Frontiers: Women Managers in a Global Economy*, Cambridge, MA: Blackwell; Miller, J.B. (1986) *Toward a New Psychology of Women* (2nd edn), Boston, MA: Beacon.

In most organisations, at present, however, one culture is dominant. In the UK organisation Body Shop, it is that of white liberal women, which favours 'feminine' values such as care for the environment and the support of equal opportunities. It is less individualistic than the surrounding society, but like that is secular, low in power distance and low in uncertainty avoidance. This is exceptional, however: the pervasiveness of the masculine culture in most Western organisations has been noted by a number of researchers. The expectations of this workplace culture are masculine heterosexual (these expectations create difficulties for gay people as well as heterosexual women). This culture is reinforced through joking, which often has a focus around three rules of sexuality: (i) the ideal, typical, real man; (ii) definitions of males as not-female; and (iii) the normalcy of heterosexuality.

Men's continuing domination of the most powerful positions in most organisations results in a widespread emphasis on power and control over people, resources, environments, and events as the only path to corporate success. Worse, in the 1980s, abrasiveness and macho approaches including working extremely long hours came to be valued for themselves in many organisations. While the 1990s have seen the pendulum swing to some degree against this, performance evaluations in many British and North American companies are still heavily based on personal power and control.[25]

Organisations with a strong dominant culture force those from the 'minority' cultures (who may or may not be in a numerical minority) to adjust their behaviour to accommodate it. Worse, they may not even be able to admit to having values which conflict with those of the dominant group. This creates stressful internal conflict for those individuals. It also sets up a climate in which creativity is hampered (because too many points of view are inhibited, thus ruling out the conditions favourable to creativity), and in which the damage done by group-think (or lack of challenge to majority views) can most readily occur.

BOX 3.7

EFFECT OF FACE AND CONFUCIAN AUTHORITY SYSTEMS ON CHINESE BUSINESS ORGANISATION

Overseas Chinese dominate commercial life throughout East Asia, although making up only 10% of the population. Most overseas Chinese firms, however huge, are still family run, despite displaying all the trappings of a modern corporation, such as professional managers or stock market listings. But boards often exist only to rubber-stamp the decisions of the founder or his immediate family, and the choicest assets are often owned by private companies and trusts. The chief asset of most companies is their *guanxi*, or connections.

3.4   **CULTURAL CHANGE AND GENERALISABILITY**

Culture changes, usually in an evolutionary fashion, although there are those who believe that accelerating technological change has speeded up the pace of cultural change generally. Occasionally, as with the fall of Communism in 1989/90 in the former USSR and Eastern Europe, a dramatic change in the culture can occur in a year or two.

BOX 3.8

IS THIS HOW CULTURAL CHANGE
IS BROUGHT ABOUT?

1. The traditional strong preference of Chinese people for boy children is being altered: 'After 15 years of state-managed family planning (supported by heavy fines and forced abortions for the rebels) many young people, male and female, now claim it does not matter to them whether their only child is a boy or a girl.'
2. Taiwan has become an industrialised economy. Social changes occur along with economic changes. Many modern symptoms such as crime (including economic crime), divorce, labour unrest, political protests, illegal immigration, pollution, congestion, to name a few, have increased drastically in the past 20 years. A demand for a better quality of life, more leisure, recreation, education, and clean air and water, have also increased rapidly.

People's attitudes have changed as well. The important traditional values – authoritarian attitude, filial piety (respect for ancestors and parents), fatalism, male superiority, and conservatism (self-restraint and control) – have made way for modern values such as democratic attitudes, independence and self-reliance, progressiveness and optimism, equality of males and females and respect for personal feelings. However, filial piety is still very important.

Sources: The Economist, 10 February 1996; Matsu, B. and Yeh, R.-S. (1992) 'Taiwan Management Communication Practices: past, present and future'. A summary of a presentation by Ryh-Song Yeh at the David Lam Centre for International Communication, Pacific Region Forum on Business and Management Communication. Posted on the Internet: http://www.cic.sfu.ca/forum/yeh.html

In the course of this chapter, some readers may have been wondering three things:

1. Given that any one individual is, as mentioned in the conclusion to Chapter 2, a member of multiple cultural and subcultural groups, how can behaviours be identified with any one type of group? While researchers like Hofstede might answer that their samples controlled for factors other than the one they were investigating, this does not answer the point that in some cases, at least, the categories interact inextricably.

2. With so many factors influencing behaviour, including genetic, epigenetic, familial, local, social (such as the environment of a particular school or a particular set of friends) and individual experience, how can we know what behaviours to attribute to culture? As Hickson and Pugh (1995)[26] point out, it is hard to determine whether a 'highly personal, verbal practice of communication [in an organisation is] due to a culture that values person-to-person contact or to illiteracy among employees who could not read written instructions'. These authors suggest that 'Perhaps it helps most to see the world as multi-causal, with many factors acting and interacting simultaneously... Whatever one's view, a sensitivity to the part likely to be played by societal cultures does aid understanding. Difficult although it may be to say exactly what that part is, the notion of culture is persistently useful and its manifestations are persistently recognizable.'

3. Are cultural differences disappearing so fast that it is unnecessary to allow for them? On this question of cultural convergence, superficially, at least, it is obvious that people increasingly buy the same products (Coca-Cola has been claimed to be the most recognised expression in the world). They use the same labour-saving, transportation and communication devices (recall the presence of Internet agencies in Trivandrum – see Box 3.1) and are entertained in the same way by television and music systems. Many now dress in Western-style clothes, live in Western-style houses, work at Western-style jobs and conduct a good many of their conversations in English. Does this mean that cultures are converging – that is, that people worldwide are increasingly sharing the same values, customs, worldview, kinship system and social organisation? It is a question that a number of researchers have addressed; not surprisingly the answer varies. Several comparative studies of values in different European countries carried out in the 1970s and 80s showed evidence of both convergence and continuing difference, according to van Dijk.[27] There appears to be little evidence of divergence.

The case for convergence is that all European countries show:

● the decreasing significance of religion as a source of moral obligation
● stable attitudes in favour of democratic political systems

BOX 3.9

CAN RELIGION AND ETHNIC CHARACTER
BE SEPARATED?

1. 'Perhaps religion is as often responsible for ethnic character as the latter is responsible for the faith.'
2. 'Perhaps the greatest difficulty which confronts the historian of the Irish is that of differentiating between the specifically Irish and specifically Catholic aspects of their lives. They have emerged into a modern world from a past in which Catholicism had played a stronger role than among any other people of Western Europe.'

Source: Wrobel, P. (1979) *Our Way: Family, Parish and Neighborhood in a Polish-American Community*, New York: University of Notre Dame Press.

- people increasingly valuing multiple social relations – with partners, friends and voluntary groups, instead of the old work/family axis
- people coming to value their work as much as they do their leisure (the educational explosion and the changing technological character of work are making it intrinsically valued, not just for the money it will earn)
- the growth of a general achievement orientation – increasing 'individualisation'
- social justice norms becoming increasingly important
- values such as 'peace', 'human rights' 'protection of the natural environment' and 'fighting poverty' which can be summarised as 'quality of life' values, becoming increasingly accepted, although in some countries there is also a backlash.

The case for continuing difference, according to van Dijk, is the following:

- There is a north/south (Sweden, Denmark and UK/France, Italy and Spain) divide over cultural needs in work organisations and society. For example, in the south there is lower tolerance for uncertainty and therefore greater liking for hierarchy and bureaucracy; also less individualism and more collectivism.
- There are culture clusters: an Anglo cluster (the UK and Netherlands), a Nordic cluster (Sweden, Denmark and Norway) marked, for example, by more 'feminine' values, such as a preference for caring for others and a pretty, clean environment over careers; a German cluster; and a Latin cluster where managers, for instance, are more likely to be seen as having a public role in the larger society and to be a business elite.

If studies which focus on an area such as Europe, which some might regard as having a common culture, show evidence of convergence and persisting difference, but not of divergence, what about the broader global picture? Hofstede's study provided little evidence of convergence, but this was based on a comparison between points of time only four years apart – 1968 and 1972. However, Hofstede concluded on more general grounds that:

> There is very little evidence of international convergence over time, except an increase of individualism for countries that have become richer. Value differences between nations described by authors centuries ago are still present today, in spite of close contacts. For the next few hundred years, countries will remain culturally very diverse.

It is arguable, in fact, that ethnic, gender, sexual orientation and religious consciousness are increasing among some groups and that the claims for 'rights' made by these groups are evidence of an increased cultural and subcultural awareness and sense of difference. In the USA, and to a lesser extent in Western Europe, the ideal of a pluralistic, multicultural society has largely replaced the old assimilationist ideal of the melting pot. Minorities which seek to preserve and enhance their sense of a separate identity are now seen to have a strong moral case, where in earlier times they were often seen by the majority as eccentric. There are backlashes, of course, as in that against feminism, but these may be regarded as signs of the strength of the challenge which the 'minority' movements present.

All in all it seems probable that cultural and subcultural differences will be persisting variables affecting both the internal and external environments faced by most people at work.

BOX 3.10

POLITICAL-CULTURAL CHANGE LEADS TO RETRAINING OF LATVIAN POLICE

Following the 1991 political changes in Latvia, four conditions made retraining of the Latvian police a priority. First, Latvia's new independence from Russia led to the need for all institutions to express the Latvian 'mentality'; second, the Latvian language was to be used instead of Russian; third, the police force was Latvianised, replacing the formerly predominant Russians; and fourth, and, most important, because 'A policeman, who maintains public order, is unable to coordinate activities of people without deep comprehension of their values, opinions and expressions. Therefore, the training program was to begin with expounding on the Latvian mentality and the cultural differences existing among minorities living in Latvia.'

Source: Meibergs, A. (1998) 'The New Approach to Police Training in Latvia after (the) Political Changes in 1991'. Posted on the Internet; http://www.ncjrs.org/unojust/policing/new601.htm.

Generalisability of concepts of culture

There seems to be some agreement among cultural scholars on the point that the term 'culture' can be applied to a much wider range of groupings than the national or ethnic. For example, Kim wrote: 'Culture is not viewed as limited to the life patterns of conventionally recognizable culture groups such as national, ethnic or racial. Instead it is viewed as potentially open to all levels of groups whose life patterns discernibly influence individual (communicative) behaviours.'[28]

Geert Hofstede wrote 'The word culture is used here in the sense of the "collective programming of the mind" which distinguishes the members of one category of people from another.' The 'category of people' can be a nation, regional or ethnic group (national culture and so on), women versus men (gender culture), old versus young (generation culture), a social class, a profession or occupation (occupational culture), a type of business, a work organization or part of it (organizational culture) or even a family.'

However, Hofstede also considered that:

Gender, generation and class cultures can only partly be classified by the four dimensions found for national cultures. This is because they are not *groups* but *categories* of people. Countries (and ethnic groups too) are integrated social systems. The four dimensions apply to the basic problems of such systems. Categories like gender, generation or class are only parts of social systems and therefore not all dimensions apply to them. Gender, generation and class cultures should be described in their own terms, based on special studies of such cultures.[29]

Surface culture differences are to be found in all types of grouping – age groups (notice the difference between the way pensioners and teenagers dress), religions (the Muslim shalwar kameez), genders (skirts), occupations (compare the relative formality of most bankers' work clothes with the shirt-sleeve approach in the creative departments of advertising agencies); however, with deep culture the case appears to be otherwise.

In this book, nationality, ethnicity and religion are regarded as full cultural divisions, to which nearly all the generalisations about cultural influences should be expected to apply, on the grounds that cultures must be marked by embedded shared values. So, for instance, a statement such as 'Culture implies a shared worldview and set of values which are largely held unconsciously because they were inculcated in childhood', would apply to most members (not all) of the same national, ethnic, or religious groups. Of these, only 'nationality' is generally accepted as 'culture'. 'Ethnicity', where it does not correspond to nationality, has not been well researched in this respect and the interaction of the two variables is not understood; while Hofstede himself disagrees that religion is a fundamental influence on culture, but sees it instead as influenced by it. However, other authors differ: Huntington, for instance, in discussing intercultural conflict includes Islamic, Hindu, and Slavic-Orthodox among the eight cultures he lists with such potential.[30]

The members of some other social groupings, such as gender, social class or occupational groups, typically conform to many of the norms and values of their dominant culture, but they also have some beliefs, attitudes, habits and forms of behaviour which deviate from those of others in their society and which are shared with members of similar groups in other societies. This reasoning leads me to treat them as subcultures. The statement in the previous paragraph would not apply easily to gender groups – women with different religious beliefs do not share a worldview; men from Japan are generally positioned differently on the individualism–collectivism dimension than men from America. On the other hand, a statement such as 'Cultural differences lead to differences in communication styles' does apply to gender, social class and occupational groups. Women communicate differently from men, working-class people differently from upper-class people, engineers from publishers across national, ethnic and religious boundaries.

Thus gender, social class, sexual orientation, age and educational, technical, professional and experiential background, although having a profound effect on the way people think and behave, do not meet the full criteria for cultures. For these societal subdivisions, some, but not all, generalisations about cultural influences will apply. Disability and sexual orientation are to some degree unknowns – some people with disabilities were born with them, and may have as a result acquired a particular worldview and values during primary acculturation, but others will not have.

All these distinctions have fuzzy boundaries, and there is substantial intragroup variation as well as intergroup difference. Not every Japanese person has a highly communalist outlook; not every woman is a feminist. The important point is to be aware of cultural and subcultural influences and how they may be affecting someone's behaviour at work, but to remember that individual variations generally modify and may outweigh those influences.

Critiques of current approaches to studies of culture at work

A fundamental and potentially devastating charge that can be made about most of what we think we have learned about culture and cultural difference is that it is nearly all based on culturally biased research, in that it has been rooted in the cultural assumptions of the West, particularly those about what constitutes knowledge. Knowledge production itself, specifically the scientific method, can be seen as reflecting values traditionally associated with masculinity and males in Western society (that is, independence, lack of emotion, objectivity, analysis, dominance, logic and rationality). Cultural analysis and comparisons, rather than reflecting universal truths, are inextricably bound to a particular time and place. If the primary aim in cultural analysis is to understand the world somewhat better, then an analysis which is itself culture dependent may be fundamentally flawed.

Scholars have also begun to point out that much organisational and management theory and research, developed in the USA in the decades after World War II, was (and still is) culture bound. In particular, it has been noted that it is gender blind in the sense that although it was created by, about and for men, this fact is seldom remarked. In the same way, it could be described as 'ethnicity blind', 'disability blind' or blind to any of the other differences between groups of people: although only one frame of reference is applied, this fact is rarely acknowledged.

Those cultural analyses that depend on the concept of 'values', however, themselves represent a deviation from the more extreme forms of Western scientific thinking – those, like behaviourism, which deny the existence of psychological constructs. The anthropologist Kluckhohn was strongly attacked by fellow anthropologists when he asserted that values are the key difference among cultures, because values fail the criterion of 'objectivity', which was being asserted by those trying to make the discipline equate to a natural science such as physics. Subsequent developments, however, which acknowledge the subjectivity of all empirical observations, opened the doors of Western culture to concepts such as values.

Currently, there is an attempt to create a new paradigm for cultural research in the context of work which will:

- accept differences across time and space as well as the understanding that these differences neither imply nor legitimate inequality
- challenge the traditional process and foundational products of organisational and management knowledge (seen as emerging from an historically 'masculine' view of the world as it exists in Western societies)
- be founded in a belief in the possibility and importance of moving beyond critiques of existing work to incorporate knowledge created from, and based on, the presumedly different experience of different groups.[31]

At present, too little has been produced following these criteria to provide a foundation for intercultural communication. What can be done? The view taken here is that the need to bridge the cultural divides and subdivides at work is now too urgent to wait. The, admittedly less-than-satisfactory, temporary solution seems to be to study what has been learned through the Western, 'masculine' paradigm, while constantly bearing in mind its limitations.

3.5	CONCLUSION

Diversity refers to the fact that people are of different sexes, genders, sexual orientations, ethnicities, nationalities, religions, social classes and educational, technical, occupational and experiential backgrounds and have or do not have disabilities. The differences in people's values and ways of communicating which may result from diversity have been analysed in terms of underlying dimensions which are theorised to be the core components of culture.

In addition, to varying but always considerable degrees, these values or dimensions are believed to influence thinking processes that are taken for granted. Hofstede, in a telling phrase, has called culture 'software of the mind'.

Cultures change (but deep cultures, unlike surface cultures, do not seem to be converging); which behaviours to attribute to culture and which to other influences is often unclear; many important societal groups do not exhibit the predominating characteristics of cultures – those of shared values – and so must be regarded as subcultures. Despite these limitations, the significance of cultural concepts is great and understanding of cultural difference is important for many reasons. These reasons include the point that cultural differences are brought with people to work and affect their behaviour there, interacting with the effects of their individual differences and the organisational culture. Another is captured in the English expression 'What can he [sic] know of England who only England knows?' which expresses the idea that we cannot know ourselves or our own culture without knowing something of other peoples' – we need at least one contrasting example for comparison. Trompenaars makes the point that cultural imprisonment can lead to arrogance and cultural imperialism as well as to an uncritical dependence on one way of thinking:

> Without awareness of the nature of the differences between cultures, we tend to measure others against our own cultural standards. An early and sometimes painful lesson is that all cultures have their own, perfectly consistent but different, logics.[32]

As a note of caution, however, it must be pointed out that acknowledgement of cultural difference should not be used, as it sometimes has been, to bring racism or other forms of prejudice in through another door. There is a phenomenon known as 'new racism' which draws attention to cultural incompatability. It confines racism to 'situations in which groups of people are hierarchically distinguished from one another on the basis of some notion of stock difference and where symbolic representations are mobilized which emphasize the social and cultural relevance of biologically rooted characteristics'.[33]

REFERENCES

1. Kroeber, A.L. and Kluckhohn, C. (1952) *Culture: A Critical Review of Concepts and Definitions*, Cambridge, MA: Harvard University Press.
2. Scollon, R. and Scollon, S. (1981) *Narrative, Literacy and Face in Interethnic Communication*, Norwood, NJ: Ablex.
3. Ruben, B. (1985) 'Human communication and cross-cultural effectiveness' in Samovar, L. and Porter, R. (eds) *Intercultural Communication: A Reader*, Belmont, CA: Wadsworth, pp. 338–46.
4. Lachman, R., Nedd, A. and Hinings, B. (1994) 'Analysing cross-national management and organizations: a theoretical framework', *Management Science*, **40**(1): 40–55.
5. Robinson, S. (1997) 'Intercultural management: the art of resolving and avoiding conflicts between cultures', AIESEC Global Theme Conference: Learning and Acting for a Shared Future'. Posted on the Internet: www.aiesec.org/link/focus/cu96 12–1.html.
6. Kluckhohn, F. and Strodtbeck, F.L. (1961) *Variations in Value Orientations*, Connecticut: Greenwood Press.
7. Hofstede, G. (1981) *Cultures and Organizations: Software of the Mind*, London: HarperCollins.
8. Trompenaars, F. (1993) *Riding the Waves of Culture: Understanding Cultural Diversity in Business*, London: Nicholas Brealey.
9. Parsons, T. (1951) *The Social System*, Glencoe, IL: Free Press.
10. Hampden Turner, C. (1991) *Charting the Corporate Mind*, Oxford: Basil Blackwell.
11. Tayeb, M.H. (1996) *The Management of a Multicultural Workforce*, Chichester: John Wiley.
12. Kim, M.S. (1988) 'Toward a theory of conversational constraints' in Gudykunst, W. and Ting-Toomey, S. (eds) *Culture and Interpersonal Communication*, Newbury Park, CA: Sage.
13. Collier, M.J. and Thomas, M. (1988) 'Cultural identity and intercultural communication' in Gudykunst, W. and Ting-Toomey, S. (eds) *Culture and Interpersonal Communication*, Newbury Park, CA: Sage.
14. Kincaid, D.L., Yum, J.O. and Woelfel, J. (1983) 'The cultural convergence of Korean immigrants in Hawaii: an empirical test of a mathematical theory', *Quality and Quantity*, **18**: 59–78.
15. Haslett, B. (1989) 'Communication and language acquisition within a cultural context' in Ting-Toomey, S. and Korzenny, F. (eds) *Language, Communication and Culture : Current Directions*, Newbury Park, CA: Sage.
16. Hall, E.T. (1976) *Beyond Culture*, New York: Doubleday.
17. Okabe, R. (1983) 'Cultural assumptions of East and West: Japan and the United States' in Gudykunst, W. (ed.) *Inter-cultural Communication Theory*, Beverly Hills, CA: Sage.
18. Weldon, E. (1997) 'Inter-cultural interaction and conflict management in US–Chinese joint ventures' in Stewart, S. (ed.) *Advances in Chinese Industrial Organization*, Vol. 4, Stamford, CT: JAI Press.
19. Ting-Toomey, S. (1988) 'Intercultural conflict styles: a face-negotiation theory' in Kim, Y.Y. and Gudykunst, W.B. (eds) *Theories in Intercultural Communication*, Newbury Park, CA: Sage.
20. Collier and Thomas (1988) op. cit.
21. Torrington, D. (1994) *International Human Resource Management*, Hemel Hempstead: Prentice-Hall.
22. Vance, C.M., McClaine, S.R., Boje, D.M. and Stage, D. (1992) 'An examination of the transferability of traditional performance appraisal principles across cultural boundaries', *Management International Review*, **32**: 313–26.

23. Hanninen-Salmelin, E. and Petajanieme, T. (1994) 'Women managers: the case of Finland' in Adler, N.J. and Izraeli, D.N. (eds) *Competitive Frontiers*, Cambridge, MA: Basil Blackwell.

24. Eagly, A.H. and Johnson, B.T. (1990) 'Gender and leadership style: a meta-analysis', *Psychological Bulletin*, **108**(2): 233–56.

25. Collinson, D.L. and Hearn, J. (eds) (1996) 'Breaking the silence: on men, masculinities and managements', *Men as Managers, Managers as Men: Critical Perspectives on Men, Masculinities and Managements*, London: Sage.

26. Hickson, D.J. and Pugh, D. (1995) *Management Worldwide: The Impact of Societal Culture on Organizations around the Globe*, London: Penguin.

27. van Dijk, J. (1990) 'Transnational management in an evolving European context', *European Management Journal*, **8**: 4.

28. Kim Y.Y. (1988) 'On theorizing intercultural communication' in Kim, Y.Y. and Gudykunst, W.B. (eds) *Theories in Intercultural Communication*, Newbury Park, CA: Sage.

29. Hofstede (1981) op. cit.

30. Huntington, S. (1993) 'The clash of civilizations,' *Foreign Affairs*, **72**: 22–49.

31. Aaltio-Marjosola, I. and Williams Jacobson, S. (1997) 'Researching the experience of women in "man"agement across cultures: a feminist standpoint approach'. Posted on the Internet: http://www.anderson.ucla.edu/research/conferences/scos/papers/aaltio.htm.

32. Trompenaars (1993) op. cit.

33. Mason, D. (1995) *Race and Ethnicity in Modern Britain*, Oxford: Oxford University Press.

4 (SUB)CULTURAL COMMUNICATION AT WORK – 1

Chapter 3 discussed ways of analysing how cultures differ and how these analyses can be applied to differences between individuals who vary by gender, social class, profession and so on. In the next two chapters, the subject is extended into a more detailed consideration of the effect of differences of background on individuals' communicative behaviour at work. In line with the conclusion to the last chapter, subcultural differences are considered alongside cultural differences.

The level of analysis in this chapter is largely that of the overt behaviour of individuals; Chapter 5 looks at behavioural factors and processes underlying communicative behaviours and at perspectives which treat communication as emerging from the interplay of individuals in encounters.

BOX 4.1

THE KOREAN WAY IS DIFFERENT

In formal Korean, the pronoun 'you' has seven different forms. A speaker must know if the person she or he is addressing is his or her superior or inferior, and to what degree, simply to use the word 'you'.

4.1 UNIVERSALS VERSUS CULTURAL SPECIFICS IN COMMUNICATION

A prior question to a discussion of how cultural differences are reflected in communication patterns and behaviours is whether there *are* significant differences in the communication patterns and behaviours of different groups.

The position taken here is the one suggested by Haslett (1989);[1] there are both universals and cultural differences in communication. Some research suggests that humans may be 'prewired' to recognise the communicative importance of language. This 'innate' recognition may, some suggest, account for the speed with which children learn to talk. In addition, all cultures use both verbal and non-verbal communication systems, including dress, adornment and other means. However, cultural differences in communication have been well-documented in non-verbal communication, judgements, intergroup communication and the processes by which a communication episode develops. Some aspects of communication differ among different subcultures, as opposed to cultures. Scollon and Scollon,[2] for instance, see virtually all professional communication as intercultural.

Systematic studies show that middle-class speakers tend to talk more, use more varied vocabulary, and employ more varied grammatical constructions than do working-class speakers. There is evidence that class differences in communication also exist on the non-verbal level – appearing already in pre-school age children; middle-class children are less affected than working-class children by whether an instruction is spoken in a 'positive', neutral or negative tone of voice. However, the notion that in some (sub)cultures language is simpler or more primitive is probably wrong. The basic structuring principles on which language is founded appear to be universal and most linguists now assume that languages do not differ greatly in their underlying structures or in their formal characteristics. In all languages, sentences are hierarchically structured and their interrelationships are equally complex. The same applies to the language of people of different socio-economic status or ethnicity – the rules for constructing sentences are of equal difficulty and complexity in all cases.

Women experience what some writers call 'linguistic discrimination' in the way they are socialised to use language. So, for example, women often adopt linguistic practices such as using tag questions (for instance 'that's a good idea, don't you think?'), qualifiers ('perhaps', or 'might' instead of 'should') and fillers to soften their messages. Some would argue that women use qualifiers and tag questions more than men do because they have been socialised to appear and feel tentative and powerless. Baker[3] reviewed a stream of research in the area and concluded that, although the situation mediates it, gender may well be related to usage of qualifiers (hedges) and tags.

4.2   BASIC COMMUNICATION ELEMENTS

One definition of communication would be 'message exchange between two or more participants which is characterised by the intentional, conscious (at some level of awareness) use of mutually intelligible symbol systems'.[4] This definition excludes the possibility of communication without conscious intent and so is not universally accepted: habits and emotions are generally regarded as sources of communication which do not involve conscious intention. Sarbaugh[5] prefers to define communication as the process of using signs and symbols that elicit meanings in another person or persons for whatever intent, or even without conscious intent, on the part of the person producing the symbols or signs.

Verbal and non-verbal communication

Verbal behaviour (speech and writing) is particularly good for communicating information and intentions, less good for communicating relationships and feelings. Words and other symbols convey meaning through being coded into messages; however, meaning is not simply transferred but must be decoded by the receiver of the message. In addition, human communication is too subtle and sophisticated for coding methods alone, so evidence must be supplied in the message to allow the receiver to infer meanings which go beyond the words.

One of the advantages of using language, instead of non-verbal communication, is that it is better at transmitting a speaker's intention – to query an assertion, make a promise, ask a question, give an order, or perform some other action. This is because language is more explicit – in an extreme case the speaker can say 'I am telling you this because…' – and also because the rules for grammar and syntax can make intentions clear when the speaker wants them to and the receiver understands the rules. However, speakers may not want clarity; receivers may not be equipped to understand; and, for both speakers and receivers, communicating in a language not fully understood may prevent the language's rules of grammar and syntax from making the speaker's intentions clear.

The problem of language is most obvious when people speak different languages. Many terms are untranslatable, because the underlying concepts differ; for example, the Bulgarian word closest to 'ambitious' never carries a negative connotation, as it does in the English term 'ambitious schemer'. Loan words can be a particular problem: for instance, in Kazakhstan the loan word 'executive' refers only to the chief executive.

BOX 4.2

THE DIFFICULTY OF TRANSLATING LITERALLY

'There is a presumption that when words are translated, meaning is also translated. However, words may often be imbued with meanings and nuances that cannot be adequately conveyed when translated. For example, "company" is translated as *"kaisha"* in Japanese, but there is a tremendous difference in the meaning of the two words. A "company" refers to a body of assets that are bought, sold, or otherwise managed to yield profits (typically short-term profits) for the benefit of shareholders. In short, a "company" is a shareholder-oriented management of assets. A "*kaisha*" refers to an organisation that is imbued with values and with relationships with suppliers, employees, subcontractors, banks, financial institutions and insurance companies. A "*kaisha*" is managed so as to ensure the harmonious maintenance of all these relationships over the long term.'

Source: Patterson, K. (1991) 'Investor Relations in Japan: How to communicate to Japanese investors.' Speech at the David See-Chai Lam Centre for International Communication, Simon Fraser University at Harbour Centre: Pacific Region Forum on Business and Management Communication; (summary by K. Patterson and L. McClanaghan).

However, differences in meaning can be just as significant when each culture uses the 'same' language. If a British native tells her American friend to put the bags in the boot, the American may not know that she means her to place the luggage in the trunk of the car. While this is an obvious example, Samovar and Porter[6] point out that objects, events, experiences, and feelings have a particular label or name solely because a community of people have arbitrarily decided so to name them.

BOX 4.3

LINGUA FRANCA?

A Polish engineer called in a British international salesman to help interpret an American manual for a machine. The problem was the term 'stick-up point'. The British salesman had never heard of it, and could not make it out from the context. When he got back to England he telephoned the company and was told the phrase meant 'point of maximum deflection'; it came from the fact that the meter needle would 'stick' in the 'up' position at that point. The US engineer was mystified that its meaning was not obvious.

Source: Author's research.

A study of the natural language descriptions employed by some American high school adolescents found that the adolescents' language was separate enough from 'mainstream American' for the researchers to term the group a 'culture'.[7]

BOX 4.4

MYTHS AND CULTURE

'Religious, mythic, philosophic, and scientific discourses construct worldviews and convey a society's values and rules. "There are no innocent, no unideological myths, just as there are no 'natural' myths. Every myth is a manufactured object, and it is the inherent bad faith of a myth to seem, or rather to pretend, to be a fact."

'Religious myths seem to be especially potent. Religion "legitimates so effectively because it relates the precarious reality constructions of empirical societies with ultimate reality".'

Source: Said, E. (1986) 'Orientalism and the October War: the shattered myths', in Baha abu-Laban and Zeadey, F.T. (eds) *Arabs in America, Myths and Realities,* Illinois: The Medina University Press, p. 83.

Non-verbal behaviour has particular communicative characteristics which makes it different from verbal communication:[8]

● Much of it, although not all, has universal meaning: threats and emotional displays, for example, may be biologically determined.
● It makes possible the simultaneous transmission of several messages – a person can smile to show friendliness, keep eye contact to show assertiveness and nod to show agreement, all at the same time.
● In many cases it evokes an automatic response – laughter, for instance, can be 'contagious'.
● Often it is emitted spontaneously and is hard to control – emotion, particularly, tends to leak out through non-verbal behaviour.

Like language, non-verbal communication is used to express meaning, but it is particularly important in revealing feelings and attitudes, especially towards the person(s) being communicated with (for example 'You bore me' or 'I like you'). It is 'the major contributor to communication of "affect" in messages'.[9] It is also used to simplify and organise the communication of specific messages and to help regulate an interaction (as when a person coughs to indicate that they want to interrupt). Most non-verbal signals are analogic, that is, the signal has preserved some of the pattern of what it stands for, whereas most words are digital (onomatoepia is an exception) in which the signals are arbitrarily related to the thing represented. It is probably for this reason that humans make more use of non-verbal communication for intensity, using more loudness, tempo and pitch to communicate greater strength of feeling or conviction, and for relationship data.

Non-verbal communication has received a good deal of scholarly attention over the past 30 years. For instance, Ray Birdwhistell was a scholar of kinesics who put forward the following propositions:[10]

- All bodily movements have potential meaning in communication contexts. Somebody can always assign meaning to any movement, even when there was no communicative intent.
- Bodily activity can be analysed, because it is patterned – the same individual will generally use the same non-verbal expression for the same emotion or purpose.
- People are influenced by the visible bodily activity of others.
- A person's use of bodily activity will have idiosyncratic features but will also be part of a larger social system shared with others. (This point is important for understanding intergroup communication.)

In the world of work, an important category of non-verbal behaviour is its symbolic use to signify occupation or status – for example the white coats of doctors symbolising hygiene, the uniforms of police constables to lend them authority and recognisability, the large office with the thick pile carpet for the chief executive. Some of the symbols are more subtle – in a full-service advertising agency, although formal suits are worn, there is a greater readiness to leave off jackets than in a bank; in a creative hot shop, clothing generally will be more 'designer' than in their more traditional competitors. People who misread these symbols may behave inappropriately – may fail, for instance, to give the chief executive his or her 'due', or may themself dress in a style which is not quite right and which will signal an alien presence to insiders.

Non-verbal behaviour differs across groups – for example voice tone. Latins tend to vary their tone a great deal, Asians tend to favour extreme monotony while Anglo-Saxons are in between. There are also differences in the way different ethnic groups sequence their communication. Anglo-Saxons, for example, tend to follow without overlapping (interrupting is rude), Latins to overlap and Asians to leave silence gaps. Women often use body language to express submissiveness – taking up less physical space in relation to their size than men, hovering in the background or lowering their eyes when looked at instead of making eye contact. Women managers, in contrast, sometimes show their understanding of the subcultural meaning of non-verbal behaviour by dressing in a masculine way or decorating their offices in a neutral 'sexless' manner.

BOX 4.5

WHY NON-VERBAL BEHAVIOUR HAS ENHANCED IMPORTANCE IN DOCTOR–PATIENT COMMUNICATION

- The patient's condition may interfere with their ability to communicate verbally.
- Patients feel they have a subordinate role during consultations and so are less verbal: for example they ask fewer questions.
- Fear and uncertainty make patients inclined to interpret, or over-interpret, the non-verbal behavior of those they assume know more than they are telling.
- Patients may not fully understand or believe verbal messages, so they look for further cues in non-verbal behavior.

Source: Buller, D.B. and Street, R.L. (1992) 'Physician-patient relationships' in Feldman R.S. (ed.) *Applications of Nonverbal Behavioral Theories*, Hillsdale, NJ: Lawrence Erlbaum Associates, p. 128.

Non-verbal behaviour is used to reinforce and communicate identity as a group member. Speech style and accent are the main non-verbal vehicles performing this function, as exemplified in the difference between middle-class and working-class speech in British English.

Proxemics, the study of the way in which people use space as a part of inter-personal communication, recognises that 'people of different cultures do have different ways in which they relate to one another spatially'.[11] Furthermore, within cultures, the use of space helps define social relationships and social hier-archies. A father traditionally sits at the head of the table in Western cultures, thus signifying his primary role in patriarchal societies. Similarly, it is widely accepted that supervisors will often exhibit a more relaxed posture than subor-dinates, or that Arabs stand very close when conversing. In fact, Arabs and Europeans differ on distance, facing, touching, loudness and eye contact.

There are universal features – there is always some norm to regulate non-verbal features of social interaction: bowing where it is used always signifies submission; similarly smiling is a universal sign of appeasement. The meaning of most non-verbal behaviours, however, varies: head nodding and shaking, hissing and spitting, although having the same meaning in many cultures, all have different meanings in at least some – for instance, spitting is a sign of affec-tion among the Masai of East Africa.

Facial expression, which has been shown to be linked to emotion, was found by Ekman and Friesen (1968)[12] to have both an innate and a cultural basis. They theorised that culture modifies innate emotional expression in three ways – by the eliciting event having different meaning (for example a funeral could be an occasion of sorrow or joy), by affecting the reaction to emotions (for example some cultures induce their members to suppress anger through 'shame') and by 'display rules' such as those which make losers in competitions act as 'good' losers.

State, trait and style in communication

Early attempts to theorise about behavioural phenomena – leadership is one example – have often included state, trait or style theories. Communication is no exception. A state is a temporary phenomenon, the result of a mood, passing need or perceived requirement of a situation; a trait is a tendency to behave in a certain way, in the judgement of the self or others. For some psychologists a bundle of traits is called a personality; the equivalent for communication theorists is communicator style. Two sets of communication states or traits are especially important in an intercultural context – rhetorical sensitivity and assertiveness.

Rhetorical sensitivity is the tendency to adapt messages to audiences. Hart and Burks (1972)[13] found that people differ in the degree to which they use sensitivity and care in adjusting what they say to allow for the knowledge, ability level, mood or beliefs of the listener. Some people stick to their personal preference for how to express themselves without variation or adjusting to others; some people mould themselves completely to what they perceive as likely to please others (they termed these speakers rhetorically reflective); rhetorically sensitive people adopt an intermediate way, showing concern for themselves, for others, and a situational attitude. Hart and Burks found, in research among nurses, that those under the age of 35 and those with more education were more rhetorically sensitive, those over 55 more rhetorically reflective, while registered nurses were the least flexible. Most people use all three types of communication – that is, they are sometimes in a rhetorically sensitive state – but show a tendency to use one more than the others; in other words they exhibit a rhetorical trait.

For Hart and Burks, rhetorical sensitivity is the most desirable trait, partly because it requires higher cognitive skill, such as the ability to accept that other people are complex, and partly because they considered it a more effective way to communicate, leading to greater understanding and a greater readiness on the part of the listener to be influenced. More rhetorically sensitive people are likely to be more adaptable intercultural communicators.

Assertiveness involves putting one's own rights forward without hampering other individuals' rights. The kinds of rights which can be asserted are these listed by Langrish (1981):[14]

- the right to make mistakes
- the right to set your own priorities
- the right to refuse requests without feeling guilty
- the right to express yourself as long as you do not infringe the rights of others
- the right to judge your own behaviour, thoughts and emotions and to take responsibility for the consequences.

Assertiveness is a middle way between submissiveness and aggression. It has been much advocated in the West in recent years as a way for women and members of ethnic minorities to communicate, especially with people who are prejudiced against them or who for other reasons are inclined to 'put them down' – and, indeed, it can be effective. However, rights are not separable from the society in which someone communicates, and assertiveness is culture relative – what is assertive in one society is aggressive in another.[15]

BOX 4.6

ASSERTIVENESS AMONG
HEALTHCARE PROFESSIONALS

1. Pharmacists rated assertion skills as the most important yet the most difficult to put into practice, especially when dealing with other professionals and with ancillary workers.
2. Nurses experience particular difficulty in being assertive, perhaps especially because their work role involves being kind, considerate, often humble and non-confrontational.

'A number of factors influence the degree, nature and effectiveness of assertion. The gender of both parties is important, since it is often easier to be assertive with someone of the same sex. In the health context, it is difficult to be assertive with seriously or terminally ill patients and their relatives, with physically or mentally handicapped people and with the elderly. It is also more difficult to be assertive with close friends and with people of high power and status... certain subcultures will expect the practitioner to be the sole decision maker... health professionals need to be sensitive to the cultural nuances of those with whom they interact.'

Sources: Morrow, N. and Hargie, O. (1987) 'An investigation of critical incidents in interpersonal communication in pharmacy practice', *Journal of Social and Administrative Pharmacy,* **4**: 112–18; McCartan, P.J. and Hargie, O.D.W. (1990) 'Assessing assertive behavior in student nurses: a comparison of assertion measures', *Journal of Advanced Nursing,* **15**: 1370–6.

There are differences in the value placed by people from different backgrounds on behaviours such as assertiveness. For example, one study found that American subjects rated assertive behaviour more highly and as more competent than Japanese subjects did. Japanese subjects discriminated more between ingroup and outgroup members in their attitudes towards performing assertive behaviours. They rated them more highly when performed by ingroup members than by outgroup members.[16]

Differences in assertiveness can be at odds with many people's preconceptions. For instance, one American study found that in interaction in mixed-gender groups of adolescents, young African-American women were more equal with African-American men overall and in terms of level of activity and of one measure of influence than white women were with white men. Some of the differences were quite marked – unassertive utterances such as 'yeah, uh-huh' made up 36% of white female adolescents' speech acts, but only 12% to 17% of those of each of the other race–gender categories of participants. This pattern suggests a speech style among the white female adolescents distinctly less assertive than that among African-American female adolescents, as well as less assertive than that among male adolescents of either ethnic group.[17]

One explanation for the greater assertiveness of African-American than white women can be based around social role theory – the theory that people's behaviour is strongly influenced by their normal social role. This theory suggests that gender stereotypes and differences in gender-related social behaviours can be traced to differing distributions of men and women into the employee role (which is associated with active (agentic) qualities) and the homemaker role (which is associated more with communal (supportive) qualities). Historically, African-American women have been more likely than white women in America to go out to work, often carrying a primary responsibility for supporting their families. These findings are an example of culture-gender interaction effects on communication.

In itself a *communicator style* is merely a signal as to how a message should be received (for example as authoritative, friendly or warm) but style theorists believe that individuals have dominant styles. Style variables that have been researched include being friendly, impression leaving, relaxed, contentious, attentive, precise, animated, open, dominant and having a positive communicator image. Robert Norton[18] held that messages communicate on two levels: an informative level and one that tells the listener how the speaker expects the message to be responded to (the style message). People have such a strong tendency to expect others to send a style message that they will infer one even if none is transmitted (an abnormal situation) and will try to identify one using their previous perceptions of the speaker's usual style. Inability to detect or infer a style message will make a listener uneasy and disrupt communication, Norton argued.

Communicator style is partly individual but also partly influenced by social background. One study of twins (Horvath, 1995)[19] found that some communicator style variables may be inherited – the most likely being openness, relaxation, dominance, and communicator image. Horvath's explanation is that these four variables (out of eleven) all relate to having a sense of confidence. To be a dominant communicator involves taking charge and being perceived as assertive; a relaxed communicator exudes confidence; open communicators have the self-confidence to disclose personal information to others, and obviously people with positive self-images as communicators generally have self-confidence. Even these communicator style variables, however, are only partially inherited: the environment still plays an important part in the evolution of communicative 'personality', which thus can be expected to vary among cultures and subcultures.

Hofstede's cultural dimensions of power distance, achievement/relationship orientation, individualism–collectivism and uncertainty avoidance can be used to predict and explain differences between communicator styles in different countries. A study by Gudykunst et al. (1996)[20] explored this question and found the following:

- High uncertainty avoidance cultures, such as those of Greece, Portugal and the Latin American countries, where anxiety ('a diffuse state of being uneasy or worried about what may happen') tends to be relatively high, are cultures where communicator styles tend to be more expressive. 'They are the places where people talk with their hands, where it is socially acceptable to raise one's voice, to show one's emotions, to pound the table' (Hofstede, 1991, p. 115).[21] Conversely, countries known for their phlegmatic style of communication, such as Great Britain, Singapore and the Nordic countries, are those which Hofstede's indices revealed as low in uncertainty avoidance.

- As would be expected, cultures with strong achievement values, like Austria, Venezuela and the Republic of Ireland, tend to more assertive and competitive forms of communication than cultures with more relational values like Sweden, Norway and the Netherlands. Japan, which ranks first on the achievement values index, is an exception here, possibly because the strength of collectivism in the culture outweighs even the powerful achievement value.

- The effect of high-power distance on communication generally is inhibitory, leading to lower levels of disclosure, openness and informality than in lower-power distance cultures. At work, it leads to greater differences according to who is communicating with whom: between managers and subordinates, the above points apply and are reinforced, with subordinates' style conveying deference and managers' condescension or paternalism. On the other hand, between co-workers low down the hierarchy, it can lead to high levels of informality, with joking, teasing and an esoteric language, as the low level of responsibility required of these workers by the value system fosters a playful or childish approach.

- Individualism–collectivism has both a direct effect on communicator styles and an indirect effect that is mediated through self-construals. In the study by Gudykunst *et al.*, it was hypothesised that cultural individualism–collectivism, self-construals and values would have separate effects on individuals' use of low- and high-context communication styles. As predicted, the results of the study suggest that independent self-construals and individualistic values mediate the influence of cultural individualism–collectivism on the use of low-context communication, and interdependent self-construals and collectivistic values mediate the influence of cultural individualism–collectivism on the use of high-context communication. The patterns for cultural individualism–collectivism are not as clear cut. The findings suggest that individual level factors (that is, self-construals and values) are better predictors of low- and high-context communication styles across cultures than cultural individualism–collectivism.

Gudykunst *et al.* conclude that culture influences communication both directly, guided by cultural norms and rules, and indirectly, through self- construals and values which influence individuals' styles of communication. Table 4.1 summarises their findings.

Table 4.1   Relations among different cultural values and communication styles

Cultural values	Communication styles	Comment
High uncertainty reduction	Expressive	
Low uncertainty reduction	Phlegmatic	
High achievement	Assertive; competitive	Except among Japanese
High relational	Supportive; cooperative	
High-power distance	High formality; low disclosure and openness	This applies to manager–subordinate interactions; depends on power balance
Low-power distance	Low formality; high disclosure and openness	
High individualism	Competitive	Mediated by self-construals
High collectivism	Cooperative with ingroup	Mediated by self-construals

---

BOX 4.7

THE POWER OF THE LAW

1. Legal training and attitudes to clients may be powerful enough to overcome the effects of national culture on communication style. A study analysed nineteen lawyer–client conversations in an Israeli legal aid office with the aim of revealing if Israeli ideological commitments to egalitarianism, solidarity and informal relationships even between strangers mean that the participatory model of professional–client relationships prevails. However, the results showed that lawyer–client behaviour resembled the authoritarian model.

2. Another study found that advocates' use of persuasive techniques in the legal discourse of a state appellate court case focused on cognitive biases, including cultural stereotypes, in their attempts to influence what happens in court readers' minds as they strive towards a case decision.

3. There is a tension between legal requirements and everyday conversational mechanisms in the management of accusations and defences, a study of Dutch courtroom interactions found.

4. There can be a cultural 'motivation' behind legal judgements – inferences in one case 'expressed' a subcultural point of view in various ways, it is claimed.

Sources: Bogoch, B. (1994) 'Power, distance and solidarity: models of professional–client interaction in an Israeli legal aid setting', *Discourse and Society,* **5**(1): 65–88; Stratman, J.F. (1994) 'Investigating persuasive processes in legal discourse in real time: cognitive biases and rhetorical strategy in appeal court briefs', *Discourse Processes,* **17**(1): 1–57; Komter, M.L. (1994) 'Accusations and defences in courtroom interaction', *Discourse and Society,* **5**(2): 165–87; Fjelstad, P. (1994) 'Legal judgment and cultural motivation: enthymematic form in Marbury v. Madison', *Southern Communication Journal,* **60**(1): 22-32.

Concepts such as rhetorical sensitivity, assertiveness and style have proved useful aids to improving individuals' communication effectiveness, in the intercultural sphere among others. As theories, though, since virtually any behaviour which is repeated can be defined as a trait, trait and style theories are weak and subject to the criticism that they do not go far enough in establishing the linkage between traits and actions. Traits are by definition stable across contexts and yet are not usually claimed to be universal, but trait theories give no account of when a predisposition will be manifested in behaviour and when it will not. They therefore downplay – indeed, many would argue that they seriously understate – the effect of the situation.

Situations

Meanings attached to both verbal and non-verbal forms of communication are determined in part by the situation in which they are produced. A communication situation is the entire communication event, including the participants, the setting and the activities taking place. People normally adjust their communicative behaviour for the situation in one or more of the following ways:[22]

- by evaluating the participants differently – for instance, a manager's behaviour will be evaluated differently by subordinates according to whether it takes place in the office or at the office party
- by adjusting their goals: what they hope to achieve from the encounter – thus most people would recognise that they are unlikely to succeed in a request for a salary raise in a large meeting where a major sales dip has been reported
- by adjusting their behaviour – for example, the degree of formality they use in addressing others, whether to make jokes or how much of the 'air time' to take.

Situational communication theorists usually consider that people are pursuing strategies to achieve their interaction goals and that in the light of their perception of the situation they adjust their strategies according to two criteria: maximising effectiveness and minimising cost, where 'cost' refers to the amount of energy and time required and to possible negative consequences. For example, if a person wanted to obtain some information about their organisation's location plans, their initial strategy might be to ask their manager in a straightforward way, as an assertion of a right. However, they might then discover that no one else had been told and the information had in fact been withheld from someone who was normally privy to all plans. This information might lead them to believe that a straightforward enquiry would be ineffective and might involve a high cost by embarrassing their manager. In this changed situation, they would probably adjust their communication strategy – perhaps adopting a special pleading approach, claiming a particular need for the information, for example, for reasons of their children's education.

Intercultural encounters are in themselves 'situations' whose characteristics affect communication behaviour. 'Two people socialized to different cultures may react to a situation differently because of differences in internalized conceptions of the content of the situation, of what is normal, what is appropriate, and so on' (Hall 1976).[23] The example given earlier that in some cultures a funeral is seen as a joyful and not a sorrowful occasion is one illustration; another is the way in which life events are seen by some religious groups as expressing 'God's Will' so that to complain about them would be sacrilegious.

The work context, too, is a situation – or, rather, a large number of different situations with some shared characteristics, such as normative expectations about focus on task, which again affect communication behaviour. The fact that work communication is different from social or other behaviour is cross-cultural, although how it differs varies from one (sub)culture to another.

> **BOX 4.8**
>
> ### APOLOGIES AT WORK USUALLY RELY ON THE SITUATION
>
> Apologies in telephone interviews conducted for a public opinion polling service were analysed to determine whether they mainly relied on the situation (I'm sorry I cannot answer your questions, I am late for work') or were personal ('I do not believe in answering polls'). Apologies range along a continuum from the most situational to the most personal. Results indicated that both interviewers and respondents use apologies at the situational end of the continuum.
>
> *Source:* Bean, J.M. and Johnstone, B. (1994) 'Workplace reasons for saying you're sorry: discourse task management and apology in telephone interviews', *Discourse Processes,* **17**(1): 59-81.

Messages

In one sense the term communication refers to the exchange of messages and the creation of meaning (for example assigning signs or interpreting messages). Only messages can be transmitted and received; meanings cannot be transmitted.

Sending messages. The non-transmittability of meaning entails that, first, senders must encode their meanings into symbols, choosing those which are likely to be familiar to their audience both in themselves and in what they stand for. Even routines such as greeting people on the street were at some point learnt and have to be retrieved from memory.

The non-transmittability of meaning also entails that it must be recreated by the receiver, often by inference. In this fact lies scope for miscommunication: there is no way for Person A to be certain that Person B means the same by 'blue' as they do. Much speech is elliptical: in ordinary work conversation Person A is quite likely to say, 'Bring me the blue folder, please', even if there are several blue folders, so long as he or she has some reason to think that the person being addressed will be able to infer which blue folder is meant.

Messages operate at multiple levels – four, according to Stohl and Redding (1987).[24] Level 1 deals with what the sender would like to convey, level 2 with what they intend to convey, level 3 with the ostensive message (what is actually verbalised) and level 4 with the receivers' interpretations. So, for instance, a sales representative might like to tell an over-demanding and intractable customer to 'Get lost', intend to say 'What you want is simply not available at that price', actually say 'I'm afraid we do not stock anything that meets your requirements', and be understood by the customer to say 'We could order this for you, if you would like us to'.

Messages also have multiple meanings, a point which may not be understood by those people who repeatedly interact with the same narrow range of others. Such people tend to receive the same information and, especially, to have the same 'reading' of a social situation reinforced (rewarded), over and over again, so gaining the view that there is only one way to interpret messages and events. Mixing with a wide range of people leads to receiving more diverse information, opinions and accounts which suggest that there can be more than one view of a situation. This in turn leads people to expect messages to be complex and to carry more than their surface meaning; such people may have an initial advantage in intercultural communication.

Message qualities are highly dependent on who is communicating. The conversation of two members of the same family, or two colleagues of long standing, will often make little sense to those who are not part of their closely connected network. Abbreviations and jargon will be used, details will be omitted, common expressions will have esoteric meanings. Against this, the conversations of people who have simple relations and communicate only about task-related concerns are more structured and explicit; background information is provided and what is being referred to is made clear. Because intercultural communication at work is mainly task related, the barriers to understanding can be lower than they would otherwise be.

Receiving messages. Message reception can be seen as involving five processes: focusing (attending, filtering); decoding (translating the symbols into the received message); integrating (making connections between data); inference (filling in the gaps); and making attributions (judging what caused the behaviour). In addition, two processes are involved in remembering a message: storage in memory and retrieval from memory. Each of these seven processes can prevent a message being understood or remembered in the way the speaker intended, so that miscommunication occurs in ways additional to those produced by the speaker's encoding practices.[25]

Recent concern with message reception in communication studies has included three areas of particular interest: message ambiguity, deception detection and the evaluation of arguments:

1. In communication studies, *message ambiguity* is usually discussed in relation to the reception of the message rather than its transmission. Thus, blatant ambiguity occurs when a receiver is confused or uncertain about the meaning of a message, because he or she cannot construct any plausible interpretation of the message or realises that there are multiple possible interpretations and cannot select which was intended. Subtle ambiguity occurs when there are two or more possible meanings to a message but the receiver is unaware of this possibility. An example of subtle ambiguity could occur if two executives, one from the UK and one from Japan, were talking and both used the term 'company'. As Box 4.2 shows, their under-

standing of what this means could diverge substantially without either being aware of the problem.

There is a commonplace assumption that message ambiguity is always undesirable at work, that to communicate well is to communicate with perfect clarity. It may be believed that successful communication avoids time being spent or resources consumed on communication processes themselves. Underlying this belief is an often false assumption about people's motivations – for instance, that all a doctor has to do is to tell a patient precisely what he or she should do and he or she will do it; and similarly for a manager and subordinate. In practice, as a substantial literature has now shown, gaining compliance is often problematic and, more generally, motivations, including communication motivations, are highly complex. Ambiguity serves many useful functions – for example, to save the 'face' of someone who makes a suggestion which is rejected, it is often advantageous for them to 'maintain deniability' through ambiguity.

2. Being able to *detect deceptions* – to know when someone is not telling the truth, or not telling the whole truth – is an important work communication skill. Lawyers, social workers and other professionals, for instance, need to be able to detect deceptions because clients do sometimes fabricate, conceal information, exaggerate or obfuscate and they need to know that this is happening. Equally, vendors may lie to purchasers, interviewees to interviewers, subordinates to their managers and negotiators and colleagues to one another.

We know from research that, to detect deception, most people use three cues:

- How plausible is the message being communicated?
- How nervous is the communicator?
- Does the communicator's non-verbal behaviour breach common expectations?

Unfortunately, research also shows that lie detection rates barely exceed chance. One study (Feeley *et al.*, 1995)[26] found that subjects who were trying to detect deceptive communicators achieved a 0.54 success rate. They did rather better in detecting truthful communicators, where accuracy was 0.70. The researchers concluded that communicators attempting to deceive are difficult to detect and that a possible explanation is that receivers of messages have a bias towards believing that others are truthful.

Suspicion on the part of someone who is being deceived, however, or who thinks they are, prompts behaviour changes which are detectable. One experiment set up interviews during which interviewees lied or told the truth and interviewers were induced to be moderately or highly suspicious (or not). The results confirmed that suspicion was perceived when present, suspicion was manifested through non-verbal behaviours (but with different behavioural patterns for moderately versus highly suspicious interviewers), and suspicion on the part of the receiver affected sender behaviour. Thus it seems that interpersonal deception is a matter of mutual influence processes.[27]

The addition of a cultural difference dimension can only make deception detection more difficult still.

3. *Judging arguments* which are being put forward by another person during a discussion or meeting is another obviously necessary message reception skill at work. People sometimes evaluate an argument in an elaborated, critical and thoughtful way (centrally) and sometimes more casually (peripherally). In the second case, they are more likely to be influenced by extraneous factors, such as a liking for the person arguing, rather than the strength of argument. However, attitude change brought about by a central process is likely to be more durable. Central and peripheral processing can both occur about the same message.

BOX 4.9

JUDGING ARGUMENTS – THE TURKISH WAY?

'When presenting to Turks, for instance to Turkish government officials about a privatisation proposal, one issue is whether to give a balanced view, referring to potential problems, or not. Generally, their history and culture predispose them to believe that any problems referred to are the tip of a very large iceberg and will actually prove fatal to the project. They are not used to working through problems; instead their experience is that problems cause failure. It makes it difficult to follow banking prudence nostrums – you do not know what to say that would make them realise you are being prudent without triggering alarm bells.'

Source: Interview with an investment banker, author's research.

The likelihood of elaboration depends on the receiver's ability – whether enough is known about the subject of the message to allow them to think critically about it – and motivation. There are at least three elements in motivation: involvement – how relevant the topic is to the receiver personally; the number of persuasive sources and different arguments used (more increases the motivation to 'elaborate' by making it harder to dismiss the matter off hand); and the receiver's personal preference for critical thinking. Three out of four of these factors can lead to cultural and subcultural differences in whether or not a given message will be processed centrally or peripherally. For example, a message about sign language is more likely to be processed centrally by a well-educated deaf person than by a school drop-out with good hearing; the former would probably know more about the subject, find it more personally relevant and be more inclined to critical thinking than the latter would.

If a person does process the persuasive message by elaboration, he or she will be more likely to be influenced if the argument is a strong one and if it is consistent with his or her pre-existing salient beliefs or attitudes. If he or she merely uses peripheral processing, source credibility, liking, fear or guilt may be stronger influences.[28]

The main evidence on (sub)cultural differences in the basic message transmitting and reception processes concerns gender. Hall (1979),[29] for instance, found that women are slightly better decoders of affect (feelings and attitudes) and considerably better encoders, especially with strangers. Overall, positive messages were decoded worst and negative messages best; but men were worse on both positive and negative messages.

Research by Gallois and Callan (1986)[30] looked at ethnic differences in conveying and interpreting positive and negative messages by comparing encoding and decoding of messages by people of Australian, British and Italian ethnicity. They found that positive messages by Australian and Italian men were decoded less accurately than positive messages by British men. On negative and neutral messages, Italian male speakers were decoded less accurately than Australian and British male speakers. There were fewer differences for female speakers.

Gallois and Callan's results indicate that the rules for encoding and decoding negative messages are clearer and more accessible to English-speaking senders and receivers than rules for positive or neutral messages, which could significantly affect how, for instance, workforces respond to management announcements of their plans. A review of the literature led Hall (op. cit.) to the conclusion that decoding and encoding are influenced by both social skills and attitudes towards the other interactors and that this may help to account for the gender differences observed in his research.

Functions of communication

Important though messages and message theories are, communication is more than just messages. It is a process – some writers would call it a 'system requiring more than one actor in an ongoing series of events'. The system adjusts – for instance, if one person increases intimacy by standing a little closer the other person will compensate to adjust the system by, for example, reducing eye gaze.[31] Within the system, any single communicative behaviour can serve a variety of communication functions, where 'function' does not necessarily imply purpose or intention but the inevitable, natural and unavoidable consequence of communication behaviour.

Five primary communication functions in this sense are to distribute communicative control, to determine the level of affiliation, to communicate content and relationship, to experience a subjective sense of social identity and community membership and for negotiation or ratification. These functions are 'primary' because they are extremely widespread elements of communication, although how they function varies across cultures and subcultures.

1.   There appears to be a near-universal need for people to *distribute control* of the direction, purpose and style of any conversation or discussion. Commonly, in Western cultures, this allocation is achieved either by a competitive process in which each participant transmits messages designed to obtain control or one in which one participant claims control through such messages and the other or others implicitly concede. 'Messages' designed to obtain control include talking more than one's partners, talking less but self-protectively questioning more, formal terms of address and pronoun usage (*vous* rather than *tu* in French) and exhibiting a relaxed posture (arms akimbo, reclining or leaning backwards, open legs).[32]

BOX 4.10

'HOW NOT TO' SELECTION INTERVIEW

An inexperienced selection interviewer observed doing twelve interviews in Bulgaria was recorded as doing nearly 80% of the talking, thus reversing the usual 20/80 talking/listening ratio for such interviews. At the end the interviewer commented that the candidates appeared to have little to say for themselves!

Source: Author's observational research.

Control is the 'constellation of constraints' people place on one another by what they say and how they structure the conversation, which in turn limit the options available to participants. It is likely that communicators usually seek optimal control distribution rather than dominance but there are exceptions. A study of doctor–patient communication showed that doctors in diagnostic interviews with patients, when a high level of openness and listening to encourage information disclosure might be expected, actually engage in heavily controlling behaviour such as doing most of the talking, initiating 90% of the utterances, posing 90% of the questions raised, asking futher questions before the patient has answered the last one, interrupting the patient more (except when the doctor is female), determining the agenda and topic shifts and determining the termination of the encounter.[33]

2. The need to *determine the level of affiliation* – intimacy, friendliness, neutrality or some degree of hostility – also appears to be a widespread characteristic of communication episodes. In the West, self-disclosure has been shown to be the most powerful strategy available to promote affiliation. It is the voluntary making available of information about the self that would not normally be accessible to the other at that moment. It serves to escalate a relationship towards positive affiliation because of what Gouldner (1960)[34] called the norm of reciprocity – the social pressure on people to produce equivalent responses. Its reverse – the refusal to reciprocate self-disclosures made by others or to respond to 'invitations' to self-disclose is, conversely, an effective way of establishing or maintaining a low level of affiliation, which may be appropriate in some work interactions.

    Teenagers are low self-disclosers; women disclose more easily and at more depth than men; Americans self-disclose more than Europeans and they, in turn, more than Asians; younger siblings more than older. People disclose more to the opposite sex, except in the case of intimate problems. The friendliness, 'acceptingness' and empathy of the listener encourage self-disclosure, which is linked to trust, even at work. Reciprocation of self-disclosures at a similar level is the norm in most situations but in the work context the subordinates, clients and patients do most of the disclosing.

3. Communication involves both *content and relationship data* – messages transmit both what is talked about (the content) and the speaker's view of the relationship between the communicators.[35] 'Where have you been?', for instance, can be simply interrogatory, critical, quizzical or pleading, depending on where the emphasis is placed and the situation. The content message is the same, but the relationship message differs. At one extreme, an accountant's report would normally be almost all content; at the other extreme, greetings are almost all relationship data with virtually no content: their purpose is to acknowledge that another person is recognised and affirm that the relationship with that person remains in being. An appraisal interview should be a mixture of the two.

    Relationships can be characterised by complementarity or symmetry. Either the response to one person's behaviour is complementary – for example, dominance is met by submission – or it is symmetrical – dominance is met by dominance. The response to a critical 'Where have you been?', for example, might be 'Sorry, the traffic was awful' (a submissive response) or 'That's my business' (a dominant response). Relationships are regulated by rules, which may be widely applicable, like the rules for work roles, in which case the relationship is social and role bound, or comparatively unique, in which case the rule structure is individualised.

There are differences in the relative value placed by different cultures on control, affiliation, content and relationship in communication. Japanese culture, for instance, places a very high value on communicating subtle aspects of feeling and relationship and a much lower value on communicating information. (This is despite the fact that the Japanese are low in relationship values – high in achievement values – the two are not necessarily correlated.) Most Japanese people also believe that the most important things cannot be communicated in language. Most Western cultures, despite some recent shifts, are the opposite. Not only do they emphasise communicating content at the expense of relationship but they tend to treat what cannot be expressed in language as not worth attending to. (Women from Western cultures, though, are closer to the Japanese in this respect.)

4. Philipsen (1989),[36] in four communities which he studied, identified four different ways in which speech was used to enable communicators to experience a subjective sense of social identity and community membership. According to Philipsen, much of what has been learned in the empirical study of speech behaviour suggests that how speech functions, in lives and societies, varies across speech communities (see Box 4.11).

5. Another difference in the functions which language in different cultures serves is in whether language is normally used for *negotiation* or *ratification*. In some societies relationships are thought of as spontaneously created by individuals and language is used to negotiate those relationships; in other societies relationships are thought of as pre-determined and set – here language performs the function of ratifying pre-existing relationships. In business negotiations, Asians, who follow the ratification model, may state their positions less extremely if they feel that not to do so would disrupt the harmony of the relationship. Westerners may assume that each party has in mind only achieving their own best advantage and may state their positions strongly even if it should cause a feeling of disharmony. These differences can lead to misunderstandings and conflict.

BOX 4.11

DIFFERENT USES OF SPEECH IN FOUR
DIFFERENT COMMUNITIES

Teamsterville. Speech here reveals and reinforces the speaker's place in a social structure which is hierarchical and socially segmented; the emphasis is on place and on using 'substandard' American English.

Nacirema. This is speech which provides a sense of reciprocal disclosure about the self and attentiveness to the disclosures of others. It reaffirms membership of a culture which values the unique self and unique interpersonal relationships between individuals.

Israel Sabra. The culture emphasises the importance of individual acts that reject the inherited culture of class relations and domination and instead affirm equality of persons in a newly created society. Speech affirms symbolically the social good over the personal.

Bond. Speech here is designed to link individuals with fellows and family who wish one another well, without any instrumental agenda. Its main purpose is to check up on one another's well-being.

Source: Philipsen, G. (1989) 'Speech and the communal function' in Ting-Toomey, S. and Korzenny, F. (eds) *Language, Communication and Culture: Current Directions*, Newbury Park, CA: Sage.

Communication strategies

Individuals adopt communication strategies to achieve their goals. Employing strategic communication should not, however, be seen as a perpetual, constant process but one which operates at higher and lower levels at different times and in differing circumstances. Although communicators rarely explicitly distinguish between the two, there is a difference between the strategies employed concerning the content of a message and the strategies used to communicate that message. For example, if a subordinate is regularly late for work, the manager's choice might be to ignore it, to reprimand accompanied by a warning but take no disciplinary action or to instigate a dismissal procedure. Whichever of those the manager chooses to do will constitute the message content strategy that he or she will communicate to the subordinate. Let us suppose that she or he decides to reprimand but take no disciplinary action. She or he is still presented with a choice of communication strategies. She or he might open by asking questions in order to 'get the facts' before reprimanding, or, if she or he feels the facts are known, might ask questions about the subordinate's attitudes;

she or he might make a firm, unequivocal statement accompanied by a warning 'Your behaviour is completely unacceptable and unless there is some improvement I shall have to...' or she or he might take a softer line 'Jeremy/Mary, you know this can't go on, don't you?' or use one of many other alternatives. The choice made is a choice of communication strategy, not content strategy.

There has been a certain amount of empirical evidence accumulating about what factors influence people's choice of communication strategy. One study concerning requests found that, before making a request for some form of help or for resources, speakers constructed a plan containing a sequence of messages. Thus, someone intending to make a request might plan first to ask a question about whether the person they were asking was able to grant the request. Two factors influenced these plans: the goals the person was trying to achieve by making the request and features of the situation.[37]

Another piece of research tested which had more influence – the person's goals or the situation – by getting subjects to write requests for fifteen hypothetical situations. Contrary to the expected results, it was found that goals have a more important influence on the communication strategies people use than the situation does[38] – a conclusion which implies that people's level of strategic adaptation for intercultural communication situations will also be low.

Power and status in choice of communication strategy. Status and power impact heavily on work communication, especially between managers and subordinates. Thompson (1993)[39] contends that managers overuse advocacy in their relations with subordinates. He argues that nowadays there is a need for organisational learning: the complexity of the issues being confronted require the knowledge of people from diverse backgrounds (both technical, functional and cultural) to be shared to help solve problems. These factors mean that the real, although often disguised, approach of 'consulting' only when the decisions have in fact been taken, will no longer work. Managers need to gain greater skill at inquiry, which involves particularly:

- asking tough questions
- admitting when something is not understood
- establishing decision rules
- drawing out people's best ideas.

The implication is that Western managers are currently defective in these communication skills, probably because of an over-concern with status. Figure 4.1 shows a continuum of communication strategies related to managers' purposes in their discussions with subordinates.

Deborah Tannen[40] argues that gender differences in communication are based in women's lower power orientation. Her research in companies across the US shows that:

Men tend to be sensitive to the power dynamics of interaction, speaking in ways that position themselves as one-up and resisting being put in a one-down position by others. Women tend to react more strongly to the rapport dynamic, speaking in ways that save face for others and buffering statements that could be seen as putting others in a one-down position. These linguistic patterns... affect who gets heard and who gets credit.

Women are likely to downplay their certainty; men are more likely to minimise their doubts.

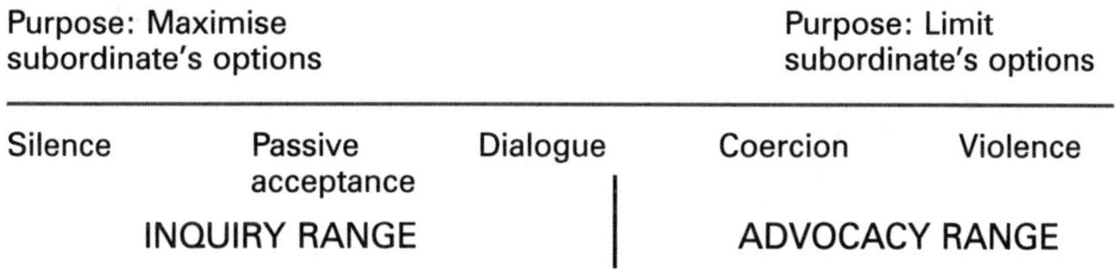

Purpose: Maximise subordinate's options			Purpose: Limit subordinate's options	
Silence	Passive acceptance	Dialogue	Coercion	Violence
INQUIRY RANGE			ADVOCACY RANGE	

Figure 4.1   Managers' communication choices based on a purpose continuum

Source: based on Thompson, M.P. (1993) 'The skills of inquiry and advocacy: why managers need both', *Management Communication Quarterly*, **7**(1): 95–106.

Differences in status are also reflected in, for example, verbal turn-taking (women let men take more of the air time and subordinates do the same for managers). Research into the traditional question of whether men dominate women in conversation, by analysing audiotapes of five meetings, found that men talked significantly more than women when there was someone in charge of the group, although not when the task setting was cooperative.[41] One researcher has argued that women's use, even in professional settings, of 'self-depowering' communication, and men's use of self-empowering ones, are strategic. These differences, it is argued, originate in the different conversational objectives of professional men and women: women are seeking affiliation, men are more instrumental. Lack of opportunity, tokenism and gender role spill over contribute to differences in both communication acts and communication expectations (including goals).[42]

BOX 4.12

CROSS-CULTURAL COMPARISONS OF MANAGERS' COMPLIANCE-GAINING STRATEGIES

Compliance gaining is the use of persuasion, especially with key subordinates to influence them to do what they are directed to do and to convince them that the task is worth doing. Such communication is common between superiors and key subordinates. Theories of compliance gaining identify seven message strategies that managers use:

1. reasoning – influencing subordinates by relying on explanations to support requests, stating the objective merits of the request
2. friendliness – convincing the subordinates to think well of the superior, creating favourable impressions
3. coalition – using social pressure to obtain compliance, mobilising other people to support requests
4. bargaining – relying on negotiations and the exchange of favours, appeals to social norms of reciprocity
5. assertiveness – employing a forceful manner, making demands, setting deadlines
6. appeal to higher authority – relying on the chain of command, using the influence of higher levels in the organisation to back up requests
7. sanctions – using rewards and punishments derived from organisational position, employing promises and threats about pay and employment conditions.

Research suggests that most of these strategies are rarely used by US or European managers. Only reasoning and friendliness are used frequently, and these are used uniformly across organisations.

Probable explanations are that these (a) reduce uncertainty more than or as much as other strategies but do not make superior–subordinate interactions more risky and (b) help both superiors and subordinates to attain their goals. What applies to Japanese managers? Theories of Japanese management suggest that five different compliance-gaining strategies would be used:

1. appeals to duty and loyalty, built by managerial communication
2. assertiveness used as an easy strategy where there is no problem of the exit alternative or need for 'voice' because of lack of a hiring market at other than entry level

3. appeals to 'wa' spirit – emphasising the need for harmony and unity of purpose within the group and in the organisation. This is based on an assumption of subordinates' willing control of self-interest in service to the group
4. indirect use of coalitions
5. appeals to authority (due to high-power distance).

However, findings based on three samples of 14, 13 and 41 Japanese managers were that:

- Reasoning is the most used strategy.
- When Japanese managers see themselves as permanent employees they resort more to the use of assertiveness, frequently setting deadlines for key subordinates, telling these subordinates that they must comply and reminding them repeatedly.
- Greater use of loyalty appeals is used when the manager is permanently employed, even when the condition does not apply to the subordinates.

Source: Sullivan, J. and Taylor, S. (1991) 'A cross-cultural test of compliance-gaining theory', *Management Communication Quarterly,* **5**(2): 220–39.

The influence of culture on communication strategies is emphasised in one communication theory – *coordinated management of meaning* (CMM) theory. It includes the following summary propositions:

- Communication is goal driven, but actors are not always aware of their goals.
- Culture defines the logic of communication.
- The implicit theories of a culture specify how to place and organise communication.
- The implicit communication theories of a culture are learned through socialisation.
- Cultures differentially value communication goals and alternative strategies for reaching those goals.
- Cultural prescriptions are used rather than followed.
- The influence of culture on communication is most evident in situations in which conventional goals and plans are 'given' to actors – in non-routine situations the influence of culture diminishes.[43]

Since intercultural encounters, especially in the early stages of a (work) relationship, are intrinsically non-routine, CMM theory implies that the influence of culture will be reduced. This somewhat contradicts other theories, described in

Chapter 7, which assert that heightened awareness of difference in such encounters increases the influence of culture.

The concept of communication strategy is employed in several intercultural communication theories and contexts which will be covered later in this book.

4.3   LANGUAGE USE

In communication with people who are familiar, language use goes on largely at a level below consciousness, with varying degrees of effectiveness; with new acquaintances or people from different backgrounds, heightened consciousness of how language is being used is needed for effectiveness. This applies widely in work situations.

Elaborated versus restricted codes

When speakers expect marked differences from other people with whom they are interacting, they use more formal language, called the elaborated code, instead of the restricted code which they use when they can assume that the receiver will understand their assumptions. An expectation of marked difference leads the speaker to express fully those meanings that are expected to be misunderstood. In other words, these meanings have to be put into words rather precisely to make them available to the listener. Therefore elaborated codes require a large vocabulary and complex syntax.

Restricted codes explicate less fully. For example, if someone approaches another person who is waiting at the side of a country road in England, the conversation might run like this: 'What are you waiting for?' 'The 10.15'. Both questioner and responder have used a restricted code – neither thought it necessary to elaborate on the fact that it was a bus that was being referred to. The same assumption of shared knowledge could not necessarily be made, even if one of them came from an English town – urban dwellers are used to bus stops being marked by a post and might not be aware that in the country they often stop at known but unmarked places. Then the conversation might run differently: the 'what' in 'What are you waiting for?' would have a wider denotation and the answer might correspondingly be 'The bus'.

Restricted codes encourage the expression of group membership rather than of individual differences. They depend on a context of shared assumptions, common social experience and shared expectations. The vocabulary used is smaller and the syntax simpler. Non-verbal communication is vital in the restricted code; in fact with their ingroup, people often express new information or individual differences solely through non-verbal communication; for elaborated codes, however, non-verbal communication is much less useful.

The distinction between elaborated and restricted codes is not between a more and less sophisticated use of language: Bernstein, who first observed it, commented that 'Let it be said immediately that a restricted code gives access to a vast potential of meanings, of delicacy, subtlety and diversity of cultural forms.'[44] The difference lies in the speakers' assumption (or otherwise) of knowledge shared with their listener and thus the degree to which they feel required to verbalise. Bernstein did note, however, that closed societies make more use of restricted codes, open societies more use of elaborated ones. People from closed societies might have more difficulty in switching to using elaborated codes when they meet outsiders. Bernstein's distinction is incorporated in intercultural communication theories to help explain differences in the ways people communicate with different others as opposed to those with whom they are familiar.

There is an obvious parallel between the 'elaborated/restricted code' distinction and Hall's high-context/low-context communication distinction (described in Chapter 3), although Hall's concept is more rigid – use of HCC or LCC is closely related to a person's culture.

Rules

Communicating involves following certain rules. 'Speaking a language is engaging in a rule-governed form of behaviour.' Grammar and syntax are, of course, basic rule systems. In addition, whether a listener finds another person coherent depends on rules being followed and understood by both parties; there are also rules for efficient communication.

Rules for coherence. Jacobs and Jackson (1983)[45] assert that there are two kinds of rules necessary for coherence:

- Validity rules establish the conditions necessary for an act to be judged as a sincere move in a plan to achieve a goal. For example, for a speaker to make a promise, the person who receives their message must believe that they sincerely intend to make a promise.
- Reason rules require speakers to adjust statements to the perspectives and beliefs of the other participants. This does not mean saying what they want to hear, but framing what is said in a way that will make logical sense within the perspective of the other person. For example, to say 'It was a big document – about a hundred thousand kilobytes' to someone who is not computer literate, would be to break the rule of reason.

The rules for coherence are not always followed: they may be deliberately violated; coherence is not always wanted and when it is, it is not always achieved, even intraculturally.

Validity rules, with their dependence on the interpretations of the receiver, are culture specific and may be hard for people from outside the culture to apply. Reason rules, with their requirement that speakers adjust their statements to the perspectives and beliefs of the listeners, place heavy demands on the perceptiveness and rhetorical sensitivity of speakers, especially in intercultural situations.

Concern with how coherence is achieved and with the rules governing it led Teun van Dijk[46] to argue that it depends on following a set of macro-rules such as these:

- Propositions unnecessary for understanding other propositions should be deleted (that is, avoid red herrings). For instance, in the sentence 'To prepare a budget, you need to forecast your level of activity and the costs of the materials you will use and budgeting is an important skill for a headmistress nowadays', the second part of the statement should be omitted.
- Propositions needed as building blocks for a higher order proposition should be included, for example 'To prepare a budget, you need to forecast' is weak in propositional coherence, because it does not include the 'building block' of what it is that you need to forecast.
- Propositions should be grouped into more general ones by their common topic and general propositions should combine the elements of lower order ones – this helps listeners find the general concept that holds individual propositions together. For example, because the three statements which follow are not grouped, with the first two clearly falling under the third, propositional coherence is lost: 'You should forecast your level of activity'; 'You should predict what your costs for materials will be'; 'You have to prepare a budget'.

It is likely that Van Dijk's set of rules for propositional coherence are somewhat culture specific – in some cultures, such as Arab culture, inclusion of 'redundant' propositions is not confusing, and in particularistic cultures (see Chapter 3), ungrouped lists of propositions are perfectly comprehensible.

Rules for efficiency. A set of communication rules which have had considerable influence in the study of language use since 1967, when Paul Grice put forward the key ideas, is his 'conversational maxims'.[47] Grice proposed that for efficiency all communicators must observe the cooperative principle – meaning that their contribution must be what is required at the stage at which it occurs by the accepted purpose or direction of the talk exchange in which they are engaged. This cooperative principle is important, because the fact that listeners will assume that speakers are being cooperative enables them to make a wide range of inferences which would otherwise not be possible; and this capability and practice of listeners enables speakers to imply a wide range of meanings without explicitly stating them. (This conversational facility is called 'implicature'.) For example, if a speaker says 'The XYZ Company has two factories', while it would be logically impossible for the statement to be true if the XYZ Company has fewer than two factories, it could be true if it has more than two factories. Therefore, to tell a listener explicitly how many factories the company has, the speaker would have to say 'The XYZ Company has two factories and only two factories' for the listener to understand that he or she means that the company has just exactly two factories. The principle of cooperativeness, however, allows the listener to assume that if the speaker means that the XYZ company has more than two factories, or if he or she thinks it might have more, he or she would say so (for example by 'The XYZ Company has at least two factories').

Cooperation is achieved by following the maxims of quality (being truthful); quantity (providing enough but not too much information); relevance; and manner (not being obscure, disorganised or ambiguous). These maxims, Grice claimed, are never violated without disrupting the flow of conversation or affecting others' perceptions in the conversation. However, the violations may be seen as intentional and implications read into that interpretation. This allows communicators to use all kinds of strategically interesting, indirect statements to achieve their purposes. For example, in the XYZ company example above, suppose the speaker is deliberately violating the rule of quantity, and that in fact the company has four factories. Why might he or she do this? One reason might be that there is a third person present whom the speaker knows to know the truth so that the implicature gives a clear signal to that third person that the speaker wishes, without lying, to deceive the apparently intended listener.

The more a culture encourages and supports the use of implicature, the more difficult it is for outsiders to follow discussions without explicit adjustment by the speakers.

In general, rules are important regulators of communication. For example, someone following a rule may be harder to persuade to act differently than someone whose behaviour in that area is not rule governed, especially if the rule is salient – that is, if it is tied to their personal standards or closely linked to their self-concept. People generally use rules to interpret what they see and hear (rules of meaning) and then act on the basis of their interpretations, employing rules (rules of action) to decide what kind of action, in this case communication action, is appropriate.[48]

Communication rules, like other rules, are affected by cultural values. For example, Japanese people generally follow a different set of rules about politeness, including showing a high level of deference to older people, than those followed by most Americans. Only by understanding the rules someone else follows can they be fully understood, while awareness of a person's own rules allows them to eliminate or adapt them, change the range of situations to which they apply or follow them more rigorously.

Rule theories can be criticised on three grounds. They lack unity and coherence – the meaning attached by rule theorists to 'rules' varies widely; they lack explanatory power – the theories merely describe what the rules are and fail to account for how they arose and how different cultural groups selected different sets of rules; and they allow too little scope for the dynamic nature of communication. However, some rule theorists distinguish conventional logic, which treats the rules as determinants, from rhetorical logic which treats communication as a way of changing the rules by negotiation. The disagreements between these theoreticians and the adherents of 'rule-governing' theories have contributed to the lack of unity of the 'school'. Despite these criticisms, at least one rule-based theory, speech act theory, has been described as 'among the most productive creations of contemporary philosophy and social science'.[49]

Speech act theory

When someone speaks, he or she performs an act; moreover, speakers have intentions about the acts they perform. This is the crux of speech act theory, which was initiated by the philosopher G. Austin and elaborated by John Searle.[50] The act, and the associated intention, may be stating, questioning, commanding, promising or a number of other possibilities. Speech is not just used to designate or describe something; it actually *does* something. Speakers do not only speak to give information: they may have one or more of a range of intentions.

If a speech act is successful, the receiver will understand the speaker's intention. If, for example, when Person A asks a question, the receiver, Person B, only understands the words, but not that A intended to ask a question, B is unlikely to give an answer, and A's speech act will not have been a successful one. Speech act theory identifies what it takes to make a successful speech act, that is, to have an intention understood. There are guidelines for how to use speech to accomplish a particular intention – for instance, if A wants something, he or she makes a request, and does it in a form which B will understand to obligate him or her either to grant it or to turn it down.

Speech acts, according to Searle, are regulated by strict rules. For communication to 'work', speakers must follow rules and those rules must be known to and understood by receivers. For example, promising involves five basic rules:

- It must include a sentence indicating that the speaker will do some act in the future.
- The receiver would rather that the speaker do the act than not do it.
- It should not be obvious that the act would be done in the normal course of events.
- The speaker must intend to do the act.
- It establishes an obligation for the speaker to do the act.

The high value placed by communication scholars on speech act theory is based on its use of intentions to explain how people structure communication. It is probable that the core propositions of the theory are universal – that in all cultures, to speak is to perform an act and that to be successful the communicative intention behind the act must be understood by the receiver. However, both intentions and the forms required to communicate them may be culture specific and hard for outsiders to comprehend. For instance, in some societies, for a guest to praise a possession of their host usually obliges the host to offer it as a gift; thus if a guest does so praise a host's possession, it must be assumed that their intention is to ask for it. For Westerners that implication of praise would not be understood without prior knowledge.

Expression and understanding of intentions

Understanding what the speaker's intentions are in saying something is crucial to a receiver. For instance, if a colleague says something like 'The post has arrived', the literal meaning is easily understood by decoding, but the receiver would want to know why she or he made this announcement. What was the intention behind saying this? It might be a simple desire to impart the information but usually the speaker also has a communicative intent – in this example, it might be that she or he wants the receiver to go to the post room to collect it or that she or he wants them to know that she or he has been to the post room (as, perhaps, her or his duties require).

Receivers will usually want to know which of the possible communicative intents apply – indeed they will need to know, or the full meaning of the message will elude them. To decide this, they will draw on a set of assumptions that they use to understand their experience – their cognitive schema. Their difficulty is to decide which of the numerous assumptions in their cognitive schema are relevant in this particular case. *Relevance theorists* assert that to make this selection receivers will apply the general principle that 'people try to maximise the effect and minimise the effort of any action'.[51]

First, they will draw on what is available in immediate memory in the particular time and place of the message being received; from the assumptions thus produced they will choose the set that allows them to infer the speaker's intentions with the least effort.

At this point, an additional subtlety is introduced into relevance theory. The receiver assumes that the speaker wants to help him or her understand their intentions. Therefore, the receiver makes an assumption of relevance – an assumption that the speaker's intention will correspond to the beliefs most likely to be relevant to the receiver. The assumptions brought to mind from the receiver's cognitive schema can therefore be tested against their relevance to the receiver and the first that works is likely to be adopted as the receiver's understanding of the speaker's communicative intention. So, to decide why a colleague has said 'The post has arrived' a receiver would probably opt for the colleague's intention being to tell them to go to the post room if that job was part of the receiver's normal duties or to tell the receiver that he or she has done it if it was part of the colleague's. Figure 4.2 presents the process as a flow chart.

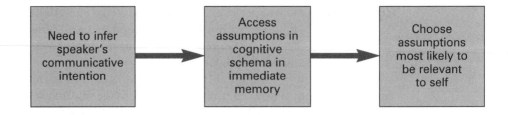

Figure 4.2 Relevance theory account of how message receivers infer speakers' intentions

Using relevance theory to understand communicative intent can, however, create problems in intercultural situations where the speaker may have a limited ability to make their intention correspond to the beliefs most likely to be relevant to the receiver. For instance, in the example given in Box 4.9, a Western banker explained that in dealing with Turkish officials he experienced difficulty in conveying an intent to be 'properly and prudentially' cautious because of a lack of knowledge of what beliefs would be relevant to them in that situation.

Language use ambiguity

This section has drawn attention to a number of quite basic language usages which may differ from culture to culture and so cause confusion interculturally. More generally, there is a problem in that language itself is fundamentally ambiguous.[52] For instance, in English, there is nothing in the words themselves to say 'This is the important point'. That emphasis is supplied by the expectations each speaker has that the other speaker will use language in the same way that he or she does – and in the case of English that means they have to grasp the subtle English use of voice modulation. For example, questions can be expressed as statements spoken in a rising voice pitch – as in 'So you went to the bank this morning' which is a statement if spoken in a level pitch and a question if spoken in a rising pitch.

Four propositions which help explain these confusions are:

1. Language is ambiguous by nature.
2. We must draw inferences about meaning – we have no choice. We do it based on two main sources: (a) the language a speaker has used and (b) our knowledge about the world. A statement like 'There is a man at the door' could mean 'There is a man sitting on the doorstep playing the guitar'. However, you are likely to discount this in favour of assuming it to mean 'There is a man at the door waiting to enter' or '... about to ring the bell'. That is, you are likely to assume that, unless a speaker states otherwise, the obvious common-sense assumption is correct. However, what constitutes 'common sense' varies across cultures.

3. Inferences are drawn very quickly. Most researchers suggest that such inferences must be drawn every time it becomes possible for speakers to exchange turns and that such occasions occur approximately once every second in normal conversation.
4. Inferences tend to be fixed, not tentative.

> The concepts and theories in this section and the preceding one derive mainly from a tradition that sees the individual human mind as the independent locus for processing information and generating and understanding messages. This individualistic, cognitive approach has been dominant in Western social science during the twentieth century; however, it can be challenged for social science generally and especially in the study of communication, which is essentially something that happens between people and so cannot be explained solely from the perspective of the individual mind.

4.4   CONCLUSION

Many of the theories described in this chapter are weak (in Popper's[53] sense of a strong theory being refutable), incomplete and lacking in parsimony. However, this does not mean that they, and more particularly the concepts they incorporate, are not useful. Trait theories are a case in point – it has already been pointed out that they lack predictive power and do not discriminate well – and they certainly fail Popper's test: it is impossible to conceive of a way of refuting that traits exist or that any particular behaviour tendency is a trait. Yet assertiveness and rhetorical sensitivity are trait concepts which have proved extremely useful for normative approaches to communication.

The value of the concepts and theories introduced here for the purposes of this book is that heightened awareness of the structure and processes of communication itself is an aid to achieving communication competence, which in turn is a prerequisite for intercultural communication competence. Awareness of communicative behaviour, or mindfulness, is widely understood to be necessary for interacting successfully with different others.

In addition, this chapter has highlighted (sub)cultural differences in communication practices. Without heightened awareness of such differences, many people (especially the members of dominant [sub]cultures) are unlikely to be able or motivated to adapt their communication in intercultural encounters.

REFERENCES

1. Haslett, B. (1989) 'Communication and language acquisition within a cultural context' in Ting-Toomey S. and F. Korzenny (eds) *Language, Communication and Culture: Current Directions*, Newbury Park, CA: Sage.
2. Scollon, R. and Scollon, S. (1981) *Narrative, Literacy and Face in Interethnic Communication*, Norwood, NJ: Ablex.
3. Baker, M.A. (1991) 'Gender and verbal communication in professional settings: a review of research', *Management Communication Quarterly*, **5**(1): 36–63.
4. Hewstone, M., Stroebe, W., Codol, J.-P. and Stephenson, G.M. (eds) *Introduction to Social Psychology*, Oxford: Basil Blackwell.
5. Sarbaugh, L.E. (1988) 'A taxonomic approach to intercultural communication' in Kim, Y.Y. and Gudykunst, W.B. (eds) *Theories in Intercultural Communication*, Newbury Park, CA: Sage.
6. Samovar, L.A. and Porter, R.E. (1985) 'Introduction' in Samovar, L.A. and Porter, R.E. (eds) *Intercultural Communication: A Reader* (4th edn), Belmont, CA: Wadsworth.
7. Baxter, L. A. and Goldsmith, D. (1990) 'Cultural terms for communication events among some American high school adolescents', *Western Journal of Speech Communication*, **54**(3): 377–94.
8. Harrison, R. (1974) *Beyond Words: An Introduction to Nonverbal Communication*, Englewood Cliffs, NJ: Prentice-Hall.
9. Gallois, C. and Callan, V.J. (1986) 'Decoding emotional messages: influence of ethnicity, sex, message type and channel', *Journal of Personality and Social Psychology*, **51**(4): 755–62.
10. Birdwhistell, R. (1970) *Kinesics and Context*, Philadelphia: University of Pennsylvania Press.
11. Hall, E.T. (1976) *Beyond Culture*, New York: Doubleday.
12. Ekman, P. and Friesen, W. V. (1968) 'Nonverbal behaviour in psychotherapy research' in Schlein, J.M. (ed.) *Research in Psychotherapy*, Vol. 3, Washington DC: American Psychological Association.
13. Hart, R.P. and Burks D.M. (1972) 'Rhetorical sensitivity and social interaction', *Speech Monographs*, **39**: 75–91.
14. Langrish, S. (1981) 'Assertive training' in Cooper, C.L. (ed.) *Improving Interpersonal Relations: Some Approaches to Social Skills Training*, London: Gower.
15. Kim, M.-S., Hunter, J.E., Miyahara, A., Horvath, A., Bresnahan, M. and Yoon, H. (1996) 'Individual- vs. culture-level dimensions of individualism and collectivism: effects on preferred conversational styles', *Communication Monographs*, **63**: 29–49.
16. Singhal, A. and Motoko, N. (1993) 'Assertiveness as communication competence: a comparison of the communication styles of American and Japanese students', *Asian Journal of Communication*, **3**(1): 1–18.
17. Filardo, E.K. (1996) 'Gender patterns in African American and White adolescents: social interactions in same-race, mixed-gender groups', *Journal of Personality and Social Psychology*, **71**: 71–82.
18. Norton, R. (1983) *Communicator Style: Theory, Applications and Measures*, Beverly Hills, CA: Sage.
19. Horvath, C.W. (1995) 'Biological origins of communicator style', *Communication Quarterly*, **43**: 394–407.
20. Gudykunst, W.B., Matsumoto, Y., Ting-Toomey, S., Nishida, T., Kim K. and Heyman, S. (1996) 'The influence of cultural individualism–collectivism, self construals and individual values on communication styles across cultures', *Human Communication Research*, **22**: 507–34.
21. Hofstede, G. (1991) *Cultures and Organizations: Software of the Mind*, London: McGraw-Hill.

22. Cody, M.J. and McLaughlin, M.L. (1985) 'The situation as a construct in interpersonal communication research' in Knapp, M.L. and Miller G.R. (eds) *Handbook of Interpersonal Communication*, Beverly Hills, CA: Sage.
23. Hall, E.T. (1976) op. cit.
24. Stohl, C. and Redding W. (1987) 'Messages and message exchange processes' in Jablin, F., Putnam, L., Roberts K. and Porter L. (eds) *Handbook of Organizational Communication: An Interdisciplinary Approach*, Newbury Park, CA: Sage, pp. 451–502.
25. Hewes, D.E. and Planalp, S. (1987) 'The individual's place in communication science' in Berger, C.R. and Chaffee S.H. (eds) *Handbook of Communication*, Newbury Park, CA: Sage.
26. Feeley, T.H. and deTurck, M.A. (1995) 'Global cue usage in behavioral lie detection', *Communication Quarterly*, **43**: 420–30.
27. Burgoon, J.K., Buller, D.B., Dillman, L. and Walther, J.B. (1995) 'Interpersonal deception: IV. Effects of suspicion on perceived communication and nonverbal behavior dynamics', *Human Communication Research*, **21**: 163–96.
28. Petty, R.E. and Cacioppo, J.T. (1986) *Communication and Persuasion: Central and Peripheral Routes to Attitude Change*, New York: Springer-Verlag.
29. Hall, E.T. (1976) op. cit.
30. Gallois, C. and Callan V. J. (1986) op. cit.
31. Argyle, M. (1973) *The Psychology of Interpersonal Behavior*, Harmondsworth: Penguin.
32. Wiemann, J.M. and Giles, H. (1988) 'Interpersonal communication' in Hewstone, M., Stroebe, W., Codol J.-P. and Stephenson G.M. (eds) *Introduction to Social Psychology*, Oxford: Blackwell.
33. West, C. (1983) 'Ask me no questions… an analysis of questions and replies' in Fisher S. and Todd A. (eds) *The Social Organization of Doctor–Patient Communication*, Washington, DC: Centre for Applied Linguistics.
34. Gouldner, A.M. (1960) 'The norm of reciprocity', *American Sociological Review*, **25**(2): 161–78.
35. Bateson, G. (1958) *Naven*, Stanford, CA: Stanford University Press. For a fuller exploration see Watzlawick, P., Beavin, J. and Jackson D. (1967) *Pragmatics of Human Communication: A Study of Interactional Patterns, Pathologies and Paradoxes*, New York: Norton.
36. Philipsen, G. (1989) 'Speech and the communal function' in Ting-Toomey S. and Korzenny, F. (eds) *Language, Communication and Culture: Current Directions*, Newbury Park, CA: Sage.
37. Meyer, J.R. (1994) 'Formulating plans for requests: an investigation of retrieval processes', *Communication Studies*, **45**: 131–44.
38. Ibid.
39. Thompson, M.P. (1993) 'The skills of inquiry and advocacy: why managers need both', *Management Communication Quarterly*, **7**(1): 95–106.
40. Tannen, D. (1990) *You Just Don't Understand: Women and Men in Communication*, New York: William Morrow, p. 42.
41. Le Poire, B.A., Burgoon J.K. and Parrott, R. (1992) 'Status and privacy: restoring communication in the workplace', *Journal of Applied Communication*, **20**(4): 419–36.
42. Baker, M.A. (1991) 'Gender and verbal communication in professional settings: a review of research', *Management Communication Quarterly*, **5**(1): 36–63.
43. Cronen, V.E., Chin, V. and Pearce, W.B. (1988) 'Co-ordinated management of meaning' in Kim, Y.Y. and Gudykunst, W.B. (eds) *Theories in Intercultural Communication*, Newbury Park, CA: Sage.
44. Bernstein, B. (1971) *Class, Codes and Control: Theoretical Studies Toward a Sociology of Language*, London: Routledge & Kegan Paul.
45. Jacobs, S. and Jackson S. (1983) 'Strategy and structure in conversational influence attempts', *Communication Monographs*, **50**: 285–304.
46. van Dijk, T. (1981) *Studies in the Pragmatics of Discourse*, The Hague: Mouton Hifflin.

47. Grice, H.P. (1975) 'Logic and conversation' in Cole, P. and Morgan, J. (eds) *Syntax and Semantics*, Vol. 3, New York: Academic Press.

48. Shimanoff, S. (1980) *Communication Rules: Theory and Research*, Beverly Hills, CA: Sage.

49. Littlejohn, S. (1996) *Theories of Human Communication*, Belmont, CA: Wadsworth.

50. Searle, J. (1969) *Speech Acts: An Essay in the Philosophy of Language*, Cambridge: Cambridge University Press.

51. Sperber, D. and Wilson D. (1986) *Relevance: Communication and Cognition*, Cambridge, MA: Harvard University Press.

52. Scollon, R. and Scollon S.W. (1995) 'What is a discourse approach?' in Scollon, R. and Scollon, S.W., *Discourse*, Cambridge, MA: Blackwell, pp. 1–15.

53. Popper, K.R. (1972) *Conjectures and Refutations: The Growth of Scientific Knowledge* (4th edn), London: Routledge & Kegan Paul.

5 (SUB)CULTURAL COMMUNICATION AT WORK – 2

The concepts and theories covered in Chapter 4 focus on overt communication behaviour and the individual; as a result, useful though they are, the level of explanation they provide is limited. In this chapter, the factors (constructs) and processes underlying the overt behaviour of individuals and the interactions between them come into focus, to provide more explanatory power. Section 5.1 considers psychological factors and processes antecedent to individual communication; Section 5.2 examines interactionist approaches; and Section 5.3 explores facework, which cuts across all three levels – the overt and underlying behaviours of the individual and the interactions between individuals, as Figure 5.1 illustrates.

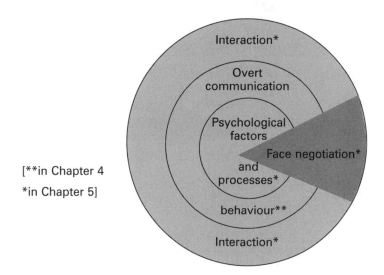

[**in Chapter 4
*in Chapter 5]

Figure 5.1 Relation between content of Chapters 4 and 5

5.1 ANTECEDENTS OF COMMUNICATION BEHAVIOUR

Communication, from one point of view, is only a particular form of behaviour. This means that we can increase our understanding of how people communicate if we understand more about the influences on their behaviour. There are two ways of doing this: by examining the 'internal factors' (actual constructs), which help explain and may even help predict what people do, and by considering the processes people go through before and during the course of communication. The internal factors are the 'self', motivations, emotions, cognitions – perceptions, expectations, beliefs and attitudes – and values. The most important process is social cognition. In this book there is no space to introduce these huge subjects (but readers are recommended to follow them up: some relevant books are listed in 'Further Reading'); instead the concentration is on how cultural differences are reflected in these constructs and processes which are antecedent to communication. Finally this section discusses the question of how – by what processes – culture affects behaviour.

Figure 5.2 gives a model of the constructs and processes covered here and their relation to communication.

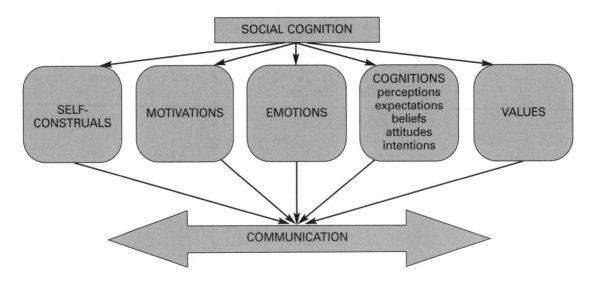

Figure 5.2   Behavioural constructs and communication behaviours

Self-construals and self-esteem

The self-construal is a mental representation of the self, derived at least in part reflexively from the interpretations of the projected perceptions of others communicated in interaction. Individualists have independent self-construals: their mental representations of the self are separate from those they have of others; in contrast, for collectivists, the self-construal is fundamentally interdependent – others are considered part of the self.[1] In individualistic Western models, the self 'comprises a unique, bounded configuration of internal attributes, such as preferences, traits, abilities, motives, values and rights, and behaves primarily as a consequence of these internal attributes'. For people with

Western self-construals, although other people are crucial in maintaining the sense of self and function as standards of comparison and sources of appraisal, the persistent concern in communicating is to express internal attributes. The collectivistic self is always aware of the nature of the relationship to others and of maintaining mutuality within those relationships.

It has also been asserted that culture influences the perceived discrepancy between the actual self and the ideal self, and lends the criteria in which self-esteem is appraised and evaluated; that self-esteem is, in essence, a cultural creation. The evidence on this point, however, is somewhat conflicting. Farh *et al.* (1991)[2] found cultural differences in self-esteem strongly reflected when they investigated modesty bias among Taiwanese and Western workers. Modesty bias means that subjects give self-ratings of work performance that are lower than supervisors' ratings; Western workers' self-ratings of performance are usually higher than ratings obtained from supervisors – they do not exhibit modesty bias. Farh *et al.* found that Taiwanese workers do exhibit modesty bias. They explained their findings in terms of broad cultural differences between Taiwanese and Western workers. However, a replication study using data from several organisations in mainland China[3] showed leniency in self-ratings – that is, self-ratings higher than supervisor or peer ratings – which suggests that broad cultural factors may not fully explain the modesty bias reported by Farh *et al.*

Women in the West may be more like people from collectivist cultures than Western men in having more interdependent self-construals: Cross and Madison (1997)[4] argue that 'many gender differences in cognition, motivation, emotion and social behaviour may be explained in terms of men's and women's different self-construals'. For US women, but not for men, a positive relationship has been found between self-esteem and prosocial and affiliative motives. Strategies for self-enhancement used by US men often involve boasting and exaggeration of their abilities, or operating with a 'false uniqueness' bias – the false belief that one's own abilities are exceptional – and over-estimating their performances against objective standards. US women are more likely to adjust their self-enhancement strategies for the feelings of others – for instance, women students with high grade point averages are more likely to take into account the assessments received by their interlocutors before talking about them. US women's greater responsiveness to feedback has also been interpreted in terms of their having more interdependent self-construals: studies show that women's self-evaluations are more responsive to the feedback they receive than are men's.

However, the fact that women are more responsive to feedback may be a function of their having lower self-esteem. Because women have lower status than men they may have lower self-confidence, leading them to be, among other things, more responsive than men to others' evaluations in achievement situations. Women may attach more value than men do to others' opinions of them, because low self-esteem leads them to placing a low valuation on their own opinion of themself. Men and women approach evaluative achievement situations differently. Men may be particularly likely to respond to the competitive nature of evaluative achievement and hence to adopt a self-confident approach that leads them to deny the informational value of others' evaluations. Women, because of their low self-esteem, may be particularly likely to approach each situation as opportunities to gain information about their abilities.[5]

The self-concepts of *people with disabilities* have been shown to be different from stereotyped portrayals and not to differ significantly from those of other people. A study was undertaken of 177 students registered with a university's disabled service and 160 other students, using five measures of self-concept validated in the literature. These are surgency (extraversion), agreeableness, conscientiousness, emotional stability and culture in the 'high culture' sense. Students with and without disability tended to rate each other in a stereotypical manner. Students with disabilities were seen by others as more conscientious and cultured than were students without disabilities, whereas students without disabilities were seen by others as more extraverted and emotionally stable than students with disabilities. When the students rated themselves, however, no such differences emerged between the groups with and without disabilities.

The researchers concluded that, although peer feedback effects may be difficult for people with disabilities, it should not be assumed that they have deficits in their self-perceptions.[6]

Motives

While general need-based models of motivation, such as those of Maslow,[7] can be applied to communication, a better account may be provided by considering a more tailored set, such as those suggested by Turner (1988).[8] Needs for security, especially for confirmation of identity, group inclusion (affiliation), avoiding diffuse anxiety, sense of a shared common world, symbolic and material gratification and predictability interact with basic drives to motivate people to interact and influence their behaviour during interactions. Needs for power, esteem and autonomy are also thought to be influences.

Motives for communicating have been found to vary with communicative traits or styles; the implication is that they influence them. One piece of research allocated communicators to one of four groups based on their assertive and responsive behaviours, where assertiveness referred to making statements in a non-aggressive, non-submissive manner and responsiveness to replying to others with rhetorical sensitivity. The four groups consisted of 'competent communicators' (defined by the researchers as high assertives, high responsives), 'non-competent communicators' (low assertives, low responsives), 'aggressives' (high assertives, low responsives) and 'submissives' (low assertives, high responsives). The findings were that competent communicators communicated from needs for affection (affiliation), pleasure (gratification) and inclusion more than any of the other three groups. Aggressive types communicated more from control (power) needs, while non-competent communicators and submissive types communicated from escape (autonomy) needs.[9]

Most current theories of motivation, including Turner's, originated in the USA and are now being criticised for being culture specific. For example, it has been argued that the needs for power, esteem and achievement, which feature strongly in Western motivational theories, are not found in all cultures. Achievement – which means individual achievement – may be a motive limited to individualistic cultures; similarly, the need for power may not motivate many people in a high-power distance culture, such as India's, where most people accept that they have a 'pre-ordained' position in a social hierarchy.

Motivational differences between the *genders* may have been exaggerated. In research into 1001 adolescents, girls were not found to have lower achievement orientations than boys. The review of research into women's and men's professional communication, however, as we saw earlier, found that women's communication motivations were more affiliative and less power orientated than men's.

BOX 5.1

THE NEEDS OF MIDDLE EASTERN STUDENTS

Needs particular to Middle Eastern students (except Israelis) include respect for their culture, close personal relationships or friendships, relaxed social relationships, hospitality accompanied by the offering of food, interaction with fellow Arabs, having a mentor from the same background, and having a satisfactory relationship with faculty and administrative advisors.

Source: Parker, O.D. (1976) 'Cultural clues to the Middle Eastern student' (ERIC Document Reproduction Service No. ED 136 604). Posted on the Internet: http://www.flstw.edu/pderic.html.

Emotions

Emotions are feelings, related to satisfaction or otherwise of needs (for example fear or happiness), responses to other people (for example love, hate), personal goals (for example anger, joy) or judgements of someone's own behaviour (for example pride, shame). A model of how emotions are elicited and manifested has the following components: antecedent events (which trigger feelings); event categorisation (for example as humiliating or flattering); appraisal of the event according to its coding (for example humiliation as harmful, flattery as pleasant); physiological reaction (like sweating or blushing); action readiness (to run, to leave the room); emotional behaviour (like insulting vengeful speech or crying); and regulation – people can either inhibit or enhance responses. A review article by Mesquita and Frijda (1992)[10] has reported that both cultural similarities and cultural differences have been found for nearly all the components of this model, from antecedent events (British traditional culture defines as funny a pavement accident caused by slipping on a banana skin – it is safe to say that some other cultures do not) to facial and vocal expression. The less overt expression of emotion by Chinese and Japanese people is widely recognised – viz. the traditional European notion of 'Oriental inscrutability'.

It was always important to try to understand the emotions that might be fuelling people's communicative work behaviour but changes in organisational attitudes (see Section 3.4) increase the legitimacy of dealing with them. In intercultural encounters at work, cultural variations in emotions have to be taken into account.

Research found differences in the emphasis placed by women and men housing managers in work-based interpersonal relationships and, as Table 5.1 shows, women managers may be more responsive to emotional issues.

Table 5.1   Gender differences in the emotional responsiveness of managers

Emphasis in inter-personal relationships	Women housing managers	Men housing managers
With own team	Understanding of people; sensitivity; care for individual feelings and development; rich perception of human beings	Supports own team; looks after their interests; defends them to the hilt
With clients	Empathy; relationships; understanding of different needs	Can use pressure groups

Source: based on Sparrow, J. and Rigg, C. (1993) 'Job analysis: selecting for the masculine approach to management', Selection and Development Review, **9**(2): 5–8.

Cognitions

These are mental constructs; they are the things people are aware of in the form of thoughts and ideas. They include perceptions, which embody an awareness of the environment (both physical and social) and beliefs, which are cognitions to which people attach a degree of credence. Beliefs include assumptions, which are taken-for-granted beliefs, and expectations, which are beliefs about the future.

Perceptions. Some writers on culture, especially those concerned with culture and management, place perceptions centrally in their understanding of the concept. For example, J. Johansson (1994)[11] defines culture as:

The underlying framework which guides an individual's perceptions of observed events and personal interactions and the selection of appropriate responses in social situations. The framework consists of objective reality, as manifested in terms of societal institutions, and also subjective reality as socialized in terms of predispositions and beliefs.

Culture as framework, according to Johansson, 'serves to highlight certain aspects of a situation and downplay others. It frames reality as observed and interpreted, and provides behavioural rules as a guide for acting on it. Culture involves behavioural constraints imposed by society. This suggests that culture is a strong determinant of observed behaviour.'

Another writer who agrees with the centrality of culture in perception is S. Robinson,[12] who argues that culture 'lies at the very roots of perception'. In fact what people perceive is strongly influenced by (Robinson says determined by) their deep culture:

One could even go so far as to say that deep culture leads to a distortion of reality. However, it would be more accurate to say that deep culture is the source of the inaccurate restructuring which takes place when things emanating from one place are perceived by people from another. Their restructuring is inaccurate because of the self-referential nature of human perception.

Box 5.2 gives some examples of the way work-related perceptions can vary with culture.

BOX 5.2

VARIATIONS IN PERCEPTIONS OF WORK AND ORGANISATION IN DIFFERENT CULTURES AND SUBCULTURES

- High-power distance may tend to make people perceive the top managers in their organisations as infallible, not expect that they themselves will necessarily attain to positions of power during their career, be motivated to work hard by loyalty to the 'godlike' chief executive and have the attitude that a steeply hierarchical work organisation is natural and fitting.
- An American manager, from a highly individualistic culture, expects to gain personal status at work from the performance, such as increased market share, higher profitability or product

> innovation produced by his or her department; to a Japanese manager, from a collectivist culture, such achievements belong to the group, and it is mainly from the development of subordinates that his or her own status derives.
> ● Where some white males perceive a hierarchical structure open to talent and energy, people from ethnic minorities, women and people with disabilities often perceive a glass ceiling.

One perceptual concept which has had considerable impact on the field of communication is constructivism, which is based on Kelly's personal construct theory (and the Kelly grid he devised to measure personal constructs).[13] The idea is that differences people perceive – such as 'x is tall' or 'y is short' – are not natural but derived from predetermined sets of opposites within an individual's cognitive system, which contains many such distinctions. Constructs allow individuals to give meaning to experiences. They are learned through interaction with other people, so that culture impacts strongly on them. For example, culture has an effect on how finely different subjects are categorised – a well-known example is the many fine gradations in types of snow which are given names in the Inuit language; another is the way there are many common names in English for different types of wild flower where the languages of desert people tend to have the one word 'flower'.

Another perceptual concept which has inspired much cross-cultural research and been incorporated into intercultural communication studies is that of 'field independence or dependence'. Witkin and Berry,[14] in a series of experiments, found that, in an adjustment task, some individuals were less distracted than others by the frame in which the object to be adjusted was placed. Those people who were little distracted they called 'field independents'; those who were more distracted they called 'field dependents'. Later findings established that 'field independent' people differed from 'field dependents' in respect of social perception, too: they were more autonomous, self-orientated, even distant compared with field dependent people, who tended to display more sensitivity to contextual cues and to be more sensitive and empathic.

Although rooted in heredity, socialisation and enculturation have a strong influence on whether someone is field independent or dependent. Field independence, for example, is more prevalent among hunter gatherers than among agriculturalists and, in general, among men than women – a finding which Witkin and Berry attributed to socialisation rather than genes.

Beliefs, assumptions and expectations. The 'knowledge' that people in different cultures and subcultures take for granted is extensive and affects their behaviour, including their communication behaviour, in multiple ways. In addition to rituals, status differentials and values it includes all the manifestations of surface culture. These include roles (what is done and not done by people in various categories, such as male/female, supervisor/subordinate, teacher/student) work (how much emphasis is placed on social interaction versus task completion, how supervisors treat subordinates) time (how late a person can be without apologising; whether it is more important to be on time for the next appointment or to complete the business at hand) and space (what constitutes invasion of someone else's 'territory'; how acceptable open-plan offices are; how many people can get into a lift before they feel crowded).

Worldview and religious beliefs are two key components of culture and so key variables in cultural difference. As far as subcultural variation is concerned, though, the issue is less clear cut. Some feminist scholars have described the female worldview as significantly different from the male worldview. Gilligan, arguing from a psychological perspective, states that 'female identity revolves around interconnectedness and relationship'. Conversely, she argues that male identity 'stresses separation and independence'. The ways in which concepts of social relationships (and their accompanying communication patterns) differ between genders are parallel to gender differences in worldview.[15] However, in this book, the view is taken that, in most cases, core beliefs are shared among the members of a culture. Religious beliefs largely cross subcultural boundaries. When they do vary within cultures, as in many Western societies, there is more variation among individual members of a society than between groups other than religious groups themselves.

Taken-for-granted beliefs, or assumptions, undoubtedly affect behaviour and are hard to detect, sometimes even by the person holding them. At work, relevant assumptions include those held by managers about their subordinates' work motivations, those negotiators hold about their opponents, and those people hold about the members of other social groups. For instance, assumptions about the stereotypical characteristics of women (emotional, sensitive, nurturing and interdependent) and men (independent, dominant, emotionally inhibited and goal directed) are strong unspoken influences on their relative treatment in terms of job segregation and career advancement.

Writing specifically in a work context, Edgar Schein actually defined culture in terms of assumptions: viz. 'I am defining culture as the set of shared, taken-for-granted implicit assumptions that a group holds and that determines how it perceives, thinks about and reacts to its various environments' (Schein, 1992).[16] Norms become a 'visible' manifestation of these assumptions, but it is important to remember that behind the norms lies this deeper taken-for-granted set of assumptions that most members of a culture never question or examine.

Schein identified two subcultures (he called them 'cultures'), based on occupational communities, which are quite stable in the assumptions they hold: the 'engineers', the practitioners of the organisation's core technology, who 'prefer solutions without people'; and 'the executives' – CEOs especially – for whom their role brings about the perception that 'financial criteria always have to be paramount'. The engineers resist the new organisational 'learning' culture (see Chapter 3) because it does not accord with their preferred type of solution and the executives resist giving time and resources to building learning capacity, which does not give quick returns; they are, Schein says, over-concerned with the control system and collude with engineers to downplay the human factor. As a result, according to Schein, 'new methods of learning or solving problems do not diffuse or even become embedded in the organisations that first used them... individual projects learn new methods of operating, but these methods do not diffuse to other groups or organisations'.

Ethnocentrism is a biased assumption or set of assumptions in favour of one's own ethnic group. To some degree, biases in favour of people's own ingroup and in opposition to their outgroups are 'natural'; there are studies which show that people from all cultures have a tendency to:

- think of what goes on in their own culture as natural and correct and what goes on in other cultures as not natural or not correct
- perceive their own customs as universally valid
- believe their own norms, roles and values are correct, particularly as concerns their own immediate ingroup or subculture
- favour and cooperate with ingroup members while feeling hostile toward outgroups.[17]

Ethnocentrism is rewarded in interactions within an ethnic group: high ethnocentrics are more likely to conform to its norms, roles and values and so to be accepted. However, the point that people are particularly likely to believe that the norms, roles and values of their own culture or subculture are correct needs some qualification. It applies where the members of a social grouping are concentrated and in day-to-day contact with other members (as in the case of, say, the Greek-Cypriot community in areas of London), even if the grouping is subordinate and low in attractiveness; it applies less strongly where the members of a subordinate social grouping are spread out among among the members of the dominant social grouping; this probably accounts for the fact that, despite feminism, we have not found it necessary to coin the term 'gendercentrism'.

A work-based task-group study found that ethnocentrism varied, depending on whether respondents were reporting on task aspects or relationship aspects of their intergroup dynamics. In some conditions groups seemed motivated to minimise or to invert usual ethnocentric tendencies. Over allocation of resources, groups minimised their advantage or emphasised their disadvantage – in 'a marked contrast to the usual ingroup–outgroup pattern in which groups see themselves favorably and others unfavorably'.[18] An obvious explanation of this last behaviour, however, is that the groups were motivated to lower the favourability of their self-perceptions in order to try to obtain more resources. Because assumptions are inaccessible to self-awareness and powerful, they are key variables in intercultural encounters.

Expectations about others' behaviour, including role expectations, normative expectations and expectations about how they will communicate all affect individuals' communication choices. These expectations are a function of knowledge, beliefs/attitudes, stereotypes, self-concepts, roles, prior interaction and status characteristics.[19] Thus the expectations someone has about the behaviour of people from another culture are related to how much they know about that culture, what they believe and what their attitude is to that culture, stereotypes of individuals from that culture, their own self-concept (for example as 'proud to be British' or as 'a citizen of the world'), roles which do or do not require interfacing with people from the other culture, previous experience of people from the other culture and their perceptions of their own and the others' relative status.

BOX 5.3

CROSS-CULTURAL COMPARISONS OF
WORK ATTITUDES

1. Tse *et al.* (1990) compared managers' attitudes in China, Hong Kong and Canada. They concluded that there are both important similarities and significant differences in orientations across the three countries. Attitudes towards strategic adaptiveness, democratic organisation and centralisation are similar, as are the perceived requirements for general management skills. However, attitudes differ towards participation, formal structure, internal competition and risk, in views about experimentation and innovation, and in values such as ascribed status, intuition and loyalty to the organisation.

2. In a Russian factory in the late 1980s, a production manager from the UK, with extended international experience, found that three-quarters of the width of an important supply road was blocked by rubbish, waste materials and so on, which slowed everything down because vehicles could not pass. He asked to get it cleared.

   A day later, he was called back by the factory manager, and shown that an area of ten feet had been cleared, exposing a huge beam of timber left there since the factory was rebuilt in 1916 when the wooden beams were replaced with metal girders.

Sources: Tse, D.K., Lee, K., Vertinsky, I. and Wehrung, D.A. (1988) 'Does culture matter? A cross-cultural study of executives' choice, decisiveness and risk adjustment in international marketing', *Journal of Marketing,* **52**: 81–95; interview with an expatriate manager, author's research.

Subcultural variations in expectations were found for example by research which showed that physician and patient groups had different role expectations of themselves and one another and that age differences affected role expectations in both groups.[20] Other research has shown that professional nurses in psychiatric wards are more likely to respond to violent patient behaviour directed against staff with a therapeutic reaction if they perceive the behaviour as arbitrary than if they perceive it as non-arbitrary. In other words, their professional role creates expectations about patient behaviour which are different from those most people would have about others' behaviour, and, if the expectations are not fulfilled, their response is affected.[21]

Attitudes

Attitudes, which are a combination of beliefs and 'affects' (or enduring positive or negative evaluations about some person, object or issue), received a great deal of attention from psychologists when it was believed that they had a strong influence on behaviour – so strong that a person's behaviour could be predicted from knowledge of their attitude. Unfortunately, it eventually became clear that looking for a direct global attitude–behaviour link was not likely to be fruitful. Instead, following Ajzen (1991),[22] attempts have been directed at establishing links between attitudes to performing a behaviour and performing it (for example attitudes to working abroad and actually seeking such an assignment); attitudes to a target person or object and acting accordingly (for example attitudes to an overseas job offer and accepting it); attitudes to the context and acting accordingly (for example attitudes to a country and seeking to work there); and attitudes to time and using it for a particular purpose (for example attitudes to one's career and taking a year out to gain international experience). All four attitudes might need to be favourable before the relevant action is performed, or one might overwhelm all the others.

Trust is an interpersonal attitude which is of particular importance – and difficulty – in dealing with people from different backgrounds from someone's own. Trust is an orientation towards another person, assumed voluntarily in order to cope with relational uncertainty. It involves accepting vulnerability in conjunction with expecting that another's actions will not be adverse. In interactions, trust influences levels of disclosure, openness and formality on the part of speakers and willingness to listen, believe and be persuaded on the part of receivers.

Nicol (1994)[23] has identified three dimensions of trust. They are referred to as the 'institutional agent' (willingness to trust an agent from outside one's group to act on one's behalf), 'caution' (setting limits to trust) and 'relationship' (setting the level of trust according to the relationship) dimensions. The relative importance of each of the dimensions is, in part, influenced by cultural conditioning. Findings from a comparative survey of 153 Mexican and 177 US subjects showed that people from individualistic cultures valued the caution and institutional agents' dimensions of trust more than people from collectivistic cultures, and people from collectivistic cultures valued the relationship dimension of trust more than people from individualistic cultures.

These findings can be explained as follows: because people from individualistic cultures are relatively more comfortable moving among different groups, they need to balance prudent caution with the potential for gaining from mixing; and because individualistic cultures generally adopt a universalistic approach to value standards and think in terms of indistinct group boundaries, they feel relatively comfortable with institutional agents external to their immediate ingroup. People from collectivistic cultures, who are prone to particularism, and to invoking different value standards for in- and outgroups, do not trust external agents and do not consider it an important form of trust. In contrast, for collectivists, the nature of the relationship and group membership is particularly relevant, and so relationship trust is the most valued.

Intentions

These mental plans of action are more closely linked to behaviour than attitudes, although the relationship is still far from one-for-one. They are high in awareness and so relatively controllable. In addition, as Chapter 4 showed, it is vital to effective communication for receivers to correctly understand speakers' communicative intent. Intentional actions, it has been suggested, are less strongly influenced by culture than routine, habitual ones or those driven by emotion; however, social perceivers usually over-estimate the intentionality of others' actions, thus under-estimating the influence of culture on others' behaviour.

Values

Values are broad tendencies to prefer certain states of affairs over others; or, to put it another way, enduring complexes of attitudes. Like attitudes, values have belief and affect components and carry the implication of acting in accordance with them. Values are usually expressed by using terms like good or evil, dirty or clean and so on. Values are generally ethical in form – that is, they have to do with someone's position on and the importance they attach to, for instance, various moral, religious, political or ecological issues.

Since differences in national values are the core concept behind findings on cultural variation, there is no need to add to the argument here (although the question of whether the values of ethnic minorities within nations align with those of the nation or the ethnic group is complex and ill-researched). Gender appears to have a rather limited effect on the core cultural values, except the achievement/relational dimension, according to Hofstede's findings, as has already been examined. However, with regard to other important values, gender differences are becoming more evident. A study which used 267 repeated policy questions examined US gender differences in policy choices and how they have changed from the 1960s to the 1980s.[24] It was found that average gender difference in preferences toward policies involving the use of force were consistently 'moderately large' throughout the period. Gender differences in opinion toward other policies – regulation and public protection, 'compassion' issues, traditional values – were approximately half as large but they also were found to warrant more attention than in the past. The researchers' analysis suggests that the salience of policy issues has increased greatly for women, and as a result differences in preferences have increased in ways consistent with the values of women and the intentions of the women's movement.

BOX 5.4

INGROUP EFFECTS ON ACADEMIC STANDARDS

A university lecturer who has worked extensively in Central Asia said when interviewed: 'A problem arises in regard to marking standards and objectivity, because these can conflict with staff members' sense of their moral obligation to support the members of their tribe or community. It is very difficult for them to fail the work of a student from their own tribe.'

Source: Interview with an expatriate university teacher, author's research.

Social class has been shown to affect values. Less educated, low-status employees in various Western countries hold more 'authoritarian' (that is, higher-power distance) values than their higher status compatriots. These authoritarian values are not only manifested at work, but are also found in their home situation. A study in the USA and Italy (Kohn, 1969)[25] showed that working-class parents demanded more obedience from their children than middle-class parents, but that the difference was larger in the USA than in Italy.

When Hofstede divided occupations within IBM into six groups according to the level of achievement or relationship (masculine or feminine) values they reported, people in unskilled and semi-skilled occupations came fifth – that is, they recorded the highest level of relationship values apart from office workers, above managers of all categories, skilled workers/technicians, professional workers and the group with the most masculine values, sales representatives. Hofstede's own explanation for this is in terms of the nature of the work – sales representatives were paid on commission, creating a highly competitive climate, whereas unskilled and semi-skilled workers have 'no strong achievements to boast' and usually work in teams, so that cooperation is important to them.[26]

The rankings certainly support such an interpretation. However, an alternative possibility is that members of less skilled occupational classes share the lower valuation of work (working to live rather than living to work) that characterises relationship (sub)cultures.

> All these variables – self-construals and self-esteem, motivations, emotions, perceptions, beliefs, assumptions, expectations, attitudes, intentions and values – are affected by many factors, ranging from genetic make-up to school environment during upbringing, from the innate element in intelligence to experiences at work. In particular, they are affected by the way people have been taught by their culture to look at the world. In turn, they affect individuals' communicative styles, functional emphases (content versus relationship, control, affiliation), strategies, and ways of using language.

Social cognition processes

Of equal interest with the cognitive constructs are the processes by which they come into being, because those processes are known to be subject to a number of distorting influences. As a process, cognition can be seen as a set of activities through which information is received, selected, transformed and organised and through which representations of reality are constructed and knowledge built. Many activities are involved, including perception, learning, memorising, thinking (thought elaboration) and verbalising. These processes are tightly interwoven: they interact continuously and strongly influence one another.

Social perception processes

Because the amount and complexity of the information people are exposed to exceeds their processing capacity, they use a number of devices to reduce the mental work involved, such as selective attention, limited arousal, categorisation and simplification. These devices are some of the sources of bias in social perception. The process which has been shown to introduce most cultural bias (or difference) into social perception, however, is attribution. This refers to a process of deciding, often subconsciously, whether another person's observed behaviour is caused by their disposition (character), the object of their behaviour or their situation. People make attributions in order to predict future events, exercise control and gain understanding. However, it has been well documented that several types of attribution bias are common:

● The fundamental attribution error refers to a tendency to over-emphasise personal explanations (dispositions) and under-emphasise situational causes;

this bias is usually accounted for either by a general proposition that other people's dispositions are more salient (more important because more relevant) to the attributor than their situation or by the assertion that societal norms may often require that internal attributions are made as part of the mechanism by which people are induced to assume personal responsibility. This second explanation is, of course, particular to individualistic cultures.

- The actor–observer error – in general, people are more likely to attribute their own behaviour to the situation and other people's to their disposition. Probable explanations are either or both of the fact that they have less information about other people's situations so that dispositional attributions are easier to make, especially as attributional 'knowledge' based on earlier observations can be carried forward; or in terms of perceptual salience – people's own situation matters more to them than other people's does, while others' disposition, which they perceive as uncontrollable, is more salient to them than their own over which they think they have control.

- The underuse of consensus – people often ignore information about how other people behave. For instance, even though evidence is presented that most other people do x, they may attribute Mary's doing x to her disposition, often in favour of an assumption that other people behave as they themselves do.

- The false consensus effect – the belief that others agree with oneself more than they actually do.

- The false uniqueness effect – the belief that one's own positive qualities are rare.

- Self-serving bias – people may be more likely to attribute successful outcomes of their own actions to themselves and failures to the situation. The self-serving bias has been found to occur more frequently in American and some north European individuals than in Asians or southern Europeans. Although an analysis of cross-cultural studies among subjects of diverse cultural backgrounds (Nurmi, 1992)[27] showed that the bias was present in most cultures, it also showed that differences do exist between cultures in relation to the extent and degree of measured bias. For example, North American subjects tend to use self-serving bias to a greater extent than do Japanese, Indian or Asian subjects (Chandler et al., 1981).[28] Perhaps more interestingly, though, Nurmi also showed that Finns use self-serving bias to a lesser extent than Americans do. In comparison to the Americans, the Finns – who stereotypically represent Western culture – are less likely to attribute good outcomes to internal, stable, and global factors. Additionally, Nurmi cites another study in which Dutch subjects are found to have exhibited a similar attribution pattern. The writer believes that some 'Western' societies may exhibit more 'collectivist' patterns of self-serving bias than originally presumed from studies of mainly Americans. According to the theory of self-esteem in attribution, self-serving bias helps to protect one's self-esteem and the extent of the need for such protection depends on cultural factors.[29]

Thinking processes

Aspects of mental processes that may differ between cultures include:

Categorising. How people, things or issues are classified or differentiated is not 'natural', but rather learned through interaction. The complexity of the categories in a child's cognitive system increases as it gains experience and in mature individuals it varies – some people differentiate more finely than others and most people differentiate more finely in regard to subjects that interest them or where they are knowledgeable than in regard to other subjects. The fact that categories used are learned during socialisation means that they are culturally influenced. For example, English uses the word 'aunt' to mean 'mother's sister' and 'father's sister'. Other cultures distinguish between the two. Chinese has different words for 'older brother' and 'younger brother', as age is an important indicator of status.

'Categorising is a fundamental and natural human activity. It is the way we come to know the world' so that 'any attempt to eliminate bias by attempting to eliminate the perception of differences is doomed to failure.'[30] The more subtle our categorical distinctions, the closer to reality our stereotypes will be. 'People should make more, not fewer distinctions – for example Europeans and Americans should divide Japanese people into male and female, rather than see both genders in terms of the same stereotype.'

Logic. Western logic can be characterised as emphasising atomistic analysis, dichotomies, deduction, induction from empirical data by an accepted set of procedures and abstraction. There are variations within Western cultures on which of these is more emphasised – French and German cultures are more concerned with ideas and abstractions than British culture – but overall, their logic systems can be contrasted with those of Eastern cultures. There, again with internal variations, holism, intuition and an emphasis on seeing the relationships between the external and internal world predominate.

Learning styles. While the capacity to learn from experience is clearly universal, there are (sub)cultural differences in what is learnt, how it is learnt and the degree to which mature adults remain open to such learning. Similarly, if people believe that it is proper to accept the world as it is rather than to try to change it, learning based on problem solving and future forecasting may be difficult. The relative emphasis placed on memorising versus understanding, knowledge versus skill acquisition and passive versus active learning similarly varies across cultures, as it has, historically, within single cultures such as Britain's.

In regard to formal learning, if, as in many central and eastern European countries, teachers are highly respected and honoured and hierarchies are important, then people may be used to learning from a lecture rather than from the give and take of a discussion. One of the many difficulties experienced by Western academics and others attempting to inculcate Western business education methods in the transition economies has been to make workshops, case studies and other participative learning techniques effective.

Many communication behaviours can only be explained in terms of an interaction among psychological, behavioural and communicative forces. An example is the interpersonal expectation effect. This is a distinctive interpersonal form of self-fulfilling prophecy. It occurs when a perceiver develops an expectation about the behaviour of some target person. Often unknowingly, the perceiver communicates their expectation to the target, probably through nonverbal behaviour. In turn, the message induces the target to act in ways which confirm the perceiver's expectations.

Purely psychological processes do not produce the effect; for example, it is not explained solely by perceptual biases leading to selective, self-confirming information processing. Moreover, the effect does not result from purely behavioural processes; for instance, it is not explained solely by perceivers acting in ways that constrain target response. Non-verbal messages conveying the perceiver's feelings and evaluations of the listener are thought to be the 'central mediating force in interpersonal expectation effects' – mediating the impact of perceptual biases and behaviour.[31]

5.2   INTERACTION THEORIES

We turn now from examining the psychological factors regarded as underlying communication, which take individual interactors as the unit of analysis, to explanations which take the interaction itself as the unit of analysis. Interaction is 'the sustained production of chains of mutually-dependent acts, constructed by two or more agents each monitoring and building on the acts of the other'.[32]

Some key interactionist propositions are:

- The meaning of a word is determined entirely by its context. In fact, there are as many meanings of a word as there are contexts. Interactionists criticise some discourse analysts for viewing language as a static, in-place, implicit system. They argue it should be viewed dynamically and that there should be a focus on the way in which specific kinds of interactional work are accomplished by the use of various improvised and conventional codes – speakers' and receivers' meanings should be placed in the centre of the analysis.[33]

- Society, or group, life is a cluster of cooperative behaviours on the part of its members. Cooperation consists of making sense of the other person's actions and intentions and responding appropriately. Communication is at the heart of social life and at the heart of communication is mutual response with the use of language: for instance, the term 'court' has no meaning apart from the interpretations of the actions of the people involved in it. (We usually think of such a word as having different meanings in different contexts – tennis court, law court or the verb for the intentions and actions of lovers. However, interactionists argue that unless we impose such contexts, the sound or the written letters are *without* meaning, like the letters 'chup' which form a pronounceable sound by the rules of phonetics but have no meaning in English.)

- As communicators, people are active planners rather than passive reactors: mind (thinking) often arises around thinking through future actions, imagining various outcomes and selecting and testing possible alternatives.

- Interactionists accept Bateson's (1958)[34] notion that all message exchanges have both content and relational characteristics, where the latter refers to the reciprocal rules of interdependence that combine the persons into an interactive system.

Convergence theory, located within the interactionist paradigm, treats communication as a process in which two or more individuals share information and converge towards a state of greater uniformity. Convergence is a process of movement towards one point, towards another person or persons, towards a common interest, or towards uniformity. Within convergence theory, some terms have particular definitions:

- Perceiving is the process of becoming aware of a physical difference through one's senses.
- Recognising is the process of identifying a previously known form or pattern that has been perceived. Interpreting is the process of understanding the meaning of a form or pattern that has been recognised. Believing is the process of accepting a particular interpretation.
- Mutual understanding is a state in which two or more individuals share to some degree a similar interpretation of information that they both have. Mutual agreement is a state in which two or more individuals to some degree jointly accept as valid a mutual understanding that has been reached.
- Action and collective action are the overt behaviour of an individual and the coordinated, overt behaviour of two or more individuals, respectively.

Perceiving, recognising, interpreting and believing are all decision processes that take place under some degree of uncertainty. A physical difference (pattern) beyond some threshold creates in an observer uncertainty that poses the question 'Is something there?' Detection of a sound, for example, would make one wonder if someone had actually spoken or not. Answering the question 'yes' reduces that uncertainty, but at the same time it creates uncertainty about what was said. Then, supposing that the answer to the question, 'What was spoken?' is the phrase, 'Excuse me', uncertainty is reduced about what it was (by a decision) creating at the same time a new level of uncertainty about what it means. And so on. Thus, residual uncertainty usually remains, which may be clarified by asking what was meant, or by taking action which tests what was meant. Both of these actions initiate another cycle of information processing in coordination with the other person: communication is social behaviour. Feedback is a diminishing series of under-and-over corrections converging on a goal.[35]

Although there is no research known to the author which investigates the possible link between culture and tendency to converge, it seem logical that people from cultures high in uncertainty avoidance would be more likely than others to pursue the information-processing cycle as far as possible, in an attempt to eliminate residual uncertainty.

The concept of convergence has been fundamental to at least one intercultural communication theory, communication accommodation theory, while the importance of uncertainty reduction is central in another, anxiety/uncertainty management theory.

All types of encounters between people are regarded in *social exchange theory* as quasi-economic transactions.[36] It says that when people meet, each hopes and expects to gain some benefit, and is prepared to give something in return. The theory assumes that individuals engaged in exchange are self-interested: they are trying to ensure a net positive balance of exchange outcomes, such that their benefits are maximised and their costs minimised. Benefits and costs are 'social', including enhancement or reduction of social identity, as well as material. Over time, the theory predicts, people with more power will do better out of their dealings with others: for example, someone who is higher in social attractiveness, which is a power source, will probably gain more friendship, esteem from others or other valued benefits than someone who is lower in social attractiveness.

In social exchange theory terms, the level of power distance accepted within a culture should affect the inputs and hence the outputs of interactions. Relatively egalitarian societies should logically produce a more even balance of benefits and costs compared to high-power distance societies. However, collectivism may counter the effects of high-power distance in some societies.

Social exchange theory provides an explanation for the tendency of people in mixed culture groups to form 'cliques' with people from their own culture: the perceived costs of interaction with people from different cultures outweigh the perceived benefits and/or the perceived balance of benefit over cost from such interactions is lower than from own-culture interactions. The theory can also be used to predict the balance of outcomes from intercultural exchanges: strangers and outsiders, meeting with insiders, are confronted with someone of higher social power and may expect to do worse from the exchange. (On the other hand, following the law of diminishing returns, the benefits that are gained by the 'outsider' may be more valued by them than the benefits gained by the 'insider' are by them, notwithstanding that the latter are 'objectively' greater.)

R.H. Turner's (1987) identity theory[37] emphasises the importance of identity self-affirmation and self-discovery in novel situations. Identity security/vulnerability is viewed as the primary dialectic of human existence: social interactions are driven forward by people's need to reduce feelings of insecurity which are related to their sense of self. Turner's theory, because of its emphasis on unfamiliar situations, is especially relevant for intercultural communication theory; on the other hand, the concept of the self which it embodies is clearly a Western individualistic one, so the 'primary dialectic' may not be so primary among members of collectivist (sub)cultures.

Brewer's (1991)[38] *optimal distinctiveness theory*, in contrast, is concerned with the idea that there are opposing drives for assimilation and differentiation in the dynamic of interaction. As Figure 5.3 shows, individuals are seen as confronted with a continuum of social life positions: in the extreme 'differentiation' position, they will suffer from a sense of isolation and stigmatisation; in the extreme 'assimilation' position, from a sense of a lack of self-definition. Only in the intermediate condition will they feel a comfortable sense of 'inclusiveness' where they are neither isolated nor suffer a loss of sense of self. It is this intermediate position, therefore, that they strive to 'negotiate' in their interactions with other people. Brewer's theory per se seems to be robust against cultural difference, although where an individual's 'comfort zone' in terms of differentiation and assimilation lies will vary between individualists and collectivists.

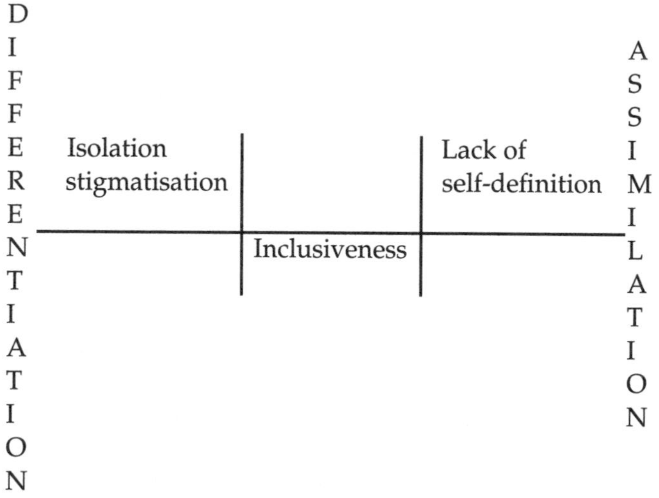

```
D
I
F                                                          A
F                                                          S
E    Isolation          |           Lack of               S
R    stigmatisation      |          self-definition  I
E                        |                            M
                        _|_____|__  I
N                        |   Inclusiveness          |   L
T                        |                          |   A
I                        |                          |   T
A                                                          I
T                                                          O
I                                                          N
O
N
```

Figure 5.3 Brewer's optimal distinctiveness theory

Source: Based on Brewer, M. (1991) 'The social self', *Personality and Social Psychology Bulletin*, **17**: 475–82.

Symbolic interactionists view social life as a process of interaction between and among individuals who use symbolic means (that is, verbal and non-verbal signifiers) to maintain, establish and modify certain systems of beliefs and conventions and to uphold certain positions and identities in encounters or episodes. As its name implies, in this perspective the meaning that people attach to their experiences derives from symbols used in interaction with others. This places communication at the centre of what it is to be a human being. This summary account can be better understood through an expanded set of symbolic interactionist propositions:

1. Understanding is a process of assigning meaning to what is received through the senses.
2. Meanings are learned in interaction with other people.
3. Meanings arise from the exchange of symbols (for example words) in social interactions.
4. Therefore, what people understand by their experiences is a function of the symbols which intervene between their sensory impressions and their perceptions. Reality is filtered through a symbolic lens.
5. Thinking is an internal conversation, using the symbols derived from social interactions. The mind can be defined as the process of interacting with oneself.
6. Overt behaviour is meaningless unless one is fully aware of the way the person behaving understands what they are doing.
7. All social institutions and structures consist of interactions between people.

Symbolic interactionists take a different view on rules for conduct or communication from analysts of language use such as van Dijk or Grice; they hold that 'It is the social process in group life that creates and upholds the rules, not the rules that create and uphold group life.'[39]

As a perspective on social life, symbolic interactionism is a universal theory: all people from all cultures use symbols in the way the theory describes. In addition, as symbols are elements of surface culture, where convergence is in evidence, some of them are coming to have 'universal' significance – for instance, the iconic signs used in airports or some brand names. However, more broadly, which symbols different peoples use and what meanings they attach to their experiences as a result of those symbols and their significance within the culture still varies and, in accordance with proposition 6 in our last list, may be fundamentally inaccessible to outsiders. For example, the full meaning of the Cross to Christians or the Crescent to Muslims is probably unfathomable by non-followers of those religions.

Historically, communication study is marked by an enduring concern with how symbolic action can serve the needs of individuals and societies. Recently increased attention has been paid by symbolic interactionists to the communal function – that is, to communication as a means for linking individuals into communities of shared identity. This comparatively new development increases the relevance of the theory for intercultural communication study (see Chapter 7).

There are two main grounds of criticism of interactionist explanations of communication. One is that their scope is too narrow – they leave out the emotions of the individual on the one hand and features of societal organisation, such as power structures, on the other. Interactionists have an answer to this criticism: for them individual emotions and societal structures alike are dependent variables, created through interaction, not independent variables causing it, although by a feedback loop they influence it.

> More problematic for interactionists is the dilemma of determinism: if meaning is created through social interaction, individuals cannot see the world in autonomous ways and so their goals and definitions of situations are only illusorily their own. This loss of free will for the individual is not acceptable to most interaction theorists and yet most have been unable to reconcile free will with their communication theory.

5.3   FACE NEGOTIATION

The concept of 'face' overlaps both interactionist and individual-level approaches. As Ting-Toomey put it 'Face is, in essence, a co-operative discourse game with ad infinitum rules.' She thus locates it within the structural-functional tradition. At the same time it is governed by interactionist constraints: 'Face is not an objective of interaction, but a condition for interaction, or a ritual constraint.' And, finally, face has particular significance in a cultural or intercultural context: 'The rules are… grounded in the socio-cultural norms of the speech community.'[40] The idea of 'face' in a cultural context is familiar to many people: for instance, it is a truism of Western concepts of Asian culture that face, and particularly avoiding loss of face, are important motivators for people from that culture. The traditional implication is that people from Western cultures do not have an equivalent motivator in their cultural baggage, or at least that it is comparatively weak. However, the large amount of recent theorising and research on face and facework has tended to blur this distinction, acknowledging that face concerns are universally powerful, although their precise nature differs from culture to culture.

Face, in the words of Goffman, is the 'positive social value people assume for themselves, the image they try to project to the public'. Goffman, like other symbolic interactionists, saw the human drive to sense making as fundamental: in any typical situation, people are asking themselves 'What is going on here?' Their answer is their definition of the situation and it is that definition which is real for them.

For Goffman, people use 'frames' to understand events; frames are definitions of sequences of activities. Thus, someone might frame the sequence of activities of leaving home, walking to a bus stop, taking a bus ride and entering a building as 'going to work'. To understand the way individuals organise their experiences, therefore, frame analysis is undertaken.

Communication activities, like all others, are viewed in the context of frame analysis. An encounter (or face engagement) is an interaction between two or more people who *perceive themselves* as mutually interacting (Goffman recognises that people may be aware of others' presence without paying one another attention). Face engagements use both verbal and non-verbal cues and the cues give signals about the nature of the relationship as well as a mutual definition of the situation. For Goffman, talkers, even in the ordinary run of conversation, 'present dramas'; they do not make bald statements of 'fact' but *present* them in an attempt to engage the listener(s). They therefore present themselves as a particular character in a particular role. A crucial concern, for the talker(s), is whether the listeners will accept their presentation (such acceptance is called 'tact') and thus endorse their character, their role and their definition of the situation, or whether they will reject it.

To achieve acceptance, interactors try to get information about the other people in the situation; they also give information about themselves. This involves impression management:

> He [sic] may wish them to think highly of him, or to think that he thinks highly of them, or to perceive how in fact he feels toward them or to obtain no clear-cut impression; he may wish to insure sufficient harmony so that the interaction can be sustained, or to defraud, get rid of, confuse, mislead, anatagonize or insult them.[41]

Later, Ting-Toomey[42] summarised the general understanding among academics of the concept of face as:

1. A claimed sense of identity in an interactive situation – that is, it describes the person someone projects themself as being when dealing with others.
2. A resource that is highly vulnerable: that can be honoured, threatened or bargained over, and that must be maintained. Even though the identity someone claims for themself is not extravagant or fraudulent in any way, making any claim exposes them to the need to have other people accept it tactfully – to honour it. If they do not seem to honour it spontaneously, the person might feel threatened by exposure; they might have to act tactfully towards the other's, possibly more unjustified, identity (face) claims to ensure that they honour their own – that means that they might have to bargain; and they will certainly have to keep up the appearances required by the identity they have claimed – to maintain it.
3. For most people, whether their sense of self-respect or self-esteem is enhanced or diminished during an interaction is affected by whether or not their face is honoured and maintained.

Face has two aspects: one is negative face, which is a claim to personal space, privacy and the right not to be distracted; another is positive face, which is a claim to be appreciated and to be approved of by others; additionally, people may be concerned, not only with supporting their own negative or positive face but also with supporting the negative or positive face of the person(s) with whom they are interacting

To support negative face, people use communication devices such as apologising, building up to making requests with a recognisable ritual and using recognised 'formulae' for such purposes as resisting compliance or giving commands. These are known as negative facework and they express the need for dissociation from another person. To support positive face, people use self-disclosure, paying compliments and making promises, all of which express the need for association and appreciation by another person. They are known as positive facework. Supporting another person's face is done, for example, by exercising tact or politeness.

In general writers on face show a clear recognition that its meaning and enactment are heavily culture dependent. For example, Ting-Toomey[43] commented that face is 'grounded in the webs of interpersonal and sociocultural variability'. Tina Katriel (1991)[44] expressed the view, based on her studies in Israel, that cultural communication orientation has a profound influence on the use of direct and indirect facework strategies.

Ting-Toomey (1988)[45] attempted to provide a face negotiation framework which is culture generic but builds in the effects of culture, as follows:

● People in all cultures try to maintain and negotiate face in all communication situations.
● The concept of face is especially problematic in uncertainty situations which call in question the situated identities of interactants.
● Individualistic–collectivistic culture will influence members' selection of one set of facework strategies rather than another.

Because the relative importance of self and group differ in individualistic and collectivistic cultures, the characteristics of an appropriate face and the nature of facework also differ. In a collectivistic culture, facework is used to present the self as an appropriate member of the social network, and people are expected to help others maintain a similarly appropriate face. In contrast, in an individualistic society, facework focuses more on maintaining one's own personal identity with little concern about helping others maintain theirs.

The concept of face and its elements have been further analysed by Ting-Toomey et al.[46] in terms of two theories of culture: Hofstede's individualism–collectivism dimension and Hall's low-context–high-context communication distinction. (The analysis assumes that individualism is correlated with low-context communication and collectivism with high context.) These variables influence the following:

● whether the person's sense of identity is 'I' or 'we'
● whether the primary face concern is for the self or the other
● the relative importance of negative or positive face need
● whether the style used is controlling, confrontational and orientated towards solving 'problems' or obliging, conflict avoiding and orientated towards maintaining positive feelings
● whether the person's communicative 'strategy' is competitive or collaborative
● whether the person's mode of expression, speech acts and non-verbal behaviour are mainly direct or mainly indirect.

Table 5.2 gives a summary of the differences in these constructs in LCCs and HCCs.

Table 5.2   A summary of low-context and high-context face negotiation processes

Key constructs of 'face'	Individualistic, low-context cultures	Collectivistic, high-context cultures
Identity	Emphasis on 'I' identity	Emphasis on 'we' identity
Concern	Self-face concern	Other-face concern
Need	Autonomy, dissociation, negative-face need	Inclusion, association, positive-face need
Style	Controlling or confrontation and solution-orientated styles	Obliging or avoidance and affective-orientated styles
Strategy	Distributive or competitive	Integrative or collaborative
Mode	Direct mode	Indirect mode
Speech acts	Direct speech acts	Indirect speech acts
Non-verbal act	Individualistic non-verbal acts, direct emotional expression	Contextualistic (role-orientated) non-verbal acts, indirect emotional expression

Sources: Based on Ting-Toomey, S. (1988) 'Inter-cultural conflict styles: a face-negotiation theory', in Kim, Y. and Gudykunst, W. (eds) *Theories in Inter-cultural Communication*, Newbury Park, CA: Sage; Ting-Toomey, S., Gao, G., Trubisky, P., Yang, Z., Kim, H., Lin, S.L. and Nishida, T. (1991) 'Culture, face maintenance, and styles of handling interpersonal conflict: a study in five cultures', *The International Journal of Conflict Management*, **2**: 275–96.

This low- versus high-context framework in face negotiation was used in Ting-Toomey's research in the USA, Japan, South Korea, China, and Taiwan. She also collected data from Australia, Thailand, and India. Her research consisted of open-ended questionnaires and interview data with nearly 1500 students and colleagues. Some of the concepts she explored are outlined below:

1.   *Face saving*. In answer to the question 'What is the meaning of face?' American subjects tended to equate the concept with saving their own face, that is, pride, reputation, credibility, and self-respect. For them face was more individualistic, low context, and associated with intrapsychic phenomena. Japanese subjects, on the other hand, understood the concept of face to be related to honour, claimed self-image, and the family/organi-

sation. For them there was more awareness of relational dynamics in the concept of face saving.

2. *Face giving*. American subjects could not offer a meaning for face giving, whereas Asian business people and students could talk about the meaning of this term. Therefore, Ting-Toomey believes, we may assume that face giving is more of an Eastern concern. To Asians, face giving means allowing room for the other person to recover his or her face – room to manoeuvre, to negotiate – so both can gain face in the end. For Westerners, face seems to be a dichotomous concept: they either lose face or save face. For Easterners, face is considered to be a mutual, interdependent concept, and is a relational and group phenomenon. Public face is a concern in at least two-thirds of the world's cultures. But in Western cultures, there is also a sense of individual self-respect, the right to be treated with respect, and not to be embarrassed.

3. *Face losing*. For Americans, loss of face means personal failure, loss of self-esteem, or loss of self-pride on an individual attribution basis. For Japanese and Korean subjects, however, loss of face means disrupting group harmony, bringing shame to their family, classmates, or company.

4. *Recovery from face loss*. For Americans and Canadians, humour is a strategy used to recover from face loss; if that does not work, as in a serious situation where humour would be inappropriate, other strategies that may be used are defensive strategies and attack strategies – clear win-lose strategies. Asian cultures, on the other hand, focus more on maintaining a win-win process.

5. *Conflict*. Conflict is face related, in that face appears to be a predictor of what conflict strategies are being used. Her American subjects, for example, tended to adopt self-face preservation and maintenance, focus on self-face issues, use control-focused conflict strategies and confrontational strategies, and display stronger win-lose orientations. Asian subjects, on the other hand, tended to use face-smoothing strategies, mutual face preservation strategies, and conflict avoidance strategies. This conclusion of Ting-Toomey, however, needs to be qualified by Khoo's (1994)[47] finding that people from collectivistic cultures are likely to be more aggressive and confrontational than people from individualistic cultures in conflicts with members of their outgroups. Khoo found that Euro-American business executives were more likely than Chinese people to use integrating, compromising, and obliging conflict styles. One possible explanation is their high concern with the task, which over-rides national cultural predilections. These business people contended that the best way to handle conflict was to avoid or minimise it to the extent possible to try to avoid possible economic loss. Among the ways to avoid or minimise conflict would be to strive towards mutually acceptable and favourable outcomes through the use of compromising and integrating conflict styles.

6. *Face issues*. The word 'shame' occurs when feelings are associated with face issues: shame arises in relation to self, parents, or group situations. However, practices differ, for instance, between Japanese and Chinese: for the Japanese, if they disgrace their organisation, they may or may not also disgrace themselves and their family; for the Chinese, any disgrace reflects on their family honour.

7. *Dimensions of face*. American subjects centre on autonomy face (freedom) where privacy or personal space is important; high-context, collectivistic cultures focus rather on 'approval' face. In low-context cultures, individual (intrinsic) accountability is emphasised; in high-context cultures, however, group accountability or group dynamics may dominate.

Some other facework researchers have included at least one cultural difference variable in their models. Lebra[48] described facework strategies used in Japan – that is, from a collectivistic perspective. She based her analysis on the idea that people in such a culture are exposed to face loss from both excessive humility (seen as lack of dignity) and excessive claims to dignity (seen as arrogant). They strive to remain in an intermediate zone in which face can be maintained (see Figure 5.4).

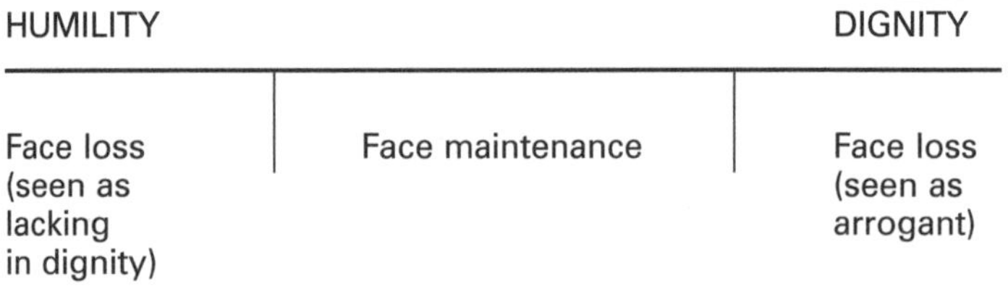

HUMILITY		DIGNITY
Face loss (seen as lacking in dignity)	Face maintenance	Face loss (seen as arrogant)

Figure 5.4   Face maintenance in Japan

Source: based on Lebra, T. (1971) 'The social mechanism of guilt and shame: the Japanese case', *Anthropological Quarterly*, **44**.

Lebra argued that strategies to protect 'own face' in a collectivist culture include:

- asking someone else to transmit a message (mediated communication)
- talking to a third person in the intended hearer's presence (refracted communication)
- acting as if a delegate – 'pretending' to be a messenger from a third person
- not expressing wishes explicitly, but expecting the other person to understand (anticipatory communication)
- corresponding by letter, so avoiding meeting face to face.

All these strategies are available to and used by people in a range of cultures, but Lebra contends that they are more often used by people from collectivist cultures. Equally, while strategies to protect one's own face and threaten the other's face, such as self-praise or arrogance, which are commonplace in highly individualistic cultures, are possible in collectivistic cultures, they are disapproved of and regarded as anti-social.

Politeness and facework

The concept of facework has been further developed by Brown and Levinson (1978),[49] who noticed that speakers often violate Gricean maxims and so may not be aiming for efficiency in message construction. Brown and Levinson speculated that instead speakers may often be guided by the requirements of politeness.

Brown and Levinson's politeness theory links a speaker's face concerns, perceived threats to face and the ways in which a speaker will express a request, explanation, disagreement or any other communication. Speakers are normally concerned both with their own face and with that of their hearer: they want to maintain their own position and at the same time not give offence to the hearer. Speakers who are indifferent to the effect of what they say on the hearer's face are poor communicators – by giving offence they reduce the chance that their message will be listened to and understood.

However, all communication risks a threat to the faces of either the speaker or the hearer or both. This is because we all have two conflicting desires: to be approved of by others – positive face need – and yet to be independent of others and their approval – negative face need. All communication therefore exposes us to the risk either of earning others' disapproval or of reducing our independence of them, on the one hand; and on the other hand of threatening the other party's desire for independence or their desire for approval. Speech acts which pose a threat to face are termed face threatening acts (FTAs).

For example, if I use an abrupt command to ask someone to do something, I threaten both their desire for autonomy (by treating them as someone dependent on me, and therefore able to be commanded by me) and their desire for approval (by showing a lack of respect for them and their feelings). However, even an obsequiously phrased request 'I'd be most grateful if you would please consider doing…' threatens their autonomy, although it is designed to placate their desire for approval. The abrupt command, however, does not threaten, indeed supports, the speaker's desire for independence and in some situations also their desire for approval – if they feel that to be 'in charge' is what is expected. The speaker who phrases their request in an obsequious way, on the other hand, probably threatens their own sense of autonomy, by expressing subservience. There is thus a trade-off between concern for own face and concern for hearer's face.

FTAs may threaten either positive or negative face for either speaker or hearer. Different communication elements are more or less threatening to either the speaker's or the hearer's face. Table 5.3 gives a typology.

Table 5.3   A typology of face-threatening acts (FTAs)

- FTAs which threaten *the hearer's positive face* include such speech acts as disapproval, criticism, contempt, ridicule, complaints, reprimands, accusations, insults, contradictions, disagreements, challenges, and expressions of violent emotions, taboo topics, bad news, or emotional topics

- FTAs which threaten *the hearer's negative face* include orders, requests, suggestions, advice, reminders, threats, warnings, dares, offers, promises, compliments, and expressions of strong emotions

- FTAs which threaten *the speaker's positive face* include apologies, accepting compliments, failing to maintain bodily control, making a faux pas, offering a confession of guilt, and failing to maintain emotional control

- FTAs which threaten *the speaker's negative face* include expressing thanks, accepting thanks, making excuses, accepting offers, responding to the hearer's gaffes, and making reluctant promises or offers

Source: based on Brown and Levinson (1978) 'Universals in language usage: politeness phenomena', in Goody, E.N. (ed.) *Questions and Politeness: Strategies in Social Interaction*, Cambridge: Cambridge University Press, pp. 56–289.

Threat is also increased by three factors: how much the communication imposes on the hearer (asking for directions is less of an imposition than asking for a loan); the status relations between the speaker and hearer (a schoolmaster is more threatened by a pupil's disagreeing with him than in the reverse case); and how well the speaker and hearer know one another – knowing one another well reduces threat.

Politeness theory defines politeness in communication as the attempt by the speaker to minimise or reduce the threat to the hearer's face, and postulates that the more intrinsically threatening the situation, the more polite the speaker will be. In other words, in order to minimise the potential social and personal emotional harm which might result from an FTA, speakers employ a variety of politeness or facework strategies. Brown and Levinson divide these facework strategies into four categories:

1. Bald-on-record: this simply involves following Grice's maxims with no actions to attend to the hearer's face needs.
2. Positive politeness: this addresses the hearer's need to maintain a sense of approval by others and generally employs inclusive language which indicates that the speaker wants the same things the hearer wants.
3. Negative politeness: this addresses the hearer's need to maintain a sense of personal autonomy and generally employs hedges (such as 'if you agree' or 'if you don't mind') which indicate that the speaker wants to avoid violating the hearer's autonomy.
4. Off-record: this addresses the hearer's need for positive and negative face (that is, social approval and personal autonomy) and generally employs evasive and ambiguous language which provides the speaker with an opportunity to deny the FTA.

BOX 5.5

POLITENESS

N. Barley, a columnist, wrote in British Airways' *High Life* magazine in March 1998, lamenting the 'demise' of the queue: 'Queues... show the acceptance of basic rules in interaction, a concept of natural justice, with little sub-rules that constitute a definition of "fairness". The halt and the lame are at no disadvantage, for pushers and shovers are restrained from using their competitive edge.'

Americans have far less respect for the queue, which they call 'standing in line', an expression which may itself express a negative attitude. Barley once heard an American woman shout in outrage at a bank teller 'Don't you understand you're stealing my life?' The author of this book once heard an American, reproved for queue jumping, shout 'You Brits, all you do is stand in line.' To which the woman reprover said 'It's called civilisation.'

But the barbarians are at the gates, according to Barley, who points to road rage and 'the unruly jostling mobs that now mill around bus stops and departure gates at airports'.

Source: Barley, N. (1998) 'British Airways', *High Life* magazine, March.

There is a fifth possible strategy – no communication – which minimises face threat but does not allow the speaker to progress towards those goals which the speaker may be able to gain through interaction.

Speakers select facework strategies based on three situational factors:

1. the social distance between the speaker and the hearer
2. the degree of power which the hearer has over the speaker
3. the relative cultural assessment of the imposition the specific FTA represents.

The speaker assesses the relative risk of damage to face and chooses a strategy which carries no greater risk than required in the situation. If a particular FTA and situation carries an excessively high degree of risk, the speaker will opt to avoid doing the FTA at all, whereas if a particular FTA and situation carries little or no risk, the speaker will opt to do the FTA as efficiently as possible, using no strategies to lessen the face threat. In situations where the risk to face for a particular FTA is greater but not overwhelming, the speaker will choose strategies which carry relatively less risk, selecting positive politeness strategies to address threats to the hearer's positive face, negative politeness strategies to address threats to the hearer's negative face, or off-record strategies to provide the speaker with the opportunity to deny the intent of the FTA.

In calculating the weight of an FTA, Brown and Levinson envision the three factors functioning as independent variables. Even if the social distance between speaker and hearer is high, and the degree of power of the hearer over the speaker is high, which together suggest that the speaker should choose a low-risk, less efficient strategy, a situation in which an FTA has an extremely high degree of urgency might sufficiently reduce the risk of face loss such that the speaker would choose a high-risk, more efficient strategy. For example, in nearly all cultures, a worker who sees the CEO about to step out in front of a speeding car would have licence to warn the CEO in as efficient a manner as possible. In other words, rather than saying, 'Excuse me, but are you aware that you are about to step out in front of a speeding car and possibly incur serious injury or death?' as the social distance and degree of power would suggest, the worker could shout, 'Look out for that car!' without risking face loss for herself or for the CEO.

Despite its great influence, Brown and Levinson's model has received some critical comment. For instance, it has been shown that in some situations the assumptions that speech acts threaten only one aspect of face, that face threats can be understood by analysing individual acts in isolation and that all face threats are intrinsic do not hold up; second, a speaker's level of cognitive development plays an important role in the way they employ various politeness strategies. There is also criticism of the theories for ignoring strategies which might address the face needs of the speaker rather than the hearer and for the focus on politeness when such speech acts as showing contempt for the other person in the interaction have clear elements of facework in their accomplishment.

Acting on these concerns such as these, Wood and Kroger (1991)[50] proposed a different method of analysing facework which accounts for both polite and impolite speech acts, and which allows researchers to consider the effects of facework on both the speaker's and hearer's face. Wood and Kroger propose a far less restrictive framework than Brown and Levinson's, consisting of two broad categories of speech acts: the central speech action (CSA), which the speaker employs to achieve some social or personal goal; and the auxiliary speech action (ASA), which the speaker employs in addition to the CSA in achieving the goal. For example, in order to borrow a book from a colleague, I might say, 'Hey, Clay, could you lend me your copy of Bakhtin? Thanks!' According to Wood and Kroger's framework, 'lend me your copy of Bakhtin' is the CSA since it expresses the goal I intend to achieve, while the greeting ('Hey, Clay') and the expression of gratitude ('Thanks') are ASAs since they serve to mitigate the imposition of the request.

Politeness theory has generated a substantial amount of research. Some of the findings are:

- Hints can be seen as manipulative.
- Increased liking is associated with increased politeness.
- The effects of power, distance and imposition are not additive.

- There are significant power-by-distance interactions, imposition-by-power interactions and imposition-by-distance interactions. As one of these variables becomes very large, the effects of other variables are reduced.

Most empirical research has concentrated on requests. Holtgrave (1992)[51] discusses other types of facework – explanations, disagreements and self-disclosures.

There are *national, ethnic and gender* differences in concepts of politeness, the amount of politeness that people use, the influence of content versus relationship concerns on politeness and the politeness of direct and indirect forms. Box 5.7 shows some differences between German and American concepts of politeness.

Women are more likely than men to use a form which minimises the threat to the hearer's face. They may:

- give their orders as requests, such as 'Please would you mind finishing this letter first?'
- make their statements sound provisional by using qualifiers
- use tag questions, as in 'I think we need to call a meeting, don't we?'
- use disclaimers – 'I may be wrong, but...'
- use supportive rather than powerful vocabulary.[52]

One researcher has found that use of politeness of the kinds described here can lead to women being rated as less intelligent and less well informed than other people, including other women who do not use them. It is difficult, however, to know whether use of polite forms 'causes' these attributions, because men who use them are not similarly downgraded in others' estimation.[53] There may be a halo effect from the gender of the polite speaker, in the same way as some occupations, such as nursing and teaching, have been downgraded in social estimation because they are largely women's occupations.

Ethno-cultural and gender effects can be multiplicative. Penelope Brown, one of the originators of politeness theory, found that women in the Mexican region of Tenejapa are constrained to be polite, cooperative and meek in their conversation. To express anger and confrontation they are obliged to emphasise only lack of agreement and cooperation with an adversary.[54]

Non-verbal behaviour in politeness. Ambady *et al.*[55] undertook research to extend the validity of politeness theory by investigating the non-linguistic aspects of politeness in two cultures. Politeness strategies expressed through different channels of communication (silent video, speech, full-channel video and audio, and transcripts of speech) were examined, and it was found that in both cultures politeness strategies were communicated non-linguistically as well as linguistically and that non-linguistic strategy usage was related to social and contextual factors.

Content and relationship in politeness. A study in two cultures – the Korean and the American – found that politeness strategies were communicated non-linguistically as well as linguistically and that non-linguistic strategy usage was related to social and contextual factors. Koreans' politeness strategies were influenced more by relational cues, whereas Americans' strategies were influenced more by the content of the message.

BOX 5.6

DIFFERENCES BETWEEN AMERICAN AND GERMAN CONCEPTS OF POLITENESS

To Americans, politeness often implies friendliness and is shown by:

- Not broaching controversial issues like politics or religion when desiring to maintain a friendly atmosphere.
- Using informal routine formulae with strangers or acquaintances: 'Hi, how are you?' 'It was nice meeting you.' 'Have a nice day.' 'Let's get together sometime.' 'It was nice talking to you.'
- Maintaining 'the customer is always right'.
- Not saying anything negative, especially to a stranger (usually).
- Expressing some willingness to talk to strangers about family situation.
- Saying 'excuse me' when touching or bumping into a stranger in public.
- Using first names straight away.
- Talking 'informally'.
- Using chitchat, small talk.

To Germans, politeness implies respect and is shown by:

- Broaching controversial issues like politics when desiring to get to know a person better.
- Using formal routine formulae: saying *'Guten Tag'* or some variant when greeting strangers, saying *'Auf Wiedersehen'* or some variant when leaving.
- Often considering salespeople experts.
- Using last names only with an earned title or Frau or Herr (Ms or Mr) when addressing strangers and people one doesn't know well.
- Using the respectful form of 'you', *'Sie'*.
- Expressing willingness to talk with tourists on the train; topics may vary.
- Expressing honesty and directness.
- Showing distaste for small talk.

Source: Ambady N., Koo, J., Lee, F. and Rosenthal, R. (1996) 'More than words: linguistic and nonlinguistic politeness in two cultures', *Journal of Personality and Social Psychology*, **70**: 996–1011.

Direct and indirect forms. While it might seem obvious that indirect forms would always be more polite and direct forms always more threatening, in fact correlations between the direct form and the perceived threat level, and between the indirect form and the politeness level vary from one culture to another: in LCC cultures – for example Germany or the USA, a direct form of behaviour probably is perceived as less threatening than an ambiguous one. In HCCs, however, such as Korea or Vietnam, direct forms of communication can be perceived as highly threatening.

Speech accommodation theory (SAT)

SAT theory takes concern with face as a given. It is based on the common observation that two or more people who are communicating face to face often adjust features of their speech or behaviour, including accent, speed, loudness, vocabulary, grammar, voice tone and gestures. Sometimes they adjust in a way which makes their speech more like the other person's (converging), at others to make it more unlike, usually in ways that accentuate their own group membership (diverging). The question, then, is why may speakers behave like this? The original formulation, by Giles (1977),[57] treated convergence, divergence and, later, maintenance, as strategies that speakers could use to signal their attitudes toward each other. Another possible reason is that people converge to gain approval or identify and diverge to distinguish themselves. There is also a possible third speaker motivation for either type of accommodation – to achieve smoother or clearer communication.

Convergence or divergence may or may not be mutual: sometimes Person A will be converging while Person B is diverging, which creates certain difficulties for both parties. The processes are thought to be largely subconscious.

Convergence is often advantageous to the converger providing their perception of the other person's speech qualities is accurate: it has been shown to increase attractiveness to the other, predictability, intelligibility and mutual involvement. On the other hand, when it is based on an inaccurate perception – as when it is based on a false stereotype, such as the stereotype that people in wheelchairs are deaf – it can be dysfunctional. Interactors' perceptions of their own and others' communication behaviour are what count (Beebe and Giles, 1984).[58] When accommodation is perceived as inappropriate, it can be evaluated as patronising, ingratiating or humiliating. When convergence is seen as violating norms, it is evaluated as negatively as divergence.

Findings on cultural variability and accommodation include the result that people in more collectivistic cultures use more politeness strategies and more formal language when facing outgroup members than do individualists, so as to demonstrate the distance between them.[59]

Relative power has a strong influence on accommodation. Subordinates are more likely to converge than bosses; convergence is not costless – it requires effort and can threaten personal identity; therefore people need an incentive to do it, which may not be present for (or may not be understood by) a manager in interactions with subordinates.

Conversational constraints (CCs)

Conversational constraints are guiding motives or criteria for selecting conversational strategies.[60]

Three CCs are commonly identified:

1. concern for clarity
2. concern for minimising threats to the hearer's face
3. concern for minimising imposition.

The last two of these concerns are, of course, derived from the facework tradition, but the first, concern for clarity, is seen as in tension with the facework concerns. The concerns are linked to interaction goals – concern with clarity is linked to the goal of getting one's own way, concern for minimising threats to the other's face with avoiding hurting the hearer's feelings. Each interaction goal/CC pair is also linked to choice of conversational strategy, particularly the choice between direct and indirect forms, as shown in Figure 5.5.

Later versions of CC theory add two more dimensions – concern for avoiding negative evaluation by the hearer and concern for effectiveness (the desire for one's communicative acts to accomplish a primary goal). A further set of relations within CC theory links CCs to a person's self-construal. Three variables are applied: independence and interdependence; need for social approval or need for dominance; and psychological gender. These variables are linked to interaction goals and hence to choice of direct or indirect communication strategy as follows:

- Interdependent self-construal leads to placing primacy on face goals; independent to emphasis on clarity goals.
- Need for social approval leads to concern for others' face; need for dominance leads to concern for clarity.
- Psychological masculinity leads to concern for clarity; psychological femininity leads to concern for other's face.

These links between the individual's self-construal, needs and psychological make-up and their choice of communication strategy makes CC theory relevant to cultural differences in communication behaviour. A study undertaken with 972 undergraduates studying in Korea, Japan, Hawaii and mainland USA found that, as expected, culture-level individualism correlated positively with the concern for clarity and promoting one's own goals in communication but not with the three relational constraints, whereas for culture-level collectivism the results were vice versa. In both cases, the researchers found that a mediating cultural variable – an independent or interdependent self-construal – was operating. 'Biculturals', who maintain both high independent and high interdependent construals, had the highest totals for the importance ratings of all the constraints combined.[61]

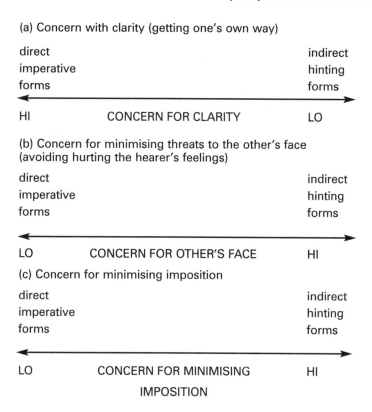

(a) Concern with clarity (getting one's own way)

direct · indirect
imperative · hinting
forms · forms

HI   CONCERN FOR CLARITY   LO

(b) Concern for minimising threats to the other's face
(avoiding hurting the hearer's feelings)

direct · indirect
imperative · hinting
forms · forms

LO   CONCERN FOR OTHER'S FACE   HI

(c) Concern for minimising imposition

direct · indirect
imperative · hinting
forms · forms

LO   CONCERN FOR MINIMISING   HI
                          IMPOSITION

Figure 5.5   Conversational constraints, interaction goals and choice of
conversational strategy

Source: based on Kim, M.-S., Hunter, J.E., Miyahara, A., Horvath, A., Bresnahan, M. and Yoon,
H. (1996) 'Individual- vs culture-level dimensions of individualism and collectivism: effects on
preferred conversational styles', *Communication Monographs*, **63**: 29–49.

However, another study within the same research project showed that participants' gender did not have any significant main effect on the perceived importance of any of the five conversational constraints; this result was found
consistently across all four societies researched.[62] This finding seems to contra-
dict assertions that men use language to assert a 'position of dominance' by
coming directly to the point (clarity), whereas women use language to create
and maintain relationships of closeness. The apparent contradiction may,
however, be more related to the distinction between preferences and behaviour;
many researchers have found gender differences in verbal styles (that is, power,
politeness, directness) but this still leaves room for males and females to be relatively homogeneous in their self-perceptions of preferred conversational styles
across cultures.

BOX 5.7

COMMUNICATION CONSTRAINTS AT WORK IN THE MINISTRY OF ENVIRONMENT

An American by birth and upbringing, resident 30 years in London, tells the following story: 'When, about ten years ago, I did a stint of work for the Ministry of the Environment here, people I knew really well, and was very friendly with, kept sending me memos addressed to 'Mr...'. Although I knew it was a cultural difference, I found it very cold and somehow wrong. So I went to them and said, 'Couldn't you call me Ed?' And they said, 'No, we couldn't.'

Source: Interview with an expatriate, author's research.

Facework, politeness, speech accommodation and communication constraints all have a processual emphasis which is a valuable contribution to the field. Interactions develop over time and are themselves often episodes in developing relationships. There is, however, a difficulty in capturing the complexity of communication development and in this respect these theories' ambitions are not matched by their achievements: they are all over-simplifications of reality (but in this, of course, they are like any model).

5.4   CONCLUSION

The purpose of this chapter has been to deepen and widen the analysis of (sub)cultural differences in communication given in Chapter 4 by exploring psychological constructs and processes underlying overt communication behaviour on the one hand and theories of interaction on the other.

The next chapter discusses the important question of whether cultural and subcultural differences really do constitute communication barriers and if so how, before Chapter 7 outlines the mainstream intercultural communication theories which both attempt to help account for those barriers and point to ways to overcome them.

REFERENCES

1. Markus, R.H. and Kitayama, S. (1994) 'A collective fear of the collective: implications for selves and theories of selves', *Personality and Social Psychology Bulletin*, **20**(5): 568–79.
2. Farh, J.L., Dobbins, G.H. and Cheng, B. (1991) 'Cultural relativity in action: a comparison of self-ratings made by Chinese and US workers', *Personnel Psychology*, **44**: 129–47.
3. Yu, J. and Murphy, K.R. (1993) 'Modesty bias in self-ratings of performance: a test of the cultural relativity hypothesis', *Personnel Psychology*, **46**: 357–73.
4. Cross, S.E. and Madison, L. (1997) 'Models of the self: self-construals and gender', *Psychological Bulletin*, **122**(1): 5–37.
5. Roberts, T.-A. (1991) 'Gender and the influence of evaluations on self-assessments in achievement settings', *Psychological Bulletin*, **109**(2): 297–308.
6. Kelly, A.E., Sedlacek, W.E. and Scales, W.R. (1994) 'How college students with and without disabilities perceive themselves and each other', *Journal of Counseling and Development*, **73**: 178–82.
7. Maslow, A.H. (1970) *Motivation and Personality* (2nd edn), New York: Harper & Row.
8. Turner, J.H. (1988) *A Theory of Social Interaction*, Stanford, CA: Stanford University Press.
9. Anderson, C.M. and Martin, M.M. (1995) 'Communication motives of assertive and responsive communicators', *Communication Research Reports*, **12**: 186–91.
10. Mesquita, B. and Frijda, N.H. (1992) 'Cultural variations in emotions: a review', *Psychological Bulletin*, **112**(2): 179–204.
11. Johansson, J.K. (1994) 'Cultural understanding as managerial skill: Japan, North America and Europe'. Presentation made at the David See-Chai Lam Centre for International Communication, Simon Fraser University at Harbour Centre: Pacific Region Forum on Business and Management Communication. Posted on the Internet: http://www.cic.sfu.ca/forum/.
12. Robinson, S. (1997) 'Intercultural management: the art of resolving and avoiding conflicts between cultures', AIESEC Global Theme Conference: Learning and Acting for a Shared Future. Posted on the Internet: http://www.eye.ch/~gtc97/intercul.html.
13. Kelly, G. (1955) *The Psychology of Personal Constructs*, New York: North.
14. Witkin, H.A. and Berry, J.W. (1975) 'Psychological differentiation in cross-cultural perspective', *Journal of Cross-Cultural Psychology*, **6**: 4–87.
15. Gilligan, C. (1982) *In a Different Voice: Psychological Theory and Women's Development*, Cambridge, MA: Harvard University Press.
16. Schein, E.H. (1992) *Organizational Culture and Leadership* (2nd edn), San Francisco: Jossey-Bass.
17. Triandis, H.C. (1990) 'Theoretical concepts that are applicable to the analysis of ethnocentrism', in Brislin, R.W. (ed.) *Applied Cross-Cultural Psychology*, Newbury Park, CA: Sage.
18. Alderfer, C.P. and Smith, K.K. (1982) 'Studying intergroup relations embedded in organizations', *Administrative Science Quarterly*, **27**: 5–65.
19. Berger, C.R. and Zelditch, M. (1985) *Status, Rewards and Influence*, San Francisco: Jossey-Bass.
20. Cichon, E.J. and Masterson, J.T. (1993) 'Physician–patient communication: mutual role expectations', *Communication Quarterly*, **41**(4): 477–89.
21. Apel, D. and Yoram, B.-T. (1996) 'Nursing staff responses to violent events in closed psychiatric wards: a comparison between attributional and cognitive neo-associanistic analyses', *British Journal of Social Psychology*, **35**: 509–21.

22. Ajzen, L. (1991) 'The theory of planned behaviour: some unresolved issues', *Organizational Behavior and Human Decision Processes*, **50**: 179–211.
23. Nicol, D. (1994) 'Trust: critical and cultural'. Posted on the Internet: http://blue. temple.edu/~eastern/nicol.html.
24. Buchanan, C.H. (1996) *Choosing to Lead: Women and the Crisis of American Values*, Boston, MA: Beacon Press.
25. Kohn, M.L. (1969) *Class and Conformity: A Study in Values*, Homewood, IL: Dorsey Press.
26. Hofstede, G. (1981) *Cultures and Organizations: Software of the Mind*, London: HarperCollins, p. 31.
27. Nurmi, J. (1992) 'Cross-cultural differences in self-serving bias: responses to the attributional style questionnaire by American and Finnish students', *Journal of Social Psychology*, **132**(1): 69–76.
28. Chandler, T.A., Shama, D.D., Wolf, F.M and Planchard, S.K. (1981) 'Multiattributional causality for social affiliation across five cross-national samples', *Journal of Psychology*, **107**: 219–29.
29. Kashima, Y. and Triandis, H.C. (1986) 'The self-serving bias in attributions as a coping strategy: a cross-cultural study', *Journal of Cross-Cultural Psychology*, **17**(1): 83–97.
30. Langer, E. (1989) *Mindfulness*, Reading: Addison-Wesley.
31. Burgoon, J. and Hale, J. (1988) 'Nonverbal expectancy theory', *Communication Monographs*, **55**: 58–79.
32. Levinson, S.C. (1983) *Pragmatics*, Cambridge: Cambridge University Press.
33. Banks, S.P. (1989) 'Pronouns and the language of intercultural understanding', in Ting-Toomey, S. and Korzenny, F. *Language, Communication and Culture: Current Directions*, Newbury Park, CA: Sage.
34. Bateson, G. (1958) *Naven*, Stanford, CA: Stanford University Press.
35. Rogers, E. and Kincaid, D.L. (1981) *Communication Networks: Toward a New Paradigm for Research*, New York: Free Press.
36. Homans, G.C. (1958) 'Social behavior as exchange', *American Journal of Sociology*, **63**: 597–606.
37. Turner, R.H. (1987) 'Articulating self and social structure', in Yardley, K. and Honess, T. (eds) *Self and Society*, Chichester: Wiley.
38. Brewer, M. (1991) 'The social self', *Personality and Social Psychology Bulletin*, **17**: 475–82.
39. Blumer, H. (1969) *Symbolic Interactionism: Perspective and Method*, Englewood Cliffs, NJ: Prentice-Hall.
40. Ting-Toomey, S. (1988) 'A face negotiation theory', in Kim, Y.Y. and Gudykunst, W. (eds) *Theories in Intercultural Communication*, Newbury Park, CA: Sage.
41 Goffman, E. (1959) *The Presentation of Self in Everyday Life*, Garden City, NY: Doubleday, p. 3.
42. Ting-Toomey (1988) op. cit.
43. Ting-Toomey, S. (1986) 'Interpersonal ties in intergroup communication', in Gudykunst, W.B. (ed.) *Intergroup Communication*, London: Edward Arnold.
44. Katriel, T. (1991) *Communal Webs: Communication and Culture in Contemporary Israel*, Albany: SUNY Press.
45. Ting-Toomey, S. (1988) 'Inter-cultural conflict styles: A face-negotiation theory', in Kim ,Y. and Gudykunst, W. (eds) *Theories in Inter-cultural Communication*, Newbury Park, CA: Sage.
46. Ting-Toomey, S., Gao, G., Trubisky, P., Yang, Z., Kim, H., Lin, S.L. and Nishida, T. (1991) 'Culture, face maintenance, and styles of handling interpersonal conflict: a study in five cultures', *The International Journal of Conflict Management*, **2**: 275–96.
47. Khoo, G.P.S. (1994) 'The role of assumptions in intercultural research and consulting: examining the interplay of culture and conflict at work'. Paper given at the David

See-Chai Lam Centre for Internation Communication, Simon Fraser University at Harbour Centre: Pacific Region Forum on Business and Management Communication. Posted on the Internet: http://www.cic.sfu.ca/forum/.

48. Lebra, T. (1971) 'The social mechanism of guilt and shame: the Japanese case', *Anthropological Quarterly*, **44**(4): 241–55.

49. Brown, P. and Levinson, S. (1978) 'Universals in language usage: politeness phenomena', in Goody, E.N. (ed.) *Questions and Politeness: Strategies in Social Interaction*, Cambridge: Cambridge University Press, pp. 56–289.

50. Wood, L.A. and Kroger, R.O. (1991) 'Politeness and forms of address', *Journal of Language and Social Psychology*, **10**(3): 145–68.

51. Holtgrave, T. (1992) 'Linguistic realisation of face management: implications for language production and comprehension, person perception and cross-cultural communication', *Social Psychology Quarterly*, **55**(2): 141–59.

52. Colwill, N. and Sztaba, T.I. (1986) 'Organizational genderlect: the problem of two different languages', *Business Quarterly*, **3**: 64–6.

53. Kim, M.-S. and Bresnahan, M. (1996) 'Cognitive basis of gender communication: a cross-cultural investigation of perceived constraints in requesting', *Communication Quarterly*, **44**: 53–69.

54. Brown, P. (1990) 'Gender, politeness, and confrontation in Tenejapa', *Discourse Processes*, **13**(1): 123–41.

55. Ambady, N., Koo, J., Lee, F. and Rosenthal R. (1996) 'More than words: linguistic and nonlinguistic politeness in two cultures', *Journal of Personality and Social Psychology*, **70**: 996–1011.

56. Yum, J.O. (1982) 'Communication diversity and information acquisition among Korean immigrants in Hawaii', *Human Communication Research*, **8**: 154–69.

57. Giles, H. (1977) *Language, Ethnicity and Intergroup Relations*, London: Academic Press.

58. Beebe, L.M. and Giles, H. (1984) 'Speech accommodation theories: a discussion in terms of second-language acquisition', *International Journal of the Sociology of Language*, **46**: 5–32.

59. Gallois, C., Giles, H., Jones, E., Cargile, A.C. and Ota, H. (1995) 'Accommodating intercultural encounters: elaborations and extensions', *Intercultural Communication Theory (International and Intercultural Communication Annual)* XIX, Thousand Oaks, CA: Sage, pp. 115–46.

60. Kim, Y.Y. (1988) *Communication and Cross-cultural Adaptation*, Clevedon: Multilingual Matters.

61. Kim, M.-S., Hunter, J.E., Miyahara, A., Horvath, A., Bresnahan, M. and Yoon, H. (1996) 'Individual- vs. culture-level dimensions of individualism and collectivism: effects on preferred conversational styles', *Communication Monographs*, **63**: 29–49.

62. Kim, M.-S. and Bresnahan, M. (1996) 'Cognitive basis of gender communication: a cross-cultural investigation of perceived constraints in requesting', *Communication Quarterly*, **44**: 53–69.

6

BARRIERS TO COMMUNICATING ACROSS CULTURES

The idea that face-to-face communication is imperfect and can lead to misunderstanding and even conflict is based in common experience. Miscommunication arises from 'noise', in the technical sense of interference, whether physical or psychological, which prevents messages being received; poor encoding by the sender; distortion by the medium; and selection, inaccurate decoding or interpretation and indiscriminate categorisation by the receiver. It is true that the two-way nature of face-to-face communication creates possibilities for reducing miscommunication by feedback (the sender can easily find out how well the receiver is understanding and responding). However, it also imposes demanding time pressure on each receiver in turn to respond, thus reducing opportunities for a 'rethink'.

Communication theorists generally take it as given that the phenomenon which they study is imperfectible. Burke,[1] for instance, who was a leading symbolic interactionist, considered that communication between people can never be perfect, because communication is only possible in the area of overlap between their essential being (what Burke calls their consubstantiality) and this is never total (or individuals would not be unique); on the other hand, some degree of consubstantiality is always present, simply because two people are both human. The actual extent of potential communication varies within this range according to the shared consubstantiality of the interactors.

In the case of communication with people from different backgrounds the sources of miscommunication are of two kinds: those such as the general problem of intergroup communication, stereotyping and prejudice which are 'universal' barriers, but which apply with particular force in intercultural situations; and those arising from the fact that, as the two previous chapters showed, differences of background, whether cultural or subcultural, ethnic, gender based or based on some other distinction, do affect how people communicate. Larkey (1996)[2] put forward a general view that cultural differences affect intercultural encounters, usually by leading to misunderstanding or conflict, at both the individual and the group level. At the individual level, as different values, beliefs or worldviews are manifested in communication behaviours and as culture creates differing expectations (especially about communication rules) and differing styles or patterns of speech, interpersonal misunderstanding and conflict can arise. At the group level, intergroup processes can be triggered by, for instance, an individual's non-verbal behaviour or ways of speaking which stereotypically represent a group. There is, however, still some debate about whether such differences actually create barriers to communication and if so how. The second section of this chapter will attempt an answer to this question; it will argue that they do and try to show how.

In this book, the term 'miscommunication' is used broadly, even to cover cases where communication is intended but none occurs – as when A speaks to B but B is not listening and does not hear. This broad definition means that miscommunication includes at least all the following cases:

- those where communication is intended but none occurs
- those where the hearer makes no sense at all of the message
- those where the hearer misunderstands the message – the speaker's meaning and the hearer's understanding of the meaning are different
- those where the speaker's communicative intention (to ask a question, make a request, make a promise and so on) is not understood
- those where information imparted by the speaker, which he or she intended to have believed, is not believed
- those where an attempt to persuade fails
- those where an attempt to exert power fails
- those where a communication is understood but provokes unintended conflict.

So broad a use of 'miscommunication' extends its usual definition, but allows it to refer to all cases where barriers to communication are effective. However, this does not mean that all cases of disagreement, for example, constitute miscommunication: a process of working through disagreement can increase understanding and, if it becomes clear that their views are fundamentally irreconcilable, people can 'agree to disagree'.

BOX 6.1

SOME EXAMPLES OF INTERNATIONAL MISCOMMUNICATION

1. A British business woman asked over the phone her Bulgarian co-workers in a project to book her into a 'middle-range' hotel in Sofia for a five-day stay. On arrival, she found they had booked her into a slightly upgraded student hostel, with no restaurant, no reception and way out of the town centre. At $20 per night, it was very cheap by Sofia standards. The explanation was that, not

knowing what 'middle range' meant to her, they had judged it by the standards of their usual visitors, who were mainly postgraduate students.

2. Two British academics spent three days in London training two visiting staff from a university in Kazakhstan in the mechanisms of a student–manager-shadowing scheme. The questions flowed freely and it appeared that good communication had been achieved. After the two Kazakhstan faculty members returned to Almaty, however, one went sick and it quickly emerged that the other had understood very little because of inadequate English. Only then did the two British attach significance to the fact that most of the questions and discussion had come from only one of the visitors.

Source: Author's research.

6.1 THE GENERAL PROBLEM OF INTERGROUP COMMUNICATION

Meetings with individuals from different ethnic backgrounds, socio-economic classes, age groups, occupational categories and so forth are termed 'intergroup' encounters. In these encounters, people may communicate with each other not just or even mainly as individuals with unique temperaments and personalities but to a considerable extent as undifferentiated representatives of social groups – for example, Person A might deal with someone as a 'Polish Catholic lawyer' or 'white male doctor' and Person B might deal with Person A as 'a Welsh Protestant client' or 'an Afro-Caribbean woman nurse'. If they do, the term 'intergroup encounter' applies even if only two people are present. This tendency to emphasise group membership is especially strong at initial meetings with a different other, which here means anyone who is believed to lack understanding of the social world inhabited by members of the other person's or people's ingroup.

Part of the explanation for treating different others as group members rather than individuals is the 'outgroup covariation effect'. People generally see their outgroups as less variable (more similar) along single characteristics, such as intelligence or cleanliness, than their ingroup. However, even perceptions of outgroup members show less covariation – more differentiation – along single characteristics, the more familiar the individual is with members of the outgroup. For instance, in research done with students, it was found that among both young and old, who in each case had only limited familiarity with the other group, there were high levels of covariation; for occupation, undergraduates differentiated less than MBA students, who had more work experience and hence familiarity with different occupational groups; while both men and women, who naturally had high familiarity with members of the other sex, were least inclined to perceive covariation in the other gender.[3]

Communicating with others as representatives of their groups creates barriers and complications in at least the following ways:

- People's group membership is not always obvious: identifying it is often a creative process in which communication 'work' must be done and group membership must be inferred.
- Intergroup encounters are complex: interpersonal factors cannot be ignored and therefore two dimensions need to be juggled, both the interpersonal and the intergroup. It can be difficult to get the right balance.
- Intergroup communication involves at least one of the individuals present being a different other. Interactions between different others and members of the ingroup can create anxiety and often are experienced by both parties as a series of crises.[4]
- When people treat an encounter as 'intergroup', they commonly make social attributions about the behaviour of the different other – that is, they use their knowledge of the group to 'decide' whether the individual's disposition or the situation is causing the behaviour. This leads them to show an increased tendency to attribute different others' behaviour to their disposition as opposed to their situation. This tendency is probably caused by a need to enhance their own social identity.[5] In addition, their knowledge of the culture of the different other's group is likely to be limited, leading them to make false attributions or, if they are aware of the problem, limited and provisional attributions.[6]
- Ethnocentrism is readily activated in intergroup encounters, leading to hostility towards the different others.

6.2	STEREOTYPING

The problems of intergroup communication are increased by the near-universal tendency to stereotype. A stereotype is a stable set of beliefs or pre-conceived ideas which the members of a group share about the characteristics of other groups. The concept of stereotype has gradually lost its earlier connotation of irrationality and prejudice; instead stereotyping is now considered an ordinary cognitive process in which people construct schemata to categorise people and entities in order to avoid 'information overload'.

BOX 6.2

SOME STEREOTYPES

'On the positive side, Germans often see Americans as friendly, open, resourceful, energetic, innovative, and, in general, capable in business... [with] greater freedom, generally happier... more productive and creative than many other people...; [and having] opportunities to succeed... [Americans find Germans] highly disciplined, well educated, neat and orderly... systematic, well-organized, meticulous, ... efficient. ...Some Americans find them hard to get to know – not unfriendly, but reserved. On the negative side... Germans are [seen by Americans as] pushy in service lines... and often insensitive to the feelings of others.'

Source: Hall, E.T. and Hall, M.R. (1990) *Understanding Cultural Differences: Germans, French, and Americans*, Yarmouth, Maine: Intercultural Press, pp. 75–6.

The outgroup covariation effect means that people and groups are more likely to create stereotypes of people who are members of groups different from themselves. Stereotypes also tend to favour the ingroup. Outgroup members are believed to be less attractive, less capable, less trustworthy, less honest, less cooperative, and less deserving than members of the ingroup.[7] As a result, people behave differently toward outgroup members.

All the major cultural and subcultural groups discussed in Chapter 2 are, of course, the objects of stereotyping by other population groups. Some are positive (see Box 6.2). Many, however, are negative: for instance, the stereotype of Scottish people as 'mean'. Others may be positive in some contexts and negative in others. For example, stereotypes that are shared by many people about gender differences have men as high in instrumental traits such as aggressiveness and independence, and women as possessing expressive traits such as sensitivity, nurturance and tactfulness. Women's stereotypical traits may well be positively regarded in the context of friendship or the home, but they are generally regarded negatively in the context of work, especially higher level executive or managerial work.

BOX 6.3

LACK OF CULTURAL AWARENESS OF MEMBERS
OF ONE SOCIETY FOR OTHER MEMBERS

It was reported in *The Economist* of 10 February 1996 that two shopping centres in Soweto, the Johannesburg township, had exposed significant misunderstandings of black shopping habits by white South African investors. For instance, unlike whites, black South Africans seldom eat out at night, which led to dfficulties for one centre's restaurant and its owners, Sanlam, a big local insurance company.

Another much smaller, more downmarket shopping centre opened in 1990 by Fedsure, a financial services group, got into difficulty by under-estimating locals' shopping sophistication.

It had been assumed that black shoppers would want relatively inexpensive stores run by fellow blacks but it emerged that they prefer to shop in smart stores that offer the same branded goods on sale in white shopping malls.

Source: The Economist, 10 February 1996.

Stereotypes distort intergroup communication because they lead people to base their messages, their ways of transmitting them and their reception of them on false assumptions. These arise in at least five ways:[8]

1. Stereotypes influence the way information is processed – more favourable information is remembered about ingroups, less favourable about outgroups; for instance, someone who has a stereotype of Scottish people as 'mean' is likely not to notice or quickly to forget if a Scottish person shows generosity.

2. Objectively, there is often more variation within groups than between them: this applies even to fundamental cultural values – not all Japanese people are 'collectivistic' – and still more to superficial characteristics such as 'meanness'. Stereotyping, however, leads to individuality being over-looked.

3. Stereotypes create expectations about 'others', and individual 'others' often feel a pressure to confirm these expectations. It may seem unlikely that Scottish people will try to confirm expectations that they are mean, although it can happen; but research has shown that schoolchildren under-perform if teachers expect less of them because of their background.

4. Stereotypes constrain others' patterns of communication – conventions and politeness may prevent people who perceive they are being treated in accordance with a stereotype from refuting it. Even if they do react, this is likely to distract them and to be a diversion from the conversation or discussion.

5. Stereotypes engender sterotype-confirming communication, thus creating self-fulfilling prophecies – a clear example is the way that, as research cited in Chapter 4 showed, women use disempowering ways of speaking to conform to stereotypes of femininity.

These points are illustrated in Figure 6.1.

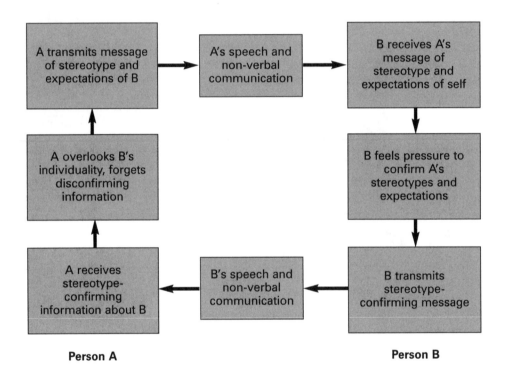

Figure 6.1   How stereotypes distort communication

The power of stereotypes has been demonstrated by research in which people are 'primed' in adopting stereotypes. Priming refers to 'the incidental activation of knowledge structures, such as trait concepts and stereotypes, by the current situational context'.[9] Many studies have shown that the recent use of a stereotype, even in an earlier or unrelated situation, carries over for a time to exert an unintended, passive influence on how people interpret the observed behaviour of members of the group to which the stereotype relates.[10]

It has been shown that people whose concept of rudeness was primed inter-rupted the experimenter more quickly and frequently than did people primed with politeness-related stimuli; people for whom an elderly stereotype was primed walked more slowly down the hallway when leaving the experiment than did those from a control group, showing that even their self-concept could be stereotypically primed; and participants for whom a negative African-American stereotype was primed reacted with more hostility to a vexatious request of the African-American experimenter than those for whom a positive stereotype was primed.[11]

The persistence of ethnic stereotyping and associated prejudice was demon-strated in a survey of 208 Dutch secondary school students. The research exam-ined the existence of ethnic stereotypes and their effect on the social distance which the subjects maintain towards minority groups.[12] (Maintaining social distance refers to avoiding intimacy or spending time with another person.) The study measured social distance and thirteen perceived characteristics of five different ethnic groups in four basic social domains: as neighbours, colleagues, classmates and (marital) partners. (The four domains used in this study imply different numbers, ages and cohesion of outgroup members; also different degrees of contact of the subjects with the members of the outgroup.) The find-ings of the research included the following:

- Domain-specific ethnic stereotypes exist and predict social distance fairly well.
- Three factors underlie the perceived characteristics of ethnic outgroups: tradi-tionalism, deviancy and low education/dark skin.
- How stereotypes predict social distance varies by domain of behaviour – for instance, the main predictor of social distance in the domains of neighbours and work colleagues for all groups except Jews was attributed deviancy; for all groups except Jews as classmates and for Turks and Moluccans as marital partners it was attributed traditionalism; for Jews as neighbours and for Jews, Spaniards and Surinamers as marital partners it was attributed low education.

In the discussion the researchers argued that how much social distance people impose as a result of stereotypes varies. Perceived characteristics also may vary when a particular set of individuals is involved – classmates were attributed low traditionalism whichever ethnic group they came from. Finally, the stereotypes themselves may predict different types of behaviour of outgroup members in different situations and therefore lead the holder of the stereotype to prefer greater or less social distance.

6.3	PREJUDICE

Prejudice is a thoughtless derogatory attitude or set of attitudes towards all or most of the members of a group. It includes racism, sexism, homophobia and ageism. Religious prejudice, too, can be as potent and thoughtless as any of these.

One major strand in approaches to the origins of prejudice is to view it as a personality trait linked to authoritarianism (measured by an F (for Fascist) scale) resulting from early socialisation. However, a cross-cultural study of prejudice in South Africa and the USA showed that racists in those countries did not necessarily have high levels of authoritarianism.[13] Furthermore, individual-level explanations of extreme prejudice fail to account for its widespread incidence in some societies. For these reasons, socio-cultural factors are now given more credence in explaining prejudice. Hagendoorn and Kleinpenning (1991)[14] consider that there is a new problem among people who will no longer explicitly deny ethnic equality but instead exhibit 'aversive racism', which is defined in terms of negative affect – feelings of discomfort and uneasiness which motivate avoiding ethnic outgroups and lead people to maintain social distance from them.

One form of prejudice, sexism, is seen by some authors as ambivalence and as composed of opposite evaluative orientations toward women: sexist antipathy or hostile sexism (HS) on the one hand and, on the other hand, a subjectively positive orientation toward women, benevolent sexism (BS) derived from three sources: paternalism, gender differentiation and heterosexuality. Hostile and benevolent sexism may co-exist in the same person. Six studies on 2,250 respondents established convergent, discriminant, and predictive validity for measures of ambivalent sexism based on individuals' levels of agreement with the statements in Box 6.4. It is possible that similar ambivalence exists in relation to other forms of prejudice, such as that against people with disabilities.[15]

A meta-analysis of research in which actual performance indicators were equalised between men and women found evidence of prejudice directed against women managers and leaders. It found an overall tendency to favour male leaders, which is real although slight. The analysis further found the tendency to be larger in the following conditions:

- Where the woman leader's style corresponds to male stereotypes (that is, is not interpersonal and participative).
- For roles usually occupied by men as against those occupied equally by both sexes or where the sex distribution is unknown.
- In some organisational contexts, such as sports and athletics coaching or business and manufacturing. There is a general slightly more favourable evaluation of male business managers than female business managers.
- Men are more likely to devalue women than women are. Women are largely neutral.[16]

BOX 6.4

PARAMETERS OF HOSTILE AND
BENEVOLENT SEXISM

Hostile sexism
   Women exaggerate problems at work
   Women are too easily offended
   Most women interpret innocent remarks as sexist
   When women lose fairly, they claim discrimination
   Women seek special favours under the guise of equality
   Feminists are making reasonable demands (reverse scoring)
   Feminists are not seeking more power than men (reverse
      scoring)
   Women seek power by gaining control over men
   Few women tease men sexually (reverse scoring)
   Once a man commits, she puts him on a tight leash
   Women fail to appreciate all men do for them

Benevolent sexism
   A good woman should be set on a pedestal
   Women should be cherished and protected by men
   Men should sacrifice to provide for women
   In a disaster, women need not be rescued first (reverse scoring)
   Women have a superior moral sensibility
   Women have a quality of purity few men possess
   Women have a more refined sense of culture, taste
   Every man ought to have a woman he adores
   Men are complete without women (reverse scoring)
   Despite accomplishment, men are incomplete without women
   People are often happy without heterosexual romance (reverse
      scoring)

Source: Glick, P. and Fiske, S.T. (1996) 'The ambivalent sexism inventory:
differential hostile and benevolent sexism', *Journal of Personality and Social
Psychology*, **70**, 491–512.

Direct effects of prejudice at work are mainly discrimination and harassment, which have been discussed in Chapter 2. Both these, in addition to their negative effects for individuals and the organisation, are intrinsically barriers to communication, but so is prejudice itself, even when it is not overt. Prejudiced people distort and misread communication from those about whom they hold prejudiced views. On the other side, people who become aware of others' prejudices about themselves or others are likely to develop negative attitudes to the prejudiced individual's opinions in general, regardless of how soundly based those other opinions may be.

Moreover, perceptions of prejudice are themselves often prejudiced: there is a tendency to believe that certain groups (such as older white male managers) are prejudiced or that its victims are members of certain groups (such as Bangladeshi women). That is, perceptions of prejudice are strongly influenced by specific expectations regarding who are the prototypic perpetrators and victims of prejudice.[17] In an interview with the author, the personnel director of a major UK car manufacturer said:

> We find that the stereotypes of who will be prejudiced are often wrong. We tend to think that it will be the older males, especially from the engineering or factory side, that will be most biased. Often, however, it's the 'young Turks' – mostly graduates – in sales and marketing. I think perhaps they see them – the women – as rivals, in a way the older ones don't.

False suspicions of prejudice can create communication problems in a wide range of organisational, work, social and educational settings.

BOX 6.5

SOME PREJUDICES AND SOME COMMENTS

1. Commenting on an article by Robert Henderson in *Wisden Cricket Monthly*, which 'argues, broadly, that Englishmen with black skin won't play for the country with the same fervour as those with white', Mike Marqusee wrote in the *Guardian* that 'Racial and national stereotyping – and especially a combination of the two – are commonplace in cricket talk. This denial of reality leads such people as Henderson… to argue, in effect, that the England cricket side will be more effective the less representative it is of the social composition of the country.'

2. 'The perception is that young people have more energy and drive and cut through the detail. The upbringing of people in their forties is seen as much more structured and dogged. As a result, there is a view that older people are less flexible and used to going in a straight line. People in their thirties seem to be more mercurial, in a positive sense, and prepared to take risks.'

3. 'On the one hand, we all know that you can't ban discrimination by legislation. But, by outlawing the expression of discriminatory attitudes, you make clear the society's disapproval of the discrimination.'

   'We have a cultural problem. We don't any longer recognise that age connotes wisdom.'

Sources: The *Guardian*, 4 July 1995; Ashley Robinson, consultant with MacNeil, a recruitment agency, quoted in *The Times* of 5 February 1996; Germaine Greer, on the radio programme *Any Questions*, 8 February 1996; Charles Moore on the radio programme *Any Questions*, 8 February 1996.

6.4 CULTURAL DIFFERENCES IN COMMUNICATION AS BARRIERS

However valid in terms of their own (sub)culture, national, ethnic, gender and social class differences in how people speak and interact can lead to them being perceived as disorganised and poor thinkers or as being insulting. For instance, in the UK for schoolchildren of Afro-Caribbean ethnic origin, and elsewhere in Europe for children of Algerian, Turkish or Indonesian ethnicity, differences in dialect, frequency of interruption, story telling and conversational rules have resulted in lower performance expectations from teachers, excessive speech/language therapy placements, and perception of communication differences as discipline problems. For the children themselves, lowered self-expectations and a perception of the school climate as negative often follow from their treatment. Gender differences in ways of talking and non-verbal behaviour can cause one sex to be seen as powerful and decisive and the other as submissive and indecisive. Differences brought about by education and professional training can cause frequent misunderstandings and misinterpretations.

This section aims to show how many of the *communication practices* introduced earlier, and some others, can lead to misunderstanding and even conflict in intercultural encounters.

Language ambiguity, which was explained in Chapter 4, causes particular confusion interculturally.[18] The subtleties of language use which enable a native speaker of a language, when acting as a receiver of messages, to draw inferences accurately about the meanings of a speaker will tend to escape the non-native speaker. Equally, the other source of inference – knowledge of the 'world' – may be defective when the speaker is from another culture, as the speaker's 'world' will be influenced by his or her culture.

Implicature presents a particular problem as the conventions governing it differ from one language group to another.

Non-verbal behaviour is prone to being wrongly interpreted in intercultural encounters. Some examples are given in Box 6.6. *State, trait and style* differences can create impediments. For instance, the point has already been made that there are cultural differences in what counts as assertiveness and the value attached to it. Using a level of assertiveness which is appropriate in one culture with interactors from another will probably be seen as aggression or, on the other hand, lack of assertion. Both *encoding* and *decoding* of messages lay traps for the unwary intercultural communicator. Gallois and Callan considered that the results of their study of message decoding in Australia (see Chapter 4) revealed that the negative attitudes of Anglo-Australians to Italian men are reflected in the difficulty they have in decoding speakers when the Italian voice and accent are present. They concluded that the listener's own goals and perception of the context as threatening may lead to an overall distortion of the speaker's messages.[19]

BOX 6.6

EXAMPLES OF COMMUNICATION BARRIERS
CREATED BY NON-VERBAL COMMUNICATION
DIFFERENCES

Kinesics. Asians in general tend to smile or laugh more readily than Westerners when they feel difficulty or embarrassment. This is then misinterpreted by Westerners as normal pleasure or agreement and the source of difficulty is missed.

Proxemics. Hall (1959) put forward the notion of a 'space bubble' in which each individual moves and feels comfortable. The size of this space bubble varies by culture: Arabs and Latin-Americans feel comfortable with a smaller space bubble than Anglos. This leads them to stand closer, creating discomfort for an interacting Anglo, who may move backwards, thus giving an impression of unfriendliness to the Arab. Responses to perceived invasion of space have been shown to differ between men and women. While men may respond aggressively, women tend to yield space rather than challenge the intruder.

Speed of delivery. Faster speakers almost always evaluate slower speakers negatively. Thus people from the southern states of the USA are often regarded as slow-thinking by Europeans and people from the northern USA.

Speech styles. Language and communication norms among young African-American males, particularly those of lower socio-economic status, are related, at least in part, to their higher rate of disciplinary problems and special education placements. Speaking ethnically based English vernaculars and the use of urban argots can be seen by such youths as markers of masculinity and defiance of white standards, but it 'virtually guarantees' academic problems and, sometimes, social problems, by conflicting with the school's communication norms.

Communicator style. A study examined the role that culture plays in communication distortion by using observation and interviewing techniques to gather data while applicants from West Africa and Westerners applied for a visa. The results suggested that speech patterns, body posture, eye contact, information disclosure and verbal aggression are interpreted differently depending on culture, which leads to communication distortion.

Sources: Hall, E.T. (1959) *The Silent Language*, New York: Doubleday; Northwest Regional Educational Laboratory: CNORSE 'Cross-cultural communication: An Essential dimension of effective education'. Posted on the Internet: http://www.nwrel.org/cnorse; Olaniran, B.A., and Williams, D.E. (1995) 'Communication distortion: an intercultural lesson from the Visa application process', *Communication Quarterly*, **43**(2): 225–40.

Between users of *low-context communication and high-context communication*, misunderstanding is hard to avoid. When a speaker uses high-context communication, the problem for a low-context receiver is literally to grasp their meaning: so much is left unsaid and they are not attuned to the implicatures and inferences being used nor to the extensive use of non-verbal communication. Indirectness and an emphasis on relationship data compound the problem. When the speaker uses low-context communication, the problem for the high-context communication receiver is less to grasp their overt meaning than to avoid over-interpreting and seeing inferences which may not be present; being affronted by directness or the 'brutality' of the concentration on hard content; and simply suffering from information overload.

It was pointed out in Chapter 4 that most people have three ways of *detecting deceptions*. One is whether the communicator's non-verbal behaviour breaches common expectations; this is even more likely to be misread by people from a different background; to a lesser degree, too, their ability to use the other two ways (assessing how plausible is the message being communicated and how nervous is the communicator) may be limited by lack of (sub)cultural knowledge. For example, most able-bodied people would not know enough about cerebral palsy to assess the plausibility of a statement about its symptoms and treatment which they were told by a person with this disability. The same problem of lack of knowledge of the (sub)culture of a different other interactor will tend to lead to *judging arguments* by peripheral processing instead of centrally and critically. Not only is peripheral processing generally less likely to lead to accurate judgements, but source credibility, which is the main cognitive criterion used in peripheral processing, is itself hard to assess interculturally; the other main variables, liking, fear and guilt, are emotions hardly likely to help in judging an argument accurately.

Differences in the *functions to which language is put*, such as distributing control and determining the level of affiliation, can set up barriers. For instance, some women see talk as the essence of a relationship while some men use talk to exert control, preserve independence, and enhance status. Tannen[20] has argued that 'Communication between men and women can be like cross cultural communication, prey to a clash of conversational styles.'

Language use, or linguistic pragmatics, can create barriers. Pragmatic errors result when people impose the social rules of their own (sub)culture in a situation where the social rules of another (sub)culture would be more appropriate. One type occurs when a speech strategy is employed which is inappropriate for the language being spoken: for instance, speaking loudly and forcefully in Japanese. Another type involves getting the balance between talk and silence wrong for the culture. Moreover, attempting to adapt to the perceived needs of the person being spoken to can itself produce problems – for instance, using a simplified 'foreigner talk' register, as the Japanese often do, even when the person they are addressing is highly competent in the language, limits discussion as well as possibly giving offence.

(Sub)cultural differences in *communication strategies* can lead to misunderstanding. For example, in discussions with men, women's communication strategies often express the subordinate, non-aggressive role allocated to women in Western society, but this can be misleading. The soft-spoken woman who uses multiple hesitations and tag questions may nevertheless be highly determined and power orientated; she may be deliberately, and even successfully, adopting a 'feminine' style or she may lack awareness of her own style and miscommunicate her attitudes or intentions.

When people realise that they are interacting with someone from a different background, they usually adapt their discourse by using *elaborated rather than restricted codes*.[21] This is necessary, but can mean that intercultural encounters are marked by a tone of formality which slows the pace at which relationships develop and which people from some (sub)cultures, such as Americans, find 'unfriendly'. In addition, the requirements for adapting to the elaborated code place heavy demands on people's communication resources. By the same token, what a person from one culture overhears in a discussion between two people from a different culture who are using a restricted code can be mystifying or misleading.

Ting-Toomey (1988)[22] states that *face* is an especially problematic issue for people in uncertain situations which call into question the situated identities of interactants (that is, their sense of 'who' they are). Obviously, meeting people from another culture for the first time, especially in important work meetings, negotiations or interviews, are examples of 'uncertain situations'. In these and other face-threatening situations, active facework is required: the parties engage in two kinds of facework: self-face concern and other-face concern. However, culture influences people's use of facework and their tendency to select one set of facework strategies and conflict styles (such as face avoiding and face obliging) rather than others (such as face threatening and face defensive). Non-alignment of facework strategies can lead to miscommunication – the people who are interacting misread each others'signals and so respond inappropriately. This can lead to spiralling conflict.

Miscommunication of *politeness* is another source of intercultural communication problems. Ambady *et al.* (1996)[23] speculate in their conclusion to research about cultural differences in politeness strategies that 'Perhaps many understandings that occur between cultures are due to the miscommunication of politeness.' What constitutes a face-threatening act varies cross-culturally. For instance, making a request is generally a less face-threatening act for Americans (as shown by their dictum 'always ask') than to many British people.

Some intercultural miscommunication is produced by *directness and indirectness* in certain situations involving greetings, farewells, compliments or negative observations, or appropriateness of subject matter. Directness perceived positively is called 'honesty'. However, if it is negatively perceived it quickly becomes 'rudeness'. Indirectness, too, can have positive or negative connotations. Indirectness in certain situations can be perceived positively as 'politeness' or 'friendliness', whereas indirectness perceived negatively is called 'superficiality' or 'insincerity'.

This issue has been found to affect communication between Germans and Americans. Americans often show politeness through behaviours and language perceived as 'friendliness', and Germans show it through what they might label 'respect'. Many Germans stress 'honesty' in encounters, while many Americans wish to maintain an agreeable attitude and do not want to disappoint their interlocutors. Thus, when they meet, if they are expecting behaviour from the others that they find in their own cultures, Americans and Germans often do not have their expectations met, and they become disappointed in the members of the other culture.[24]

The topic–comment structure of a communication refers to the fact that speakers may first give the context of what they want to say and then their main point or vice versa. For example, 'Reaching the factory involves taking the ring road' puts the topic, background or reason first and the main point, suggested action or comment second, whereas 'You take the ring road to go to the factory' puts the main point, suggested action or comment first and the topic, background or reason second.

Topic–comment order varies between cultures and this can cause confusion, especially in languages like English which (unlike Japanese, for instance), have no semantic way of marking the main subject. Research in a major East Asian city studied situations which could be considered to require professional communication.[25] It found that among people from American/European cultures, it was usual to put the comment, main point or suggested action first and then give the topic, background or reason. People from Asian cultural backgrounds did the reverse: they put the topic, background or reason first and then their main point, comment or the action they were suggesting.

For example, an American might say, 'We could announce price cuts on 100 items for the next three months – we'd run a big press campaign and an in-store sales promotion, try to get lots of publicity [suggested action]. That way we'd really cut the ground out from under our competitors with their selective weekly price cuts [reason].' An Asian listener, expecting to hear the reason for any action first, might find this abrupt, or might interpret the opening sentence as the reason and become confused. By contrast, an Asian speaker would be more likely to say 'Our competitors are launching a campaign of weekly price cuts. This could have very serious consequences for our sales and market share [reason]. We could look at announcing price cuts on 100 items for the next three months [suggested action].' An American listener might grow impatient, especially if the reasons are elaborated, as they might well be, and be inattentive when the speaker reaches the point of proposing action.

Only limited evidence is as yet available for cultural differences in specific aspects of communication – it must necessarily be the case, therefore, that the evidence that such differences constitute barriers to intercultural communication is still more limited. Nevertheless, this section has attempted to establish a prima facie case that they do and that such barriers can be a serious cause of miscommunication.

6.5 BEHAVIOURAL BARRIERS TO INTERCULTURAL COMMUNICATION

Both *deep and surface culture* can be problematic in intercultural communication: deep culture because communication which conflicts with others' values is very likely to be misunderstood, rejected and offensive; surface culture because it determines matters such as what is and is not polite (for instance, in the West to proffer the left hand for a hand shake is a mere error; to do it in Arab countries is a grave offence against manners). Sometimes the problem is one of false interpretation: Example 1 in Box 6.7 illustrates such a case: a difference in the conventions governing eye contact can lead to Westerners finding Indians untrustworthy. At other times, there are genuine differences in values or attitudes that, when accurately communicated, create negative responses: Example 2 in the same box may reflect such a situation: it is probable that differences in education and upbringing between the French and British (both of which may be rooted in differences in their cultural levels of uncertainty avoidance) do lead at least some of the people of these two nations to approach issues differently and it is also quite possible that both have low tolerance for the others' approach.

BOX 6.7

ILLUSTRATIONS OF NATIONAL DIFFERENCES AS BARRIERS

1. Many Indians look down when acknowledging authority, an attitude that many North American and European managers interpret as untrustworthiness.
2. The British find the French analytical approach arid; the French find British pragmatism confused.
3. Giving public reprimands is acceptable in US culture, even effective, but probably in few others.
4. The Argentinians and other South Americans need time to elapse for trust building before doing deals; this is in conflict with North Americans' need not to waste time because 'time is money'.
5. A fertiliser manufacturer lost a lot of money in West Africa because of failing to realise that it is women who are the farmers there and that they would not want to grow more than neighbours for fear of being suspected of witchcraft.
6. The Germans value experience/seniority/age so to send a young manager to deal with seniors is a mistake; also jokes are felt to be inappropriate in a business setting.
7. It is easy for people visiting Africa to give offence by taking photographs of local people. First, for Muslims, there is a Koranic prohibition on representations of the person; second, 'local colour' to them is the backward aspect of their society; third, some people may associate being photographed with becoming a victim of witchcraft.

Sources: Adler, N. (1991) *International Dimensions of Organizational Behavior* (2nd edn), Belmont, CA: Wadsworth; Smith, M.G. (1986) 'Pluralism, race and ethnicity in selected African countries', in Rex, J. and Mason, D. (eds) *Theories of Race and Ethnic Relations*, Cambridge, Cambridge University Press.

All of the *underlying psychological factors* which were shown to vary cross-culturally in Section 5.1, are capable of 'producing' behaviours which disturb effective intercultural communication. Different concepts of the *self* between people from individualistic and collectivist cultures mean that

Each group is likely to make false assumptions about members of the other group. Asians will possibly overestimate a Westerner's concern about his [sic] group's response to an issue, while a Westerner is likely to assume a greater degree of independence on the part of an Asian with whom he is negotiating.[26]

Between people from different sides of these cultural 'divides', communication can be inhibited by non-acceptance of the others' *values*. For example, the 'natural' attempt on the part of someone with high power in a *high-power distance* society to receive the attentions 'due' to their status will grate on people from more egalitarian communities – witness the dislike expressed by a British university lecturer for the Asian practice of staff and students bowing out the institution's president as he departed (see Box 9.8). On the other hand, the egalitarianism between students and staff which is now usual in British universities is regarded by many university lecturers in Central Europe as undermining the learning process by undermining their authority; this has led to cases where lecturers from Britain, working for a semester in a Central European country to help introduce Western business studies or management courses, have found themselves isolated as their local colleagues distance themselves. Numerous similar examples could be cited to show how differences in the other core values lead to miscommunication broadly defined.

Universalism and particularism, as Chapter 3 explained, contrast a preference for drawing general principles versus a preference for the anecdotal or itemised; there can be tendency for people who use 'universal' modes of thinking and speaking to under-rate the quality of thinking of those who think and speak particularistically. Conversely, particularistic thinkers can regard universalistic thinkers as 'academic' and out of touch with the real world. In both cases, these attitudes lead to poor listening – a lack of serious attention and consideration of the views being expressed or the information being imparted. When these attitudes to others are transmitted, often unintentionally, to the person to whom they apply, a natural reaction is for them to 'withdraw', reducing the amount of communication they offer, or to get angry (probably ostensibly about an issue under discussion). Either reaction can lead to a breach in communication.

People from *specific* cultures, 'with their small areas of privacy clearly separated from public life, have considerable freedom for direct speech'. This may result in 'insulting' people from *diffuse* cultures, for whom the principle of losing face is 'what happens when something is made public which people perceive as being private'. The importance of avoiding loss of face is 'why in diffuse cultures so much more time is taken to get to the point: it is necessary to avoid private confrontation because it is impossible for participants not to take things personally'.

Several of the core cultural values have the property of constituting barriers to communication in themselves, regardless of whether intercultural communication is at issue. For example, if everyone were an *individualist*, one might predict a world of poor communication – individualists show low concern for 'other face'; if all were *collectivists*, one could predict poor communication and conflict between groups – collectivists erect barriers to communication with outgroup members, regardless of whether those outgroup members are themselves collectivists or not. People in *high-power distance* cultures erect barriers with those in a different power position from themselves, although their communication with those in a similar power position to their own may be enhanced, because similarity fosters liking, acceptance and persuasibility. High *uncertainty avoidance* leads to reluctance to engage in uncertain communication situations regardless of whether they are with culturally different people. High *masculinity* as a trait (as opposed to a value) has been shown in this book to have been found to correlate with low ability to 'read' others' emotional states or to express emotion; it seems probable that the equivalent value tends to lead to similar communication deficiencies.

Making false *assumptions* based on the situation in someone's own culture can lead to giving or taking offence by, for example, not giving deference where it is expected or expecting it where it will not be granted. Who is important, whom it would be useful to get to know, who is to be respected may be different in one culture than it is in another. A religious leader may be more important in one culture, and someone with wealth in another. Blacks may be the insiders in one culture and South Asians in another. People who are 'insiders' in their own culture, due to their economic, professional, or educational status, may be outsiders in another culture, because their skills are not important there, or because of race or gender, or simply because they are from another culture and never will really be fully accepted in the host culture.

Probably more disagreement arises over differences in conscious *beliefs* than anything else. Although disagreement should not be confused with miscommunication, even on a broad view, some writers (for example Sarbaugh)[27] consider the worldview, which encompasses a set of beliefs about the nature of life, the purpose of life and our relation to the cosmos, to be the behavioural element most resistant to change, and therefore heterogeneity of worldviews to be the most long-lasting barrier to communication across cultures. To the degree that conflict can be taken as a measure of miscommunication, the amount of conflict throughout history and still raging today around issues of religion is an indication of how this aspect of worldview produces barriers.

When examples of belief which lead to hostility are examined, often one of two elements (or both) seem to be present: one is that the belief itself incorporates the idea that holders of other beliefs are not just mistaken, but 'evil'; the other is a refusal to contemplate the possibility of error. As Kincaid has expressed it: 'Absolute certainty renders communication inoperable... At times, intercultural communication seems to approach this extreme, when the intercultural assumptions are so divergent and the intracultural certainty so high that communication is very ineffective or does not work at all.'[28]

Trompenaars[29] contends that the amount of visible *display of feeling* is a major difference between cultures. A further aspect of this difference is the degree of separation from 'objective' and 'impersonal' matters. Americans, for example, are high in emotional expression but also high in separation; Italians are high in emotional expression but low in separation, the Dutch and Swedes are low in emoting visibly and high in separating.

BOX 6.8

EURO-AMERICAN MISALLIANCE

A franchiser of top-of-the-market 'mail box' services, supplying clients with a postal address, secretarial, packaging, dispatch and document delivery services, is extremely successful in the USA. When the company decided to expand into Europe, they began with the country most like the USA, England, and followed their usual procedure of appointing a 'master licensee' for the country, who was to sell the individual franchises.

'In the US,' one of their managers said, 'only someone really motivated to succeed and having the necessary skills would take on a master licence for this product. It would be known to be really hard work to build up the business in a competitive market.' In Europe, the company found, to its dismay, that conditions were different. The UK master licence was bought by a rich Spanish family to provide a junior member of the family with an occupation. This wealthy scion was not only completely ignorant of the product and business generally, he was a playboy. That was the first problem.

The second problem was that the British man appointed as chief executive of the main franchise 'Only wanted the plaque on his desk saying "Managing Director". He didn't want the work either.' Eventually, when things went really badly and the franchiser realised that their brand image worldwide might be damaged, the US manager was sent to the UK on a renewable two-year contract to sort things out. He succeeded partly, but found the obstacles to working as he was used to in the USA so great and the difficulty of cooperating with the two unmotivated people at the top of the organisation so frustrating that he refused to renew at the end of the two years and, when interviewed, was planning to return to America.

Source: Interview with an expatriate manager, author's research.

These differences in culturally inculcated rules for emotional display can create severe difficulties for participants in intercultural encounters. The English, with their famous 'stiff upper lip' have traditionally been embarrassed, to the point where their ability to empathise or sympathise was subverted, by the more demonstrative displays of affection and grief shown by Mediterranean people. The same applies to subcultures – men in Western cultures often fear the 'emotionalism' of women (and so take the dysfunctional route of avoidance) although the gender differences here may be more closely related to culturally induced differences in what it is legitimate to display than in the real level of emotion.

In addition to the obstacles created by these cultural differences, the intercultural encounter itself often engenders emotions which can create further barriers. For example, in a report posted on the Internet in 1995, a group psychotherapy facilitator wrote about sessions working with medical students to try to achieve a greater ability to perceive, introspect and express oneself so as to bridge the distance between the doctor/student and patient, specifically looking at different emotions to do so. The therapist reported having been told that medical students do not do well in group psychotherapy because 'they won't be vulnerable' and having found there to be some truth in this. There was a particular problem with the emotion of fear, because 'As emotions are infectious, this particular emotion produces a tremendous amount of anxiety when examined closely.' Another example concerns communication between people with and without disabilities. Coleman and DePaulo (1991)[30] showed that anxiety, as well as negative stereotypes and expectations, affect both parties in such encounters and lead to miscommunication.

Most people experience the state of *fear of communicating* in some circumstances – it may be public speaking or asking for a favour or – a common one among managers – having to reprimand a subordinate. For some people, however, fear of communicating (also known as communication apprehension) extends to so many circumstances that it can be both dysfunctional and painful for them. Fear of communicating with the opposite sex, with people from a different national, ethnic or educational background or with people with disabilities exists to an unrecognised degree among people at work and can make life difficult for both them and their colleagues.

James McCroskey,[31] who researched fear of communicating, believed that the cause is primarily cognitive: that people have expectations about how encounters will turn out and, if they have a number of experiences which disconfirm their expectations, they become fearful of future interactions of the same type. Thus fear of communicating is essentially a kind of learned helplessness, which is treatable through systematic desensitisation techniques. William Douglas[32] found that individuals who experience communication apprehension ask few questions during the first minute of an interaction, engage in high levels of self-disclosure, and are considered less competent by their communication partners. Self-reports suggest that individuals who experience communication apprehension are high in global uncertainty and lack expertise when playing out acquaintance scenarios.

However, there is evidence that who suffers from communication fear and when is not stereotypical. The results of one study indicated that Middle Eastern and European subjects in the USA reported levels of apprehension well *below* statistical norms previously established by US subjects, while Asian and Latin-American subjects reported levels just slightly below those norms when communicating in their native languages. All groups indicated that communication anxiety was more of a problem when speaking in English, with Asians and Latin-Americans reporting the highest levels. Females were slightly more apprehensive overall when communicating in either language, but women in the Latin-American sample reported less apprehension than males in every context except public speaking. Neither the subjects' number of years speaking English nor the length of time living in the USA correlated with communication fear, suggesting that neither competency nor skill in a second language is related to the amount of apprehension experienced.[33]

Brislin *et al.* (1986)[34] identified five 'problem' emotions which are common in intercultural encounters:

1. *Disconfirmed expectations* – being upset not because a situation is bad, in and of itself, but rather because it is not what was expected.
2. *Not belonging* – not being part of the 'ingroup' of a culture; always feeling like an outsider. For example, some British people who are tall and fair skinned can feel more comfortable in a country like Slovakia, despite not speaking the language and being confronted with a largely unknown culture, than in the south of France, even if they speak good French. Many of the Slavic people of Slovakia are also generally tall and fair skinned, unlike the often darker, shorter people of the south of France, where people who are tall and fair are conspicuous.
3. *Ambiguity* – not being sure what is 'going on' – how to interpret events.
4. *Confrontation with one's own prejudices* – in being socialised into their own culture, people learn to categorise people as 'like me' and 'not like me' on some criteria, and develop ways of treating people in those two groups differently. In another culture, where the majority of people are 'not like me', they have to rethink how they treat other people – and sometimes are unpleasantly surprised to discover how prejudiced they are. (This point relates particularly to sojourning.)
5. *Anxiety* – feeling anxious because of not knowing if a given behaviour is appropriate, what is safe, how to negotiate a situation and so on. Anxiety is so important that Gudykunst's theory of intercultural communication, described in Chapter 7, gives a central place to managing it.

Other common negative emotions in intercultural situations include a need to be dependent or a feeling of being overwhelmed and a need to withdraw. It is not, of course, the emotion itself which constitutes a communication barrier: it is how the individual responds to that emotion. If their response is withdrawal or aggressiveness, communication is impeded. Having strong emotional reactions to intercultural situations is normal, and one of the skills of becoming interculturally competent is learning how to deal with such emotions in productive ways.

Violations of expectations, including role and norm expectations, are among the most common causes of miscommunication at work. People have expectations about both the verbal and the non-verbal behaviour of others, based on social (cultural) norms, previous experience with the situation and, where applicable, previous experience of the other person. These expectations are both descriptive, referring to how they think others do behave and normative, referring to how they think others should behave. However, as norms for behaviour vary from social group to social group, these expectations can sometimes be violated. For instance, Burgoon and Hale (1988)[35] pointed out that in the European American middle-class subculture of the USA:

One expects normal speakers to be reasonably [sic] fluent and coherent in their discourse, to refrain from erratic movements or emotional outbursts and to adhere to politeness norms.

What counts as reasonable fluency and coherence, erratic movement, emotional outburst or politeness varies considerably from one culture (and subculture) to another, so European-American middle-class people interacting with many other groups in the world are likely to have their expectations violated. Insofar as interactions with people from outside someone's own social circle are often expected to be more 'costly' in terms of effort than 'rewarding' in terms of social gain,[36] people may be more inclined to evaluate violations by different others negatively.

BOX 6.9

PROBLEMS OF ARAB–WESTERN BUSINESS COMMUNICATION

There are at least three ways in which misunderstandings can arise in business communication between people from Saudi Arabia and Westerners:

1. They have different concepts of time – Saudis do not 'budget' it in the way Westerners do.
2. They have different senses of how business deals are made: Saudis spend time in small talk (and perhaps over several meetings) in order to build trust before discussing business.
3. Aspects of negotiations which a Westerner might regard as confidential and therefore as taking place only between the main participants might be attended in Saudi Arabia by members of the negotiator's family. Business is in the public domain and therefore not treated with the intense privacy to which the personal is subjected.

Inferring the *intentions* of a speaker, which, as Chapter 4 showed, is crucial to communication, is highly problematic for receivers from another culture. (Some of the problems were noted in the discussion of language ambiguity.)

The *processes of social cognition* are subject to difficulties and errors particular to intergroup and intercultural encounters. *Differences in logical systems*, such as those described in Section 5.2, obviously impede mutual understanding. The increased tendency to make errors when making intergroup attributions has already been discussed. *Categorisation* is another error-prone process; the available evidence suggests that it is one which varies from individual to individual as well as (sub)culturally. Some people categorise narrowly and both some of them and some others categorise rigidly. Narrow categorisers group together only cases which are closely similar on a particular criterion: for instance, a narrow categoriser might only apply the label 'manager' to people who are responsible for the work of others. Broad categorisers, in contrast, allow more cases to fit into the same category by using an increased number of criteria – so broad categorisers might count as managers people who manage budgets or brands as well as those who manage people. Both narrow and broad categorisers might be flexible or rigid categorisers – willing or unwilling to shift their category 'definitions' on receiving new information – although there is a tendency for rigidity and narrowness to go together. Rigidity and narrowness, especially when combined, create obstacles to intercultural communication by leading people to over-emphasise differences and ignore similarities and by reducing their willingness to search for appropriate interpretations of different others' behaviour.

6.6	OTHER BARRIERS TO CROSS-CULTURAL COMMUNICATION AT WORK

In the work context, in addition to the problems caused by the general intercultural communication barriers already described, two areas have attracted particular attention: the effects of the heterogeneity of problem solving and task groups; and conflict.

Heterogeneity of work groups

Because organisations are increasingly moving to team-based job design, communication within both task groups and decision-making groups is increasingly important. This has led to an amount of research being undertaken into the effects of heterogeneity in work groups on how well people working in them communicate and on related matters such as their creativity.

According to McLeod and Lobel[37]: 'Research on creativity in groups has generally supported the notion that heterogeneity along a variety of dimensions leads to original and high quality ideas and problem solutions.' They suggest there are two mechanisms for this:

BOX 6.10

AGE AND COMMUNICATION BARRIERS AT WORK

A 1989 study showed that similarity in age influences the likelihood of technical communication between co-workers, but not all that strongly: the coefficient of determination between age similarity and communication with other project members was 0.18 (in a study of a 92-member technical project group).

Source: Zengler, T. and Lawrence, B. (1989) 'Organisational demography: the different effects of age and tenure distributions on technical communication', *Academy of Management Journal.*

1. Cross-fertilisation of perspectives and attitudes resulting from different experiences: empirical support for this proposition has come from studies of personality and gender, attitude but not ability and groups with open memberships (changing over time) but not closed groups.
2. Ideational (creative) ability; this has been shown to vary and also the presence of individuals with high ideational ability has been shown to raise the creativity of a group as a whole.

It is also possible, McLeod and Lobel claim, that 'Creative thinking ability may be related to ethnicity.' The argument here is that previous work found that Asian-Americans, Hispanic-Americans and African-Americans are bicultural; many are bilingual or biglossal (able to switch languages freely during the course of one conversation):

> Based on the flexibility and divergent thinking associated with bilingualism and biculturalism, we might expect to see greater creativity in groups that have members from those backgrounds than in groups from the predominant Anglo culture, which is typically not bilingual or bicultural.

Ethnicity differences are associated with behavioural differences and these affect group outcomes. More ideas, more unique ideas and more ideas rated as effective and feasible come from ethnically diverse groups. Also, groups composed of people from collectivist ethnic backgrounds are found to be more cooperative on a choice-based dilemma task than groups composed of people from an individualist ethnic background.

However, the findings of a 17-week longitudinal study into the interpersonal processes and performance of culturally homogeneous and culturally diverse groups (with at least two nationalities and three ethnic groups) were less clear cut. Groups were controlled for age, gender, years of work experience and educational achievement. Initially, homogeneous groups scored higher on both process and performance effectiveness:

> A high degree of cultural diversity did appear to constrain process and performance among group members in newly formed groups (up to 9 hours)... The diverse groups reported more difficulty in agreeing on what was important and in working together and more often had members who tried to be too controlling, which hindered member contributions.[38]

Over time, however, both types of group showed improvement in process and performance and between-group differences converged. By week 17, there were no differences in process or overall performance, although heterogeneous groups scored higher on two task measures out of four – identifying problem perspectives and generating solution alternatives – but lower on problem identification, choosing the most effective of the solutions generated by the group and justifying their choice.

There is a case for arguing that communication failure in heterogeneous work groups can lead to higher staff turnover rates as some people leave. The results of a study of 20 actual work units with 79 respondents suggested that heterogeneity is associated with lower levels of groups' social integration which in turn is associated with individual staff turnover. The study focused on age heterogeneity. It found that more distant group members are the ones likely to leave. 'Individuals in an age-heterogeneous (work) group have higher turnover rates as do individuals distant in age from an otherwise homogeneous group.'[39] One possible explanation comes from an earlier finding that, after controlling for an individual's demographic characteristics, the greater the difference in superior–subordinate dyads, in terms of age, education, race and sex, the lower the supervisor's rating of the subordinate's effectiveness and the higher the subordinate's role ambiguity. If subordinates experience 'prejudiced' assessments when they are in a mixed work group or when they are different in background from their supervisor, they may decide that the easiest solution is to leave.

Conflict

There is clear evidence for poor work relations in intercultural situations. For instance, studies of Chinese/American joint ventures reported the following:

1. 'Workers... evaluated Chinese managers by a simple standard: whoever quarreled with Americans the most aggressively would be considered a comrade in arms, and whoever cooperated with the Americans would be nicknamed "Er Gui Zi" (fake foreigners).'[40]

2. 'American managers complained that the Chinese do not recognize the importance of deadlines and schedules; that the Chinese are not proactive and will not take risks; that the Communist party representative at the firm often has more power than the Chinese managers; and that the hardship of working in China is a chronic stressor, which exacerbates inter-cultural conflict. The Chinese managers complained that Americans do not try to understand and learn from the Chinese; that the American management style is too abrupt; that Americans fail to recognize the importance of relationships; and they overemphasize the importance of formal rules and regulations.'

BOX 6.11

YOUR BIAS IS SHOWING BUT YOU CAN'T SEE IT

An interethnic conflict recorded on videotape during a university student organisation meeting was analysed from a number of perspectives. The findings suggested that although the participants claimed that neither race nor gender was involved in the conflict, the conflict could be explained on the basis of cultural differences in behaviour and interpretations of the behaviour of members of the other ethnic group.

Source: Speicher, B.L. (1995) 'Interethnic conflict: attribution and cultural ignorance', *Howard Journal of Communication*, **5**(3): 195–213.

---

3. 'The atmosphere [at Beijing Jeep] became so tense that even the most trivial business dealings between the American and Chinese became bogged down in charges and countercharges.'[41]

BOX 6.12

UNITED EUROPE?

1. Two Danes, two Britons, one Icelander (who had lived for eight years in the USA) and one Belgian met for the first time to try to work out a proposal to collaborate under an EU initiative to help ethnic minority young people make the transition from school to

---

work. (The Danes and the Belgian worked in schools concerned with Turkish first- or second-generation immigrants, the Britons for a charity helping members of ethnic minorities mainly from the Commonwealth, the Icelander for a government department dealing with Vietnamese families.) At several points the meeting almost broke up in disagreement over a range of issues. Questioning revealed that a majority of the problems were attitudinal, based on cultural differences in approach:

● The Britons and the Icelander felt that the ethnic minority people would be 'short-changed' if they did a lot of work and got no qualification; the Danes, who had been resisting pressure from their government to introduce assessment in their work, felt it put unfair pressure on the participants.

● The Belgian and the Britons wanted to emphasise vocational preparation, such as business computing; the Danes and the Icelander preferred language training and an emphasis on developing the whole person through arts and leisure activities which build confidence and integration into society generally; the Belgian wanted to make extensive use of multimedia; the Danes saw this as over-mechanical.

● Some problems were caused by differences in approaches to groupwork, again based on culture: the Danes and the Icelander experienced as 'hostility' and 'conflict' what the Britons and the Belgian saw as 'debate'; the Britons had come with a clear programme of what they wanted to do through the project; all the others felt they were being hustled into supporting someone else's project. The Britons found the others woolly and unprepared; and, when some aspects of their proposal were rejected, concluded that the others were being 'negative'.

2. 'As to the police cooperation in Europe in particular, this means that we have to consider the rather unconscious differences of basic assumptions, values, experiences, habits and traditions that guide the application of law. My thesis is that the so-called adaptation or homogenization of law is not useful because it meets cultural obstacles. Even if the European countries would stipulate identical police laws, the actual, every-day application of these laws by the police officers in their practical work would differ from one country to the other. The inertia of the Schengen process is a good example. In this as well as in other fields, police cooperation makes less progress than the international cooperation of criminals.'

Sources: Author's research, observational study; Koch, U. (1996) 'Intercultural human resource management for police cooperation in Europe; policing in Central and Eastern Europe: comparing firsthand knowledge with experience from the West', College of Police and Security Studies, Slovenia. Posted on the Internet: http://www.ncjrs.org/unojust/policing/inter103.htm.

Larkey (1996)[42] proposed that there are five dimensions of interaction in culturally diverse groups at work. Because they are dimensions, they naturally have positive as well as negative poles, but there is a clear implication that it is the negative poles that are most often associated with workforce diversity. The dimensions are inclusion/exclusion, convergence/divergence, varied ideation/conforming ideation, understanding/misunderstanding and positive/negative evaluation.

Inclusion/exclusion

Exclusion in the workplace is the practice of marginalising members of certain groups by limiting contact and restricting entry into certain job arenas. One possible explanation for exclusion practices is the concept of reflexivity – the more groups interact within their membership group and limit interaction with outsiders, the more the groups become differentiated from each other, which further affects patterns of interaction. Another explanation is that economic self-interest creates power/status groups which are then maintained through institutionalised practices and ideologies, the exclusion of already disadvantaged employees from mentoring and development and established, dual labour system pay scales. The resulting communication behaviours, according to Larkey, include simple inclusion or exclusion from conversations, by avoidance or starting them only when selected individuals are present or by non-verbally or linguistically excluding outsiders who are present; changes in the content of information, especially to include/exclude individuals from job-related information, either deliberately or by the assumption that they are not appropriate recipients; the use of privileged forms of discourse; and exclusion from the normative expectations.

Convergence/divergence

This is the Kincaid concept[43] already introduced in Chapter 4 (and further explained in Chapter 7) whereby convergent communication means adjusting ways of speaking (such as style, dialect, rules and primary language choice) to match those of a partner perceived as different or to show a wish for affiliation; divergence is adherence to one's own way in spite of perceived differences. It is open to individuals in diverse work groups to diverge deliberately in order to increase social distance. However, Larkey considers that the communication behaviours are difficult to predict because there are so many different influences on the patterns.

Varied ideation/conforming ideation

Conforming ideation means the suppression of divergent points of view and convergence towards normative views in decision making. Varied ideation is the reverse. The pressure for conformity is explained by the experimental findings of Sherif (1936)[44] and Asch (1965).[45] A climate of conforming ideation is likely to lead to suppression of the views of 'minorities'.

Understanding/misunderstanding

Understanding is the matching of expectations and meanings for people in interaction; misunderstanding is the mismatch. Misunderstandings can result from the way language is used, unexpected or misinterpreted communication patterns and linguistic cues, different values and belief systems and cognitive incongruities – culturally based schemas in both employees' and managers' minds predispose each to interpret the communication of others according to specific expectations. For instance, 'definitions' of a good leader or a good employee may vary substantially, leading to misinterpretations of the behaviour of individuals in those roles. Among the resulting communication practices are complaints of inappropriate responses or expectations.

Positive/negative evaluations

Negative evaluations can be explained by perceptions of ingroup/outgroup membership and associated responses to social identity, reinforced by stereotyping (the communication of even positive stereotype beliefs may elicit negative responses from those being categorised). The resulting behaviours include harassment, overt statements of negative stereotyping and stories with negative implications.

Figure 6.2 shows the relations between cultural diversity in groups and the five communication practices.

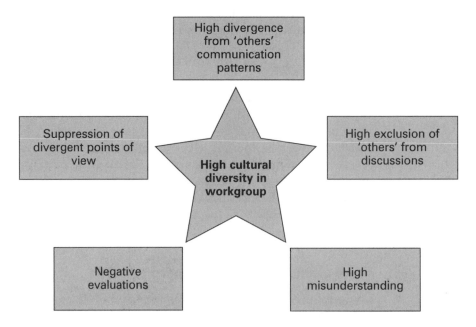

Figure 6.2 Sources of communication problems and conflict in diverse work groups

Source: based on Larkey, L.K. (1996) 'The development and validation of the workforce diversity questionnaire', *Management Communication Quarterly,* **9**(3): 296–337.

6.7 CONCLUSION

It is, perhaps, fortunate that it has been possible to make this chapter, which is concerned with sources of intercultural miscommunication, a comparatively short one. Nevertheless, the barriers are real in their consequence and seem often to have their greatest effect for not being perceived. When they are recognised, people often try to overcome them, and often succeed.

Cultural and subcultural differences in the ways in which people from different backgrounds communicate were shown to create these barriers to communication, while associated behaviours such as stereotyping, prejudice and harassment, ingroup/outgroup differentiation and discrimination increase them. At work, some of the results of these barriers are misunderstandings, often resulting in emotional distress and reduced performance, between individuals, whether in the roles of colleagues, professionals and their clients or suppliers and their customers. Other consequences are that heterogeneous work groups, while potentially more creative, take longer to perform and are more likely to break down and that trans-national negotiations and business operations can be fraught with conflict.

REFERENCES

1. Burke, K. (1966) *Language as Symbolic Action*, Berkeley, CA: University of California Press.
2. Larkey, L.K. (1996) 'The development and validation of the workforce diversity questionnaire', *Management Communication Quarterly*, 9(3): 296–337.
3. Linville, P.W., Fischer, G.W. and Yoon, C. (1996) 'Perceived covariation among the features of ingroup and outgroup members: the outgroup familiarity effect', *Journal of Personality and Social Psychology*, 70: 421–36.
4. Wiemann, J.M. and Giles, H. (1988) 'Interpersonal communication', in Hewstone, M., Stroebe, W., Codol, J.-P. and Stephenson, G.M. (eds) *Introduction to Psychology*, Oxford: Blackwell.
5. Hewstone, M. and Jaspars, J. (1984) 'Social dimensions of attributions', in Tajfel, H. (ed.) *The Social Dimension*, Vol. 2. Cambridge: Cambridge University Press.
6. Detweiler, R. (1975) 'On inferring the intentions of a person from another culture', *Journal of Personality*, 43: 591–611.
7. Hewstone, M. and Giles, H. (1986) 'Social groups and social stereotypes in intergroup communication: review and model of intergroup communication breakdown', in Gudykunst, W.B. (ed.) *Intergroup Communication*, London: Edward Arnold.
8. Ibid.
9. Power, J.G., Murphy, S.T. and Coover, G. (1996) 'Priming prejudice: how stereotypes and counter-stereotypes influence attribution of responsibility and credibility among ingroups and outgroups', *Human Communication Research*, 22: 323–48.
10. Bargh, J.A., Chen, M. and Burrows, L. (1996) 'Automaticity of social behavior: direct effects of trait construct and stereotype activation on action', *Journal of Personality and Social Psychology*, 71, 230–44.
11. Power, J.G., Murphy, S.T. and Coover, G. (1996) op. cit.

12. Hagendoorn, L. and Kleinpenning, G. (1991) 'The contribution of domain-specific stereotypes to ethnic social distance', *British Journal of Social Psychology*, **30**, 63–78.
13. Pettigrew, T.F. (1958) 'Personality and sociocultural factors in intergroup attitudes: a cross-national comparison', *Journal of Conflict Resolution*, **2**: 29–42.
14. Hagendoorn, L. and Kleinpenning, G. (1991) op. cit.
15. Glick, P. and Fiske, S.T. (1996) 'The ambivalent sexism inventory: differential hostile and benevolent sexism', *Journal of Personality and Social Psychology*, **70**: 491–512.
16. Eagly, A.H., Makhijani, M.G. and Klonsky, B.G. (1992) 'Gender and the evaluation of leaders: a meta-analysis', *Psychological Bulletin*, **3**(1): 3–22.
17. Inman, M.L. and Baron, R.S. (1996) 'Influence of prototypes on perceptions of prejudice', *Journal of Personality and Social Psychology*, **70**: 727–39.
18. Scollon, R. and Scollon, S.W. (1995) 'What is a discourse approach?', in Scollon, R. and Scollon, S.W., *Discourse*, Cambridge, MA: Blackwell, pp. 1–15.
19. Gallois, C. and Callan, V.J. (1986) 'Decoding emotional messages: influence of ethnicity, sex, message type and channel', *Journal of Personality and Social Psychology*, **51**(4): 755–62.
20. Tannen, D. (1990) *You Just Don't Understand: Women and Men in Communication*, New York: William Morrow.
21. Bernstein, B. (1971) *Class, Codes and Control*, St Albans: Paladin.
22. Ting-Toomey, S. (1988) 'Intercultural conflict styles: a face-negotiation theory', in Kim, Y.Y. and Gudykunst, W.B. (eds) *Theories in Intercultural Communication*, Newbury Park, CA: Sage.
23. Ambady, N., Koo, J., Lee, F. and Rosenthal, R. (1996) 'More than words: linguistic and nonlinguistic politeness in two cultures', *Journal of Personality and Social Psychology*, **70**: 996–1011.
24. Wierzbicka, A. (1991) *Cross-Cultural Pragmatics: The Semantics of Human Interaction*, Berlin: Mouton de Gruyter.
25. Yum, J.O. (1987) 'Asian perspectives on communication', in Kincaid, D. (ed.) *Communication Theory: Eastern and Western Perspectives*, New York: Academic Press.
26. Ibid.
27. Sarbaugh, L.E. (1988) 'A taxonomic approach to intercultural communication', in Kim, Y.Y. and Gudykunst, W.B. (eds) *Theories in Intercultural Communication*, Newbury Park, CA: Sage.
28. Kincaid, D.L. (1987) 'The convergence theory of communication, self-organization and cultural evolution', in Kincaid, D. (ed.) *Communication Theory: Eastern and Western Perspectives*, New York: Academic Press.
29. Trompenaars, F. (1993) *Riding the Waves of Culture*, London: Nicholas Brealey.
30. Coleman, L. and De Paulo, B. (1991) 'Uncovering the human spirit: moving beyond disability and "missed" communication', in Coupland, N., Giles, H. and Wiemann, J. (eds) *'Miscommunication' and Problematic Talk*, Newbury Park, CA: Sage.
31. McCroskey, J.C. (1977) 'Classroom consequences of communication apprehensions', *Communication Education*, **26**: 27–33.
32. Douglas, W. (1991) 'Expectations about initial interaction: an examination of the effects of global uncertainty', *Human Communication Research*, **17**: 355–84.
33. Allen, J.L. (1985) 'The relationship of communication anxiety, avoidance and competence of non-native English speakers in the US'. Paper presented at the 35th Annual Meeting of the International Communication Association, Honolulu, HI. ERIC Document Reproduction Service No. ED 261 448.
34. Brislin, R., Cushner, K., Cherrie, C. and Yong, M. (1986) *Intercultural Interactions*, Beverly Hills, CA: Sage.
35. Burgoon, J. and Hale, J. (1988) 'Nonverbal expectancy violations', *Communication Monographs*, **55**: 58–79.
36. Hoyle, R., Pinkley, R. and Insko, C. (1989) 'Perceptions of social behavior', *Personality and Social Pscyhology Bulletin*, **15**: 365–76.

37. McLeod, P.L. and Lobel, S.A. (1992) 'The effects of ethnic diversity on idea generation in small groups', *Academy of Management Best Papers Proceedings*, **92**: 227–36.
38. Watson, W.E., Kumar, K. and Michaelson, L.K. (1993) 'Cultural diversity's impact on interaction process and performance: comparing homogeneous and diverse task groups', *Academy of Management Journal*, **36**: 590–607.
39. O'Reilly, C.A. III, Caldwell, D.R. and Barnett, W.P. (1989) 'Work group demography, social integration and turnover', *Administrative Science Quarterly*, **34**: 21–37.
40. Grub, P.D. and Lin, J.H. (1991) *Foreign Direct Investment in China*, New York: Quorum Books, p. 194.
41. Mann, J. (1989) *Beijing Jeep: The Short, Unhappy Romance of American Business in China*, New York: Simon & Schuster, p. 180.
42. Larkey, L.K. (1996) op. cit.
43. Kincaid, D.L. (1987) op. cit.
44. Sherif, M. (1936) *The Psychology of Social Norms*, New York: Harper & Row.
45. Asch, S.E. (1965) 'Effects of group pressure upon the modification and distortion of judgments', in Proshansky, H. and Seidenberg, B. (eds) *Basic Studies in Social Psychology*, New York: Rinehart & Winston.

7 INTERCULTURAL COMMUNICATION THEORIES

Having established in Chapter 6 that differences between groups at work can create obstacles to communication in numerous ways, we can begin to look for approaches which can help in overcoming those obstacles. This chapter will discuss a range of theories which address intercultural communication, mainly in terms which are generalisable to communication between members of different subcultures.

The sequence in which these topics are taken is:

- how states, traits, styles and situations affect the nature and effectiveness of intercultural communication
- theories concerned with the cognitive and affective responses of individuals in intercultural situations: communication resourcefulness, episode representation, constructivist approaches which emphasise individuals' goal-seeking behaviours, expectations states and anxiety/uncertainty management
- theories concerned with intercultural interactive behaviour: identity negotiation, communication accommodation theory and Ellingsworth's intercultural adaptation theory
- network theories.

Several of these theories incorporate a large number of prior variables to enable hypotheses to be generated about circumstances in which effective communication will and will not take place.

Before beginning the account of the theories, however, it is important to draw attention to one notable omission and the reason for it: there are no theories in this chapter directly concerned with messages, rules, speech acts or other aspects of language use. This is despite the statement by Forgas (1976)[1] that 'Of all forms of cultural knowledge, none is more typical or important to understanding intercultural communication than knowing the rules and norms governing recurring everyday interactions or social episodes.' The reason is that, to date, such theories appear to have contributed only to our understanding of the barriers to intercultural understanding covered in the last chapter – a useful contribution, but an incomplete one. This may be accidental, or it may be the result of the criticism put forward by McGregor (1991)[2] of the assumption that discourse can be characterised in terms of units and rules. This assumption, according to McGregor, suggests a number of quite misleading models for the intercultural context. He states that the problem with these models is that they focus 'euphemistically' on *systems* in contact (or conflict), rather than on people and groups of people in contact (or conflict), each having different agendas and strategies for achieving them. The result, he claims, is that only two of many commonly held hypotheses about intercultural communication derived from discourse analysis – that there are regularities in discourse patterns and that these differ across cultures – withstand critical examination: the others are found to be 'seriously wanting'.

Implications of the theoretical approaches covered in this chapter for how to be skilled in intercultural communication at work and for sojourners are given in Chapters 8 and 9.

7.1   DEFINITIONS AND CONCEPTS

The subject of intercultural communication has been of interest to communication scholars since at least the 1960s. Samovar and Porter (1985)[3] define intercultural communication as occurring 'whenever a message producer is a member of one culture and a message receiver is a member of another'. For Collier and Thomas (1988)[4] intercultural communication is contact between persons who identify themselves as distinct from one another in cultural terms. These contrasting definitions – one treating membership of a culture as ascribable by others, the other as avowed by the person themself – point to a range of disagreements between scholars in the field. There is also an emerging tendency to treat intercultural communication as a special case of interpersonal communication and, therefore, focus on group similarities and differences in general rather than on cultural similarities and differences in particular. 'All communication is intercultural to an extent and the degree of interculturalness depends on the degree of heterogeneity between the experiential backgrounds of the individuals involved.'[5]

A preliminary question, asked by Rogers and Kincaid,[6] is 'How do people decide/define interactions as intergroup?' Their answer (see Figure 7.1) is that they use:

- *Interethnic comparisons:* If someone recognises another individual as coming from a different ethnic background, she or he may treat the interaction as an intergroup one. The same would probably apply if she or he recognised other salient background differences, such as religion or gender. However, the difference might not be salient, either because of the individual's personal attitudes or because of the purpose of the interaction – for example, perceived religious difference might have no bearing on a discussion of software capability.
- *Perceived ethnolinguistic vitality:* If the other individual(s) appear to speak a major foreign language as mother tongue, interactors are more likely to

perceive the interaction as intergroup than if their mother tongue is perceived as a minor one. The implication here is that whereas, for instance, interactions with French speakers would probably be perceived by English people as intergroup, those with speakers of Welsh, in contrast, might not be. Ethnolinguistic vitality is generally based on three factors: the status of a language-speaking group (its social prestige and economic power), demographic factors such as the number of mother-tongue speakers of the language and the amount of institutional support the language receives in the form of representation in and control over media, religious, educational and political contexts.

- *Perception of ingroup boundaries:* There is variation in where an interactor defines the boundaries of his or her own and the other interactor's ingroup. A French person might, on some occasions, perceive his or her ingroup as 'European' and thus not regard an encounter with a German as intergroup (as opposed to intragroup).

- *Status:* An interactor may disregard social group differences if she or he perceives the status of the other person's ingroup as high, identifies with other groups (for example for emotional reasons) or perceives an overlap in social categories ('You may be an English businesswoman, but, like me, you are a woman').

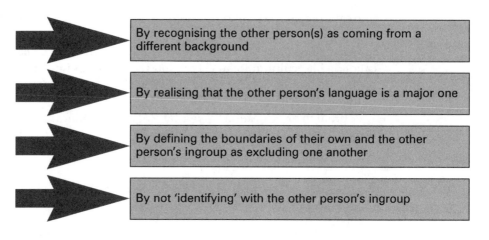

Figure 7.1 How people define an encounter as intergroup

Source: Based on Rogers and Kincaid (1981).

7.2   STATES, TRAITS, STYLES AND SITUATIONS

In addition to the characteristics identified in Chapter 4 as relevant to all communication, a number of *states* and *traits* have been positively associated with willingness to participate in, experiencing a low level of difficulty in and effectiveness in, intercultural communication. These states and traits include self-monitoring, cognitive complexity, tolerance for ambiguity, cultural relativism, attributional confidence, second-language competence and ethnolinguistic identity strength.

Self-monitoring means 'watching yourself' – being guarded and careful about the impression made on others, sensitive to the feedback from others and adapting behaviour accordingly. Being high in self-monitoring can be a state: for instance, most people are higher in self-monitoring in a job interview than normally; however, it is usually considered that it is also a trait: some people are generally low self-monitors – they are less sensitive to themselves and others and less concerned with making impressions.[7]

Cognitive complexity concerns the number and interrelatedness of the categories in an individual's cognitive constructs. It is generally regarded as consisting of two components: variety of elements (or aspects) and overlap between them. At the root of all accounts of the construct of complexity lies the idea of 'spreading activation': the idea that if one cognitive aspect is activated it will 'spill over' and activate other aspects, to the extent that the aspects overlap (that is, have in common some of their features). The greater the overlap, the greater the spill over of activation.

A study by Chen (1996)[8] investigated conversations between members of the same culture (US American) or between members of different cultures (US American–East Asian). Its findings provided some support to the notion that in both situations communicators with high cognitive complexity are better able than those with low complexity to empathise with another person and adapt their messages to the latter's needs. In a work context, high cognitive complexity is linked to skilled leadership.

Tolerance for ambiguity refers to an ability to accept indeterminacy and lack of clarity in situations. It enables people to take action or make decisions with incomplete or imperfect information; it is therefore a valuable attribute for organisational decision makers, who make most of their decisions under such conditions. People who are high in tolerance for ambiguity:

- react to new, different, or unpredictable situations with little discomfort or irritation
- manage feelings associated with ambiguity
- are observant until they determine how to approach a new person or situation
- are flexible
- use trial and error rather than the same formula until they find what works
- seek objective information rather than information which will support them emotionally.

Cultural relativism is the 'opposite' of ethnocentrism – it means accepting that one's own culture and its consequences, such as worldview and values, are one among many and that others are equally valid in their own terms.

Biculturalism refers to maintaining both independent and interdependent self-construals (which were explained in Chapter 5). Such a person may be able to modify his or her behaviour appropriately and successfully when moving from one culture to another.

Attributional confidence refers to willingness to draw inferences about another's behaviour, especially about whether it is 'caused' by the situation or by the other person's dispositions. Attributional confidence can be either a state or a trait: people generally have higher attributional confidence with culturally similar others but individuals vary in their levels of the factor. Increases in attributional confidence reduce anxiety in encounters.

Second-language competence increases an individual's ability to cope with uncertainty when meeting people from the culture in which that language is spoken. It may also increase confidence more generally.

Ethnolinguistic identity strength. According to Beebe and Giles (1984)[9] ethnolinguistic identity strength influences second-language competence and intergroup attitudes/stereotypes. Levels of ethnolinguistic identity strength are associated with ease of sojourner adaptation (see Chapter 9). Ethnolinguistic vitality, as described earlier, is a factor in determining whether or not an individual has high or low ethnolinguistic identity strength, but other individual-level factors also affect it.

Communicator style

As Chapter 4 showed, communicator style is an individual's usual coding behaviour, including their verbal pattern (ranging from word choice and statement structure to accustomed use of a particular dialect or language) and non-verbal behaviour (ranging from voice quality, volume, and articulation through kinesic and proxemic mode to contact rituals). When and how people adapt their communicator style during intercultural encounters is the subject of communication accommodation theory and Ellingsworth's adaptation theory[10] which will be covered more fully later in this chapter.

Situations

The situation is, of course, the essence of the intercultural encounter, which *consists* of the situation in which two or more people from different backgrounds meet and try to communicate. However, within the overall similarity of intercultural situations, there still remain situational differences which affect communication and behaviour. These include the extent of shared networks, the stage of relationship and the level of exposure to another culture.

Shared networks are related to attributional confidence and so to lowering anxiety even when the communicators are culturally dissimilar. Shared networks also directly reduce anxiety about interacting with members of outgroups.[11] That is, if, for instance, an interactor finds that she or he has previously worked with a colleague of someone from a different background with whom she or he has to do business she or he will experience less anxiety over the encounter.

Levels of anxiety and the significance of cultural norms vary at different *stages of a relationship*. Initial interactions are particular sources of anxiety and so are a focus of attention in some intercultural communication theories such as anxiety/uncertainty management theory. Most interpersonal relations (such as acquaintanceship or work role relations) are guided by cultural norms – that is, the parties follow the 'rules' of their own culture. However, friendships are less influenced by normative expectations; similarly, cultural stereotypes are broken down in later stages of relationships, so the level of cultural similarity between two people comes to have a lesser impact.

The more intense the exposure to another culture the greater its effect will be. People exposed to the radical situation of immersion in a new culture generally experience alienation and other psychological disturbances, known as culture shock. One effect of these is to reduce their tolerance for ambiguity (see Chapter 9 for a fuller discussion of culture shock).

With regard to the communication episode itself, research has shown that in an intercultural setting people rely on topics evoked by the situation to a greater degree than in an intracultural setting. These might include the weather, the location, the office furniture and so on. As they converse more on such topics (either through direct questions or information volunteered about themself), they learn more about each other and expand their shared knowledge. The value of such gains in knowledge is one among several reasons for undertaking 'social conversation' at the start of an intercultural work meeting.

Joint effects of traits, styles and situations

Chapter 4 showed that aspects of the situation and the individual combine to influence communication behaviour. This also applies in intercultural settings. One variable which falls into this category is regarded by many intercultural communication theorists as a crucial dimension, that is, the level of *interpersonal or intergroup salience*.[12] In an interpersonally salient encounter, unique features of the participants, such as their personal mannerisms, attributed intentions and so on are attended to; in an intergroup-salient encounter, on the other hand, interpersonal features receive less attention in favour of intergroup ones, such as social class membership or gender, with their attendant stereotypical features. One important implication of the distinction is that if participants in intergroup contacts see the encounter mainly in interpersonal terms, it is unlikely that any resulting attitude change, such as coming to see a particular Scot as generous, will generalise to the outgroup as a whole – this will happen only when intergroup differences are salient.[13]

As Figure 7.2 shows, intercultural encounters can potentially fall into any of the four quadrants produced by the intersection of the dimensions of interpersonal salience and intergroup salience.

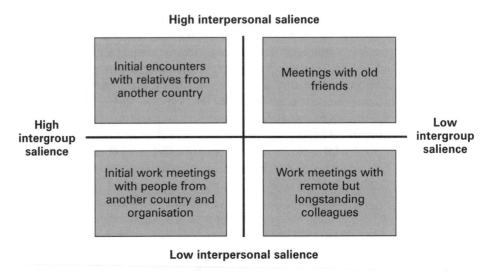

Figure 7.2   Salience of different encounters

> Consideration of states, traits, styles and situations in intercultural encounters reveals a large number of variables which may be linked to how difficult people find such interactions, whether they adapt their communication behaviour and how effectively they communicate within them. Among the most significant of these variables are the level of a person's self-monitoring, tolerance for ambiguity and the degree to which they see encounters as salient in interpersonal or in intergroup terms.

The next four sections look at theories which concern the effects of individual-level variables on intercultural communication.

7.3   COMMUNICATION RESOURCEFULNESS

Communication resourcefulness can be defined as the knowledge and ability to apply cognitive, affective (emotional) and behavioural resources appropriately, effectively and creatively in diverse interactive situations.[14] Like other forms of resourcefulness, it is related to the degree to which novel situations are approached as learning experiences.[15]

Cognitively whether someone views an intercultural encounter as an identity challenge opportunity or as an anxiety-ridden event has a profound influence on how they approach interaction with strangers. If one person conveys a sense of identity security it tends to evoke the sense of security in the other.

The *emotions* of an intercultural encounter are either ego focused or other focused – or more often some combination of the two. Culture plays a major role concerning the emotional meanings and reactions attached to encounters. For individualists, ego-focused emotions are most common: they are concerned with 'justice', revolve around conflicting claims between the self and others and can be resolved by invoking impartial rules, principles or standards. Conversely, other-focused emotions mainly experienced by collectivists revolve around issues of relationships and they can be approached through the activities of caring. In both cases, demands are made on the individual's affective resourcefulness to resolve emotional issues. Both cultural and gender variations influence an individual's self-concept and morality construction.

To deal with the diverse identity needs of different persons in different situations, intercultural interactors need the *behavioural* resourcefulness to develop a wide range of verbal and non-verbal repertoires. Being responsive to strangers and open to learn from them are other aspects of behavioural resourcefulness.

This theory has been criticised for its exclusive focus on the coordination between interlocutor identities. It is also only incidentally a model of intercultural communication, being primarily a generic communication model, although its originator, Stella Ting-Toomey, has herself emphasised its applicability to intercultural encounters, and, of course, only a model which can comprehend such encounters can lay claim to being generic.

7.4 EPISODE REPRESENTATION THEORY

One theory of intercultural communication places cognition at its centre. Forgas (1983)[16] argued that the critical issue in intercultural communication is that partners do not have matching and shared cognitive representations about 'social episodes' – that is, they think of them in different terms or images. Social episodes are 'typical recurring interaction units within a specified culture or subculture, which constitute "natural units" in the stream of behaviour, and about which members of a given culture or subculture have a shared, implicit cognitive representation'. Forgas proposed that cognitive representations of interaction episodes differ in terms of several major features including:

- the degree of intimacy, involvement and friendliness that the interaction entails

- self-confidence
- the positive or negative evaluation felt about each encounter
- the importance of task orientation versus relationship orientation
- anxiety
- cultural values such as communality/individualism and achievement/relationship.

Forgas' theory asserts that the greater the differences between communicators' representations, the harder it is for them to understand one another. Cultural and subcultural differences are one major source of such variations but other variables are also present in intercultural encounters and some of these, such as common technical expertise, favour intercultural understanding; in addition, by creating shared representations, interactors can overcome the barriers. Therefore, the effectiveness of an intercultural communication is directly related to the degree to which *shared* episode representations can be created between the people taking part. 'For interaction to succeed, participants must essentially agree in their social situation definition' (Leodolter and Leodolter, 1976, p. 327).[17]

Only one piece of research appears to have directly tested an aspect of Forgas' intercultural communication theory: this was a comparative study of more successful and cohesive and less successful and cohesive student teams. The more cohesive group had more complex episode representations (three dimensions: friendliness, intimacy and activity) than the more fragmented group (two dimensions: evaluation and friendliness). However, other research findings lend support to particular elements of the theory. For example, a comparative study of students and housewives showed that for housewives, episodes were mainly thought of in terms of intimacy and friendliness, self-confidence and positive or negative evaluation. Results are not given for students, but it is implied that they were different (Forgas, 1976).[18] A comparative study of faculty, research students and other staff showed that decreasing status was associated with an increasing role for anxiety in episode perceptions; involvement was a criterion used mainly by faculty; and students were least evaluative but placed the greatest importance on task orientation.

Another finding is that the level of social skill a person manifests is significantly related to his or her episode representations. High socially skilled individuals see episodes more in terms of the evaluation and intensity dimensions, while low socially skilled persons primarily rely on the anxiety dimension.

BOX 7.1

CULTURAL DIFFERENCES IN PERCEPTIONS
OF SOCIAL EPISODES

Leodolter and Leodolter (1976) researched perceptions of social episodes among Chinese and Australian subjects. They found that Chinese subjects perceived episodes more in terms of communal values while Australians placed implicit emphasis on competitiveness and individualism in their representations. Age, sex and personality predicted how social episodes were seen in both cultures, but the pattern of such links were culture specific. They also found that, by comparison with the Australian respondents, the Chinese respondents perceived social episodes more in power distance terms and in terms of usefulness rather than pleasantness. These findings help confirm the hypothesis that cultural differences play an important role in how people think about social episodes.

Source: Leodolter, R. and Leodolter, M. (1976) 'Sociolinguistic considerations on psychosocial socialisation', in McCormack, W. and Wurm, S. (eds) *Language and Man*, The Hague: Mouton, p. 327.

7.5 A CONSTRUCTIVIST APPROACH TO INTERCULTURAL COMMUNICATION

The constructivist approach argues that what is needed is not a theory of intercultural communication, but, at base, a coherent theory of communication whose focus of convenience encompasses the impact of historically emergent forms of group life on the various forms and functions of everyday communication[19] – that is, that intercultural communication is part of communication more generally and that there should be a theory of communication broad enough to capture it.

Following Heider (1958)[20] much current social science research uses a metaphor of person-as-naive-scientist attempting to make sense of his or her world; the constructivist approach, on the other hand, argues that in the interpersonal domain inferences and behaviour are aimed less at predicting or even understanding the self and others than at accomplishing personal or situation-induced goals. People in communication can be viewed as 'toolmakers'. When people respond to each other they typically are less concerned with understanding why others behave as they do (to allow prediction) than in understanding the immediate implications of what others do and say for their ability to achieve their own goal(s). Often the goal is simply to respond appropriately and keep the conversation on track.

In routine situations, communication is dominated by conventional goals and plans 'given' to interactors. For instance, at the end of routine work meetings, people discuss and decide the date of the next meeting without thinking about why or how. It is in such situations that the influence of culture and cultural differences on communication is most evident. Thus, in a high-power distance culture, the forward engagements of the most senior person present will be the deciding factor on the date of the next meeting; in a more egalitarian culture, a gap will be sought in everyone's diary. (This makes convening staff meetings in UK universities a very difficult task!) However, because these conventions are so implicit, people entering into intercultural communication often are unaware of the differences distorting their communication. The implications, then, are that the influence of culture on communication may be strongest, as well as least recognised, not in initial interactions but in later stages of work relationships. This conflicts with most other views of the influence of the stage of relationship.

Cultural rules, conventions and codes serve as resources in actors' pursuit of goals. In routine contexts they may be all that is needed, but even then they should be seen as used rather than followed. More demanding situations, like those involved in intercultural communication, require speakers to use person-centred messages, which recognise other people's perspectives, take others' feelings into consideration and acknowledge them when appropriate, explain the reasons for requests or orders in terms of the other's perspective and seek to obtain information about the other's attitudes, beliefs and values by open questioning. Person-centred messages are more complex than non-person-centred messages and they demand more cognitive complexity of the communicator; in constructivist terms, they 'reflect an integration of process-orientated communication competencies'. They have been shown to be more effective in gaining others' compliance.

Constructivism offers a partial explanation for individuals' motivations within intercultural interactions, although, being goal based, it is a highly cognitive one, which leaves 'needs theories' out of account. It also provides little explanation for why people enter such encounters in the first place or how their motives in entering interaction relate to their goals within them.

7.6	EXPECTATIONS THEORIES

The core idea of *expectation states theory* is the influence of expectations, which were introduced in Chapter 5, on behaviour in interactions. People 'choose among various communication strategies on the basis of predictions about how the person receiving the message will respond'.[21] Three types of information are used in making predictions: cultural, social (roles and group memberships) and personal. (North Americans use more personal than social information; Japanese vice versa.) We saw in Chapter 5 that the expectations people have about how others will respond to what they say strongly influence their communicative behaviour. Expectations themselves are a function of knowledge, beliefs/attitudes, stereotypes, self-conceptions, roles, prior interaction and status characteristics.[22] Figure 7.3 shows the relationships among these variables, some of which require further explanation in an intercultural context, although none of the ideas behind them will be new to the reader.

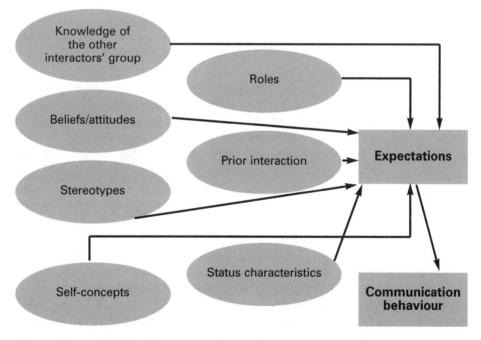

Figure 7.3 Expectation states theory: factors influencing expectations and behaviour in intercultural encounters

The *knowledge* referred to in the model is mainly knowledge of the group to which people who are being met for the first time are thought to belong. When someone meets 'strangers' without any previous knowledge of the strangers' group, she or he predicts how they will behave by watching and listening to what they do and say. These observations are, of course, selective, and the impressions gained are influenced by the individual's own cultural framework. Those observed and interpreted behaviours are then treated as 'typical' and inferences are drawn from the impressions.

The need to make inferences is greater when dealing with people who are unfamiliar; this can lead to extreme predictions and expectations. The more previous knowledge people have about the other group, the less they are inclined to over-interpret small samples of behaviour, such as are observed on first meeting. Thus, prior knowledge affects expectations and so behaviour. If this knowledge is accurate, the effect is likely to be beneficial. If, however, they have false beliefs or the 'knowledge' consists of simplified and inaccurate stereotypes, the resulting expectations can distort behaviour with adverse effects on communication. Manusov and Hegde (1993)[23] found from videotaped conversations between 46 US students and confederates from India that there were significant differences in the Americans' communication behaviours depending on their pre-existing knowledge or beliefs about India.

People employ one or more of three strategies for gaining information about another group. One is a passive strategy such as watching TV (which is the strategy most likely to lead to over-reliance on stereotypes), or observing directly but without interacting. The second is an active strategy of asking others from their own group about the other (sub)culture, and the third is an interactive strategy of meeting members of the other (sub)culture, asking them questions, self-disclosing and trying to detect deceptions. This last sounds on the surface like the best information-gathering strategy, and it can be. However, to gain accurate information, contacts with other (sub)culture members must be made under conditions that do not increase prejudice.

Self-concepts and roles link communication to personal identity. The self-concept has three components: personal, social and human. In a particular situation a person may choose (consciously or not) to define himself or herself as a unique person (a personal definition) or as a member of a group (a social definition). When communicative behaviour is based mostly on personal identities, interpersonal communication takes place; when on social or role identities, intergroup communication occurs. When people relate to one another as individuals, their expectations about the other person's behaviour will be less influenced by their beliefs about and attitudes to that person's culture than when they define the situation as intergroup.

Status is widely used in all cultures as input to the expectations individuals form about others with whom they will interact. In general, a wider range of behaviour is expected and tolerated from a high-status person than others. Status is assessed from external factors (for example race, ethnicity, sex, attractiveness, education, occupation) and expressive cues (for example dialect, eye contact, speech styles, skin colour) or indicative cues (such as someone's statement that they grew up in Mexico). Although these factors are used in all cultures to assess status, they are not used in identical ways. In Japan, professional position is so important that people need to know it in order to know how to address one another correctly and an introductory exchange of business cards is de rigueur. In the USA, in contrast, questions directed at ascertaining someone's professional status can be rude, and physical attractiveness is often a key status factor for both sexes, even at work.

BOX 7.2

DIFFERENCES IN PATIENTS' EXPECTATIONS OF MALE AND FEMALE DOCTORS

A two-part study looked at patients' expectations about male and female physicians' instructions to patients and found that patients expected female physicians to use less aggressive strategies in their verbal communication. The second part of the study suggested that male physicians might increase patient compliance by using more non-aggressive communication.

Source: Burgoon, J.K., Birk, T.S. and Hall, J.R. (1991) 'Compliance and satisfaction with physician–patient communication: an expectancy theory interpretation of gender differences', *Human Communication Research*, **18** (2): 177–208.

In communication with different others, intergroup attitudes, stereotypes and prejudice affect expectations and so do emotional responses triggered during the interaction. These emotional responses are particularly likely to be aroused if expectations are violated, so there is a feedback loop operating. Expectations may be based on knowledge of the different other's group but where such knowledge is missing or inadequate, the expectations of the person's own (sub)culture are likely to prevail – and are, of course, highly vulnerable to violation. This issue has attracted the attention of Judith Burgoon, who has generated *expectancy violation theory* to explain it. The theory is particularly concerned with non-verbal behaviour, although it may well be generalisable to verbal behaviour.

When another person's behaviour is in accordance with a perceiver's expectations, awareness of it is low and the perceiver is likely to judge the 'message' or their interactor themselves according to their 'usual' methods – for instance in line with their view of the communicator and attributions for their behaviour. However, when the other person's behaviour violates expectations – which Burgoon and Le Poire call 'expectancies' – the perceiver is distracted by it, attends to it and is aroused by it.[24] This effect can change evaluations, most commonly by strengthening them: a positively evaluated message will be evaluated more positively and so will the person with whom it originates; and vice versa for a negatively evaluated one. How the violation and the person committing it are evaluated is affected also by the degree to which the other person provides rewards for the receiver such as enhancing their self-esteem. Expectations are more likely to be violated, and the cost/reward trade-off is less likely to be favourable, during interactions with people from different backgrounds to someone's own,[25] so expectancy violation theory implies a higher rate of negative evaluations of partners in intercultural encounters compared with intracultural encounters.

Expectations theories make predictions about others' responses the main intervening variable between behaviour in intercultural encounters and a range of independent variables. In doing so, they inevitably leave out the possibly equally powerful variables put forward in other theories – goals, for instance, or episode representations.

| 7.7 | ANXIETY/UNCERTAINTY MANAGEMENT THEORY (AUM) |

The emotions, as well as the cognitions, of intercultural encounters, are the concern of anxiety/uncertainty management theory (AUM). Like others in the field of intercultural communication, AUM emerges from a blending of a number of more general theories. Its origins lie in the hypotheses of Berger and Calabrese[26] that individuals attempt to reduce uncertainty in initial interactions with strangers, especially when the strangers will be encountered in future, can provide rewards and act in a deviant fashion in the terms of the individual's own culture or subculture. Berger put forward seven axioms and 21 theorems about the relations among uncertainty and the amount of communication, non-verbal affiliative expressiveness (the degree to which people show warmth to one another by body language such as smiling, eye contact or touching), information seeking, intimacy level of communication, reciprocity, similarity and liking. (In general each of these relations is inverse – thus, the greater the amount of communication and the higher the similarity, the lower the uncertainty – but information seeking is higher in the presence of high uncertainty.)

Berger also suggested that people adopt one of three general strategies for reducing uncertainty: a passive strategy – doing nothing in the hope that as time passes things will become clearer; an active strategy – finding out as much as possible from outside sources; and an interactive strategy – seeking out opportunities to interact with people about whom uncertainty exists and using those occasions to obtain as much information as possible. (As readers will realise, this element of Berger's theory also surfaces in expectation states theory.)

Thus from the beginning AUM was particularly focused on initial interactions and the early stages of acquaintanceship. This makes it particularly valuable for understanding those aspects of communicating across barriers at work which involve meeting strangers, such as introductory interviews between professionals and clients or international negotiations. The core of AUM theory is the proposition that individuals experience uncertainty and anxiety in initial interactions with strangers and are motivated to reduce both through communication. The theory purports to show what promotes or inhibits effective communication as well as describe what takes place.[27]

Effective communication in AUM theory means that participants attach similar meanings to the messages transmitted – this is a matter of degree. Misunderstandings occur when receivers attach different meanings to messages from those attached by the speakers. Research has shown that when black and white people interact in public meetings, the interactors 'believe that the meanings they are assigning to all (these) matters are the same, and, therefore, that the (negative) motives they are ascribing to each other – based on this assumption – are justified'.[28] However, they often in fact assign different meanings, so that the negative motives they ascribe may not be justified. Effective intercultural communication also requires that individuals from one culture can make attributions that are isomorphic with individuals from the target culture – that they are the same that a native of that culture would make under the same conditions.

The core elements of AUM theory are the concepts of the stranger, uncertainty, anxiety, initial encounters and mindfulness, which has been explained earlier in this chapter:

- *Strangers* are people who are different because they are members of other groups. When strangers act in a way that is deviant in terms of an individual's own culture, the individual experiences uncertainty and, especially when those strangers will be encountered in future or can provide rewards, anxiety.
- *Uncertainty* is of two distinct types: not being able to predict what strangers' attitudes, feelings, beliefs, values and behaviour will be; and not being able to explain why they behave in the way they do. When uncertainty is too high for comfort, people will either try to reduce it by gaining information or end the interaction. When uncertainty is too low for comfort, people may be too bored to act effectively.
- *Anxiety* refers to the feeling of being uneasy, tense, worried or apprehensive about what might happen – this is an affective (emotional) response, whereas uncertainty is a cognitive (thought process) one. Anxiety is usually based on people's negative expectations, such as that their self-concepts will be damaged or that they will be negatively evaluated. When anxiety is too high for comfort, people either avoid encounters or their attention is distracted from the communication. Then they rely on information like stereotypes to predict other people's behaviour, and therefore misinterpret it. When anxiety is too low, people may not care what happens in the interaction, not pay attention and miss important cues.

Thus, for communication effectiveness, optimal levels of uncertainty and anxiety are intermediate between too high and too low. However, in interactions with strangers, both are normally too high for effective communication. In these cases, achieving effective intercultural communication is a matter of reducing uncertainty by information seeking and controlling anxiety through tension-reducing behaviour. In other words, attempts to adapt to the ambiguity of new situations involve a cyclical pattern of tension-reducing and information-seeking behaviours. Uncertainty reduction is a social cognitive process, anxiety control is largely an affective process.

● *Initial encounters.* It was noted earlier that culture forms an 'implicit' theory (about the 'rules' being followed and the 'game' being played) that individuals use to guide their behaviour and interpret others' behaviour. Much within cultural behaviour is habitual and therefore not 'conscious' (Triandis, 1980).[29] The matter is different, however, in the initial stages of intercultural communication. When interacting with a stranger, individuals become aware that the stranger does not share their own implicit theory about the rules or the game. Therefore they become more conscious of that implicit theory. The result is that interactions between strangers take place at high levels of behavioural awareness.

BOX 7.3

A POSSIBLE EXAMPLE OF AUM IN OPERATION

The UK representative for a charity undertaking an urban renewal project in the north of the Czech Republic was meeting the mayor of the town concerned for the first time. It was, in fact, the representative's first visit to Central Europe, and first contact with anyone from a former Communist country. In such circumstances, AUM theory would predict that the uncertainty and anxiety she felt would both be very high. She would be unable to predict how the mayor would behave or how he would respond to anything she said, or what his attitudes would be. She would also tend to rely on any stereotypes she might have about officials of towns in former Communist countries. Since avoidance was not possible, she would try to gain information as quickly as possible, and to lower the tension by, for instance, smiling and making eye contact and seeking occasions for sharing humour. The representative was in fact observed doing these things, although it is hard to say whether the cyclical pattern that would be predicted by AUM theory in fact occurred.

Source: Observed by the author.

AUM axioms

In a recent formulation of the theory, only anxiety and uncertainty act directly on communication effectiveness (although uncertainty is partly mediated through behavioural intentions).[30] However, both these are influenced in turn by a large number of other variables, grouped under the headings of self-concept, motivation, cognitive capacity, social categorisation, situational processes, connections to strangers and mindfulness. These have been used to generate an 'eclectic' 47 linking axioms – as, for instance, Axiom 11: 'An increase in our sense of security in our personal and social identities when we interact with strangers will produce a decrease in our anxiety and an increase in our confidence in predicting their behaviour', or Axiom 27: 'An increase in the informality of the situation in which we are communicating with strangers will produce a decrease in our anxiety and an increase in our confidence in predicting their behaviour.'

Cultural differences between interacting strangers enter the AUM theory as variables affecting those which directly influence uncertainty and anxiety levels. The theory uses the four core Hofstede variables of power distance, uncertainty avoidance, achievement/relationship orientation and individualism–collectivism to capture cultural differences. The addition of the cultural variables leads to another 47 axioms. Some are fairly obvious, such as Axiom 48: 'An increase in individualism will be associated with an increase in the degree to which personal identities influence behaviour when interacting with strangers', or Axiom 92: ' An increase in uncertainty avoidance will be associated with an increase in anxiety about interacting with strangers.' Others are less obvious, such as Axiom 65: 'An increase in collectivism will be associated with an increase in the ability to adapt communication when interacting with strangers', or Axiom 75: 'An increase in power distance will be associated with a decrease in the cooperative structure of the goals on which work occurs with strangers.'

Figure 7.4 shows the elements of AUM theory. Box 7.4 summarises the assumptions and axioms behind the 1988 theory. The assumptions and axioms listed in Box 7.4 are important in terms of intercultural communication skill improvement; they will be discussed in this light in Chapter 8.

BOX 7.4

A SUMMARY OF AUM THEORY (1988)

Assumptions:

1. At least one participant in an interpersonal encounter is a stranger *vis-à-vis* the group being approached.

---

2. Strangers' initial experiences with a new ingroup are experienced as a series of crises; strangers are not sure how to behave – that is they experience uncertainty – and they feel a lack of security – that is anxiety.
3. Uncertainty and anxiety are independent dimensions of intergroup communication.
4. Strangers' behaviour takes place at high levels of awareness.
5. Both intergroup and interpersonal factors influence all communication.
6. Strangers over-estimate the influence of group membership in explaining members of the group's behaviour.

Axioms:

Factors producing a decrease in strangers' uncertainty about the behaviour of members of the other group and a decrease in the anxiety they experience when interacting with members of other groups:

1. an increase in strangers' positive expectations
2. an increase in similarity between strangers' ingroups and the other groups
3. an increase in the networks strangers share with members of other groups
4. an increase in the interpersonal salience of relationships formed with members of other groups
5. an increase in strangers' second-language competence
6. an increase in strangers' self-monitoring
7. an increase in strangers' cognitive complexity
8. an increase in strangers' tolerance for ambiguity
9. an increase in strangers' attributional confidence leads to an increase in intergroup adaptation and effectiveness
10. a decrease in anxiety leads to an increase in intergroup adaptation and effectiveness
11. an increase in collectivism will produce a decrease in uncertainty in outgroup communication relative to ingroup communication
12. an increase in uncertainty avoidance will produce an increase in anxiety and a decrease in intergroup adaptation and effectiveness
13. an increase in the strength of ethnolinguistic identities leads to an increase in confidence but also an increase in anxiety, although only when members of the outgroup are perceived as typical and ethnic status is activated.

Source: Gudykunst, W.B. (1988) 'Uncertainty and anxiety', in Kim, Y.Y. and Gudykunst, W.B. (eds) *Theories in Intercultural Communication*, Newbury Park, CA: Sage, pp. 123–56.

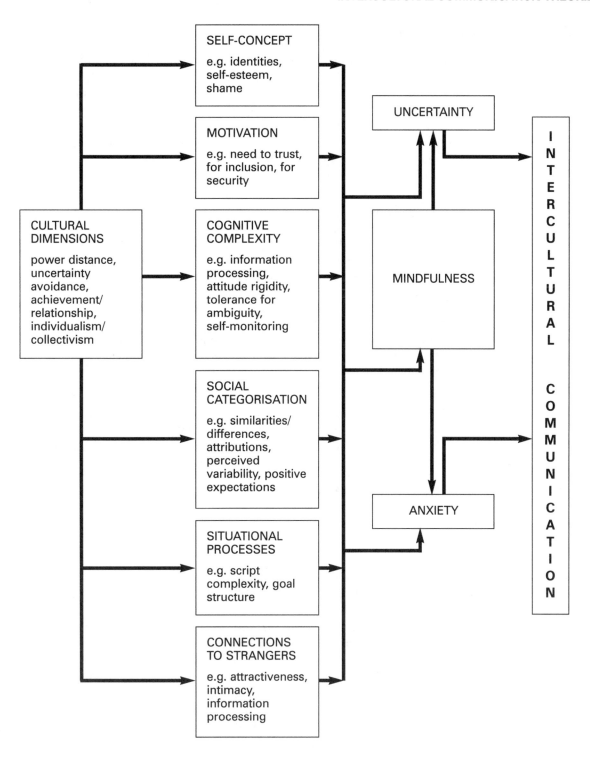

Figure 7.4   The elements of anxiety/uncertainty management theory

Research to test AUM axioms

AUM has attracted a considerable effort of research and testing – although it is so complex a theory that many areas remain untested. Support for the existence of uncertainty reduction as part of the dynamic of interaction with strangers has come from research which showed it applies to both low-context communication and high-context communication cultures,[31] friendship relations across cultures[32] ethnic differences in interactions between blacks and whites in the USA[33] and interethnic communication generally in the USA.[34]

One study of Japanese and Caucasian subjects in Hawaii[35] found that, as AUM would predict, ethnicity, stage of relationship, shared networks and ethnolinguistic identity strength influenced how much interactors self-disclosed, how many questions they asked, whether their body language expressed affiliation, whether they saw one another as similar and how confident they were in making attributions about the causes of a stranger's behaviour, using both high- and low-context measures.

Anxiety/uncertainty management theory is a complex set of assumptions and axioms linking a large number of factors to intercultural communication effectiveness through the intervening variables of anxiety and uncertainty. These are assumed to be too high for effectiveness in encounters with people who are perceived as 'different' in salient ways. Therefore, by changing the factors which affect anxiety and uncertainty in such encounters so as to reduce them, people can increase their intercultural communication effectiveness.

The theory is static and takes the individual interactor as the unit of analysis. The next three theories to be considered, cultural identity negotiation theory, communication accommodation theory and Ellingsworth's adaptation theory, are processual, include dynamic elements and take both the individual interactor and the interaction itself as the units of analysis.

7.8 CULTURAL IDENTITY NEGOTIATION THEORY

Tajfel (1978)[36] formulated a social identity theory which assumes that individuals seek positive social identities in intergroup encounters. This is a key theory from which identity negotiation theory is derived. Social identity is 'that part of an individual's self-concept which derives from his (or her) knowledge of his (or her) membership in a social group (or groups) together with the value and emotional significance attached to that membership' (p. 63). That part of the self-concept not accounted for by social identity (SI) is personal identity (PI).

The concepts of cultural identity theory have been introduced in Chapter 5. Cultural identity negotiation theory concerns the way in which cultural identities are created and negotiated with others. Throughout an intercultural encounter, people negotiate meanings, such as that this particular meeting is a social gathering, not a business meeting, concepts of time, rules, activities and so on, which differ from one (sub)culture to another. Only if they succeed in reaching implicit agreement on these kinds of points will the encounter be useful and successful. If it is successful, the culturally different identities of the participants will be positively enhanced.[37]

Intercultural communication is seen as contact between persons who identify themselves as distinct from one another in cultural terms. Identity negotiation theorists believe that the extent to which communication is intercultural is in large part decided by the interpretations of the persons present in a given encounter. Cultural identities are always a potential frame in which interactors may interpret communication. Whereas interpersonal communication refers to contact in which the distinctiveness or uniqueness of a person is emphasised, especially their person-specific qualities, intercultural comunication refers to contact in which a person's cultural identity is emphasised. Figure 7.5 shows the elements of the model.

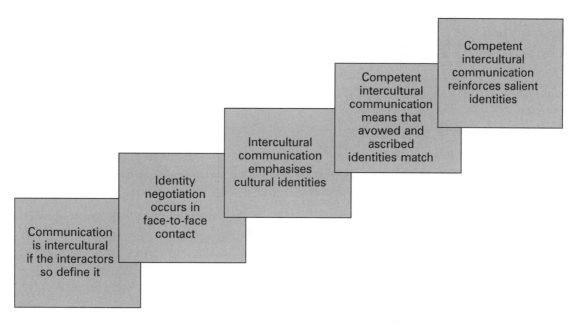

Figure 7.5 Key tenets of intercultural identity negotiation theory

The cultural identity negotiation approach acknowledges that all individuals have many potential (sub)cultural identities. It can be used to identify similarities and differences in behaviours, interpretations and norms. It also treats an individual's culture, not as static and unaffected by intercultural interactions, but as influenced by the dynamic of their encounters.

7.9	COMMUNICATION ACCOMMODATION THEORY (CAT)

This theory is a development of speech accommodation theory, introduced in Chapter 5. It, too, deals with moves of speech convergence and divergence and maintenance, that is moves to increase, decrease or maintain communicative distance, but covers non-verbal communication as well as speech. It postulates that communication involves a constant movement towards and away from others. CAT is concerned with the communication moves speakers make in interactions relative to the social and psychological contexts that are operating and relative to each other's communication characteristics.[38] Figure 7.6 gives an example of the basic CAT processes.

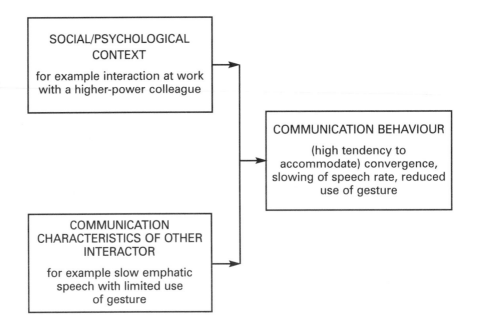

Figure 7.6   An example of the basic processes of communication accommodation theory

Source: based on Gallois, C., Franklyn-Stokes, A., Giles, H. and Coupland, N. (1988) Communication accommodation in intercultural encounters in Kim, Y.Y. and Gudykunst, W.B. (eds) *Theories in Intercultural Communication,* Newbury Park, CA: Sage.

Recent work on CAT has incorporated a number of additional concepts in the theory, which expand its ability to capture intercultural encounters.[39] These include the impact of the situation, the interactors' initial orientation, the social/psychological states of speakers, addressee focus and the evaluation that interlocutors take away from the encounter. Figure 7.7 shows the accommodation elements of an intercultural encounter.

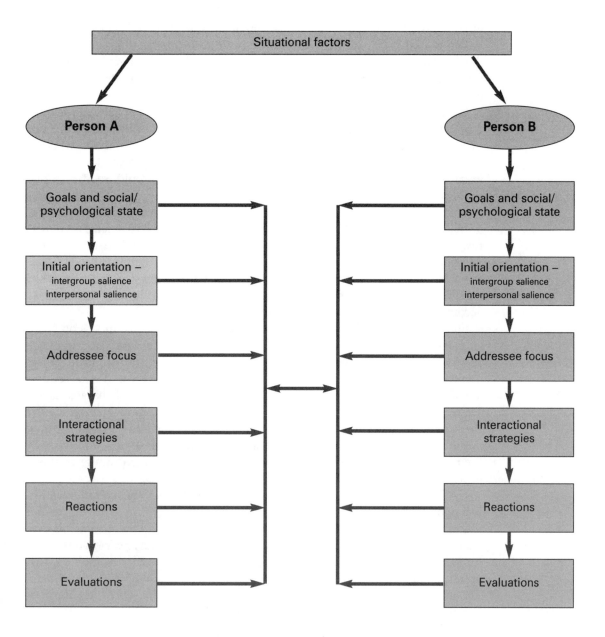

Figure 7.7   Intercultural encounters in communication accommodation theory

Situational factors. In status-marked situations, such as work meetings (which are competitive) or interviews (which are formal), norms are strict and salient and behaviour deviations of members of outgroups are negatively evaluated. Threat, which may come from the topic, or outside, also increases sensitivity to group memberships. In high-status-marked, high-threat situations, therefore, people are more likely to define the situation as intercultural (or intergroup), behave strictly in accordance with group norms, and interpret the behaviour of others in intergroup terms. In low-status-marked, low-threat situations, on the other hand, like a party with friends from outside work, people are less likely to define the situation as intercultural (or intergroup), behave strictly in accordance with group norms, and interpret the behaviour of others in intergroup terms. This is so even if the other people are from a different ethnic, gender or other group.

Within an interaction the *speakers' initial social/psychological states* include their motivations at the start of the encounter. These are affected by whether or not the participants regard the encounter as significant in intergroup terms; whether or not they think there is much potential for conflict in the encounter; and how great is their long-term motivation to accommodate to (build good relations with) people from the group of the encounter partner.

So if, for instance, a French Euro-MP is meeting a British Euro-MP to discuss a subject on which their two countries have differed in the past, such as progress towards a single European currency, she or he is likely to 'reason' that the meeting is significant in intergroup terms, that there is potential for conflict in the encounter and that the long-term importance of having good relations with the British is high; these considerations would motivate him or her towards accommodating behaviour – communication convergence.

Since Tajfel (1978),[40] interpersonal or intergroup salience is understood as a crucial dimension: in an interpersonal-salient encounter, unique features of the participants are attended to and vice versa. When people first meet, group membership is always potentially salient (important) because they have high awareness of differences in their values, codes and background characteristics. There are, however, individual differences in the way group members view their own situation, which influence their *initial orientation*. In particular, if they are relatively dependent on their ingroup, and if their sense of solidarity with their group is high, they will be more likely to define the encounter in intergroup terms.

CAT distinguishes the initial orientations, and thus the communication behaviour, of members of dominant and subordinate groups. This makes the theory particularly relevant to situations in organisations where some people, such as white males, who are 'dominant' through numbers, near-monopoly of top echelon positions or because of supremacy within the society, interact with others, such as women or members of ethnic minorities, who are subordinate. The interaction of dependence and solidarity produces the sets of initial orientations for members of subordinate groups shown in Figure 7.8.

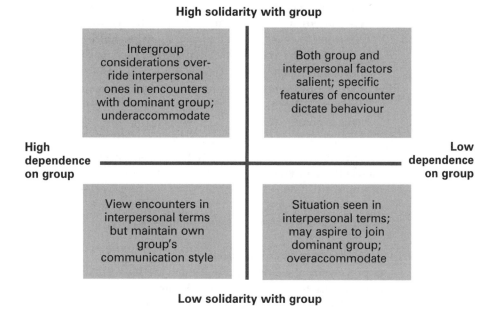

High solidarity with group

Intergroup considerations over-ride interpersonal ones in encounters with dominant group; underaccommodate	Both group and interpersonal factors salient; specific features of encounter dictate behaviour
View encounters in interpersonal terms but maintain own group's communication style	Situation seen in interpersonal terms; may aspire to join dominant group; overaccommodate

High dependence on group — **Low dependence on group**

Low solidarity with group

Figure 7.8   Initial orientations of subordinate group members

For dominant groups the corresponding initial orientations are as follows:

- High dependence, high solidarity: as for subordinates; they may be high ethnocentrics and so have stricter and less tolerant norms for 'minority' group speech (behaviour).
- High dependence, low solidarity: as for subordinates – react to outgroup members as individuals.
- Low dependence, high solidarity: as for subordinates, except that the absence of threat and intergroup alliance orientate them to maintaining their distinctive dominant group style.
- Low dependence, low solidarity: as for subordinates, orientate interpersonally.

One additional factor influences the degree to which group membership is salient in the initial orientation. This is relative deprivation, or the extent to which people feel that they as individuals are disadvantaged (egoistic deprivation) or their group is disadvantaged (fraternal deprivation). High relative deprivation increases the salience of group membership. Orientations may change during the course of the interaction.

The way in which one speaker pays attention to the needs or behaviours of another is their *addressee focus*. They may focus on the skills and competence of the partner, on their conversational needs, or on role relations in the interaction. Which of these they focus on will affect not whether they converge or diverge but how they do so. For instance:

- An addressee focus on the skills and competence of the partner, or stereo-types about it, will lead among other things to slower speech, more use of questions to check understanding and the choice of familiar topics.
- A focus on the partner's conversational needs will lead to sharing of topic choice and development as well as shared conversational register.
- A focus on the role relations in the interaction will lead to the use of inter-ruptions, honorifics and the like to keep the other person in role or allow them to change role.

As the encounter proceeds, initial orientation and situational factors become modified by interactors' reactions to one another and the process. Some factors promote attuning – that is, moves to converge; others promote countertuning, or moves to diverge.

Factors which promote attuning include:

- the desire for social approval
- perceived 'costs' of attuning which are lower than the perceived rewards
- the desire to meet the perceived communication needs of recipients
- the desire for a mutual self-presentation
- the desire for equal-status role relations.

These factors might apply for example in the case of an interviewee who is an internal candidate for a competitive promotion.

Factors which *promote countertuning* include:

- the desire to communicate a self- or group image which contrasts that of the other person
- the desire to dissociate personally from the other party or their definition of the situation
- the desire to signal differences in experience/knowledge/intellectual capa-bility/communicator style
- the desire to achieve or maintain a high-status role.

These factors might apply in the case of an interviewer of an internal candidate for a competitive promotion.

In encounters which are salient in interpersonal terms, attuning will be to the behaviours of the partner which are seen as personal; in encounters which are salient in intergroup terms, it will be to the behaviours of the partner which are seen as 'group'. The degree of attuning or countertuning used depends on the speaker's repertoires, his or her norms about maximal and minimal degress of attuning, the relative weight of individual, social and contextual factors and the extent to which the receiver's actual communication matches the speaker's expectations.

Reactions to the other speaker's behaviour affect future orientations for the rest of the interaction or future encounters. Reactions include labelling the behaviour as accommodating or not and attributions about why the behaviour occurred. *Evaluations* may be positive or negative, and the other individual may be seen as typical or atypical of his or her group.

CAT, it is claimed, has both an objective and a subjective focus: an objective focus on predicting communication outcomes such as competence or adaptation and a subjective focus on understanding the interactive process of communication. The essential vocabulary used in the other objective theories tends to reduce interaction to a state of individual achievement, but CAT predicts the motivated communication processes of convergence and divergence.

It is also claimed for it that it meets an essential requirement of intercultural communication theories: that they must at least take into account both intergroup and interpersonal factors and give equal importance to each of them. CAT is complex, but, in the author's view, highly practical: a careful study of what is involved in attuning, for instance, yields clear ideas on how to improve intercultural communication.

7.10   ELLINGSWORTH'S ADAPTATION THEORY

Ellingsworth has proposed a theory which, like CAT, is concerned with the conditions under which individuals interacting interculturally make more or less effort to adapt; in particular it concerns how responsibility for adapting is allocated between two participants. However, unlike in CAT, Ellingsworth regards adaptation as a burden which the participants will assume equally or differentially according to various factors, most of which are related to their relative power in the interaction (or their relative dependence on it for desired outcomes).[41] Adaptations are the changes that individuals make in their affective and cognitive identity and in their behaviour as they interact in a new cultural environment. The extent and nature of the adaptation depends on their motivation.

The theory asserts that when people have a purpose in an interaction, as opposed to merely engaging in a casual conversation (that is, when they have a motive for the communication to be successful), they are more likely to adapt their communicator style. If the purpose is shared, if, for instance, both are trying to 'get to yes' in a negotiation, both participants will adapt; if only one participant has a purpose which will be served by adaptation, then only that person will adapt. Purposes arise from needs for cooperation, participation or agreement in such areas as commerce, manufacturing, defence, education, science, technology, politics, agriculture, medicine, the arts, and scholarly research.

When adaptive behaviour occurs but is ineffectual the other participant will respond by invoking culture-based differences in belief. (Ellingsworth's concept of culture-based beliefs is derived from the work of Rokeach (1973)[42] that beliefs have a cultural base growing out of nurture and conditioning.) So, if a European in negotiation with someone from China suddenly starts 'stone-walling', in a clumsy attempt to adopt what she or he regards as a Chinese negotiating style, the Chinese person might ascribe the behaviour to Western deviousness, if that is part of his or her culture-based belief about Europeans. Invocation of culture-based beliefs will disrupt adaptation by the other participant (in this case by the European negotiator); in its absence, other impediments such as status differences or the effects of problems with the purpose of the interaction are more likely to be overcome. Another example which can illustrate the disruptive power of invoking culture-based beliefs is the case referred to by the investment banker in Box 4.9: invoking the Western beliefs that any problem is soluble and any difficulty only a challenge to be met might well alienate the Turkish officials with their different cultural beliefs.

Adaptation theory concerns first-time encounters, which are less predictable than later ones, and whose outcomes determine in part whether contact will be renewed. In first-time encounters, the theory states, people will probe one another's beliefs, especially those related to the task or purpose of the meeting, in order to identify areas of commonality or disagreement.

Ellingsworth put forward a number of propositions which express his intercultural communication theory:

- An increase in the amount of functional adaptive behaviour will speed up progress towards task completion.
- When adaptive behaviour occurs and proves to be non-functional, the other participant will respond by invoking culture-based differences in belief, which are likely to be disruptive.
- A shift from inequity toward parity in adaptive behaviour will accelerate progress toward task completion.
- When participants share a purpose or goal, they will move towards equity in adaptation, regardless of status differences or territorial advantage.
- When interaction reveals that only one person will benefit from task completion, that person will accelerate adaptive behaviour.
- When one person has a territorial advantage, it will have limited effects on adaptation unless invoked; then the other person will display an increase in adaptation.
- When the initiator has more status or power than the other participant, he or she will initially use that advantage as a substitute for adaptive behaviour and may continue to do so throughout the interaction.
- The more adaptation displayed by a participant, the more change will occur in their attitudes to and perceptions of the other and the culture they 'represent'. (This is because behaviour affects attitudes at least as much as attitudes affect behaviour.)
- The more adaptation displayed by a participant, the more change that will occur in that person's perceptions of themselves and the culture she or he represents.

BOX 7.5

ON AVOIDING INVOKING CULTURE-BASED BELIEFS

1. 'My job involves negotiating for London Electricity with big customers in Wales. Sometimes the people I deal with are quite upset at the idea of getting their power from a London-based company – it offends their nationalist sympathies. They never mention it, but it affects their overall attitudes.'

   Question: 'Would you ever bring the issue out into the open?'

   Answer: 'Never. It would be and look unprofessional. I keep cool and concentrate on the task in hand.'

2. 'In my work as a computer trainer, I often encounter people who, because of my skin colour and because I'm in my twenties, doubt my authority and expertise – sometimes they ask to "speak to the boss" – I am the boss.'

   Question: 'Do you bring it out into the open and try to resolve it?'

   Answer: 'No. It would take all my time, first; second, it's not my job to educate them. Instead, I let the fact that I do know what I'm talking about impress them.'

Source: Interviews with a consultant and a computer trainer, author's research.

Thus, Ellingsworth's theory focuses on process, which centres on adaptation through intercultural communication. It also focuses on outcomes, of which an important one is reinforcement or modification of prior cultural stereotypes – learning which will become a part of the cognitive resources for future encounters. Whether such learning proves to be functional or non-functional depends on the extent to which the next such stranger conforms to the stereotype. Experience does not necessarily increase competence in intercultural communication, although it has the potential for doing so. Also important is self-examination. Adaptation involves confronting not only the other, but also the self. In this process, the personal cultural stereotype is reinforced or modified, and this learning also becomes part of the background of the individual's future intercultural encounters.

In view of the large amount of attention given to power in Western accounts of behaviour, especially work-related behaviour, it was to be expected that a power-based account of intercultural communication would emerge. It has the strengths and weaknesses of most power-based accounts – power is part of the story, but is over-emphasised and power is objectified instead of treated as subjectively perceived. This last is a particular weakness as an account of inter-cultural encounters, where cultural differences will lead participants to perceive power bases differently. However, Ellingsworth's account of the outcomes of adaptation is convincing and useful.

7.11	NETWORK THEORY

In contrast to the theories discussed so far in this chapter, which take the individual or the dyad as their primary unit of analysis, network theory is concerned with the way that individuals are embedded in networks of social relations that are both created and maintained by the exchange of information; it takes these networks as its unit of analysis.

Communication networks are differentiated into local areas of relatively greater density of connections inside their boundaries rather than outside. Because the members of such locally bounded networks tend to share the same information over time (compared to those outside it), communication results in a convergence among members towards a state of greater uniformity. This basic theorem of communication is considered a prerequisite for cultural evolution (Kincaid, 1987).[43]

Network theory takes as its premise the idea that human behaviour can be explained by analysing the relationships between and among individuals, as opposed to the characteristics of the individuals themselves. It focuses on positions and social relations, rather than beliefs or norms, and on a series of inter-connecting relations, not static, bounded groups. Individual members of a social system are seen as actively choosing, creating and manipulating their networks and in turn being influenced by such networks.

Network theory has developed in part as 'a critique of the normative view of social action' (Anderson and Carlos, 1976, p. 38)[44] but networks are not completely free of normative forces: we often keep network relations because of societal norms such as *uye-ri* (long-term faithfulness) in Korea or *mezia* (reciprocity) in Tunisia.

The main sources of network analysis are role theory, exchange theory, and action theory. More recently, convergence theory from the field of communication provides an alternative theoretical foundation. The *roles* in network theory are positional roles within a network as a whole rather than socially prescribed as in role theory. According to *exchange theory*, introduced in Chapter 5, the exchange relation, not each individual behaviour or single transaction, is the unit of analysis. The concept of reciprocity is central to exchange theory; the origins of a network are exchange and reciprocity. In turn, interpersonal networks connect individuals in a series of communicative, economic, manipulative and other types of strands.[45] *Action theory* holds that social life is like a game involving continuous 'scheming, struggling and making decisions'.[46] Network theory postulates a network of relations into which a person is born and which she or he constructs, tries to manipulate and through which she or he is manipulated. *Convergence theory*, as already described, holds that communication is a process in which two or more people share information and converge towards greater mutual understanding. The emphasis is placed on the differences between individuals rather than on individuals per se. Communication is the process by which such differencess are reduced by feedback.[47]

Network analysis theorems

Network theory assumes that the variance between cultural groups is greater than the variance within them. On the basis of this assumption it puts forward the following theorems:

- Intercultural network patterns will be more likely to be radial than interlocking compared to intracultural networks. (A radial personal network is one in which an individual interacts with a set of dyadic partners who do not interact with each other.)
- Intercultural networks are less dense than intracultural networks. (The density of a network is the ratio of actual direct links among members of a network to the total possible number of such links.)
- Intercultural networks are less likely to be multiplex than intracultural networks. (Multiplexity is the degree to which multiple message contents flow through a dyadic link between two individuals and hence the degree to which those two individuals have multiple role relationships. Multiplex relationships require more time to establish than uniplex relations, even within a single culture; usually intercultural relations are initiated as uniplex links. People will usually try to meet relational needs within their own cultural group, because it is easier.)
- Intercultural network ties are more likely to be weak ties than strong ties.
- The roles of liaison and bridge will be more prevalent and more important for network connectedness in intercultural networks than in intracultural networks. (A liaison is an individual who links two or more cliques in a system, but is not a member of any clique. A bridge is an individual who links two or more cliques in a system from his or her position as a member of one of the cliques.) Aldrich (1982)[48] suggests that intermediary or broker roles are a natural result of actors' attempts to minimise transaction costs. Connecting two culturally different groups would cost more than connecting similar cultural groups and therefore connecting roles such as liaisons and bridges will perform a much more important function in intercultural network structures than in intracultural network structures.

BOX 7.6

NETWORKING IN CHINA

It is advisable for foreigners in China to employ a go-between, a facilitator or guide. A go-between may be from various levels in an organisation, depending on the level of those involved in the situation. The role of a go-between, or intermediary, includes:

1. Ensuring that nobody loses face if the request, invitation or proposal is refused.
2. Arranging introductions.
3. Providing appropriate interpretations of sensitive situations.
4. Carrying messages and information that cannot be transmitted in a face-to-face setting.

Even Chinese people often take facilitators with them when they pay official business calls, or use a contact person in working the network of relationships. The presence of a trusted intermediary will make an official meeting more relaxed.

Source: An interview with a Chinese banker working in London, author's research.

● Transivity will play a much smaller role in creating intercultural networks than intracultural networks. (Transivity operates when my friend's friends are my friends and my friend's enemies are my enemies: an extension of loyalties which implies normative sanctions. In intercultural situations, people share fewer cultural values and relations are uniplex and weak, so strong normative sanctions and emotional obligations are not present. Also these relations have lower visibility.)

Research findings based on network theory include some which treat networks as the independent variables; some which treat them as dependent variables.

As independent variables networks have been used in explaining social behaviour in diverse cultural settings: for example, the impact on contraceptive use in 24 Korean villages, plus Nuer political organisation, conflict among industrial workers in Zambia, personal networks in Malta, interethnic attitudes,[49] ethnic tolerance[50] and the diffusion of innovation in India, Bangladesh, the Philippines, Mexico, Korea, China, Taiwan and Nigeria. This contradicted the notion that adoption is solely an individual decision as opposed to a process located in networks and involving group initiation, group pressure and sometimes even group decision making.

In research treating networks as *dependent variables*, Yum (1987)[51] proposed that differences in network patterns result from general cultural differences. In a comparison of Eastern Asian and Western communication patterns, Yum suggested that as a result of Eastern Asians' emphasis on social relationship, their societies have developed more closely knit networks with stronger boundaries between ingroups and outgroups.

Networks at work

Network theory has been advocated as particularly relevant to understanding communication in organisations, as in *Weick's organisational enactment theory*,[52] which contends that in organisations, people's behaviours are interlocked so one person's behaviour is contingent on another's. Organisations are something that people are always accomplishing through interaction. Organising happens at the level of the double interact – an act followed by a response followed by an adjustment. The executive asks the secretary to type a letter, the secretary asks for clarification and the executive explains. A network is a large system of interaction patterns and organisations are nothing more or less than a series of networks (structure and process go hand in hand).

Networks are social structures created by communication among individuals and groups. As people communicate with others, contacts and links are made, and these channels become instrumental in all forms of social functioning, in organisations and in society at large.

Network theory provides an account of the structures and functions of an organisation. It addresses the means by which social reality is constructed within the organisation, illustrating that networks are not only instrumental but also cultural. In addition, networks are the channels through which influence and power are exerted, not only by management in a formal way but also informally among organisational members.

The main advantage claimed for network analysis is that it is context based and automatically includes some aspect of the social environment. It provides an important alternative to dominant communication theories that focus on the individual and on psychological effects rather than on groups and social effects:

> The field of intercultural communication is more sensitive to both process and relationship issues than other communication fields... intercultural communication networks are made up of interpersonal relations, but the analysis and related theory goes beyond the dyadic level to the level of triads, cliques and subgroups and intact social systems. Under network theory, acculturation can be treated as network formation, maintenance and expansion.[53]

| 7.12 | INTERCULTURAL COMMUNICATION EFFECTIVENESS |

Clearly any work on communication needs a framework which allows an examination of whether or not any particular piece of communication or episode has been effective. Communication studies should aim to explain what works and what does not work in various situations; behaviour that is typical may not be effective. The discussion of how to achieve skilled intercultural communication (see Chapter 8) will rely on an understanding of what counts as effective interpersonal communication.

The framework offered by the communications literature is mainly in terms of *communication competence*. Competence, unlike skill, carries the implication of being adequate to preserve a relationship within a desired definition but not necessarily to do more than that. Communication is an activity in which perfection is probably unattainable.

Communication theorists' understanding of communication competence not surprisingly varies according to their understanding of communication itself. Thus for *linguistic pragmatists*, communication competence includes a capacity for using language, but it is important to avoid assuming that all situations make identical demands on language, so competence must be evaluated in terms of some particular social circumstance. Communication requires both linguistic knowledge (for instance participants must attach similar meanings to the messages transmitted, which is a matter of degree, or the effective use of implicatures and violations) and non-linguistic knowledge. A fairly minimal requirement for competence is that the individual is being cooperative in Grice's (1975) sense of cooperation (see Section 4.3) – that is, makes his or her contributions, as and when needed, according to the purposes of the interaction.[54]

Communication competence can be measured either *situationally* or *dispositionally*. That is, it can be seen as particular to a given encounter or as a property of an individual. Cupach and Spitzberg (1983)[55] showed that these are separate variables. They also found that situational measures of competence predicted 'feel-good' reactions after an encounter better than dispositional measures.

To proponents of the *communication theory of identity*, interpersonal communication refers to contact in which the distinctiveness or uniqueness of a person is emphasised, especially their person-specific qualities. Competence is defined as the successful enactment of identity and interpersonal competence is seen as mutually appropriate and effective conduct in particular contexts – that is, communication which validates the identities of the participants. Communication is considered to be thoroughly saturated with issues of identity.[56]

Cognitive communication theorists define competence in terms of the mental processes required to achieve effective and efficient communication. A review of literature by Duran and Spitzberg (1995)[57] indicated that there are four discrete mental processes essential to cognitive communication competence:

1. anticipation of contextual variables that may potentially influence communication choices
2. perception of the consequences of communication choices

3. immediate reflection
4. general reflection upon the choices made.

However, Duran and Spitzberg's own research yielded by factor analysis a slightly different set of five mental processes as being linked to communication competence. These were:

1. *planning* (thinking before a conversation what people might be going to talk about, mentally practising what to say, during a conversation thinking about what topic to discuss next)
2. *modelling* (watching who is talking to whom when first entering a new situation, and trying to 'size up' the event; generally, studying people and being aware of people's interests)
3. *presence* (during a conversation being aware of when a topic is 'going nowhere', of when it is time to change the topic, paying attention to how others are reacting to what is said)
4. *reflecting* (after a conversation thinking about what you said, what you could have said, your performance and how to improve it and about what the other person thought of you)
5. *consequence* (thinking generally about how others might interpret what you say, how what you say may affect others and about the consequences of your communication).

Another view on how communication competence is achieved, which also focuses on individual mental processes, is brought to bear with a concept discussed earlier, that of *mindfulness*.

Writers on *communication strategy*, on the other hand, argue that it is grounded in rational efficiency, rather than just effectiveness, that 'Given a desired end, one is to choose that action which most effectively, and at least cost, attains the end, *ceteris paribus*.'[58] In other words, both inputs and outputs must be considered in understanding strategy use. Effectiveness is an 'output' consideration; it focuses on the results of strategy used and not on what effort or other resources it takes to employ a strategy. Efficiency, by contrast, focuses on both inputs and outputs; it considers the effort and resources that are used to achieve a given result.

There is an alternative view of communication competence that it consists, not in the attributes or performance of an individual, but in a given *relationship*.[59] According to this view, an individual may be socially skilled, but only particular communication relationships will be competent. This is because even the most skilled individual will certainly experience some failures of communication, and even the most unskilled will certainly experience some successes when they find people with whom they are congruent. This assertion receives some support from the research just cited which found that situational factors prevailed over individuals' dispositions. However, while this point is accepted, the term 'effectiveness' can still be used for analysis of communication relationships, 'competence' and 'skill' for the performance of each of the participating individuals.

Understandings of *intercultural communication competence and effectiveness* also vary, naturally, according to the theoretical perspective of the scholar. Thus, for supporters of communication resourcefulness theory, it is defined as effective identity negotiation; for Forgas, as noted in Section 7.4, as related to the degree to which shared episode representations can be created between the people taking part. Within *cultural identity negotiation theory* (see Section 7.8) intercultural communication competence refers to contact in which an interactor's ascriptions of another's cultural identities appropriately and effectively match those that the other person ascribes for themself – that is, where there is a good match between an individual's own beliefs about his or her own cultural identity and those of the people with whom she or he interacts. Communication can be more or less interpersonal and simultaneously more or less intercultural. Intercultural competence is the demonstrated ability to negotiate mutual meanings, rules and positive outcomes. This means that in order to create intercultural competence:

- Discursive meanings must be shared; for instance, an encounter must be mutually understood as a social gathering. People must negotiate relational meanings, concepts of time, activities and so on, throughout the gathering.
- Rules (norms) must be agreed and adhered to; rules are communication prescriptions that specify when and how actions are to be performed for communicative purposes such as politeness, offering proper evidence and how to be properly assertive. Rules vary in scope and salience – so Mexican-Americans hold similar rules for appropriate conduct whether talking with another Mexican-American or an Anglo, but black and Anglo-North Americans use different rules for intra- and intercultural conversations with acquaintances.
- Communication is functional to the extent that positive outcomes are experienced, regardless of whether or not the 'intended' goal was accomplished. Positive outcomes include self-concept reinforcement, affirmation of cultural identity, desire to maintain the relationship and goal accomplishment.[60]

The *facework* approach to intercultural communication competence is a developmental model: there are four stages in reaching it:

1. Unconscious incompetence implies fundamental ignorance on the cognitive and behavioural levels.
2. Conscious incompetence means that behaviour is understood but not synchronised, so, for example, an interactor may be aware that there are too many awkward pauses and silences but not be able to correct this.
3. Conscious competence or the 'grave, mindful, acute' stage means cognitively understanding communication differences, the patterns and variations of different cultures, and working on behavioural facework competence.
4. Unconscious competence is the final, fully effective stage: there is an analogy with driving a car or swimming; at a certain point, it becomes spontaneous and natural. Spontaneity is part of practising facework: adjustment and adaptation occur without conscious effort. The individual becomes 'grave, mindless, acute'. [61]

An atheoretic treatment of intercultural communication competence is provided through the dimensions of the *intercultural behavioural assessment indices*. The seven dimensions are: display of respect, interaction posture, orientation to knowledge, empathy, relational role behaviour, interaction management and tolerance of ambiguity. A study which examined 149 international students (mainly from the Far East, Asia, Middle East, Africa, and Europe) at a large midwestern university in the spring of 1986 revealed significant positive correlations between the linear combination of the dimensions of intercultural behavioural assessment indices and the linear combination of personal attributes, communication skills, psychological adaptation, and cultural awareness, as shown in Figure 7.9.[62] The study used both self-ratings and third-person ratings of the variables.

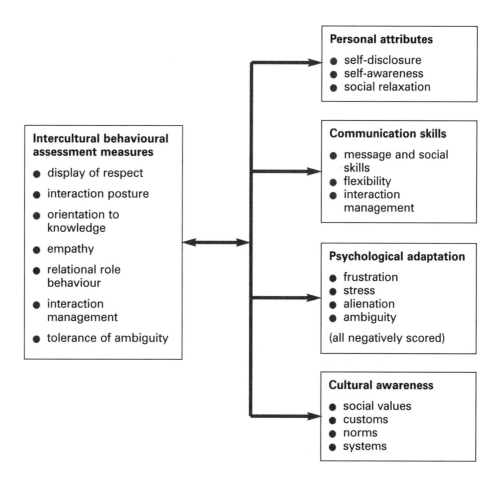

Figure 7.9   Intercultural communication competence measures

Source: based on Chen, G.M. (1988) 'Relationships of the dimensions of intercultural communication competence'. Paper presented at the 79th Annual Meeting of the Eastern Communication Association, Baltimore, MD.

Finally, there are, of course, cultural variations in what counts as communication competence and effectiveness, whether intercultural or not. Using low-context communication in a high-context culture counts as incompetent – too many words, too little use of silence; the reverse is also true – in a low-context culture high-context communication may be seen as inarticulate and hesitant. Indirectness is ineffective where directness is the rule and vice versa; an emphasis on relationship data is seen as 'soft' where content data are usually predominant (and, as the case of women illustrates, conveys a lack of authority and assertiveness); an emphasis on content data in a (sub)cultural milieu that prefers an emphasis on relationship data may be seen as an incompetent lack of subtlety and refinement.

7.13	CONCLUSION

The main psychological constructs, individual-level processes and interactive processes incorporated in the theories described in this chapter are set out in Figure 7.10.

It would be wrong to create the impression that these intercultural communication theories are non-problematic. Jehn and Weldon (1992),[63] for example, criticised the ethnocentric assumption that Western theories can be applied in any culture. Although their criticism focused on conflict management theories in particular, there is every reason to believe that it applies equally to the intercultural communication theories discussed in this chapter. They wrote:

> The problem centers on the way that conflict management behavior is conceptualized, and the way it is measured in studies of cross-cultural differences. In each case, a theory of conflict management behavior developed in the West is adopted. These theories focus on dimensions that differentiate strategies of conflict management... These (Western-originated) dimensions of conflict management behavior are then linked to dimensions of cultural variability.

These shortcomings, they argue, suggest that research based on these theories provides little useful information. To produce useful information, Western-based measures must be discarded, and an inductive search for *etic* dimensions (outsiders' descriptions of what people do and why they do it, developed using the tool kits of linguistics and anthropology) and *emic* constructs (what people themselves tell you about what they do and why they do it) must be conducted. Discovering true etics allows meaningful comparisons across cultures on a set of common dimensions, and the discovery of emics contributes to a full understanding of each culture.

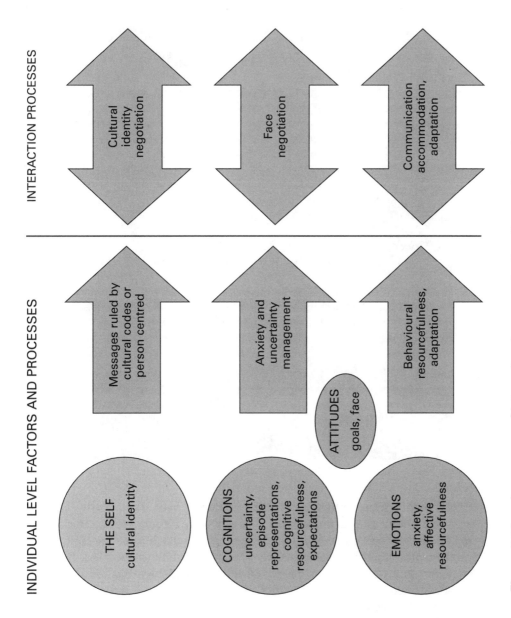

Figure 7.10 A summary of intercultural communication theory elements

BOX 7.7

GOING BEYOND COMMUNICATION –
NEGOTIATING THE SPECIFIC–DIFFUSE
CULTURAL DIVIDE

'Doing business with a culture more diffuse than our own feels very time consuming. Some nations refuse to do business in a mental subdivision called "commerce" or "work" which is kept apart from the rest of life. In diffuse cultures, everything is connected to everything. People from diffuse cultures do not accept that you can use logic to force someone to agree with you. In other words, specificity and diffuseness are about strategies for getting to know other people. For people with a diffuse orientation, it is the relationship between two people that increases or reduces output, not the other way round.'

'Reconciling specific–diffuse cultures
This is perhaps the area in which balance is most crucial, from both a personal and a corporate point of view. The specific extreme can lead to disruption, the diffuse extreme to a lack of perspective: a collision between them results in paralysis. It is the interplay of the two which is the most fruitful, recognising that privacy is necessary, but that complete separation of private life leads to alienation and superficiality; that business is business, but stable and deep relationships mean strong affiliations.'

Source: Trompenaars, F. (1993) *Riding the Waves of Culture*, London: Nicholas Brealey, p. 89.

Other difficulties with these theories are that they are partial and yet each theory stands alone as if its proponents believe it to be a complete account. Little effort has so far been made to integrate them and, with limited exceptions, insights from other theorists' and researchers' work are not incorporated. However, this defect is probably characteristic of a young and vigorous subject area in the social sciences and while it reduces the immediate value of the work, it may well be productive for the further development of the field.

In addition, there are some obvious gaps in the variables covered. With the exception of communication accommodation theory (CAT), theories of motivation – why some people and not others are motivated to achieve effective intercultural communication – are weak or lacking; in one case, motivational analysis is reduced to the proposition that 'length of sojourn' is the key underlying variable (see Chapter 9). Little attempt has been made so far to draw on motivational theories from psychology and social psychology.

More surprisingly, perhaps, there is a lack of recognition of cultural difference in some of the theories. With the partial exception of anxiety/uncertainty management theory, they are silent on such questions as whether collectivists are more or less likely than individualists, those high in power distance than those low in power distance, universalists than particularists to perceive interactions in terms of cultural identity, to have their expectations violated, to adapt and so on. (It is true that one of the reported pieces of research on CAT relates part of the theory to cultural variability, but the theory per se does not incorporate this.) Equally, only cultural identity theory presents cultural difference as in any way a dependent variable, affected by the process of intercultural interaction. There is clearly potential for including cultural differences in the various models by a fairly simple logic, but the work has not yet been done, or is not yet published.

Despite these criticisms, collectively the intercultural communication theories and research presented in this chapter have carried our understanding of the phenomena a considerable way forward and many of them have the benefit of being readily applied in practice, as the following two chapters aim to show.

REFERENCES

1. Forgas, J. P. (1976) 'The perception of social episodes: categorical and dimensional representations in two different social milieus', *Journal of Personality and Social Psychology*, **33**: 199–209.
2. McGregor, W. (1991) 'Discourse analysis and intercultural communication', *Australian Journal of Communication*, **18**(1): 13–29.
3. Samovar, L.A. and Porter, R.E. (1985) 'Introduction', in Samovar, L.A. and Porter, R.E. (eds) *Intercultural Communication: A Reader* (4th edn), Belmont, CA: Wadsworth.
4. Collier, M.J. and Thomas, M. (1988) 'Cultural identity: an interpretive perspective', in Kim, Y.Y. and Gudykunst, W.B. (eds) *Theories in Intercultural Communication*, Newbury Park, CA: Sage.
5. Kim, Y.Y. (1988) 'On theorizing intercultural communication', in Kim, Y.Y. and Gudykunst, W.B. (eds) *Theories in Intercultural Communication*, Newbury Park, CA: Sage.
6. Rogers, E. and Kincaid, D. (1981) *Communication Networks: Toward a New Paradigm for Research*, New York: Free Press.
7. Snyder, M. (1974) 'Self-monitoring of expressive behavior', *Journal of Personality and Social Psychology*, **30**: 526–37.
8. Chen, L. (1996) 'Cognitive complexity, situational influences, and topic selection in intracultural and intercultural dyadic interactions', *Communication Reports*, **9**: 1–12.
9. Beebe, L.M. and Giles, H. (1984) 'Speech accommodation theories: a discussion in terms of second-language acquisition', *International Journal of the Sociology of Language*, **46**: 5–32.
10. Ellingsworth, H.W. (1988) 'A theory of adaptation in intercultural dyads', in Kim, Y.Y. and Gudykunst, W.B. (eds) *Theories in Intercultural Communication*, Newbury Park, CA: Sage.

11. Gudykunst, W.B. (1983) ' Similarities and differences in perceptions of initial intra-cultural and intercultural encounters: an exploratory investigation', *The Southern Speech Communication Journal*, **49**: 49–65.

12. Tajfel, H. (1978) 'Social categorization, social identity, and social comparison', in Tajfel, H. (ed.) *Differentiation Between Social Groups*, London: Academic Press.

13. Gudykunst, W.B. (1986) 'Ethnicity, types of relationship, and intraethnic uncertainty reduction', in Kim, Y.Y. (ed.) *Interethnic Communication: Current Research*, Beverly Hills, CA: Sage, pp. 201–24.

14. Spitzberg, B. and Cupach, W. (1984) *Interpersonal Communication Competence*, Beverly Hills, CA: Sage.

15. Ting-Toomey, S. (1989) 'Communicative resourcefulness: an identity negotiation perspective', in Asante, M.K., Gudykunst, W.B. and Newmark, E. (eds) *Handbook of International and Intercultural Communication*, Newbury Park, CA: Sage.

16. Forgas, J.P. (1983) 'Social skills and episode perception', *British Journal of Clinical Psychology*, **22**: 26–41.

17. Leodolter, R. and Leodolter, M. (1976) 'Sociolinguistic considerations on psychoso-cial socialisation', in McCormack, W. and Wurm, S. (eds) *Language and Man*, The Hague: Mouton, p. 327.

18. Forgas, J.P. (1976) op. cit.

19. Applegate, J.L. and Sypher, H.E. (1988) 'A constructivist theory of communication and culture', in Kim, Y.Y. and Gudykunst, W.B. (eds) *Theories in Intercultural Communication*, Newbury Park, CA: Sage.

20. Heider, F. (1958) *The Psychology of Interpersonal Relations*, New York: Wiley.

21. Miller, G. and Steinberg, M. (1975) *Between People*, Chicago: Science Research Associates.

22. Berger, C.R. and Zelditch, M. (1985) *Status, Rewards and Influence*, San Francisco: Jossey-Bass.

23. Manusov, V. and Hegde, R. (1993) 'Communicative outcomes of stereotype-based expectancies: an observational study of cross-cultural dyads', *Communication Quarterly*, **41**(3): 338–54.

24. Burgoon, J.K. and Le Poire, B.A. (1993) 'Effects of communication expectancies, actual communication and expectancy disconfirmation evaluations of communica-tors and their communication behavior', *Human Communication Research*, **20**(1): 67–96.

25. Hoyle, R., Pinkley, R. and Insko, C. (1989) 'Perceptions of social behavior', *Personality and Social Psychology Bulletin*, **15**: 365–76.

26. Berger, C.R. and Calabrese, R.J. (1975) 'Some explorations in initial interactions and beyond', *Human Communication Research*, **1**: 99–112. See also Berger, C.R. (1987) 'Communicating under uncertainty', in Roloff, M.E. and Miller, G.R. (eds) *Interpersonal Processes*, Newbury Park, CA: Sage.

27. Gudykunst, W.B. (1988) 'Uncertainty and anxiety', in Kim, Y.Y. and Gudykunst, W.B. (eds) *Theories in Intercultural Communication*, Newbury Park, CA: Sage, pp. 123–56.

28. Kochman, T. (1983) *Black and White: Styles in Conflict*, Urbana: University of Illinois Press.

29. Triandis, H.C. (1980) 'Values, attitudes and interpersonal behavior', in Page, M. (ed.) *Nebraska Symposium on Motivation 1979*, Vol. 27, Lincoln: University of Nebraska Press.

30. Gudykunst, W.B. and Tsukasa, N. (1994) *Bridging Japanese/North American Differences*, Thousand Oaks, CA: Sage.

31. Gudykunst, W.B., Nishida, T., Koike, H. and Shiino, N. (1986) 'The influence of language on uncertainty reduction: an exploratory study of Japanese–Japanese and Japanese–North American interactions', in McLaughlin, M. (ed.) *Communication Yearbook*, Vol. 9, Beverly Hills, CA: Sage.

32. Gudykunst, W.B., Yang, S.M. and Nishida, T. (1985) 'A cross-cultural test of uncertainty reduction theory: comparisons of acquaintance, friend and dating relationships in Japan, Korea and the US', *Human Communication Research*, **11**: 407–55.
33. Gudykunst, W.B. and Hammer, M.R. (1988) 'Strangers and hosts: an uncertainty reduction based theory of intercultural adaptation', in Kim, Y.Y. and Gudykunst, W.B. (eds) *Intercultural Adaptation*, Newbury Park, CA: Sage.
34. Gudykunst, W.B., Nishida, T. and Chua, E. (1986) 'Uncertainty reduction in Japanese–North American dyads', *Communication Research Reports*, **3**: 39–46.
35. Gudykunst, W.B., Sodetani, L.L. and Sonoda, K.T. (1987) 'Uncertainty reduction in Japanese–American/Caucasian relationships in Hawaii', *Western Journal of Speech Communication*, **51**(3): 256–78.
36. Tajfel (1978) op. cit. p. 63.
37. Collier, M.J. and Thomas, M. (1988) op. cit.
38. Kim, Y.Y. (1988) *Communication and Cross-cultural Adaptation*, Clevedon: Multilingual Matters.
39. Kim, Y.Y. (1989) 'Intercultural adaptation', in Asante, M.K. and Gudykunst, W.B. (eds) *Handbook of International and Intercultural Communication*, Newbury Park, CA: Sage, pp. 275–94.
40. Tajfel, H. (1978) op. cit.
41. Ellingsworth, H.W. (1988) 'A theory of adaptation in intercultural dyads', in Kim, Y.Y. and Gudykunst, W.B. (eds) *Theories in Intercultural Communication*, Newbury Park, CA: Sage.
42. Rokeach, M. (1973) *The Nature of Human Values*, New York: Free Press.
43. Kincaid, D.L. (1987) 'The convergence theory of communication, self-organisation and cultural evolution', in Kincaid, D. (ed.) *Communication Theory: Eastern and Western Perspectives*, New York: Academic Press.
44. Anderson, R.J. and Carlos, M.L. (1976) 'What is social network theory?', in Burns, T. and Buckley, W. (eds) *Power and Control*, London: Sage.
45. Cook, K. (1982) 'Network structures from an exchange perspective', in Marsden, P. and Lin, N. (eds) *Social Structure and Network Analysis*, Beverly Hills, CA: Sage.
46. Boissevain, J. (1974) *Friends of Friends: Networks, Manipulators and Coalitions*, Oxford: Blackwell.
47. Rogers, E. and Kincaid, D.L. (1981) *Communication Networks: Toward a New Paradigm for Research*, New York: Free Press.
48. Aldrich, H. (1982) 'The origins and persistence of social networks', in Marsden, P. and Lin, N. (eds) *Social Structure and Network Analysis*, Beverly Hills, CA: Sage.
49. Yum, J.O. (1982) 'Communication diversity and information acquisition among Korean immigrants in Hawaii', *Human Communication Research*, **8**: 154–69.
50. Alba, N. (1978) 'Ethnic networks and tolerant attitude', *Public Opinion Quarterly*, **42**: 1–16.
51. Yum, J.O. (1987) 'Asian perspectives on communication', in Kincaid, D. (ed.) *Communication Theory: Eastern and Western Perspectives*, New York: Academic Press.
52. Weick, K. (1969) *The Social Psychology of Organizing*, Reading, MA: Addison-Wesley.
53. Yum, J.O. (1988) 'Network Theory', in Kim, Y.Y. and Gudykunst, W.B. (eds) *Theories in Intercultural Communication*, Newbury Park, CA: Sage.
54. Banks, S.P. (1989) 'Pronouns and the language of intercultural understanding', in Ting-Toomey, S. and Korzenny, F. (eds) *Language, Communication and Culture: Current Directions*, Newbury Park, CA: Sage.
55. Cupach, W.R. and Spitzberg, B.H. (1983) 'Trait versus state: a comparison of dispositional and situational measures of interpersonal communication competence', *Western Journal of Speech Communication*, **47**(4): 364–79.
56. Collier, M.J. and Thomas, M. (1988) op. cit.

57. Duran, R.L. and Spitzberg, B.H. (1995) 'Toward the development and validation of a measure of cognitive communication competence', *Communication Quarterly*, **43**: 259–75.
58. Ting-Toomey, S. and Korzenny, F. (1989) *Language, Communication and Culture: Current Directions*, Newbury Park, CA: Sage.
59. Kim, Y.Y. (1991) 'Intercultural communication competence: a systems–theoretic view', in Ting-Toomey, S. and Korzenny, F. (eds) *International and Intercultural Communication Annual*, Newbury Park, CA: Sage, pp. 259–75.
60. Collier, M.J. and Thomas, M. (1988) op. cit.
61. Wiemann, J.M. and Giles, H. (1988) 'Interpersonal communication', in Hewstone, M., Stroebe, W., Codol, J.-P. and Stephenson, G.M. (eds) *Introduction to Social Psychology*, Oxford: Basil Blackwell.
62. Chen, G.M. (1988) 'Relationships of the dimensions of intercultural communication competence'. Paper presented at the 79th Annual Meeting of the Eastern Communication Association, Baltimore, MD. ERIC Document Reproduction Service No. ED 297 381.
63. Jehn, K. and Weldon, E. (1992) 'A comparative study of managerial attitudes toward conflict in the United States and the People's Republic of China: issues of theory and measurement'. Paper presented at the Academy of Management, Las Vegas, NV.

SKILLS FOR WORKING WITH DIVERSITY

This chapter is concerned with the practicalities of face-to-face communication with different others at work. It both looks at communication theories when applied in practice and draws on empirical sources to provide guidance.

The topics covered are:

- inclusive language – ensuring that barriers are not created, even inadvertently, by words or phrases that exclude or give offence
- behaviours and traits which promote good intercultural communication
- applying general and intercultural communication theories.

8.1   INCLUSIVE LANGUAGE

None of the ways of overcoming intercultural communication barriers described later in this chapter is likely to work if, whether unintentionally or out of a perverse or misguided intention not to be 'politically incorrect', biased language is used. Biased language has been shown to affect adversely the self-image of members of the group excluded or negatively portrayed. There is therefore a strong argument from social justice (equal opportunity) in avoiding it. In addition, it naturally provokes resentment among members of such groups, which contributes to social disharmony and disrupts intercultural communication. It reinforces barriers to the full participation of all members of an organisation or society in its work and undermines policies aimed at benefiting from diversity.

Biased language is of three main kinds:

1. Using generic masculine words or titles to refer to all persons.
2. Using terms or expressions that reinforce inappropriate, outdated, or demeaning attitudes or assumptions about persons or groups based on age, disability, ethnicity, gender, national origin, religion, or sexual orientation.
3. Misusing stereotypes, which too often represent an oversimplified opinion, subjective attitude or uncritical judgement. They become particularly offensive and demeaning when used to make assumptions about the intel-

lectual, moral, social or physical capabilities of an individual or a group. Although characteristics such as age, disability, ethnicity, gender, national origin, religion and sexual orientation help define people as individuals, none of these characteristics should be mentioned, nor should an individual be designated as a member of his or her group, unless it is specifically relevant to the topic under discussion. To reflect individuality and diversity, it is best to choose language that accords with a receiver's expectations and self-image. 'Inclusive language' aims to respect the wishes of the group to or about which the communication is taking place.[1]

Ethnicity

Grouping people by ethnicity is a social and political phenomenon, and, as such, these categories are not fixed. As society changes, so do the labelling conventions that define groups. Within broadly drawn groups, individual members may not agree about which term they feel best defines them. In the UK, 'white' and 'black' (sometimes distinguishing 'black-Caribbean' and 'black-African') are current; Indian, Pakistani and Bangladeshi are generally used specifically, although 'Asian' also occurs. Interestingly, the equivalents of terms such as 'black-American' or 'Asian-American' – for example 'black-Briton' or 'Asian-Briton' are not current, which perhaps points to a lack of inclusiveness in British social attitudes.

Gender

Traditionally, terms such as 'man' and 'mankind' and the masculine pronouns 'he', 'him' and 'his' have served as generic words, referring to both sexes. However, it has more recently been acknowledged that this grammatical convention has two costs: ambiguity and exclusion. Careless use of these terms requires the listener or reader to determine whether the reference really does include women as well as men. More seriously, studies have shown that girls and women do feel excluded by this usage. Feeling excluded from history books, policy statements, professional titles and the like can have a powerful impact on the self-image and aspirations of women.

Stereotyping by gender often takes the form of assigning complementary and opposing characteristics to men and women, such as active/passive, strong/weak and rational/emotional. In these formulations, it is usually the characteristic associated with masculinity that is viewed as more positive and desirable, at least in a work context. Men and women should be treated primarily as people, not as members of different genders. Their shared humanity and common attributes should be stressed. Neither gender should be stereotyped. Both men and women should be represented as whole human beings with *human* strengths and weaknesses, not masculine and feminine ones.

Age

In many countries, people are living longer in good health, but language has yet to catch up with these facts. Just as some people in their twenties and thirties are not as vigorous as others of their age, people in their sixties and seventies differ greatly in their physical health and abilities. Expressions such as 'even at 75, x can do y', or 'octogenarian w still does y' are ageist; even describing someone as 'old' depends on a judgement which may be prejudiced.

At the other end of the scale, young men and women should not be referred to as 'boys' and 'girls'. Always giving the age of individuals in reports, as newspapers do (especially for women), reinforces ageism (and sexism). Unless age is the topic being written or spoken about, it is generally preferable not to refer to it.

Disability

People with disabilities prefer that others focus on their individuality, not their disability, unless, of course, it is the topic which is being written or spoken about. The term 'handicapped' is falling into disuse and should not be used. The terms 'able-bodied', 'physically challenged', and 'differently abled' are also discouraged and so is the article 'the' with an adjective (for example 'the deaf') to describe people with disabilities. The preferred usage, 'people with disabilities' ('people who are deaf'), stresses the essential humanity of individuals and avoids objectification. Alternatively, the term 'disabled people' ('deaf people') may be acceptable, but still defines people as disabled first and people second.

It is important to be careful not to imply that people with disabilities are to be pitied, feared, or ignored, or that they are always somehow more heroic, courageous, patient or 'special' than others. The term 'normal', in contrast, should never be used.

Sexual orientation

Most people feel, and authorities agree, that sexuality is determined early in life, and, as a rule, cannot be changed. Thus, 'sexual orientation' is a more accurate term to describe a person's sexuality than 'sexual preference' or 'choice'. The clinical term 'homosexual' may be appropriate in certain contexts, but generally the terms 'gay men', 'lesbians' and 'gay people' are preferable. The euphemisms 'lifestyle' or 'alternative lifestyle' should be avoided, because gay men and lesbians, like heterosexuals, have a variety of lifestyles. The term 'domestic partner' is being used increasingly to refer to the person with whom someone shares a household on a permanent basis, whether married or not.

Although during conversation finding the acceptable term for members of a group may be tricky, it becomes easier with practice. Overall, the message conveyed here may be summarised quite simply: when speaking about any group or individual, concentrate on the person's essential humanity, not on characteristics such as age, ethnicity or gender.

8.2 GOOD INTERCULTURAL COMMUNICATION BEHAVIOURS

Many factors may affect the success or failure of face-to-face intercultural communication; some of these are not within a person's immediate control – for instance their status in the eyes of the person with whom they are interacting or the prejudices of other participants. However, there is an opportunity to control one thing which impacts very directly: and that is one's own behaviour during the interaction. This section looks at how to *develop* behaviours which help intercultural communication; it covers mindfulness, cultural relativism, biculturalism, predicting others' behaviour and responses accurately, self-monitoring, tolerance for ambiguity, managing anxiety and communication fear, being nonjudgemental, showing empathy, achieving clarity, showing concern for relationship as well as task, appropriate assertiveness, avoiding and proscribing harassing and discriminatory behaviour, coping with others' harassment, prejudice or discrimination and helping change others' stereotypes about outgroup members. The crucial antecedent behaviour of improving intercultural social perception is also covered here.

Mindfulness

To correct the tendency to misinterpret others' behaviour, people need to become more aware of communicative behaviour – more 'mindful'. Mindfulness means tuning in consciously to habituated mental scripts; mindlessness is the rigid reliance on old categories, whereas mindfulness means the continual creation of new ones. Mindfulness carries a certain degree of existential vulnerability (openness). As shown in Figure 8.1, it occupies an intermediate zone between uncaringness and monitored constraint – between not caring about learning or improving and an inhibited caution which is defensive and closed to new ideas. Mindfulness is linked to cognitive resourcefulness and consists of:

1. creating new categories
2. being open to new information
3. being aware of more than one perspective.[2]

Uncaringness	Monitored constraint

– mindfulness +

Figure 8.1   The cognitive resourcefulness continuum

Cultural relativism and biculturalism

A vital shift for achieving real intercultural communication requires moving away from a position in which the norms, roles, values and behaviours into which a person was socialised are seen as uniquely valid and into one in which those of others are seen as equally valid in themselves, possibly beneficial and eligible for consideration and possible adoption. Unfortunately, it is difficult to achieve: following norms into which one was socialised is reflexive and requires little effort; not following them, or following others, is non-reflexive and requires substantial effort. The key skill required is mindfulness, which, with practice, can become habitual.

BOX 8.1

ADVICE FROM A CATERING MANAGER – SHOWING RESPECT FOR OTHERS' BELIEFS IS CRUCIAL

An Australian catering manager interviewed by the author said, 'One of my biggest difficulties in dealing with staff from different backgrounds stems from religion. I find it nearly impossible to understand why someone cannot make a ham sandwich or push a dog out of the restaurant. But I never try to force the situation. I'll make the sandwich or deal with the dog myself if necessary. I accept that, although I don't understand them, these religious rules are for them like the law is for me – they have to be obeyed. Staff are your biggest asset and they must have faith in you – and that means you must respect their beliefs.'

Source: Author's research.

To achieve cultural relativism involves trying to understand different others according to their own frame of reference. Biculturalism goes beyond this and involves accepting role taking as part of the human condition, avoiding stylised verbal behaviour, being willing to accept the strain of adaptation, being well aware of conversational constraints and showing flexibility in conversational adaptation.[3]

Predicting others' behaviour and responses accurately

This skill is needed to guide choices of communication strategy, to avoid giving offence inadvertently and to keep the flow of discussion smooth. Without necessarily being fully aware of doing so, all communicators make such predictions repeatedly during interactions. Often, however, their predictions are inaccurate. This is especially likely if they are a member of a dominant subculture interacting with a member of a 'minority' subculture, as the latter may conceal negative responses to the behaviour of their interlocutors out of fear or a wish to ingratiate. As a result, members of dominant subcultures often receive little feedback about their communication performances, especially if they as individuals are in positions of power. Sadly, too, such individuals are often not high in awareness or sensitivity. Everyone, however, relies on stereotypes and rules based on past experience to predict others' responses and these necessary simplifications often produce inaccuracy.

BOX 8.2

CULTURAL AWARENESS PROBLEMS OF DOMINANT GROUPS

A research study showed that 'Blacks reported more discussion about racial issues, both within their own group and outside it, than whites did... Members of the minority group are forced to deal with intergroup issues and to come to grips with their relationships in intergroup terms. Members of the majority group can overlook group forces and can attempt to explain their relationships mainly in terms of the individuals involved.'

Source: Alderfer, C.P. and Smith, K.K. (1982) 'Studying intergroup relations embedded in organizations', *Adminstrative Science Quarterly*, **27**: 5–65.

To increase predictive accuracy calls for obtaining as much information as possible both before and during interactions, heightening awareness of sensitive issues, language and non-verbal behaviour, examining and modifying stereotypes, implicit theories and rules and encouraging others to give feedback.

Self-monitoring

There is substantial research evidence for the positive effects on intercultural communication of the habit of self-observation and analysis which is known as self-monitoring.[4] High self-monitors are better able to do all the following:

- discover appropriate behaviour in new situations
- have control over their emotional reactions
- create the impressions they wish
- modify their behaviour to changes in social situations
- make more confident and extreme attributions
- seek out information about others with whom they anticipate interacting
- initiate and regulate conversations more.

They also have a greater need to talk and are more likely to be leaders – this applies to both genders.

Tolerance for ambiguity

To achieve tolerance for ambiguity involves managing the feelings associated with unpredictability: it is not suggested that discomfort or other negative feelings should not be experienced when confronted with uncertain situations, but that both those feelings and their display can be controlled. Individuals with a higher tolerance for ambiguity, that is, who can feel comfortable in situations where what is happening, or why, or what the outcome is likely to be, are unclear, are more inclined to seek out 'objective' information, which means that their intercultural behaviour is more likely to be based on a realistic appreciation. People with lower tolerance for ambiguity tend to seek supportive rather than 'objective' information – that is, to select and distort in such a way that they feel less psychological discomfort.

Some behaviours that support being or becoming tolerant of ambiguity are: delaying the decision on how to approach a new person or situation until as much information as possible has been gained by observation; having flexible short-term aspirations or goals (for instance, not being fixated on achieving a particular goal in the present encounter – being willing to try again at a later date if necessary); using trial and error rather than the same formula until what works becomes clear; consciously relaxing muscles, especially those in the back and neck; avoiding tense behaviours such as frowning, growling, pacing, sounding exasperated, clenching teeth, fidgeting, talking fast or pounding anything (remembering that how someone behaves affects how they feel as much as the reverse); projecting confidence to oneself through positive messages ('I feel confident, I can handle this, I feel relaxed').

Other traits related to being tolerant of ambiguity are uncertainty orientation: uncertainty-orientated individuals seek cognitive information more than certainty-orientated individuals; and field independence: people whose sense of self is not too much affected by their environment experience less stress on entering a new culture than field dependents.[5]

Managing anxiety and dealing with communication fear

In contrast to assertiveness, described later, it seems likely that it is always desirable to control the level of anxiety or fear experienced in intercultural communication. There are three main reasons: fear will make interaction unpleasant or painful, it will make it difficult to concentrate enough to behave in a skilled way and it will communicate itself to interlocutors and at best puzzle them, at worst lead them to despise or take advantage of their conversational partner.

Ability to manage anxiety and communication fear should mainly be developed away from interaction itself, through introspection, observation and the following practices: identifying, as precisely as possible, situations that give rise to communication fear; observing carefully, from memory if possible and from future interactions, just how, if at all, past expectations were proved wrong (the fear usually originates in past experiences of disconfirmation of expectations); taking equally careful note of when expectations were confirmed (there is a tendency to notice our failures but not our successes, which undermines confidence unnecessarily); checking that when a situation requiring communication gives rise to apprehensiveness in future, the problem is not caused by over-generalising. Communication situations have multiple aspects: two people may be from different continents, but both be mothers; the discussion may be about accounts, which make a person nervous, but with fellow students to whom they can talk without fear on other subjects. Instead of concentrating on the difficulties, it is more effective to concentrate on the easy aspects.[6]

Being non-judgemental

Judging others' behaviour or them as people, especially early in initial meetings, risks making errors of judgement and so basing one's own behaviour on false premises. It also leads to being over-influenced by stereotypes and to communicating the fact that they are being judged to interlocutors with, probably, negative consequences for their attitudes to the speaker.

Behaviours that support and communicate a non-judgemental perspective include: withholding preconceived opinions – asking, not telling; framing questions openly 'What do you think?', 'What do you mean by...?', 'Can you give me an example of...?'; soliciting feelings specifically: 'How do you feel about…?'; asking questions to find out explanations of others' behaviour that may be deep seated in an individual's values or culture; when expressing views, making it clear that it is understood that they are only opinions which may be disagreed with; acknowledging different values, beliefs and perceptions as valid; listening openly; listening to another's view without interrupting or criticising; acknowledging the other's point of view as valid: 'I see what you mean'; providing reassurance: 'Don't worry – this won't be taken as agreement'; avoiding calling a view which is disagreed with bad or wrong; sorting 'objective' facts from more subjective feelings, perceptions, and stereotypes; avoiding over-generalisations; making statements in a form which acknowledges one's own subjectivity, such as, 'I feel uneasy when Mr Ling does not appear to react to what I am saying', rather than generalising or laying claim to objectivity, as in 'Chinese are hard to read'.

Showing empathy

Being empathic means accurately understanding the thoughts and motivations of another person in an interaction and putting oneself in another's shoes when making a judgement about them. It does not necessarily mean agreeing with them or sympathising with them – rather, it implies really trying to understand them. Total empathy with another person is probably impossible, even when both come from the same culture and subcultures. However, most people's communication with others would be more successful if they could increase their ability to empathise and, equally importantly, if they could convey to their interlocutor an intention to empathise.

BOX 8.3

EMPATHY IN ACTION

A talk with a European who had spent many years working with Aboriginals in Australia suggested the value, for successful intercultural communication, of empathy with the beliefs of people from other cultures – or at least of not rejecting their worldview. For example, to teach them about the physics of electricity, he had talked in terms of 'the spirit of electricity' and 'the spirit of water'. Further, he did not find their beliefs altogether alien even when he first began the work: for instance, their belief in telepathy. 'My own father and mother communicated telepathically,' he said, 'When my brother and sister and I were children we took it for granted that they could do it.

For ten months in the war my father was posted missing, presumed dead, but my mother never believed it, because at certain times she could "feel" him sending messages to her. After the ten months were up, he was reported in a German prisoner of war camp. Later they communicated telepathically about quite banal things. They trained for it, and structured it – arranging to "speak" to one another at set times. Anyway, this meant that I did not find Aboriginal telepathy strange at all.'

Source: Author's research.

To communicate empathy effectively involves asking open-ended questions, such as 'What was the experience like for you when…?'; listening actively; paraphrasing the other person's words (for example 'What I think I hear you saying is…' 'Is this what you mean?') to check for understanding and to show a sincere attempt to understand; checking out verbal and non-verbal cues to find out what another is feeling: 'I sense you are feeling… angry… sad… glad… afraid. Am I reading you correctly?'; paying attention to any of one's own non-verbal messages that may make another person uncomfortable; mirroring elements of the other person's body language, tone and pace, as appropriate.

Achieving clarity

Communicating clearly is often, although not universally, an important communication objective, especially in work-based situations where the requirements of the task demand it. For instance, for a doctor, important though it is to communicate empathy and concern for relationship, clarity is even more important because of the importance of accuracy in diagnosis and in patients' following of instructions.

To achieve clarity involves stating points clearly and precisely; adjusting to the other person's level of understanding without being demeaning; simplifying language; explaining jargon; where possible and acceptable, using the idiom of the other (sub)culture; avoiding slang; slowing down (but not speaking louder); starting from where the other person is 'at'; using progressive approximations rather than escalation; dividing projects and expectations into smaller, more specific pieces; repeating in alternative ways; getting the other person to ask questions; giving short answers – stopping after a partial reply and waiting for their response; and checking understanding to ensure messages are communicated clearly and completely: for example by asking 'Am I being clear?', 'Will you say it back to me in your own words?', 'Let me show you what I mean', 'Why don't you give it a try now?'

Communicating a relationship as well as a task orientation

People from individualistic cultures are at risk of provoking a culture clash if they act with people from collectivist cultures according to what may be their usual priority of getting on with the task 'regardless'. It is well known that Arabs and other Middle Easterners prefer to do business by building a relationship and then, when trust has been established, proceeding to the negotiation or discussion. The same applies to people of many other nationalities and ethnicities. Equally, men who wish to move away from the position in which their dominance imposes a style which may be inimical to their women colleagues, clients or patients and/or counterproductive for the organisation (as described in Chapter 6), should be trying to increase the amount of 'relationship' orientation they communicate at work.

Methods include: remembering people's names and small details about them learnt unobtrusively or by asking; using their names according to their culture (for example patronym first); initiating conversations on non-work topics; being sensitive to nuances; initiating and reciprocating acts of consideration; using humour appropriately and with care; finding common ground with counterparts; supporting others' communication; bringing others in to discussions; thanking others for their work or contribution; praising above-standard work (in public or private according to the other person's culture); where appropriate giving candid feedback (in private).

Communicating appropriate assertiveness

The point was made in Chapter 5 that assertiveness, while fundamentally desirable as a communication attribute, is a variable; the level appropriate in one culture appears as aggressiveness in another and submissiveness in another again. There is a matter of judgement here – some people may be unwilling to compromise their own assertiveness level even if they are aware that the other person is likely to regard their behaviour as aggressive (this is a common problem for women dealing with men) or, if for instance, they have an Eastern background and are dealing with a Westerner, over-submissive. However, the optimal intercultural communication approach is to seek the appropriate level of assertiveness for the culture or style of the person being interacted with.

> **BOX 8.4**
>
> ## RESPONSIVENESS MAY BE MORE WIDELY ACCEPTABLE THAN ASSERTIVENESS
>
> One study found that, overall, when students perceived teachers as more assertive and/or more responsive, they trusted them more; as a student's trust of a teacher is regarded as an important factor in determining the degree to which the student will be open to being taught by that teacher, this finding endorses, in general, the value of assertiveness in teaching. However, when the students themselves were shy, timid or reserved, increased assertiveness from the teacher was associated with reduced trust, but increased responsiveness was associated with increased trust even among these unassertive students.
>
> *Source:* Wooten, A.G. and McCroskey, J.C. (1996) 'Student trust of teacher as a function of socio-communicative style of teacher and socio-communicative orientation of student', *Communication Research Reports*, **13**: 94–100.

Avoiding and proscribing harassing and discriminatory behaviour

Any kind of harassing or discriminatory behaviour is not only wrong and unacceptable in itself, it also creates barriers to communication, not only with its victims but with all who perceive and condemn it. Although these subjects have been covered in Chapters 4 and 6, they are so important that a reminder at this point is worthwhile. Some kinds of harassment, especially sexual harassment, are not always understood as such by the perpetrators.

The European Commission identifies five categories of sexual harassment:

1. non-verbal (for example pin-ups, leering, whistling and suggestive gestures)
2. physical (unnecessary touching)
3. verbal (unwelcome sexual advances, propositions or innuendo)
4. intimidation (offensive or superfluous comments about dress, appearance or performance)
5. sexual blackmail.

As the 1995 film *Disclosure* famously showed, not all harassment at work is done by men to women; however, the majority is. While awareness of some of these behaviours as harassment has increased and most men avoid them, others continue to be a problem.

Coping with others' harassment, prejudice or discrimination

While sexist, racist and other prejudiced behaviours are not the fault of the victims and the responsibility for preventing them and putting them right is primarily the perpetrators' and secondarily any relevant managers', organisations' or institutions', victims often do need to handle them in order not to be damaged emotionally or in their ability to communicate and maintain relationships generally.

BOX 8.5

COPING ON CAMPUS

From first to senior year, US undergraduate women's academic and career aspirations have been reported to decrease, and despite their superior performance in high school, women in college typically earn lower grade point averages than do men.

Two factors that have been implicated are:

1. loss of self-esteem
2. inequities in the campus environment.

Bernard (1988) argued that '"down-putting" behaviours directed against women in academic environments cause them to accept the potentially crippling belief that they are inferior to men'.

Some authors have suggested that the ability to perceive differential treatment and externalise blame to the perpetrators of the inequities are vital survival skills for women in academic settings. There is evidence that selection of women rather than men as a reference group (that is, the standard against which one compares one's values, beliefs and actions) predicted positive feelings about themselves for a group of female science majors.

Source: Bernard, J. (1988) 'The inferiority curriculum', *Psychology of Women Quarterly*, **12**: 261–68.

Box 8.6 outlines a developmental process by which women and other 'minority' groups can learn to cope with others' damaging behaviours. Other suggestions are:

- having clear parameters and consistent commitment to fair treatment
- judging when to 'let it go' and when to react strongly
- recognising allies in the oppressing categories
- getting a mentor
- getting better qualifications and experience than the 'competition'
- accepting the need to prove oneself over and over.

BOX 8.6

THE STAGE MODEL OF SELF-DEFINITION FOR MEMBERS OF 'MINORITY' GROUPS

Black writers advocate a staged progression of self-definition among black people (Cross, 1971). It is contended that the process is similar for gender, social class, sexual orientation and so forth. The womanist model (as opposed to the feminist) says that weakness results from using external standards to govern identity development. Therefore to become a womanist, women must overcome the tendency to use male (*or* female) social stereotypes of womanhood and define for themselves what being a woman means.

In Stage 1, pre-encounter, a person conforms to societal views about their group, holds a constricted view of their group's roles, and non-consciously thinks and behaves in ways that devalue their own group and esteem 'opposing' groups as reference groups.

In Stage 2, encounter, she or he begins to question the accepted values and beliefs of the pre-encounter stage as a result of contact with new information and/or experiences that heighten the personal relevance of membership of their group.

In Stage 3, immersion–emersion, she or he actively rejects supremacist definitions, idealises group activists, seeks self-affirming definitions of, and intense affiliations with, their group.

In Stage 4, internalisation, the person incorporates into his or her identity constellation a positive definition of their group based on personal attributes, views other members and their shared experiences as a source of information concerning their role, but refuses to be bound by external definitions.

Studies have found that women with high internalisation levels have lower perceptions of gender bias. Likely explanations are that:

- To develop internalisation attitudes, women learn to screen out environmental cues concerning what is appropriate for them as women (intellectualisation is a primary defense strategy in other minority-status theories [Cross, 1971]).
- Women with high levels of these attitudes elicit more positive cues.
- Women develop their own support systems (for example joining groups).

Sources: Ossana, S.M., Helms, J.E. and Leonard, M.M. (1992) 'Do "womanist" identity attitudes influence college women's self-esteem and perceptions of environment bias?', *Journal of Counseling and Development*, **70**: 402–8; Cross, W.E. (1971) 'Negro-to-black conversion experience. Toward a new psychology of black liberation', *Black World*, **20**(9): 13–27.

Helping change others' stereotypes about outgroup members

The points made earlier about the effect of harassment and discrimination, even for people who are neither perpetrator nor victim, draw attention to the possible need, in order to promote a good atmosphere for intercultural communication in an organisation, to influence co-members of an ingroup to change their stereotypes of other (sub)cultural groups. The piece of research quoted in Box 8.7 suggests one way in which this can be done.

Another approach is based on attribution theory. Counterstereotypic behaviour by one member of an outgroup often fails to change outgroup stereotypes because it can be dismissed as an exception to the rule. Thus, for instance, Mrs Thatcher's behaviour as UK Prime Minister failed to change many men's stereotypes of women because they chose to regard her as an 'honorary man', that is, not a typical woman. However, a study has shown that the impact of an individual outgroup member's behaviour on stereotypes can be increased if it is attributed to a stable internal cause such as personality (rather than to an external cause, such as 'luck' or an unstable internal cause such as mood) and the outgroup member is seen as typical, because in other ways their behaviour is similar to the behaviour of many members of the outgroup. Thus, by dressing in a feminine way to confirm male stereotypes of women but consistently making the 'hard' decisions, women managers increase their chances of shifting their male colleagues' stereotypes of women. Unfortunately, however, negative beliefs are often more resistant to change than positive ones.[7]

BOX 8.7

INFLUENCING CO-MEMBERS OF AN INGROUP BY REFERENCE GROUP INFLUENCE

Research has shown that members of an attractive ingroup can help shift stereotypes held by other members – that they can have a stronger influence than other influencing factors would suggest. A study reported in the *British Journal of Social Psychology* in 1996 discussed referent information influence – the motivation individuals have, where their social identity is salient and they define themself in terms of a shared group membership, to agree with (that is, share the beliefs of) other group members. Where disagreement occurs in these circumstances, individuals may be motivated to reduce the subjective uncertainty that arises from disagreement with people with whom they expect to agree. Then they may change their views in one of three ways. They may alter them to become consistent with other ingroup members (for example by shifting their own stereotypes – as in 'My sister Mary does a lot of work with Asian women and she says they are not nearly as submissive as people think – she could be right'); attribute the disagreement to perceived relevant difference in the stimulus situation (for example as in 'My sister Mary does a lot of work with Asian women and she says they are not nearly as submissive as people think – but she's talking about the ones who've been brought up in the West – they're different'); or recategorise the disagreeing ingroup members as an outgroup (for example as in 'But Mary's always had some peculiar ideas – she's not like the rest of our family').

Source: Haslam S.A., Oakes, P.J., McGarty, C., Turner, J.C., Reynolds K.J. and Eggins, R.A. (1996) 'Stereotyping and social influence: the mediation of stereotype applicability and sharedness by the views of in-group and out-group members', *British Journal of Social Psychology*, **35**: 369–97.

Improving intercultural social perception

A first stage in skilled communication behaviour is reaching a level of understanding of the values, motives, beliefs, attitudes and intentions of an interlocutor. As Figure 8.2 suggests, some factors which influence work behaviour are relatively easy for strangers to access, others are more difficult. In an intercultural context, this means attaining not only interpersonal understanding but also intercultural understanding. The five main elements required for such understanding are developing awareness of and escaping from own social category imprisonment, awareness of cultural sensitivities, awareness of contexts and awareness of barriers to intercultural communication, including harassing behaviour. These are the topics covered in this section.

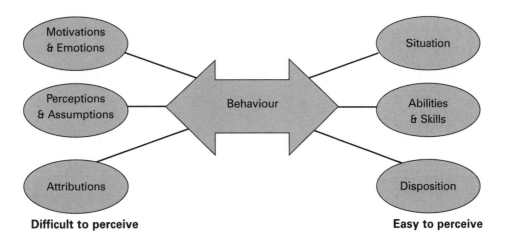

Figure 8.2 Ease and difficulty of perceiving factors influencing others' behaviour at work

Increasing self-awareness

The point has already been made that, without exposure to at least one other culture, most people remain unaware of the degree to which their own behaviours, attitudes and beliefs are culture specific. Therefore, a first step towards better intercultural understanding is to seek out such exposure at work or at leisure. Learning from such experiences then needs to be enhanced and speeded up by reflective observation, either alone or in discussion, remembering that the knowledge sought is reflexive – you are trying to understand yourself, your own stereotypes, prejudices, ethnocentrism, values and attitudes as much or more than those of others. Some trainers in intercultural communication now consider that working to enhance self-awareness is the most essential preparation for intensive work in another culture as in sojourns or international assignments.

Awareness of cultural sensitivities

As the example in Box 8.8 shows, it is easy, when one is ignorant of the sensitivities of another culture, not only to set up barriers to good communication but even to cause serious offence. The problem is how to avoid such situations. Obviously, the answer which is easy to give is to study the culture of the people with whom you interact sufficiently to know what sensitivities they are likely to have; and this is certainly something to aim for. However, there are two barriers which many professionals, particularly, face in achieving this aim:

1. They may interact with people from a wide range of cultures and subcultures. For instance, if the computer teacher quoted in Box 8.8 worked in a central London university, she might find in her classes people from several different European, African and Asian nations, from several different British ethnic and religious minority religious groups (for example Bangladeshi, Indian, Pakistani, Afro-Caribbean, Jewish, Muslim, Sikh, Catholic, Church of England), plus, of course, different genders, sexual orientations and levels of physical ability. In addition, all these groups could be represented, without notice, on her first day of teaching.

2. Often the answer to the question 'How can I learn about culture X?', is the discouraging information that there is no comprehensive book (or list) available on culture X.

BOX 8.8

DANGERS OF BREACHING OTHERS'
CULTURAL TABOOS

'I had a student from an African nation. He was having problems with understanding the English and computer terms. I paired him with another man who was a jolly soul who loved computers. One day this African man discovered the connection between the commands and the purpose for giving them in DOS (before windows). He was so excited, I reached over and gave him a hug. The poor man got hysterical, screamed and ran out of the class. I was shocked and his partner went to check on him. He was crying hard in the hall, and I couldn't figure what I had done so wrong. Moral of the story. A young white woman hugged him. That was a death sentence in his home town. A young woman touched him, he had to marry her (me) or I would be shamed. Yicks, his partner calmed him down, told him no one would kill him, I didn't have to marry him and everything was OK.'

'It wasn't a fun lesson to learn, the young man dropped my course. I now have learned the art of praise without a touch, or just a touch of hands. A hard lesson, but fair when you work in an university environment that has many cultures.'

Source: Frazier, J. (1996) 'Stories from a computer teacher'. Posted on the Internet: FRAZIER@CCIT.ARIZONA.EDUÁÁ.

There is, anyway, no substitute for experience in gaining knowledge of other cultures. However, realistically, few service providers are likely to be able to visit all the countries represented among their students, patients or clients or even to get well acquainted with all the ethnic or religious groups so represented. There is no easy solution, but there are a number of principles which can be applied:

1. The best, and most neglected, source of information on a culture is the representatives of the culture with whom you interact in the course of work. Setting aside time to talk with as many of them as possible about the sensitivities inculcated through their culture is an excellent use of time. Few, in the author's experience, will be unwilling to help if you explain that you know you know all too little about their culture and you want to know more, both in order to understand better out of respect and to avoid giving offence to them or others. If the people concerned are clients, patients, advisers, customers or suppliers it may be necessary to arrange a special time for the discussion; if they are colleagues, students, or others with whom you are in regular, repeated contact, opportunities may arise naturally in the course of the work. Even in the latter case, however, it is advisable to make the purpose of the discussion explicit, in the way already described, rather than to ask the questions you want answered without explaining why.

2. The following set of caveats should be kept in mind:

    - Firsthand experience is necessary to understand many subtleties of any culture.
    - What is logical and important in a particular culture may seem irrational and unimportant to an outsider.
    - In describing another culture, people tend to stress the differences and overlook the similarities; however, in interacting with people from another culture, they tend to assume more similarity than actually exists.
    - Stereotyping may be inevitable among those who lack frequent contact with another culture but an understanding of the limited truth of stereotypes is essential.
    - Personal observations of others about another culture should not be taken as objective evidence.
    - Many subcultures often exist within a single ethnic group, language group, religion or nationality, differentiated by education, age, gender, socioeconomic status, education, and exposure to other cultures. Highly educated people of a given cultural group are less likely to reveal indigenous language and communication patterns than less educated persons.
    - All cultures have internal variations.
    - Cultures are continually evolving. Understanding another culture is a continuous process.
    - To understand a culture best, one should understand the language of that culture.

Awareness of contexts

All talk takes place within a context. Katriel (1989),[8] observing that ethnographic studies have pushed towards a greater recognition of the situated nature of talk, has argued that the context fundamentally affects the knowledge requirements of encounter participants. The context of talk has at least four dimensions, each of which can magnify, reduce or have neutral impact on how aware the participants are of their (sub)cultural differences.

The dimensions are:

1. Socio-political factors. These can create a sense of social distance, such as that which might be felt between a British aristocrat and his or her tenant farmer.
2. Cultural assumptions defining the 'rules of the game'. As a 1987 British study showed,[9] in intercultural contact between white and black people, the white person is typically the gatekeeper – the controller of access to valued resources – and the black person is typically the powerless client. (The authors concluded, gloomily, that 'This is the socio-political context in which cross-cultural encounters take place: one in which there is no possibility of an equal exchange between black and white.')
3. Attitudes, based on biographical experiences.
4. The role the participants assign to the immediate encounter. For instance, if two colleagues of different sexes, ethnicity and professional status were discussing their annoyance at the inconvenience of a photocopier breakdown they would probably have lower awareness of their (sub)cultural differences than they would if they were negotiating with one another over the pay of one of them.

An appreciation of the context of an encounter is a useful tool in increasing intercultural effectiveness. Intercultural encounters have distinctive characteristics and texture, according to their context; for instance, touristic encounters, unlike some others, essentially celebrate, rather than try to overcome or pacify, the experience of cultural difference. When Western tourists tell stories of bargaining in 'native' stores, they are relating their enjoyment of what is, to them, an unusual experience. International trade, diplomacy and scholarly exchanges are other examples of encounters with their own distinctive characteristics and texture. All these contexts, Katriel would argue, create differences in the expectations of the parties to encounters and the requirements for effective communication. The nature of the task, in work encounters, also has a strong contextual influence.

Another contextual factor influencing the characteristics of intercultural encounters is the stage which has been reached in acquaintanceship between the participants, with initial encounters being among the most problematic. Not surprisingly, the influence of cultural norms and stereotypes diminishes as acquaintance grows. Therefore, being able to communicate successfully when the level of cultural dissimilarity is high matters most on first acquaintance or in formal settings. (These, of course, are highly relevant to work communication.) For this reason, most studies have focused on the early stages of intercultural relationships.

It has already been pointed out that, when interacting with a stranger, individuals become aware that the stranger does not share their own implicit theory about the rules of the game. Therefore they become more conscious of that implicit theory. The result is that interactions between strangers take place at high levels of behavioural awareness. This will apply to your counterpart as well as to you.

Work contexts can sometimes reduce intercultural communication difficulties, because where both parties concentrate on the task, the near-universalism of 'technology' (in its broadest sense) creates a bridge. However, there has often been an over-reliance on this factor with resulting poor work relations between people from different cultures.

BOX 8.9

ADVICE FROM A FEMINIST

Although there may be cultural differences between the sexes, it is not productive to assume that all men love sports any more than it is constructive to assume that all Irish consume extraordinary amounts of alcohol. The tendency to evaluate another's culture as inferior to our own is perhaps the most difficult stumbling block to avoid, especially when applying it to gender communication. So, instead of becoming annoyed by a male's aggressive communication style, we should recognise that it is a style which is as much a part of his identity as an ethnic cuisine or a religious tradition is part of a culture. The task in improving intercultural communication is awareness and respect rather than evaluation.

Source: Mulvahaney, B.M. (1994) *Gender differences in communication: an intercultural experience.* Posted on the Internet: http://snyside.sunnyside.com/cpsr/gender/mulvaney.txt

---

Awareness of perceptual barriers to intercultural communication

In intercultural communication, being aware of stumbling blocks can also help in avoiding them. A discussion of these problem areas was given in Chapter 6, but those which fall under the heading of social perception can be summarised as:

- assumed similarity
- language
- non-verbal misinterpretations

- preconceptions and stereotypes
- tendency to evaluate.

Intercultural communication is improved by learning not to assume that others have the same values and attitudes, by becoming more sensitive to differences in others' verbal and non-verbal language, more aware of societal preconceptions and stereotypes which portray other groups from our own as 'different', or in the case of the other gender as 'opposite', and by reducing the tendency to evaluate another's culture as inferior.

Learning and unlearning

Increasing all the forms of awareness described so far is really a matter of learning and unlearning. Unlearning may often be a necessary preliminary to improving social perception – it means being freed from past attitudes, preconceptions, prejudices and expectations in order to absorb new ideas and information. Unlearning is, of course, learning by another name; but it is a difficult type of learning because it involves a change in self-organisation – in the perception of oneself – which is threatening and tends to be resisted.

Certain conditions, according to Carl Rogers,[10] make learning (and hence unlearning) easier: when the subject matter is perceived as having relevance for someone's own purposes – therefore learning about cultural difference and intercultural communication comes more easily at times when you are likely to be going abroad, when you want to make overtures to someone of a different gender or sexual orientation or when you need to build bridges to a colleague from a different background. In addition, when external threats are at a minimum, learning which is threatening to the self is more easily assimilated, because there is a maximum total level of threat which most people can tolerate.

Certain behaviours also facilitate learning:

- Activity – much significant learning is acquired by doing (see the Kolb learning cycle in Figure 9.1 to understand why and how).
- Responsible participation by the learner in the learning process (abjuring models of learning in which the learner is a passive recipient of input in favour of those in which the learner drives and steers the process – in other words, for active learning).
- Self-initiated learning which involves the whole person – feelings as well as intellect – is most lasting and pervasive.
- Formative evaluation by the learner: this is more helpful than summative evaluation by others; that is, if learners can assess, somewhat objectively, their own progress, strengths and weaknesses as they go along, they will gain independence, creativity and self-reliance as well as knowledge.
- Learning how to learn by a continuous openness to experience and incorporation into oneself of the process of change.

A wide range of behaviours and traits can contribute positively towards achieving effective intercultural communication. Some of these fall into the category of 'self-management'; others are directed at reassuring interlocutors of having good intentions and a desire to establish good relations. Perhaps most effort, initially, should be directed at improving intercultural social perception.

8.3 APPLYING THEORY TO IMPROVE INTERCULTURAL COMMUNICATION

At this point, we can examine the implications of the theories set out earlier in this book for improving intercultural communication skills. These theories include both the general communication theories described in Chapters 4 and 5 and those specifically focused on intercultural communication described in Chapter 7.

Applying general communication theories

To make practical use of communication theories in intercultural encounters, individuals need to adapt their behaviour and expectations. For example, in encounters between people from individualist and collectivist cultures, the tendency of the individualist to use the elaborated code may be functional, and the majority adaptation needed is from the collectivist; on the other hand, the individualist needs to adapt his or her expectations about the input from the collectivist. Against this, the individualist needs to increase the amount of 'relationship' and 'other-face concern' in his or her communication and the collectivist to lower his or her expectations on these dimensions.

Behaviour shifts can range from minor adaptations to complete adoption of others' language practices. Unfortunately, this area is both complex and little researched. We simply do not know, for example, in what circumstances it is more effective to try to adopt the topic–comment order used by someone from another culture or to stick to one's own, or when mirroring others' non-verbal communication behaviours (which is, in fact, quite a 'natural' thing to do) creates an improved level of understanding and liking or is alienating. Although both rhetorical sensitivity research and convergence theory imply that adaptation generally promotes intercultural communication, they are not specific enough to determine whether they apply to particular aspects of communicative behaviour such as the use of routine formulae or the use of disclosure to promote affiliation.

Currently, therefore, in relation to the many aspects of language use which were introduced and shown to vary cross-culturally in Chapter 4, the best overall guidance that can be given is to work to gain heightened awareness of them and their effects so that variations are more easily noticed; adjust expectations regarding others' behaviour, so that responses will be affected by fewer violations of expectations; and cultivate sensitivity to when and how adaptation of language use will be beneficial.

Some of the specific communication theories covered in earlier chapters, do, however, carry direct implications for skilled intercultural communication.

Interactionist theories

These theories contribute the idea that sustaining interaction successfully depends on accomplishing two things – systematically interweaving your actions with those of another person or persons and observing the social 'rituals' required by the particular set of participants or situation. While the theories give limited help on how to accomplish these two actions, it is likely that mindfulness, described in Section 8.2, is an essential behaviour.

Interactionist concepts of identity security/vulnerability, self-affirmation, self-discovery and the opposing drives for assimilation and differentiation help intercultural communicators gain better understanding. This applies not only to what the other party may be experiencing but also to their own feelings. Thus they can make sense of what may often appear to be contradictory behaviours.

Burke's symbolic interactionist theory of consubstantiality (or identification)[11] carries implications both for understanding the barriers to intercultural communication and for ways to overcome them. Communication, according to Burke, itself increases identification because through communication shared meaning increases, thereby improving understanding. Identification, in turn, can be a means to persuasion and effective communication, although it provides intrinsic satisfactions too. There are three kinds of identification:

1. material, resulting from having similar possessions and lifestyle
2. ideational, (idealistic) from similar feelings, attitudes or values
3. formal, from participating in the same organisation, structure or event.

The 'opposite' of identification is division or difference; both are always present in some degree between two people, but communication is more successful when identification is greater than division. For people from the same (sub)cultures, the level of initial ideational identification is likely to be higher than it is for people from different (sub)cultures and the same may be true for material identification. However, formal identification resulting from participating in the same task, event or organisation can be high in intercultural encounters at work. People try to achieve identification and use a very wide range of strategies for achieving it – one way to advance your ability to communicate successfully with them is to work out what strategy they are using and reciprocate.

Face theories

According to Ting-Toomey, the process of achieving facework competence requires:

- Face co-orientation, that is, mutual knowledge of each other's face expectations, face claims and face intentions. It therefore requires cultural sensitivity, gender sensitivity and interpersonal knowledge of face vulnerability and face threshold level.
- Facework coordination, that is, synchronising, signalling interest and showing willingness to develop intact social bonds.
- Facework attunement, that is, joint attention to thoughts, feelings, intentions and motives.

Some further points, based on Ting-Toomey's work, are as follows:

1. The first application of face negotiation is critical.
2. The possibility of face giving (that is, sharing in the other's gain or loss of face), as well as face saving, should be borne in mind.
3. When face is negotiated in collectivist cultures, there are usually larger group implications.
4. There is a link from face to power as well as social esteem.
5. Business cards and formal introductions allow people from collectivist cultures to place an interlocutor appropriately and so to treat them appropriately in their own terms.
6. In many cultures, using intermediaries serves a critical function.
7. In high-context cultures, role image appropriateness is critical.
8. Face is long term.[12]

Goffman's concept of 'face' carries two intercultural implications: the importance of exercising 'tact' in receiving different others' presentations or definitions of the situation and the importance of reciprocity.

Applying intercultural communication theories

This subsection includes ideas based on applying the theories of identity negotiation, episode representation, expectation states, uncertainty/anxiety management, communication resourcefulness, communication accommodation and adaptation, as well as coordinated management of meaning and constructivist ideas.

Identity negotiation theory

To achieve intercultural competence within the framework of this theory, people at work need to:

- Assess, as realistically as possible, whether a particular interaction is inter-cultural. Is the frame in which this interaction is viewed, by the other party as well as yourself, that of their cultural identity or is it primarily interpersonal?

- Negotiate mutual meanings (for example an encounter must be mutually understood as a social gathering or a medical consultation), rules, concepts of time, space, activities and positive outcomes with the other party. In formal meetings, some of these aspects should be clarified in the course of setting the agenda – which should not, therefore, be determined unilaterally. Even so, the process of negotiation will continue throughout the meeting. It may be advantageous to make this process explicit – for instance by asking 'When you say that, do you mean...?' At other times, the negotiation will be implicit but there should be an endeavour to reach a higher level of awareness of how it is proceeding and whether understanding and agreement is being reached.

- Learn to evaluate encounters in terms which go beyond task accomplish-ment. Positive outcomes can include self-concept reinforcement, affirmation of cultural identity and desire to maintain the relationship, as well as goal accomplishment.[13]

Episode representation theory

The main implication of this theory is that the way someone thinks about encounters affects – or at least is related to – social skill in the encounter. Highly socially skilled individuals see episodes more in terms of evaluation and inten-sity, while low socially skilled persons are primarily affected by anxiety in their mental representations of social episodes. This reinforces the value of managing anxiety in the ways implied by Gudykunst's anxiety/uncertainty management theory, which are set out later and in the next chapter.[14]

Expectation states theory and expectancy violation theory

Expectations influence the ability to understand different others. The attitudes someone has about a particular other (sub)culture or other (sub)cultures in general create expectations about experiences in interactions with different others. The stereotypes someone has about the people also affect expectations. Someone who is open to other (sub)cultures, has a positive attitude toward the specific (sub)culture, and has positive stereotypes about the people of the (sub)culture will probably have positive expectations about their experiences, and vice versa.

Negative attitudes and stereotypes create negative expectations. Negative expectations, in turn, tend to create self-fulfilling prophecies; that is, lead to interpreting the behaviour of members of the other (sub)cultures negatively and therefore to having negative experiences. Similarly, expectations transferred without mindfulness from the 'own' culture are particularly likely to be violated. These are further reasons for avoiding, or at least postponing, evaluating the behaviour of 'different other' people.[15]

Constructivist theory

Constructivist theory contends that in non-routine contexts, cultural rules, conventions and codes are insufficient for actors to achieve their communication goals – instead they need to use person-centred messages.[16] Since intercultural encounters are usually non-routine, communicators should expect to use more inquiry, less advocacy and more attempts to see and acknowledge the other's point of view and emotions than they do in routine situations.

Anxiety/uncertainty management theory

To adapt successfully to working with different others, individuals usually need to reduce the uncertainty they experience about others' behaviour and the anxiety they feel about interacting with different others. This means that they must be able to understand the different others (uncertainty reduction) and be able to manage their emotional reaction to the differences (anxiety reduction).[17]

Several factors contribute to the ability to reduce uncertainty and anxiety. These factors include:

- having knowledge of the other's culture or subculture – for instance, its communication rules, or behavioural norms
- having open, flexible, and accurate stereotypes
- having positive attitudes towards the other (sub)culture and its members
- having intimate and rewarding contact with members of the other (sub)culture
- perceiving similarities between own (sub)culture and the (sub)culture of the different others
- sharing communication networks with members of the (sub)culture
- having a positive cultural identity (because if you have a negative cultural identity, the insecurity and anxiety stimulated by intercultural contact will seem greater, perhaps too great, leading to avoidance).

Individuals have control over many of these factors – they can modify or change them. The theory, therefore, can be used as a guide for communicating more effectively with members of other cultures and/or adapting to living in a new culture.

The skills which AUM theory suggests are required for good intercultural communication are:

- ability to be mindful
- ability to tolerate ambiguity
- ability to manage anxiety
- ability to empathise

- ability to adapt behaviour (through cultural relativism and biculturalism)
- ability to make accurate predictions.

These skills, with some suggestions on how to develop them, were described in Section 8.2.

Communication resourcefulness

To increase communication resourcefulness, there are three aspects to work on. These are cognitive, affective and behavioural resourcefulness:[18]

- Cognitive resourcefulness increases as someone becomes more 'mindful' (see the beginning of this chapter) and as they are able to regard encounters as identity challenges rather than sources of anxiety.

- Affective resourcefulness increases as a person achieves an acceptable and appropriate balance between ego concerns and other concerns in interactions. This also means achieving a good balance between relying on principles, rules and procedures for guidance and regulation of the encounter and relying on trust and caring – a relationship approach. Highly individualistic, achievement-orientated people are often deficient in the 'other' dimension of affective resourcefulness and should attempt to shift in that direction; other groups, including many women, may gain in affective resourcefulness by more emphasis on their own needs and on principles rather than feelings.

- Behavioural resourcefulness increases as an interactor develops a wide range of verbal and non-verbal repertoires to deal with the diverse identity needs of different persons in different situations. Another key theme is behavioural adaptation and flexibility, which refers to the importance of both behavioural responsiveness to strangers and behavioural openness to learn from the strangers or relational partners.

Communication accommodation theory

1. It will be recalled from Chapter 7 that in CAT theory the main process by which people from different cultures (or groups) increase their ability to communicate is by attuning.[19] Attuning consists of:

    - using increasingly similar phrasing and vocabulary, formality levels, and non-verbal behaviour
    - sharing of topic selection and turn-taking, back-channelling, face maintaining
    - minimising interruptions, correction and evaluations
    - adjusting speech rate, loudness, framing and focusing moves to maximise ease of understanding for the partner.

Other important processes include:

2. Learning when to expect people to behave more in intergroup terms and more in accordance with their norms and to be more careful about breaches of norms. This means learning to:

    - discriminate status-marked interactions from others
    - recognise people who are highly dependent on their group and whose sense of solidarity with their group is high
    - recognise people who feel that they or their group are disadvantaged and be aware of that possibility and its implications
    - distinguish members of dominant and subordinate groups and know how that status is likely to affect their initial orientations
    - treat initial encounters as particularly eliciting and requiring 'intergroup' behaviour.

3. Being aware that the long-term motivations of interactors to build relationships or otherwise will affect how much they are likely to accommodate.

4. Paying attention to others' needs and behaviours.

5. Noticing the degree to which interlocutors pay attention to the needs and behaviours of others.

6. Monitoring interactors' communication strategies to identify them as convergence, divergence or maintenance; becoming aware of the possibility of using a wider range of strategies than are normally used; trying to gain the level of personal control which will allow using an appropriate strategy rather than simply adopting a strategy unthinkingly.

7. Being sensitive to the other party's evaluations of one's own interactive behaviour as accommodative or not and attributable to oneself, one's situation or one's group; monitoring one's own equivalent evaluations and ensuring they are soundly based.

8. If a counterpart is attuning, being aware that this probably implies one or more of the following on their part:

    - they desire social approval
    - they perceive the 'costs' of attuning as lower than the perceived rewards
    - they desire to meet the perceived communication needs of their interactor(s)
    - they desire a mutual self-presentation and equal-status role relations.

Similarly, the presence of these factors suggests that attuning can be expected.

9.   If a counterpart is counter-tuning, be aware that this probably implies on their part that:

- they desire to communicate a contrastive self- or group image
- they desire to dissociate personally from their interactor or their definition of the situation
- they desire to signal differences in experience/knowledge/intellectual capability/communicator style
- they desire to achieve or maintain a high-status role.

10.   Knowing the counter-intuitive findings on people's use of interaction strategies – for instance, the one that people from collectivistic cultures use politeness to create distance.

Ellingsworth's adaptation theory

The implications of Ellingsworth's theory relate mainly to initial encounters. They are that it is beneficial to:

- Be aware that both interactors may be wrongly diagnosing the intercultural situation through erroneous identification of the 'kind' of foreigner, incomplete or inaccurate knowledge of the cultural stereotype with which the other has been identified (correctly) and the extent to which the individual actually conforms to the stereotype.
- Expect beliefs to be probed for areas of agreement and disagreement; understand the importance of agreement for relationship building.
- Anticipate that the other party will assume, reject or intend to share the 'burden' of adaptation in accordance with the degree to which they see the interaction as purposeful, its purposes as common, the benefit as mutual or theirs, the 'territory' as theirs or another's and their power and status as higher or lower than another's.
- Understand that adaptation itself is likely to change the attitudes and perceptions of the adapter both concerning the other party culturally represented and towards that person's perceptions of self and the culture he or she represents.
- Avoid invoking culturally based beliefs which may conflict with an interactor's.

To speed progress with the task it is beneficial to:

- Offer more functional adaptive behaviour; if there is inequity in adaptive behaviour, shift towards parity (that is, assume more of the 'burden' than would be 'natural').
- Expect the major beneficiary of task completion to take responsibility for accelerating adaptive behaviour.
- Disregard favourable status differences or territorial advantages; or invoke them to increase the amount of adaptation the other party will supply.[20]

Coordinated management of meaning theory

Thus the two most evident practical implications of this theory are that communicators are often unaware of the differences distorting communication. Intercultural working to heighten awareness is beneficial and so is a focus on developing flexible and integrative strategic means for accomplishing goals.[21]

Network theory

Possibly the most far-reaching application of network theory in intercultural situations is that an understanding of how intercultural networks are likely to differ from intracultural networks will change expectations and so reduce the impact of violations of expectations and culture shocks. The differences have been set out in Chapter 7.[22] Lack of interlocking relationships, few actual links compared to the potential total, uniplexity with its consequence of low potential for meeting relational needs, weak ties and the absence or reduced presence of normative sanctions and emotional obligations could all be disturbing experiences for the unprepared, especially for the unprepared sojourner.

Other implications are that the importance and use of intermediaries (as liaisons and bridges) are not just a function of working in a collectivist culture; network theory shows that they apply in intercultural situations generally, to reduce 'transaction costs' (which may be economic, emotional or social). Lastly, the processes of adaptation and acculturation can be seen as processes of forming, maintaining and expanding networks.

8.4   CONCLUSION

As Box 8.10 illustrates, in diverse communities appropriate intercultural communication can help organisations win goodwill, attract the best talent, gain government business, do business with people from 'other' (sub)cultures, and have good industrial relations.

For individuals, intercultural communication skills are an essential tool for providing services to, working as colleagues with or doing business with, people from backgrounds different from the individual's own.

Undoubtedly, the techniques and approaches suggested in this chapter present individuals with a more complex interactional task than they may have understood to be necessary. However, the probability is that such individuals have been living in a 'fool's paradise' in which lack of understanding, offence and even hostility went unrecognised; or that they have been imposing their 'definition of the situation' as members of a dominant group in an undemocratic and damaging way. An investment of energy and commitment is needed to move through the stages from unconscious incompetence to unconscious competence, but it may be considered that there is a moral duty as well as a performance motivator for making it.

BOX 8.10

ADAPTING TO CHANGE IN SOUTH AFRICA DEMANDS A CHANGE IN COMMUNICATION PRACTICES

In South Africa, since the end of apartheid, the teaching of Zulu, the most widely spoken of the country's nine black languages, has surged in the boardrooms of businesses. 'In the old days, few white managers bothered with African languages, on the assumption that all blacks could speak English or Afrikaans. Now that they have to deal with emerging black businesses more often, these managers have made the startling discovery that they can win goodwill by speaking to their black peers in their own language. Indeed, companies that are seen to fail to make at least an effort to be more African are in danger of being snubbed by the best black talent and losing out on government contracts and black business deals. A more pressing reason to change has been industrial relations, or rather the lack of them. The ability to understand each other matters much more now that one side is not formally superior to the other.'

Source: The Economist, 24 February 1996, p. 105.

REFERENCES

1. This section is developed from The Human Relations Code of the University of Maryland at College Park. Posted on the Internet: http://www.inform.umd.edu/Student/Diversity_Resources.
2. Langer, E. (1989) *Mindfulness*, Reading, MA: Addison-Wesley.
3. Kim, M.-S., Hunter, J.E., Miyahara, A., Horvath, A., Bresnahan, M. and Yoon, H. (1996) 'Individual- vs culture-level dimensions of individualism and collectivism: effects on preferred conversational styles', *Communication Monographs*, **63**: 29–49.
4. Snyder, M. (1974) 'Self-monitoring of expressive behavior', *Journal of Personality and Social Psychology*, **30**: 526–37.
5. Gudykunst, W.B. (1988) 'Uncertainty and anxiety', in Kim, Y.Y. and Gudykunst, W.B. (eds) *Theories in Intercultural Communication*, Newbury Park, CA: Sage.
6. McCroskey, J.C. (1984) 'The communication apprehension perspective', in Daly, J.A. and McCroskey, J.C. (eds) *Avoiding Communication: Shyness, Reticence and Communication Apprehension*, Beverley Hills, CA: Sage, pp. 13–38.

7. Cross Cultural Communication: An Essential Dimension of Effective Education Northwest Regional Educational Laboratory : CNORSE. Posted on the Internet: http://www.nwrel.org/cnorse.

8. Katriel, T. (1989) 'From "context" to "contexts" in intercultural communication research', in Ting-Toomey, S. and Korzenny, F. (eds) *Language, Communication and Culture: Current Directions*, Newbury Park, CA: Sage.

9. Mason, D. (1995) *Race and Ethnicity in Modern Britain*, Oxford: Oxford University Press.

10. Rogers, C. (1951) *Client-centred Therapy*, London: Constable.

11. Burke, K. (1966) *Language as Symbolic Action*, Berkeley, CA: University of California Press.

12. Ting-Toomey, S. (1992) 'Cross-Cultural Face-Negotiation: An Analytical Overview'. Pacific Region Forum on Business and Management Communication: summary by Beverly Matsu and Stella Ting-Toomey. Posted on the Internet: http://www.cic.sfu.ca/forum.

13. Collier, M.J. and Thomas, M. (1988) 'Cultural identity: an interpretive perspective', in Kim, Y.Y. and Gudykunst, W.B. (eds) *Theories in Intercultural Communication*, Newbury Park, CA: Sage.

14. Forgas, J.P. (1976) 'The perception of social episodes: categorical and dimensional representations in two different social milieus', *Journal of Personality and Social Psychology*, **33**: 199–209.

15. Burgoon, J.K. and Le Poire, B.A. (1993) 'Effects of communication expectancies, actual communication and expectancy disconfirmation evaluations of communicators and their communication behavior', *Human Communication Research*, **20**(1): 67–96.

16. Applegate, J.L. and Sypher, H.E. (1988) 'A constructivist theory of communication and culture', in Kim, Y.Y. and Gudykunst, W.B. (eds) *Theories in Intercultural Communication*, Newbury Park, CA: Sage.

17. Gudykunst, W.B. (1988) 'Uncertainty and anxiety', in Kim, Y.Y. and Gudykunst, W.B. (eds) *Theories in Intercultural Communication*, Newbury Park, CA: Sage, pp. 123–156.

18. Ting-Toomey, S. and Korzenny, F. (1989) *Language, Communication and Culture: Current Directions*, Newbury Park, CA: Sage.

19. Kim, Y.Y. (1988) *Communication and Cross-cultural Adaptation*, Clevedon: Multilingual Matters.

20. Ellingsworth, H.W. (1988) 'A theory of adaptation in intercultural dyads', in Kim, Y.Y. and Gudykunst, W.B. (eds) *Theories in Intercultural Communication*, Newbury Park, CA: Sage.

21. Cronen, V.E., Chin, V. and Pearce, W.B. (1988) 'Co-ordinated management of meaning', in Kim, Y.Y. and Gudykunst, W.B. (eds) *Theories in Intercultural Communication*, Newbury Park, CA: Sage.

22. Rogers, E. and Kincaid, D.L. (1981) *Communication Networks: Toward a New Paradigm for Research*, New York: Free Press.

SKILLS FOR WORKING ABROAD

In business, owing to factors such as increasing international competition and the resulting need to market products worldwide, international merger and acquisition activity and new market access opportunities (for instance in Eastern Europe), more and more managers and other staff will be confronted at least once in their careers with the opportunity to take on an international assignment or become an expatriate working and living in a foreign country.

Globalisation of telecommunications, the rapidly increasing prevalence of English as a *lingua franca* and specific developments such as the Erasmus programme of the European Union have created similar international opportunities for a wide range of non-business personnel, from students to doctors, footballers to musicians. Young people, particularly, have shown themselves increasingly eager to seize these opportunities for international experience. However, any international assignment poses challenges in terms of adaptive capabilities and cultural sensitivity; longer-term assignments require the person to cope with culture shock and the processes of sojourner adaptation as well as dealing with new roles and responsibilities in an unfamiliar environment.

This chapter is concerned with how people who are working abroad can learn to cope with and in their new cultural environment. Clearly, all encounters taking place in an overseas host culture occur in a different context from those with different others in the 'home' country. Equally clearly, overseas visitors staying for a few days before returning home or moving on to another country are in a different situation from sojourners – people who are staying for at least a month in another country, either for work or study. (Emigrants are in a different situation again.) Therefore the chapter considers first the needs of all visitors who go to another country to work: Section 9.1 addresses cultural orientation skills, with particular emphasis on knowledge – of the host country and culture and what problems to expect – and on learning how to learn from incountry experience; Section 9.2 covers cultural adaptation – dealing with culture shock, sojourner adjustment, acculturation, training and preparation. (Chapter 8 is, of course, just as relevant and important to the subject of this chapter.)

BOX 9.1

ADVICE FROM A FOREIGN CORRESPONDENT

'There are things that are never spoken about but that you have to deal with. For instance, in South East Asia, quite often people I interview do not like the look of a middle-aged, European man like me. And first impressions are vital. So I do something to deflect attention, like wearing a funny, colourful tie. That arouses curiosity; they ask questions; that entitles me to ask questions in return.

'In those countries, how long you have to wait before asking meaningful questions depends on whom you are interviewing: if it's a general, you reckon on about twenty minutes; if it's only a major, ten to fifteen might be enough.'

Source: Interview with a journalist, author's research.

| 9.1 | **CULTURAL ORIENTATION SKILLS** |

The difficulty of intercultural communication on an international level was observed by Belay in 1993. He wrote: 'Physical interconnectedness and interdependence among cultures and nations has reached a much higher level of development than the awareness and competency required from both individuals and institutions to handle this new reality positively.'[1] Belay was drawing attention to the fact that working internationally gives rise to problems of mutual understanding and appropriate self-presentation and that experiencing these difficulties can be stressful for the individuals concerned. Belay was also pointing out that institutional responses to the consequent needs of the individuals whom they send abroad to work are inadequate – training and preparation systems are generally poor.

Before going on to consider how people can learn to cope on foreign assignments or as expatriates, we need to understand what we mean by being able to cope – what we would recognise or define as coping behaviour in these circumstances. The answer given by Gudykunst is that there are three behavioural dimensions to intercultural effectiveness: the abilities to establish interpersonal relations with people from the other culture, communicate effectively and deal with psychological stress.[2] For Gudykunst, ability to cope in another culture is affected by knowledge of the culture and its language, stereotypes of and attitudes towards people in the other culture, being able to suspend evaluation of other people's behaviour and understanding the self as a cultural being (for example, being aware of one's own cultural identity).

Knowledge of the culture and its language are necessary to understand the behaviour of people in another culture. There are several ways to gain knowledge about the other culture. These include reading books or articles, watching TV programmes or films, talking to people who have had extended contact with people from the other culture or talking directly to people from the other culture. Other ways of gaining information are by observing the members of the other culture interacting among themselves and by observing their behaviour when interacting with them.

One of the best ways to learn about people in other cultures, Gudykunst suggests, is to study their language. Without understanding some of the host language, it is not possible to understand their behaviour. This does not mean that it is necessary to speak the language fluently, but that the more of the language is understood, the more of the culture can be understood. Also, making an effort to speak the language usually is taken as a positive sign by the host nationals, and attempts to use the language increase their desire to get acquainted. Two major factors that tend to affect the amount and type of knowledge people obtain about other cultures are their motivation to adjust to living in the other culture and the nature of the contacts they have with people in the culture.

Knowledge of the other culture is necessary for working out how people in the culture interpret and evaluate their own behaviour. For example, in Western countries, people greet each other with a handshake (and there are rules for what constitutes an appropriate handshake). In Japan, people generally do not shake hands; rather, they bow (and there are rules as to what constitutes an appropriate bow). Both behaviours (shaking hands and bowing) perform the same function of greeting another person, although they are very different. In another case, people may engage in the same behaviour, but use different rules. To illustrate, people may shake hands, but the rules for shaking hands appropriately may differ (for example, in some cultures two hands are used). While knowledge of general cultural similarities and differences, such as whether another culture is collectivist or individualist, particularist or universalist, is vital for interpreting the behaviour of interactors in another country accurately, knowing specific similarities and difference, such as those just described, is needed for knowing in detail how to behave.

It is clear from both common sense and the writings of various authors that having appropriate *attitudes* to intercultural encounters, is vital to working effectively abroad. Thus, Tayeb suggests, the culture's own way of working probably represents the best way of doing things within a particular cultural context. He adds:

> Once there is respect for different points of view as equally valid, there can develop a genuine desire to create new ways of working together. So long as individuals only accept the validity of their own view of the world, international working becomes a battle to get the French to follow the systems or to explain again to the Chinese that you are working to a deadline.[3]

BOX 9.2

WORKING IN TAIWAN AND CHINA

1. 'I did a job in Korea, then decided to check up on things in Taipei on my way home, so my visit was unexpected, but I did ring our agent from the airport, so he had about an hour's warning. When I arrived, I went to see the agent and asked "How are things at EE?" (a major customer). The answer was "I don't know – I suppose OK." "Haven't you been down there recently?" "No, not for ten days." "I think we'll go down." "You're tired." "No, I'll go."

   I walked down, the agent disappeared. It turned out there was a tricky problem with the machine at EE. However, the customer said "I knew you would be here today."' (That is, the agent had told the customer that the international executive would be coming, but had manipulated him into going alone without asking him to.)

2. 'I've just been doing business with the Chinese. I like their politeness – there is no danger of anyone being rude to you. You have to learn their rules and conventions and abide by them and then things are quite easy. You just have to learn the rules of their game. With the Chinese, you always sit down before them, whether they're host or guest, in order not to have your head at a higher level than theirs; you never cross your legs; you never show the soles of your feet; you never usher them through a door. And so on.'

Source: Interview with an international executive, author's research.

Respect towards the other culture is one necessary attitude; another is respect for the individuals with whom one interacts. These two attitudes can sometimes be lacking in, for instance, expatriates working in the former Soviet countries; the obvious deficiencies of some of the systems which operate (such as those referred to in Box 9.3) are translated into a broad disrespect for the entire culture and all its people, as in 'They have no initiative' or 'They can all be bribed'. Such attitudes communicate themselves to the people among whom the expatriate is living and working. Naturally they elicit responses which make the expatriate's life more difficult and thus more stressful.

It is also important to be willing to change one's own attitudes, sometimes in quite fundamental areas. One example is attitudes towards what constitutes success or failure; for instance in the situation quoted in Box 9.3, the conference, seen as a failure by the UK organiser, was regarded as a success by the Hungarians, who understood its purpose not as networking (reasonably enough, since that had not been explicitly stated) but as giving information.

BOX 9.3

THE HUNGARIAN WAY WITH
CONFERENCES IS DIFFERENT

A conference in Hungary, jointly organised by UK and Hungarian staff, had the following features:

- Ninety-three invitations were sent out, only six replies were received by the start of the conference, 72 people attended. The Hungarian staff said, 'Hungarian people have a bad habit: they do not reply to invitations.'
- The conference was intended as a participative workshop. The Hungarian staff, in charge of on-the-ground arrangements, scheduled six presentations an hour for four hours, with no time allowed for questions. This was to be followed by a one-hour 'discussion period'. The venue was the most formal room in the city's largest hotel; the seating was arranged round tables forming a huge hollow square. When the discussion period arrived (an hour later than scheduled) it was impossible to rearrange the room for group work, and, in plenary, discussion was stilted and consisted only of questions and comments addressed to the chair.
- The conference was ended sharply at six o'clock because 'Hungarians always want to rush off home.'

The UK organiser felt the workshop had been 'hijacked' and had failed to fulfil its main purpose, which was networking. However, it had been impossible to insist on other arrangements because the local people were obviously trying so hard according to their own preconceptions.

Source: Author's research.

As a result of the conference, the participants had been informed about the programme with which the conference was concerned. They had also demonstrated their interest by seizing on all the brochures and other literature supplied at the venue and making follow-up enquiries by telephone.

Describing others' behaviour before evaluating generally leads to understanding; evaluating prematurely leads to misunderstanding. There is a 'natural' human tendency to evaluate others' behaviour. Such evaluation, however, is inevitably based upon an individual's own cultural standards.

Using personal cultural standards to evaluate others' behaviour often inhibits the ability to understand them.

To understand others, what is needed is first to describe what is observed; next, to look at alternative interpretations of the behaviour and then to try to work out which interpretation is most appropriate in the other culture. (To do this the knowledge gained about the other culture is needed.) Only then is it possible to evaluate the behaviour, and even then the major reason for doing so is if it is necessary to take a decision on whether or not to engage in it personally. Suspending judgement of others until the cultural logic behind their behaviour is understood is critical to making good decisions on how to react and behave towards them in various situations.

The dangers of cultural imprisonment were pointed out in Chapter 8. *Cultural self-awareness* is related to a necessary state of awareness that usual approaches may be inappropriate.

Dinges (1983),[4] following a review of the literature, suggested that cultural knowledge, cross-cultural understanding and a number of intercultural behavioural skills and situational variables are important in fostering good intercultural relations. This would mean that sojourners and short-stay international visitors alike should focus on three areas of objective:

1. *Behaviour objectives* – to be able to act in accordance with another culture's norms, or to create new 'third culture' patterns which incorporate elements of both home and host cultures.
2. *Skills objectives* – including communication and group process skills and skills of coping with cultural differences. Some personal qualities, such as openness, flexibility, a sense of humour and pluralistic values and attitudes are also helpful.
3. *Knowledge objectives* – Dinges considered that knowledge objectives should be focused on:

    ● Realistic expectations of the target culture(s), of which the most important are those which involve different attributions or interpretations of behaviour.
    ● Information about roles and role relationships. Dinges considered this more useful than information about, for instance, economic, political and educational systems.
    ● What problems to expect. Anticipating problems of the kind quoted in Box 9.4 comes with experience; the reported experience of others can also be relevant, providing the possibility of bias is borne in mind.

In an overseas host culture, there is a need both for specific knowledge of the kinds given in Box 9.4, and the more general understanding of cultural difference and similarity derived from the kinds of analysis presented in Chapters 3, 4 and 5.

> ## BOX 9.4
>
> ### COMMUNISM'S RESIDUES IN CENTRAL ASIA
>
> 'The settlement of our hotel bill was predictably exciting, since they tried to charge us $10 more than the quote for the room, and a dollar each for unsuccessful phone calls (which constitute an estimated 90% of calls in Central Asia). The manager refused to take any responsibility for the error in the price quoted by the reception clerk, and when we insisted, he asked if he should punish the clerk by making her pay the extra $20! Appalling, of course, but this was classic Soviet policy, in which every employee was held personally responsible for errors in his [sic] work. This led to such practices as employing an extra staff person in a five-teacher English faculty, just to keep watch over and be responsible for the equipment and furniture of the faculty office and classrooms (a true example from Samarkand), and the absolute refusal of most employees to even consider performing the duties of an absent co-worker, which could expose them to additional liability.'
>
> *Source:* Correspondence with a US aid worker in Uzbekistan, author's research.

Ethical issues

There can be a dilemma over how far to accommodate to another culture when issues of principle are involved. For instance, although Japanese women are often highly educated, they are not widely accepted in the upper echelons of the corporate world. To send a woman, however senior, to negotiate in Japan is likely to prejudice the outcome. Yet for many Western organisations it is unthinkable to deny a woman such an assignment just on the grounds of her gender. Readers might wish to consider whether they would regard the solution advocated in Box 9.5 as ethical.

In cases such as these, changing one's own attitudes, however desirable from the point of view of intercultural communication, may present not only psychological problems but also ethical or philosophical ones. One of the most difficult aspects of sojourning for work is trying to behave ethically when in another culture, particularly if that culture has values which are different from one's own. An 'honest' business person in a culture where bribes are routine, a non-drinker whose Russian host brings out a bottle of vodka to celebrate his or her arrival, or a vegetarian for whom they bring out caviar – such instances create real tensions between the need to be polite and the ethical need to adhere to one's own values. In addition, the elements of culture are interconnected; if someone thinks one element of culture should be resisted or changed, they need to consider whether it can be changed or resisted in isolation.[5]

BOX 9.5

DEMOTING – CHINESE STYLE

'To transfer... Chinese incumbent managers to lower or other positions, BGB (a UK/Chinese joint venture) can use the tactic of "luring the tiger out of the mountain". Once the "tigers" are out of their lairs, they will become less powerful. For example, a training program can be offered to them and while they are out studying or even sightseeing, a small non-production unit... can be set up. After their return, they suddenly realise that they have been sent to the newly created unit. Although they will not be so pleased with the arrangement, they may feel it much better than involuntarily being put under the leadership of a newcomer.'

Source: Wenhui Wang (1996) 'Management development in Sino-foreign joint ventures', London Business School. Unpublished MBA dissertation.

Coping with negative emotions provoked by overseas encounters

In Chapter 6 an account was given of the five negative emotions identified by Brislin *et al.* (1986)[6] which are common in intercultural encounters – anxiety, the emotions attached to disconfirmed expectations, alienation, ambiguity and being confronted with one's own prejudices. These emotions and others, such as being dependent, or feeling a need to withdraw, are usually heightened when the intercultural encounter occurs outside one's own country as part of an international assignment or sojourn.

The ability to deal with and/or manage emotional reactions in interactions with people from another culture is vital to successful adjustment.[7] Anxiety and stress are natural reactions to interacting intensively with members of other cultures or living in another culture. Everyone experiences them to some degree. The degree to which someone adjusts depends upon how they cope with the stress and anxiety, not whether they experience them. Anxiety and stress, therefore, are not 'bad' in and of themselves. In fact, anxiety provoked by unexpected reactions can have positive consequences, by serving as a cue that something is not right, and motivating thinking about how to adjust.

There are many ways to cope with the anxiety and stress. 'Fighting' the other culture and looking down on its members, or 'taking flight' and interacting only with other members of the own culture are both dysfunctional. The most successful way to cope is to try to be flexible. This means adjusting behaviour to the situation by first observing the way things are done in the culture, keeping in mind that all members of the host culture do not behave in the same way. There can be tremendous variation in acceptable behaviour within a culture. These variations may occur because of education, age, social status or gender differences.

Armed with knowledge of how things are done in the host culture, new behaviours can be tried out; then the degree to which they were successful and enjoyable should be reflected on. Based upon reflection, a decision is made on whether or not to continue the new behaviour or try something different.

Equally, the same coping mechanisms used in the base culture to deal with anxiety and stress can generally be used in another culture. Functional mechanisms include formal and informal relaxation techniques, exercise, talking to a friend about the problems, temporarily leaving the stressful situation, using humour and ensuring that you have at least one 'comfort zone' – one area of life which is continuous with your previous existence. Dysfunctional mechanisms include taking tranquillisers or other drugs, drinking too much coffee or cola or eating, smoking and drinking alcohol too often. Creativity in solving adjustment problems is also valuable.

Learning how to learn from incountry experiences

Hughes-Weiner[8] used Kolb's learning cycle[9] as a model for how cultural differences affect what the sojourner needs to do to learn from incountry experience. Kolb's model, shown in Figure 9.1, proposes that people who learn effectively from experience go through a recurrent cycle of concrete experience, reflective observation, abstract conceptualisation and active experimentation. For example, the first time that native English-speaking sojourners enter on a discussion in English with someone for whom it is a second language, they might speak very slowly, using simple words and sentence structures. If the local person's response uses more sophisticated words and phrases and is spoken more quickly than expected, the sojourners might reflect that this indicates that they are more fluent in English than anticipated and that a slow, emphatic style might have been somewhat insulting – this would be reflective observation. The sojourners might go on to think that in general it would be better to obtain as much information as possible about other people's level of English language competence before giving away their expectations – this would be abstract conceptualisation. Next time they meet a 'stranger' for a discussion in English they might try to ask one or two open questions initially, to encourage the stranger to speak. This would give them the opportunity to listen and gauge the other's language competence before themself saying much – this would be active experimentation.

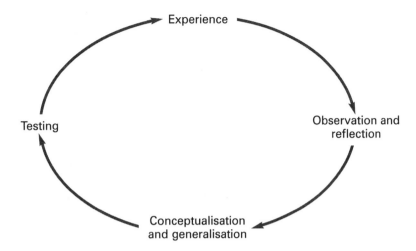

Figure 9.1 Kolb's model for learning from experience

Kolb argues, and research based on his model has confirmed, that the process of learning from experience can be speeded up, and more can be learnt, by actively engaging in this cycle – seeking more experience, reflecting on it more, generalising from it more and testing the resulting 'model' more. Hughes-Weiner, however, points out some cautions which the enthusiastic user of Kolb's model needs to bear in mind, especially if they are using it as a vehicle to understand different others.

- Concrete experience: people with different backgrounds, such as those from other cultures, are likely to have had quite different experiences.
- Reflective observation: due to the variety of behaviour patterns, artifacts and institutions in different cultures, people from different societies are likely to acquire different bodies of knowledge and to make different assumptions about what is true.
- Abstract conceptualisation: since people from different cultures have different cognitive frameworks, there is a risk of using inappropriate frameworks in cross-cultural situations or of focusing on irrelevant information, while ignoring important cues, resulting in incorrect interpretations.
- Active experimentation: since cultures differ in behavioural patterns, cross-cultural situations may be misdiagnosed, resulting in inappropriate responses. Alternatively situations may seem unfamiliar and confusing, in which case sojourners may not know how to respond. Even when they know what to do, new behaviours may be difficult to perform smoothly.

These rather negative points can be made positive aids to learning how to learn from incountry experience, however, by regarding them as areas to which the learner needs to give particular attention. In this way they will enhance awareness of areas where intercultural misunderstanding can occur.

Unrewarding or punishing experiences of any kind, as behaviourist learning theory teaches, can lead people to avoid or suppress the kind of behaviour which they associate with the negative reinforcement. For example, if a person suffers embarrassment in an intercultural encounter because of ignorance of cultural norms, he or she may have a tendency to reduce exposure in future. This tendency, according to Kolb's model, will reduce his or her speed and eventual level of intercultural orientation. One way to overcome this is by increasing knowledge in the areas where embarrassment is likely; another is to pursue a conversational strategy designed to minimise exposure to embarrassment; a third is to 'condition' the self to such embarrassment as an inevitable and productive element in gaining intercultural understanding – the arousal created by embarrassment will, according to cognitive learning theory, enhance the ability to learn.

> The effects of face-to-face adaptation, functional or non-functional, represent part of each individual's learning experience, thus partially conditioning the nature of future cross-cultural contacts with the same or different people. Time out from interacting can be used to engage in activities, such as introspection, reading, use of mass-media and so on to prepare for future interactions.

9.2	SOJOURNING

Sojourners are people who:

- grew up (had their 'primary socialisation') in one culture and moved, temporarily, but for at least a month, into another
- depend to some extent on the host environment for meeting their personal and social needs
- are engaged in firsthand, continuous experiences with the host environment.

The real difficulties inherent in being a sojourner are demonstrated by studies which have shown that 16–50% of US expatriates fail on the foreign assignment. (Failing is defined as returning to the home country before the assignment is completed successfully – therefore not counting those who fail to perform satisfactorily but still stay on.) European and Japanese expatriates do better – 59% of a European sample of organisations reported failure rates below 5%, 38% reported rates of 6–10% and 3% reported rates of 11–15%.

Baumgarten (1995)[10] found that 70% of US expatriates are sent abroad without any cross-cultural training and 90% of their families the same, although the inability of the partner to adapt to the foreign environment is one, if not the most, important cause of expatriate failure. Most of the US companies that did offer training provided only brief environmental summaries and some cultural and language preparation. Sixty-nine per cent of correspondents in Baumgarten's Western European sample sponsored training programmes to prepare candidates for foreign assignments – and the level was about the same in Japan. Mostly, however, training was only for people sent outside Europe or the USA, plus Eastern Europe.

BOX 9.6

WORKING IN MAGNITOGORSK

'It takes about a month, anywhere in the world, before people begin to accept you. During that time, you wonder what on earth made you go there and how you're going to stand it. Then it gets better. I was asked at 7pm one Saturday in Scarsdale, New York, where, if I could have my pick, I'd like to be at this time. I said Magnitogorsk in the bar. It's the unpredictability – anything could happen, but the most likely is that someone will do this to you (here he pressed the skin under his jaw), which means a party with the vodka flowing and the talk the liveliest on earth.'

Source: Interview with an international executive, author's research.

Another factor that may have contributed to poor adjustment is that, across many countries, job knowledge and technical or managerial ability appear to be the primary factors that are used in selecting international assignees. This means that little attention is paid to the factors that contribute to being able to cope in an 'alien' culture. One study[11] which sheds some light on what these factors might be took as subjects 338 international assignees from 26 diverse countries and 45 organisations, assigned to 43 diverse countries and performing diverse jobs. International assignees were defined as individuals posted from their home office to a host country subsidiary or branch. Five factors were identified by the international assignees themselves in the following descending order of importance:

1. family situation
2. flexibility/adaptability
3. job knowledge and motivation
4. relational skills
5. extra-cultural openness.

Importance ratings were not influenced by job type (managerial/non-managerial status) but they were by organisation type; in general, service organisation personnel ascribed more importance to relational and psycho-social factors (perhaps because they have more contact with the local community and host country nationals). The five-factor solution explained 50.28% of the variance. The significance of family situation was emphasised by the finding that, unlike the other factors, its importance was not influenced by the independent variables examined – that is, job or organisation; it was consistently important across all conditions.

Where two cultures are relatively similar, sojourning is easier with no change in behaviours; but where cultures are very different and adaptation is necessary, individuals who are successful in their home culture may not be able to adjust their behaviour patterns sufficiently. This proposition is in line with much anecdotal evidence from various organisations, although whether it would stand up to research is less clear. It does, however, point to the value of seeking some degree of match between individuals' culture and the culture of the country in which they will sojourn.

BOX 9.7

CHALLENGES OF STUDYING ABROAD

Large numbers of students now spend periods of a semester or a year or more abroad as part of their courses. There is, therefore, not surprisingly, an emergent body of research into their problems in such sojourns and how they cope. This research is of value for them, their tutors and cousellors and in some cases more widely:

1. Sandhu and Asrabadi (1991) found by scaling 128 international students for stress that they were psychologically at risk on perceived deprivation/alienation, loneliness/homesickness, hate, fear, stress due to change and guilt.

2. A study of 412 foreign graduate students in USA investigated their (1) perceptions of the stressfulness of role demands and (2) abilities to cope with those demands. Results indicated that students associated (lack of) English language skills and cultural distance with stress and language, academic, and problem-solving skills with coping capacity.

3. At the University of Maryland, 248 first-year international students were tested for factors linked to grade point average (GPA) and persistence:

  - 'Self-confidence' and 'availability of a strong support person' consistently predicted GPA.
  - Persistence, however, was related to an aggregate of variables, but was consistently predicted by 'understanding racism' and 'involvement in community service'. These findings suggest that the academic performance of international students is related to individual variables while persistence may require an additional adjustment to environmental variables.

4. Another US research study of 245 students from Korea, the Arab nations, and Nigeria was conducted to determine whether there are significant relationships between any of three measures of the level of stress (anxiety, depression, and somatic complaints) among international college students. Variables analysed in the study included: English-language proficiency; social interaction with Americans, co-nationals and other internationals; health; financial conditions; nationality; length of stay; and marital status. The main significant relationships were found with the following:

  - English-language proficiency
  - social interaction with Americans
  - duration of stay
  - marital status
  - health conditions.

5. Surdam and Collins investigated the adaptation of 143 international students in USA in relation to individual and family variables. Results suggested successful adaptation was related to:

  - spending leisure time with host nationals
  - adequate knowledge of English
  - coming from better educated families
  - religious participation.

6. A study of a group of foreign graduate students ($n=29$) who participated in a study skills and cultural-orientation programme at a British university found that in comparison with a group not participating ($n=26$), and contrary to expectations, participating students had more homesickness and psychological difficulties.

The findings cast doubt on the common view that culture shock is ameliorated by such programmes.

Sources: Sandhu, D.S. and Asrabadi, B.R. (1991) 'An assessment of psychological needs of international students: implications for counseling and psychotherapy'. Paper presented at the Annual Convention of the American Association for Counseling and Development, Reno, NV. ERIC Document Reproduction Service No. ED 350 550. Posted on the Internet: http://www.flstw.edo/pderic.html; Wan, T. *et al.* (1992) 'Academic stress of international students attending US universities', *Research in Higher Education*, **33**: 607–23; Boyer, S.P. and Sedlacek, W.E. (1987) 'Noncognitive predictors of academic success for international students: a longitudinal study' (Research Report No.1–87). College Park: University of Maryland, Counseling Center. ERIC Document Reproduction Service No. ED 284 499. Posted on the Internet: http://www.flstw.edo/pderic. html; Cho, S. (1988) 'Predictive factors of stress among international college students'. ERIC Document Reproduction Service No. ED 322 822. Posted on the Internet: http://www.flstw.edo/pderic.html; Surdam, J.C. and Collins, J.R. (1984) 'Adaptation of international students: a cause for concern', *Journal of College Student Personnel*, **25**: 240–45; McKinlay, N.J. *et al.* (1996) 'An exploratory investigation of the effects of a cultural orientation programme on the psychological well-being of international university students', *Journal of Higher Education*, **31**: 379–95.

Culture shock

Part of the reason for the failures of international assignees and the difficulties of international students just described is expressed in the term 'culture shock'. This refers to feelings of anxiety and tension due to loss of familiar customs and social interactions.

'Culture shock' can appear in a number of guises, varying from mild to severe homesickness, feeling frustrated and suffering alienation and isolation. These feelings can be brought on by the language barrier, loneliness, difficulty in penetrating the host society, not knowing how to react in a difficult situation and always being the centre of attention.

The main characteristics consistently listed as negative factors for cultural adjustment include:

- national origin and perceived discrimination: in the USA, for instance, sojourners from African or Asian countries have more adjustment problems than do Europeans
- depression
- locus of control.

BOX 9.8

SOJOURNING IN JAPAN

'Japan's emphasis on "belonging" to the group often tends to make newcomers feel isolated. Many foreigners I know, despite learning the Japanese language to a high level, and having many Japanese friends, still feel like an "outsider". Just little things reinforce this feeling; for example, when a young child points at me in the street and says "*gaijin, gaijin*" I often feel a little upset. I realise that the child is pointing out the obvious that I "look" different, but I am also surprised that at such an early age a child can distinguish between non-Japanese and Japanese. The very term "*gaijin*" also creates problems, as it is often literally translated as "outsider" or "alien"; both words in English have negative connotations.'

Source: Posted on the Internet: http://www.shirakawa.or.jp/~takagawa/NecHome/i_cult01.html.

The last two characteristics – depression and locus of control – point to 'personality' factors as being among those affecting susceptibility or resistance to culture shock.

Common symptoms of culture shock that have been identified include irritability, loneliness, depression and rigidity. Parallel symptoms to those induced by culture shock have been described in the 'learned helplessness' literature.

Therefore, one author suggests, the application of reformulated, learned helplessness to cultural adjustment can contribute to the understanding of culture shock.[12] Learned helplessness is a person's belief that what happens to them and the outcomes of what they do are independent of what they do and how they do it; people suffering from learned helplessness attribute negative events internally, stably and globally ('global' here means that the cause is believed to operate on a large number of things, not just one). If people suffering from learned helplessness have a bad experience, they will tend to think it is caused by them, that the cause is long lasting and unchangeable and that the cause will make other things bad, too. (The Turkish officials referred to in Box 4.9 could be described as suffering from learned helplessness.) An individual's use of stable/unstable, global/specific, and internal/external attributions can affect his or her adjustment to a new culture. Figure 9.2 flow charts the possible relationship between learned helplessness and culture shock.

BOX 9.9

WORKING IN A 'TIGER' ECONOMY

A UK expatriate university lecturer described how he found working in a university in one of the Asian 'tiger' economies:

'It's a bit like a communist state, but there aren't the stresses and strains because the population is so compliant – it's their culture. On the other hand, people are very competitive. The first thing they want to know is your grade and education.

'*The Far Eastern Economic Review* is only allowed to sell a limited number of copies here as a punishment for opposing the government. I'm allowed one, but I had to sign an undertaking not to allow any articles from it to be distributed. Another expatriate warned me not to breach this – it would get back. So I don't.

'I was appointed as a regional economist. When I first arrived I gave a presentation – an overview; this country came close to the top in growth terms, and so on, but not at the very top. I was hauled in by my boss and told this was unacceptable.

'When the President leaves the building, you get a call so you can go to your door and bow him out. When he's away, nothing gets decided. In the university, Personnel is all-powerful: they decide on hiring and firing, terms and conditions, everything, and, of course, the expat is very vulnerable – you've probably lost some ground in career terms at home by coming here in the first place, and if you return before your contract expires, the position can become irretrievable. Or, at least, people think it can, which has the same effect. So we are effectively bullied by the bureaucrats of Personnel. Not that they are vindictive, but they are absolutely rigid. For instance, a Canadian lecturer had failed to renew his medical insurance (done through the university) on the due date. When he tried to correct this, about a week later, he was met with an absolute stonewall: "Too late". He contacted the insurance company that ran the scheme, found out that there was no reason why it should not be backdated, and pointed this out. No use."Too late." He asked to be referred to her superior, but this was refused. So, in the end, he asked her how she spelt her name, so that he could name her in the letter he was writing to the President of the university. She agreed to let him renew.

'We expats debate all the time how best to handle it. Some say you should be all sweetness and light. Others that you should conform to the stereotype of Westerners here – that is, you should shout, make demands and threaten. You get to devise ways of getting round the situation. For instance, the students rate the staff, and if you get a poor rating on any item, you are in trouble.

'One of the items concerns whether you give summaries, which you are supposed to do – they are spoon-fed. So, after the first semester, when I gave summaries but still got poor ratings on it, I strongly emphasised in the first session that I would give them summaries in each session, and made them write this down. When I gave them out, I said, each time – "Here is today's summary; make sure you note it down under the heading SUMMARY"; and in the last session, I said, "You've had a summary for every session. Does anyone not agree?" Now I get asked by other staff how I manage to get such high ratings for my summaries.

'The country is run entirely by the elite – the top 5%. But I teach that group in this elitist university and by the time they get to the third year of their studies they are incapable of thinking for themselves. There's no crime, no drugs, it's clean. But after three years I don't raise my voice if I'm criticising the regime – not even when I'm abroad, like now – it's become an instinct.

'Personnel in international companies (80% of businesses are foreign-owned) are insulated from the real world – they're not affected by the restrictions.'

Source: Interview with an expatriate university teacher, author's research.

Martin[13] has pointed out, however, that sojourners should realise that culture shock and the need for a painful process of cultural adjustment are 'universal aspects' – individuals are commonly disorientated when undergoing a transitional experience and the accompanying stress. Realising that what they are undergoing is 'normal' helps many individuals to tolerate stress and eventually cope.

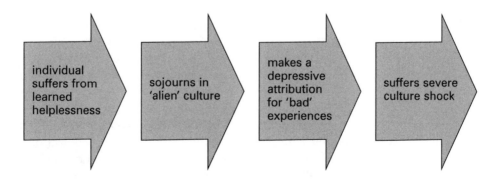

Figure 9.2   Learned helplessness and culture shock

BOX 9.10

ON JAPANESE SOJOURNERS IN LONDON

Shigeo Niwa, administrator of the Nippon Club for Japanese people working in London: 'For Japanese businessmen [sic] who are on their first assignment to the UK, the reality comes as a total culture shock. It takes them a year and a half just to get used to it. We encourage them to immerse themselves in British culture, but, because of the pressure of work, a lot of them don't have time. In any case, they know that after two or three years the company will call them back to Japan. You can hardly blame them if they go for the easier option [mixing mainly with other Japanese].'

Lady Marks of Broughton, the former wife of Lord Marks, who relinquished her Japanese citizenship 18 years ago to settle in London and whose newspaper, the *Nichi-Ei Times*, comes out fortnightly in Japanese, commented: 'The language is a barrier, but the bigger barriers are in people's minds. On one level Japanese people are fascinated with British culture, but they still want to buy British goods from a Japanese shop assistant in a Japanese store. In the morning they read a Japanese newspaper and in the evening they go home and watch Japanese satellite TV. Most of them are living in exactly the same way as they would in Tokyo... when I arrived I made sure I lived with English people. It's the only way to become part of the culture.'

Source: Evening Standard, 21 August 1995.

Sojourner adjustment/adaptation

Despite problems of culture shock, most sojourners do eventually adjust to the point where they are coping and effective. How do they do it and can it be speeded up? One approach is to recognise a series of stages which are usually gone through in the process of adjustment. In one such model the stages are:

1. *Fascination*: In the early days 'buffers' such as getting set up with work, accommodation and so on prevent real contact with the host culture.
2. *Hostility and aggression*: As the buffers reduce, contact occurs and usually anger towards everything and sometimes everyone in the host culture occurs. This is a critical point where the shock can develop into a rejection of the host culture or acceptance and adjustment to new surroundings.
3. *Acceptance*: The person then accepts the host culture as much as they can. This is never total, but is sufficient to make life comfortable.

4.   *Adaptation*: In spite of difficulties a person does his or her best to adjust to the new culture and refuses to give in to culture shock.

Motivation to adapt is perhaps the most important factor determining the speed with which individuals pass through these stages. Motivation to adapt depends in part on expected length of stay – the longer the higher the motivation. Support programmes can ease on-arrival difficulties but, in the longer term, adaptation must occur primarily in the individual, not in the host society.

According to Ady (1995)[14] sojourner adjustment is a relatively short-term, individual and time-based process that is conceptually distinct from cultural or ethnic assimilation, adaptation and intercultural communicative competence. Ady defines sojourner adjustment as a function of the extent to which the sojourner judges that he or she is meeting environmental demands and that his or her needs are being met in the new environment. Global measures of satisfaction, Ady argues, may be too problematic to be practical. Ady prefers domain-specific measures; domains are numerous but can be classifed as:

- task domains (employment and daily structuring tasks)
- social support domains (friendships, interaction with host nationals)
- ecology domains (physical aspects of the new environment).

In each separate domain, adjustment occurs as a function of the sojourner's judgement of how well he or she is meeting the demands of the environment and how well the environment is meeting his or her needs; total adjustment is a function of adjustment in all three domains. Figure 9.3 shows the model.

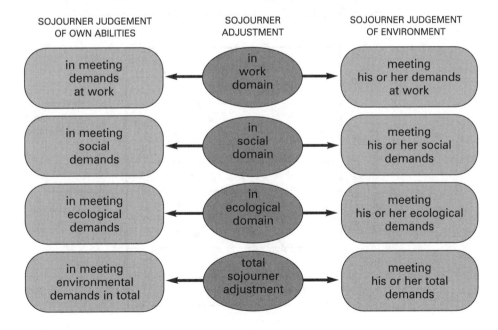

Figure 9.3   Ady's domain model of sojourner adjustment

Ady puts forward four axioms concerned with sojourner adjustment:

1. Adjustment is multidimensional.
2. Adjustment varies across domains and over time; some happens quickly, some more slowly.
3. Adjustment is experienced by sojourners as happening through a series of crises.
4. Adjustment is experienced by sojourners as non-gestalt.

Ady also contends that adjustment is highly salient to sojourners – while it is going on the problems and solutions associated with it are often central in the sojourner's consciousness.

There is a pessimistic model of sojourner adjustment, represented by a U-shaped curve as illustrated in Figure 9.4. This hypothesises that after an initial 'honeymoon' stage sojourners often become frustrated with day-to-day living and retreat to the stability and comfort of home-culture friendships. Strom (1994)[15] reports a study which, he argues, tends to support this hypothesis. Fifty-eight pairs of students, of whom half were from abroad and studying in an ESL (English as a second language) programme and half were home-country students in a university intercultural communication class, met for ten weeks in a cultural partners programme. During the programme, they conversed in English and were encouraged to make friends. The ESL students were tested at weeks two and ten for English proficiency, intercultural communication competence, interest in learning about culturally different others, interest in making friends with culturally different others, their number of cross-cultural acquaintances, number of cross-cultural friends and homophily.

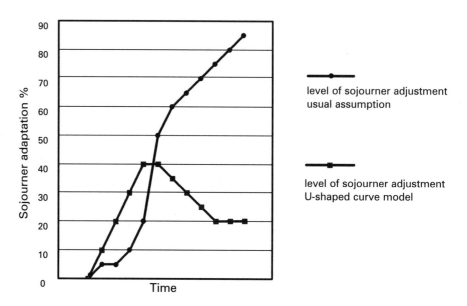

Figure 9.4 Sojourner adjustment over time: U-shaped curve hypothesis

The overall impact of the cultural partners programme, Strom reported, appeared negligible:

- The intercultural communication skills of ESL students did not improve.
- Their desire to learn about other cultures did not increase.
- The only increase in intercultural friendships was with their programme partners.
- The university students were not perceived as having become better intercultural communicators either.

There are a number of possible explanations for these findings: one is that the time spent together was too short, another that the students were reacting to unmet expectations (the programme had been explained to them as a social exercise). However, a third explanation, Strom suggests, is that the findings go to confirm the U-curve adjustment hypothesis. He concludes that 'Competence is a transactionally created phenomenon between unique communicators in specific contexts and not easily defined as an enduring trait across contexts.' That is to say, people cannot acquire a generic skill of adjusting to new cultural environments, but must repeat the learning process and curve with each new sojourn.

Kim,[16] however, proposed a more optimistic model of sojourner adaptation than the 'universal' U-shaped curve. She suggested that it is reasonable to make the following assumptions about the adaptation process: that humans have an inherent drive to adapt and grow; that adaptation to one's social environment occurs through communication and that adaptation is a complex and dynamic process.

She argued that the process involves at least the following elements:

1. Unlearning of at least some old cultural habits (called deculturation).
2. Learning new responses (acculturation).
3. A stress-adaptation-growth dynamic:

    - In new environments, people find that they have difficulty in coping – they suffer from 'information overload', uncertainty about others' expectations, difficulty in interpreting others' communicative behaviours and so on. These disequilibrating experiences are stressful. An initial response to stress, for many individuals, is to resort to defence mechanisms, such as selective attention, self-deception, denial, avoidance, withdrawal, hostility, cynicism and compulsively altruistic behaviour. Fortunately, these responses, which are not helpful to adapting, are temporary in most cases.

    - Other responses to the new environment are adaptation responses – assimilation (acting on the environment so that aspects of it may be incorporated into their internal structure) and accommodation (responding to the environment by adjusting their internal conditions to the corresponding external realities). This occurs through learning elements of the new culture and unlearning elements of the 'old'.

- The adaptation responses lead to growth – in particular to an increased ability to adapt to further environmental changes. As they gain experience at making the transition to a new host environment, people get better at it.

BOX 9.11

WOMEN MAKE HIGHLY SUCCESSFUL
INTERNATIONAL MANAGERS

In a study conducted by Nancy J. Adler of 52 international female managers who had worked in Asia, it was found that they were overwhelmingly successful. Most of these women were the first female expatriates to be sent abroad (to the role); only 10% followed another woman into the international position. Therefore, few rules or role models existed and the decision process leading a company to send a female manager to Asia could be described as one of mutual education between management and the employee. The following is a quote from Adler's study by a American female manager based in Hong Kong: 'It doesn't make any difference if you are blue, green, purple, or a frog. If you have the best product at the best price, they'll buy.'

The thrust of Adler's study was that American female expatriates were viewed first as '*gaijinå*' (foreigners), then as women.

Source: Adler, N.J. (1994) 'Competitive frontiers: women managing across borders' in Adler, N.J. and Izraeli, D.N. (eds) *Competitive Frontiers: Women Managers in a Global Economy*, Cambridge, MA: Blackwell.

As they begin to adapt successfully, sojourners show increased functional fitness (they can perform more effectively, both at work and in living), improved psychological health (they start to feel more cheerful), which is directly related to an increased ability to communicate, and an expanded and more flexible sense of themselves as a person (they begin to have an intercultural identity).

However, sojourners go through the processes of intercultural adaptation at different rates – some adapt quickly, others more slowly, a few not at all. There are reasons for these differential rates – some are related to the individual; but many, research suggests, are more closely related to the host environment: some countries and organisations are easier to fit into than others. Figure 9.5 shows the main influences.

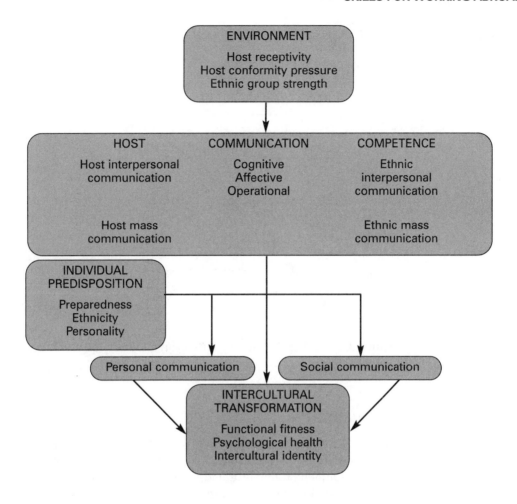

Figure 9.5   Factors affecting differences in individuals' rates of intercultural adaptation

Within individual predispositions to adapt successfully, strength of sojourner's ethnic identity seems to be a key variable. A strong ethnic identity tends to mean that adjustment initially occurs quite rapidly but then declines – there is a U-shaped curve; a weak ethnic identity is more likely to produce a slow but steady increase in adjustment. Figure 9.6 illustrates the difference.

Some empirical support for this model of sojourner adaptation can be found, as follows:

● Host mass communication has been observed to facilitate the adaptation of strangers.

● Empirical evidence shows that the extreme stress reactions in the form of escapism, neurosis and psychosis are most often seen among those whose native culture radically differs from that of the host community. However, personality factors like openness and strength reduce stress reactions.

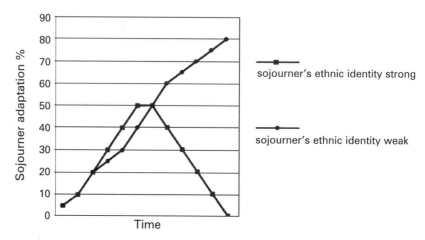

Figure 9.6   Effects of sojourner's ethnic identity strength on intercultural adaptation

Acculturation

Acculturation is the establishment of an 'intercultural identity' for an immigrant, sojourner, or international assignee who successfully integrates into a new environment. Intercultural identity (Kim, 1992)[17] is achieved when an individual grows beyond their original culture and encompasses a new culture, gaining additional insight into both cultures in the process. It involves understanding 'better the norms and values, and… adopt[ing] salient reference groups of the host society'. Acculturation and acquiring an intercultural identity presuppose that the visitor's simplified view of the host society is replaced with a complex view which is more realistic. Competence in the language of the host country, being highly motivated to achieve acculturation and having access to interpersonal and mass communication experiences are the three factors which have most bearing on gaining more complex perceptions of the host country.

One somewhat controversial aspect of Kim's later work is her contention that additional stress might result in faster and more effective acculturation. She gives examples suggesting that Canadians in Kenya 'who would ultimately be the most effective in adapting to a new culture underwent the most intense culture shock during the transition period'. Kim accounts for this by arguing that, when stress is extreme, 'human plasticity' is activated to form the person more fully into a more complete intercultural identity: in longer stays (those of immigrants for instance) initial high stress levels result in more complete acculturation, an earlier adoption of an intercultural identity and lower stress levels eventually.

Evidence to support Kim's proposals on acculturation came from Ward and Kennedy (1993),[18] who found in studies of international students that those students with the most host–national contact also showed the most adaptation, that 'psychological stress is found in individuals who attempt to integrate' and that longer stays resulted in more acculturation. Ward and Kennedy also found support for language ability being correlated with feeling at ease and satisfied with an international student experience. This is further support for Kim's proposal that host language ability is related to acculturation.

De Verthelyi (1995)[19] provides additional evidence that initial stress can lead to eventual acculturation. In studies of the spouses of international students, de Verthelyi found widespread stress. 'Initial feelings of sadness, loneliness, self-doubt, confusion, and frustration were present in their descriptions of the first weeks and months of the sojourn.' Language difficulties made this initial stress worse, supporting Kim's theory that language competence is necessary for acculturation. De Verthelyi found that a 'positive change of mood usually happened within the first 3–6 months from arrival', thus confirming Kim's (1988)[20] view that 'in time strangers become increasingly proficient in managing their life activities in the host society'.

Countering Kim's view, Martin *et al.* (1995)[21] provided some evidence that successful exchange student experiences are more related to expectations than acculturation. Their work indicated that 'Sojourners consistently reported that expectations were met or positively violated.' This led them to discount the value of stress to acculturation, as well as the value of acculturation to a successful experience. 'The notion of self-fulfilling prophecy accounts for the similarity between expectations and fulfillment of these expectations.'

In anxiety/uncertainty management theory, anxiety and the resulting stress is expected to drive the individual toward uncertainty reduction, and eventual acculturation and comfort in the new milieu. Witte (1993)[22] considers that this results only when acculturation into the new milieu appears to be manageable. The stress of culture shock will result in acculturation only if acculturation appears to be a possible outcome of the experience. If the danger in a situation provoking fear appears to be manageable, the preferred adaptive response of the individual is to take action to reduce the danger. If the danger in a fear-provoking situation seems to be too large to handle, however, or danger reduction strategies are absent, fear reduction takes over and the danger is ignored or rationalised out of salience. Similar responses to new cultures would result in maladaptive seclusion, and not result in acculturation of the individual or the society.

Witte argues that 'When anxiety is greater than attributional confidence, then anxiety control processes will dominate.' But when there is too little anxiety and/or uncertainty, Gudykunst and Kim (1992)[23] note that people are not motivated to adapt or communicate effectively because the interactions are boring, tedious or unfulfilling.

Training for international assignments and sojourns

Clearly, the better prepared sojourners are for their visit to a country with a markedly different culture from their own, the more likely they are, other things being equal, to succeed in adjustment, adaptation or acculturation. The increasing evidence on sojourner failure and distress therefore makes training an intervention of increasing concern to those responsible for sending people abroad. Much training to date has concentrated on cultural content: the ways in which the host culture, especially its surface manifestations, differs from the sojourner's home culture.

However, as Martin[24] pointed out as early as 1986, 'There are variables other than cultural content that need to be considered in designing and implementing orientation programs.' Moreover sojourners cannot be taught everything there is to know about the target culture – much will have to be learned from experience on or after arrival. Sojourners need to recognise that 'cultural diversity is not an intellectual endeavor but laden with values, beliefs and interpersonal complexities'; Martin argues that the objective of sojourner training should be to enable trainees to develop intercultural skills to the level where they can use them in an independent manner.

Bennett (1986)[25] criticised the most popular 'model' of sojourner preparation of the time, the so-called 'orientation' model, for its failure to help sojourners learn and adapt once in the host country. 'Orientation' models generally provide sojourners-to-be with culture-specific information about the host culture – their implicit assumption is that adaptation is a primarily intellectual process. In fact, however, it is likely to be the emotional and behavioural adjustment that will give sojourners most difficulty. Bennett wrote: 'If the trainee has only learned specific bits of data and generalizations about a culture, his [sic] everyday experience with individual members of that culture will quickly invalidate a major portion of the content knowledge he [sic] has received... This difference between teaching for knowledge and teaching for performance and adaptation comprises the fundamental criticism of this model.'

Once in the host country, Bennett points out:

- Trainees will be experiencing a new environment and will need to understand approaches to deriving information from new stimuli – new ways to categorise the information, internalise it and use it to accomplish new goals or solve problems.
- They will be shifting their learning environment from the classroom to an experiential environment, that of existence in another culture.
- The experiential learning environment is intrinsically learner-centred (that is, it requires adjustment from the learner).
- Sojourners will be in an environment where:
  - all cultural cues are ambiguous, if not intimidating
  - their language skills may not be adequate to meet their needs
  - they are deprived of the ordinary reinforcement routinely received in the home culture.

The simulation or area training model tries to accommodate these considerations – it relies on reproducing for the participants situations and conditions which closely duplicate the actual overseas site and assignment. However, the drawback of this model is that opportunities to participate in a ten-week intensive residential training programme abroad are few.

Another attempt is the self-awareness model, which is based on the principle that sojourners who understand themselves better will understand their culture better and consequently be more effective abroad: 'Cultural self-awareness stands as an important prerequisite component to learning the other culture's world view.'[26] These models use T-group and role-playing training methods. However, Bennett points out that the T-group is an American invention, built on the American values of openness, equality, individuality and directness. For individuals from non-American cultural backgrounds, T-groups can be too challenging and, therefore, unhelpful. Another variant, 'sensitivity groups' are 'in all probability... counterproductive in intercultural training' according to Bennett.

In cultural awareness models, in contrast to self-awareness models, the emphasis is on cultural insight, with individual awareness an expected by-product. One type is the 'Contrast home culture' model, which aims to assist in recognising the sojourner-to-be's own culture's values as a first step in relating across cultures and so focuses primarily on cultural filters. Usually the contrasting culture is not intended to be seen as any specific one. Another type is an intercultural communication workshop which focuses on the communication which results in a context of value differences. These workshops usually feature a small group experience with members of at least two different cultures, led by trained facilitators. The group experience becomes a laboratory in which members observe themselves.

Table 9.1 summarises three different approaches to sojourner preparation.

Table 9.1   Three different approaches to sojourner preparation

	ORIENTATION	TRAINING	EDUCATION
GOALS	Cognitive Behavioural	Affective Behavioural	Cognitive Affective Behavioural
CONTENT	Culture specific	Culture specific	Culture specific Culture general
	Who, what, when, where	Who, what, when, where and how	Who, what, when, where how and why
PROCESS	Intellectual	Experiential	Experiential Intellectual

Source: Based on Bennett, J.M. (1986) 'Modes of cross-cultural training: conceptualising c/c training as education', *International Journal of Intercultural Relations*, **10**: 117–34.

9.3	CONCLUSION

Both working internationally and sojourning, which means medium-term residence and, usually, working or studying in a foreign country, make high demands on individuals' ability to cope. Many international assignees actually 'fail' and return home, a problem believed to be caused by lack of appropriate selection – ignoring cultural adaptation potential – and lack of preparation and training. Nearly all sojourners will experience culture shock, although susceptibility to its more extreme effects appears to be reduced in the presence of certain factors, including host-country language competence, prior sojourning experience, and the absence of learned helplessness. Adjusting and adapting to a new culture and dealing with culture shock are assisted by an understanding that it is normal and also recognising that stress can lead to adaptation and growth. The techniques for coping with stress and experiential learning can be used to facilitate adaptation.

REFERENCES

1. Belay, G. (1993) 'Toward a paradigm shift for intercultural and international communication: new research directions', *Communication Yearbook*, **16**: 437–57.
2. Gudykunst, W.B. (1988) 'Uncertainty and anxiety', in Kim, Y.Y. and Gudykunst, W.B. (eds) *Theories in Intercultural Communication*, Newbury Park, CA: Sage.
3. Tayeb, M.H. (1996) *The Management of a Multicultural Workforce*, Chichester: John Wiley.
4. Dinges, N. (1983) 'Intercultural competence', in Landis, D. and Brislin, R.W. (eds) *Handbook of Intercultural Training*, Vol. 1, New York: Pergamon Press.
5. Katriel, T. (1989) 'From "context" to "contexts" in intercultural communication research', in Ting-Toomey, S. and Korzenny, F. (eds) *Language, Communication and Culture: Current Directions,* Newbury Park, CA: Sage.
6. Brislin, R., Cushner, K., Cherrie, C. and Yong, M. (1986) *Intercultural Interactions,* Beverly Hills, CA: Sage.
7. Gudykunst, W.B. and Hammer, M.R. (1988) 'Strangers and hosts: an uncertainty reduction based theory of intercultural adaptation', in Kim, Y.Y. and Gudykunst, W.B. (eds) *Cross-cultural Adaptation: Current Approaches*, Newbury Park, CA: Sage.
8. Hughes-Weiner, G. (1986) 'The "learning how to learn" approach to cross-cultural orientation', *International Journal of Intercultural Relations*, **10**: 485–505.
9. Kolb, D.A., Rubin, I.M. and McIntyre, J.M. (1973) *Organizational Psychology: An Experiential Approach*, Englewood Cliffs, NJ: Prentice-Hall.
10. Baumgarten, K. (1995) 'Training and development of international staff', in Harzing, A.-W. and Ruysseveldt, J.V. (eds) *International Human Resource Management*, London: Sage.
11. Arthur, W. (Jr) and Bennett, W. (Jr) (1995) 'The international assignee: the relative importance of factors perceived to contribute to success', *Personnel Psychology*, **48**: 99–114.
12. Reinicke, M.J. (1986) 'Cultural adjustment of international students in the US: A reevaluation using reformulated learned helplessness', ERIC Document Reproduction Service No. ED 274 939.

13. Martin, J. (1986) 'Training issues in cross-cultural orientation', *International Journal of Intercultural Relations*, **10**: 103–16.
14. Ady, J.C. (1995) 'Toward a differential demand model of sojourner adjustment', in Kim, Y.Y. (ed.) *Intercultural Communication Theory* (*International and Intercultural Communication Annual XIX*), Thousand Oaks, CA: Sage.
15. Strom, W.A. (1994) 'The effects of a conversational partners program on ESL and university students', *Howard Journal of Communications*, **5**(1 & 2), 138–56.
16. Kim, Y.Y. (1988) *Communication and Cross-cultural Adaptation: An Integrative Theory*, Philadelphia, PA: Multi-Lingual Matters.
17. Kim, Y.Y. (1992) 'Development of intercultural identity'. Paper presented at the annual conference of the International Communication Association, Miami, FLA.
18. Ward, C. and Kennedy, A. (1993) 'Psychological and socio-cultural adjustment during cross-cultural transitions: a comparison of secondary students overseas and at home', *International Journal of Psychology*, **28**(2): 129–47.
19. de Verthelyi, R.F. (1995) 'International student's spouses: invisible sojourners in the culture shock literature', *International Journal of Intercultural Relations*, **19**: 387–411.
20. Kim, Y.Y. (1988) 'Facilitating immigrant adaptation: the role of communication', in Albrecht, T. and Adelman, M. (eds) *Communicating Social Support*, Newbury Park, CA: Sage, pp. 192–211.
21. Martin, J.N., Bradford, L. and Rohrlich, B. (1995) 'Comparing pre-departure expectations and post-sojourn reports: a longitudinal study of US students abroad', *International Journal of Intercultural Relations*, **19**: 87–110.
22. Witte, K. (1993) 'A theory of cognition and negative affect: extending Gudykunst and Hammer's theory of uncertainty and anxiety reduction', *International Journal of Intercultural Relations*, **17**: 197–215.
23. Gudykunst, W.B. and Kim, Y.Y. (1992) *Communicating With Strangers: An Approach to Intercultural Communication* (2nd edn), New York: McGraw-Hill.
24. Martin, J. (1986) op. cit.
25. Bennett, J.M. (1986) 'Modes of cross-cultural training: conceptualising cross-cultural training as education', *International Journal of Intercultural Relations*, **10**: 117–34.
26. Bennett, J.M. (1986) op. cit.

APPENDIX: EXTRACTS FROM USA STATE DEPARTMENT'S HUMAN RIGHTS REPORTS 1996

FRANCE

Statutes ban discrimination based on race, religion, sex, ethnic background, or political opinion, and the government effectively enforces them.

Women

While the law requires that women receive equal pay for equal work, this requirement is often not the reality. A 1994 study (latest available data) found a mean discrepancy between wages of women and men of 20% in the private sector and 18% in the public sector. The same study found that the unemployment rate for women averaged about four points higher than that for men.

The law prohibits sex-based job discrimination and sexual harassment in the workplace. Thus far these laws have encountered difficulties in implementation. Women's rights groups criticise the scope of the law as narrow, and the fines and compensatory damages as often modest. For example, the law limits sexual harassment claims to circumstances where there is a supervisor–subordinate relationship, but fails to address harassment by colleagues or a hostile work environment.

People with disabilities

There is no discrimination against disabled persons in employment, education, or in the provision of other state services. The government announced several measures in 1995 to boost employment opportunities for the disabled. A 1991 law requires new public buildings to be accessible to the physically disabled, but most older buildings and public transportation are not accessible.

Religious minorities

The annual NCCHR report released in March, 1996, noted a 50% decrease in the number of threats or attacks against Jews, from 169 in 1994 to 78 in 1995 (latest available data). However, ...[there is a] perception that racist/anti-Semitic violence is a serious problem.

National/racial/ethnic minorities

Anti-immigrant sentiments sparked incidents including occasional attacks by skinheads on members of the large Arab/Muslim and black-African communities. The annual NCCHR report noted that racist attacks and threats had doubled in one year, from 207 in 1994 to 454 in 1995 (latest available data). The government strongly condemns such actions and attacks, has strict anti-defamation laws, and prosecutes perpetrators whenever possible. Government programmes attempt to combat racism and anti-Semitism by promoting public awareness and bringing together local officials, police, and citizen groups. There are also anti-racist educational programs in some public school systems.

GERMANY

The law prohibits denial of access to shelter, healthcare, or education on the basis of race, religion, disability, sex, ethnic background, political opinion, or citizenship. The government enforces the law effectively.

Women

While violence against women occurs and is almost certainly under-reported, it is prohibited by laws that are effectively enforced. It is condemned in society, and legal and medical recourse is available. Police statistics on rape showed a slight increase to 6,175 cases in 1995 (latest available data) from 6,095 in 1994.

The government has conducted campaigns in the schools and through church groups to bring public attention to the existence of such violence and has proposed steps to counter it. The Federal Government has supported numerous pilot projects throughout Germany. There are, for example, 330 'women's houses' in Germany, over 100 in the new states in the East, where victims of violence and their children can seek shelter, counselling, and legal and police protection. Germany supported the appointment of a special rapporteur on violence against women at the UN Human Rights Commission.

In recent years, the Federal Ministry for Women and Youth commissioned a number of studies to gain information on violence against women, sexual harassment, and other matters, producing for example a special report on violence against women in 1995.

People with disabilities

There is no discrimination against the disabled in employment, education, or in the provision of other state services. The law mandates several special services for disabled persons, and the government enforces these provisions in practice. The disabled are entitled to assistance to avert, eliminate, or alleviate the consequences of their disabilities and to secure employment commensurate with their abilities. The government offers vocational training and grants for employers who hire the disabled. The severely disabled may be granted special benefits, such as tax breaks, free public transport, special parking facilities, and exemption from radio and television fees.

The Federal Government has established guidelines for attainment of 'barrier-free' public buildings and for modifications of streets and pedestrian traffic walks to accommodate the disabled. While it is up to the individual states to incorporate these guidelines into building codes, all 16 states now have access facilities for the disabled.

Religious minorities

Anti-Semitic acts decreased, with 380 incidents reported in the first six months of 1996, compared with 634 incidents in the same period in 1995. There were only 17 cases involving the use of force. Over 90% of these anti-Semitic incidents involved graffiti, the distribution of anti-Semitic materials, or the display of symbols of banned organizations. The perpetrators of the 1995 firebombing of the Lübeck synagogue were deemed mentally ill and sent for treatment. There were no anti-Semitic bombings in 1996.

National/racial/ethnic minorities

Data from the Federal Office for the Protection of the Constitution show the number of violent offenses by rightwing extremists against foreigners decreased by nearly 50% in the first six months of 1996 compared with the same period in 1995. This continues a significant downtrend since 1992. According to police data, all violent acts against foreigners, regardless of the political leanings of the perpetrators, also declined by roughly 50%. Ethnic Turks continue to complain credibly about societal and job-related discrimination.

Perpetrators of rightwing violence were predominantly young, male, and low in socio-economic status, often committing such acts while inebriated. As in the past, most acts of violence against minority groups were committed spontaneously. There continued to be evidence in 1996 that neo-Nazi groups were making efforts to achieve greater coordination among themselves.

In addition to voicing condemnation of the violence, the government recommended tougher anticrime legislation and law enforcement measures, as well as measures aimed at the societal roots of extremist violence and other crime. Eastern state governments have also taken efforts to reinvigorate enforcement of laws against violence by extremists. For such projects, however, state governments have thus far allocated only limited funds in their tight budgets.

The police in the eastern states continued to become better versed in the federal legal system, better trained, and more experienced. They continued to move toward reaching the standards of effectiveness characteristic of police in the rest of Germany. The level of rightwing activity in the new states continued to decrease. Sinti and Romani leaders expressed satisfaction at the signing by the government of the Council of Europe Convention on Minorities. Germany submitted an interpretation of the Convention in which Sinti and Roma were explicitly mentioned as ethnic minorities in Germany, providing them the recognition that they had long sought.

ITALY

The law prohibits discrimination on the basis of race, sex (except with regard to hazardous work), religion, ethnic background, or political opinion, and provides some protection against discrimination based on disability, language, or social status. However, societal discrimination persists to some degree.

Women

Legislation to protect women from physical abuse, including from members of their family, was updated and strengthened in February 1996. The law regards spousal rape the same as any other rape.

Media reports of domestic violence are common, and Telefono Rosa, a prominent non-governmental organization, reported that its hot-line for assistance in cases of violence against family members received 1,621 calls in 1995 (latest available figures). The same organization reported that rape cases filed with the courts were 1,863 for 1995, compared with 1,689 for 1994 (latest available figures).

Law enforcement and court officials are not reluctant to bring perpetrators of violence against women to justice, but victims sometimes do not press charges due to fear, shame, or ignorance of the law. The legislation passed in February, 1996, makes prosecution of perpetrators of violence against women easier and shelters women who have been objects of attack from publicity.

There are a number of government offices that work to ensure women's rights. The Prodi Government created a new cabinet-level position, the Office of Minister for Equal Opportunity, and named a woman to this position. In addition there is an Equal Opportunity Commission within the Office of the Prime Minister. Another such commission is in the Labour Ministry and focuses on discrimination and women's rights in the workplace. The Labour Ministry has a counsellor who deals with these problems at the national level, and similar officials serve with regional and provincial governments. Many of these counsellors, however, have limited resources for their work.

Some laws intended to protect women from hazardous work keep them out of jobs such as night shifts or underground work in mines, quarries, or tunnels. Maternity leave, introduced to benefit women, does add to the cost of employing them, with the result that employers sometimes find it advantageous to hire men instead.

Women generally receive lower salaries than men for comparable work. They are underrepresented in many fields, such as management or the professions (women, for example, account for only 25% of magistrates and only 10% of police officers). Women are often laid off more frequently than men.

While the law does not specifically prohibit sexual harassment, labour agreements covering broad sectors of the economy, in both the private and public sectors, do contain clauses that address the problem.

Women enjoy legal equality with men in marriage, property, and inheritance rights.

People with disabilities

The law forbids discrimination against disabled persons in employment, education, or in the provision of state services. Legislation requires enterprises with more than 35 employees to draw on the disabled to staff 15% of their workforce, directs that public buildings be made accessible to persons with disabilities, and spells out a number of specific rights for the disabled. Compliance with these requirements, however, is still only partial.

National/racial/ethnic minorities

Immigrants and other foreigners face societal discrimination. Some are even subjected to physical attack. The Romani people encounter difficulties finding places for their groups to stay. The city of Rome has opened three camps for them so far and others are expected to be opened. The Romani population around Rome is between 5,000 and 6,500.

The Forum of Foreign Communities continues its work on behalf of immigrants and foreign residents. It has a hot-line to report incidents of violence against foreigners. Other non-governmental agencies, such as Caritas, provide a broad range of assistance to immigrants throughout the country.

UNITED KINGDOM

The Race Relations Act of 1976 prohibits discrimination on the basis of race, color, nationality, or national or ethnic origin and outlaws incitement to racial hatred. No legislation exists to specifically outlaw racial discrimination in Northern Ireland. Discrimination on grounds of religious or political opinion is unlawful in Northern Ireland but not in Great Britain. Discrimination on the basis of religion is only illegal in Great Britain when its effect is to discriminate against a member of a minority ethnic group. The government respects and enforces all extant anti-discrimination laws, which concentrate on employment and the supply of goods and services.

Women

Statistical and other evidence indicates that most victims of societal violence are women. Domestic violence constitutes one-third of all reported crimes against women and accounts for almost 25 % of all reported violent crimes. The government believes that the problem of stalking is becoming so acute that it promised to introduce a new law that could result in stalkers being jailed for up to 5 years.

The law provides for injunctive relief, personal protection orders, and exclusion orders for women who are victims of violence. The government provides shelters, counselling, and other assistance for victims of battery or rape, and it offers free legal aid to battered women who are economically reliant upon their abusers. The government actively prosecutes perpetrators of domestic violence, and the law provides for their imprisonment. The courts have held that non-consensual marital sex can constitute a criminal offense. A 1994 law abolished the warning that judges had previously been required to give juries to the effect that a victim's testimony alone should not be adequate for a rape conviction. The Criminal Justice and Public Order Act of 1994 made sexual (as well as other intentional) harassment a criminal offense.

The law provides for equal opportunity between the sexes, but women experience some discrimination in practice. Nevertheless, according to the Equal Opportunities Commission, there has been significant progress in equal opportunity for women at work since the Commission was set up following the passage of the Sex Discrimination Act. The Equal Opportunities Commission supports persons who bring discrimination cases before industrial tribunals and courts, and it produces guidelines on good practice for employers. Women in Britain earn approximately 20% less than their male counterparts in comparable positions. A government minister co-chairs the Women's National Commission, a forum for women's organizations that presents women's views to the government.

The 1975 Sex Discrimination Act as amended in 1986 prohibits indirect as well as direct discrimination in training, education, housing, and provision of goods and services, as well as in employment. Women have equal rights regarding property and divorce.

People with disabilities

The Disability Discrimination Act passed in 1995 outlaws discrimination against disabled persons in provision of access to public facilities, by employers of more than 20 workers, service providers (apart from those providing education or running transport vehicles), and anyone selling or renting property. The 1993 Education Act imposes specific duties on local education authorities to make provision for the special educational needs of disabled children. Disabled rights groups continued to complain that the government had declined to create an enforcement body for the Discrimination Act.

Rights Now, a consortium of over 50 independent organizations campaigning for laws to end discrimination on the grounds of disability, reports that employers are six times more likely to turn down a disabled person for a job interview than a non-disabled applicant with the same qualifications; that only 80,000 wheelchair-accessible houses were available, and that in the last general election 88% of polling stations were inaccessible to disabled people.

Access to buildings is improving but inadequate. Many buildings and train stations are so old that they do not have elevators. Since 1985 government regulations have required that all new buildings meet the access requirements of all persons with impaired mobility. In 1992 the government put in place similar regulations for sensory-impaired persons. Government regulations mandate that by the year 2000 all taxis be accessible to wheelchairs.

Religious minorities

Despite government efforts, the unemployment rate for Catholic men in Northern Ireland remained twice that for Protestant men. The Fair Employment (Northern Ireland) Act of 1989, as amended, aims to end even unintentional or indirect discrimination in the workplace. A fair employment tribunal adjudicates complaints. All public-sector employers and all private firms with over ten workers must report annually to the Fair Employment Commission on the religious composition of their work force and must review their employment practices at least once every three years. Non-compliance can bring criminal penalties and loss of government contracts. Victims of employment discrimination may sue for damages. While critics of the act have asserted that its targets and timetables are too imprecise, most leaders of the Catholic community have praised it as a positive step.

There have been improvements in fair housing, education, and provision of goods and services, although there is no legislation to prohibit discrimination on the basis of religion in Great Britain.

While active recruitment of Catholics by the Northern Ireland civil service has produced rough proportionality in overall numbers, the service has acknowledged that Catholics remain significantly underrepresented in its senior grades, and in 1993 it declared its intention to overcome this imbalance. Service-wide employment cutbacks have thus far hampered its efforts. Government efforts to increase recruitment of Catholics into the police force (currently 92%

Protestant) and related security fields in the province have been hampered by IRA assassinations and death threats, as well as widespread antipathy in the Catholic community to the security forces. The number of Catholics joining the RUC increased somewhat during the August, 1994, to February, 1996, ceasefire period but has fallen since, despite continuing recruitment efforts.

National/racial/ethnic minorities

Although the law prohibits discrimination based on race (except in Northern Ireland), persons of African or south Asian origin face occasional acts of societal violence and some discrimination. Incitement to racial hatred is a criminal offense punishable by a maximum of two years' imprisonment. The government strictly enforces the laws and regulations in this area.

The UN Committee on the Elimination of Racial Discrimination noted with serious concern in March, 1996, that among the victims of death in custody in the UK were a disproportionate number of members of minority groups; that police brutality appeared to affect members of minority groups disproportionately; and that allegations of police brutality and harassment were reportedly not vigorously investigated and perpetrators, once guilt was established, not appropriately punished.

A government-appointed but independent Commission for Racial Equality (CRE) provides guidelines on good practice, supports persons taking court action under the Race Relations Act of 1976, and may initiate its own court action. After investigating a complaint, the CRE may issue a notice requiring that the discrimination be stopped. The CRE monitors the response to such a notice for 5 years.

Following a two-year examination of the army's household cavalry, the CRE in March found that there had been racial discrimination in recruitment and transfer and racial abuse and harassment in individual cases. The Ministry of Defence agreed to take steps, including monitoring of ethnic recruitment and prompt investigation of complaints, to redress these problems.

Source: United States State Department. Posted on the Internet: http://www.rferl.org/nca/hr/index96.html.

FURTHER READING

General foundations

Forgas, J.P. and J.M. Innes (eds) (1989) *Recent Advances in Social Psychology: An International Perspective*, Amsterdam: Elsevier.

Guirdham M. (1995) *Interpersonal Skills At Work* (2nd edn), Hemel Hempstead: Prentice-Hall.

Hewstone, M., Stroebe, W. , Codol, J.-P. and Stephenson, G.M. (1988) *Introduction to Social Psychology*, Oxford: Basil Blackwell.

Huczynski A. and Buchanan, D. (1991) *Organizational Behaviour: An Introductory Text* (2nd edn), Hemel Hempstead: Prentice-Hall.

Littlejohn, S.W. (1996) *Theories of Human Communication* (5th edn), Belmont, CA: Wadsworth.

Roloff, M.E and Miller, G.R. (eds) (1987) *Interpersonal Processes*, Newbury Park, CA: Sage.

(Sub)culture and work

Adler, J. (1991) *International Dimensions of Organizational Behavior*, Belmont, CA: Kent.

Adler, N.J. and Izraeli, D.N. (1994) *Competitive Frontiers*, Cambridge, MA: Basil Blackwell.

Hofstede, G. (1994) *Cultures and Organizations: Software of the Mind*, London: HarperCollins.

Jackson, T. (1993) *Organizational Behaviour in International Management*, Oxford: Butterworth-Heinemann.

Tayeb, M. H. (1996) *The Management of a Multicultural Workforce*, Chichester: John Wiley.

Intercultural communication

Gudykunst, W.B. and Kim, Y.Y. (1992) *Communicating With Strangers: An Approach to Intercultural Communication* (2nd edn), New York: McGraw-Hill.

Kim, Y.Y. and Gudykunst, W.B. (eds) (1988) *Theories in Intercultural Communication*, Newbury Park, CA: Sage.

Samovar, L. and Porter, R. (eds) (1991) *Intercultural Communication: A Reader* (6th edn), Belmont, CA: Wadsworth.

Ting-Toomey, S. and Korzenny, F. (eds) (1989) *Language, Communication and Culture: Current Directions*, Newbury Park, CA: Sage.

Other

Pirsig, R.M. (1991) *Lila: An Inquiry into Morals*, London: Bantam.

AUTHOR INDEX

AUTHOR INDEX

Scollon, R. 50, 77, 80, 114, 116, 190
Scollon S. 50, 77, 80, 114, 116, 190
Searle, J. 110, 116
Sedlacek, W.E. 155, 284
Shama, D.D. 156
Sherif, M. 187, 191
Shiino, N. 234
Shimanoff, S. 116
Shirakawa 285
Singhal, A. 114
Smith, K.K. 45, 155, 242
Smith, M.G. 13, 44, 175
Smolinski, C. 24, 45
Snyder, M. 233, 268
Sodetani, L.L. 235
Sonoda, K.T. 235
Sperber, D. 111, 116
Spitzberg, B. 226–7, 234, 235
Stack, B. 37
Stage, D. 77
Steinberg, M. 234
Stephenson, G.M. 114
Stohl, C. 93, 115
Stratman, J.F. 91
Street, R.L. 85
Strodtbeck, F.L. 52, 58, 77
Stroebe, W. 114
Strom, W.A. 290–1, 299
Sullivan, J. 105
Surdam, J.C. 284
Sypher, B.D. 10
Sypher, H.E. 234, 269
Sztaba, T.I. 157

T

Tajfel, H. 212, 216, 234, 235
Tannen, D. 102–3, 115, 172, 190

Tayeb, M.H. 59, 77, 272, 298
Taylor, C. Jr 24, 45
Taylor, S. 105
Thomas, M. 59, 77, 193, 233, 235, 236
Thompson, M.P. 102, 103, 115
Ting-Toomey, S. 60, 77, 114, 139, 140–4, 156, 172, 190, 199, 234, 261, 269
Tompkins, P.K. 5
Torrington, D. 66, 77
Triandis, H.C. 155, 156, 208, 234
Trompenaars, F. 1, 55–9, 76, 77, 78, 177, 190
Trubisky, P. 156
Tse, D.K. 127
Tsukasa, N. 234
Tung, R. 2, 7
Turner, J.C. 252
Turner, J.H. 120, 155
Turner, R.H. 136, 156

V

van Dijk, J. 70–1, 78, 108, 115
Vance, C.M. 77
Vertinsky, I. 127
Violanti, M.T. 10
Virdee, S. 28

W

Wallman, S. 45
Walther, J.B. 115
Wan T. 284
Wang, W. 277
Wanous, J.P. 7
Ward, C. 295, 299
Watson, W.E. 184, 191
Wehrung, D.A. 127
Weick, K. 225, 235

Weissman, M. 18, 45
Weldon, E. 60, 77, 236
West, C. 115
Wiemann, J.M. 115, 189, 236
Wierzbicka, A. 190
Williams, D.E. 171
Williams Jacobson, S. 67, 78
Wilson, D. 111, 116
Witkin, H.A. 124, 155
Witte, K. 295, 299
Woelfel, J. 77
Wolf, F.M. 156
Wood, L.A. 148, 157
Wooten, A.G. 248
Wrench, J. 28
Wrobel, P. 71

Y

Yang, S.M. 235
Yang, Z. 156
Yeh, R.S. 69
Yong, M. 190, 298
Yoon, C. 189
Yoon, H. 114, 157, 268
Yoram, B.-T. 155
Yu, J. 155
Yum, J.O. 157, 190, 235

Z

Zelditch, M. 155, 234
Zengler, T. 183
Zorn, T.E. 10

SUBJECT INDEX